This book is due for return on or before the last date shown above: it may, subject to the book not being reserved by another reader, be renewed by personal application, post, or telephone, quoting this date and details of the book.

HAMPSHIRE COUNTY COUNCIL
County Library

100% recycled paper

Georges Feydeau
Plays: One

Heart's Desire Hotel, Sauce for the Goose, The One That Got Away, Now You See It, Pig in a Poke

Feydeau was the most successful French dramatist of the *belle époque* and is now widely regarded as one of the greatest of farcewriters and a worthy successor to Molière and Labiche. His series of dazzling hits matched high-speed action and dialogue with ingenious plotting. Reaching the heights of farcical lunacy, his plays nevertheless contain touches of barbed social comment and allowed him to mention subjects which would have provoked outrage in the hands of more serious dramatists. This volume of new, sparkling translations by Kenneth McLeish contains his two masterpieces, *Heart's Desire Hotel* (*L'Hôtel du libre échange*) and *Sauce for the Goose* (*Le Dindon*), and three other plays from the peak of his career, *The One That Got Away* (*Monsieur chasse!*), *Now You See It* (*Le Système Ribadier*) and *Pig in a Poke* (*Chat en poche*).

Georges Feydeau was born in Paris in 1862, the son of the novelist Ernest Feydeau. His first one-act play, *Love and Piano*, was performed when he was 18 and he had his first success with *Tailleur pour dames* in 1887, when he also married an heiress. Among his many plays his best known are perhaps *Le Système Ribadier* (1892), *Monsieur chasse!* (1892), *Un Fil à la patte* (1894), *L'Hôtel du libre échange* (1894), *Le Dindon* (1896), *La Dame de chez Maxim* (1899), *La Puce à l'oreille* (1907), *Occupe-toi d'Amélie* (1908), and *On purge bébé* (1910). He contracted syphilis and was committed to an asylum in 1919 and died in 1921.

by the same author

FEYDEAU PLAYS: TWO
(The Girl From Maxim's, She's All Yours, A Flea in Her Ear, Jailbird)

GEORGES FEYDEAU

Plays: One

Heart's Desire Hotel
Sauce for the Goose
The One That Got Away
Now You See It
Pig in a Poke

Translated and introduced by Kenneth McLeish

Methuen Drama

METHUEN WORLD CLASSICS

1 3 5 7 9 10 8 6 4 2

This collection first published in the United Kingdom in 2001 by
Methuen Publishing Limited
215 Vauxhall Bridge Road, London SW1V 1EJ

These translations first published in 2001
Copyright © 2001 by the Estate of Kenneth McLeish

Collection and introduction copyright © 2001 by the Estate of Kenneth McLeish

The right of the translator to be identified as the
translator of these works has been asserted by him in accordance
with the Copyright, Designs and Patents Act, 1988

Methuen Publishing Limited Reg. No. 3543167

A CIP catalogue record for this book
is available from the British Library

ISBN 0 413 76170 3

Typeset by Deltatype, Birkenhead, Merseyside
Printed and bound in Great Britain by
Cox & Wyman Ltd, Reading, Berkshire

Caution

Contents

Georges Feydeau
Chronology

1862   Born in Paris, December 8

1874   Death of father, Ernest

1871–9   Attended boarding schools

1879   Joined a law firm as clerk

1880   Began to write and recite monologues

1881   *Par la fenêtre* (*Through the Window*), first play to be professionally performed, produced by Rosendaël

1883   *Amour et piano* (*Love and Piano*), Théâtre de l'Athénée
        Took post as secretary to Théâtre de la Renaissance

1883–4   Military service

1884   *Gibier de potence* (*Jailbird*), produced by Le Cercle Volney

1887   *Tailleur pour dames* (*Tailor to the Ladies*), Théâtre de la Renaissance – his first hit
        La Lycéenne (*The Schoolgirl*), Théâtre des Nouveautés

1888   *Un Bain de ménage* (*A Household Bath*), Théâtre de la Renaissance
        Chat en poche (*Pig in a Poke*), Théâtre Déjazet
        Les Fiancés de Loches (*The Fiancés of Loches*), Théâtre Cluny

1889   Married Marianne Duran
        L'Affaire Edouard (*The Edward Affair*), Théâtre des Variétés

1890   *Le Mariage de Barillon* (*Barillon's Marriage*), Théâtre de la Renaissance

1892   *Monsieur chasse!* (*The One That Got Away*), Théâtre du Palais-Royal
        Champignol malgré lui (*Champignol in Spite of Himself*), Théâtre des Nouveautés
        Le Système Ribadier (*Now You See It*), Théâtre du Palais-Royal

1894   *Un Fil à la patte* (*On a String*), Théâtre du Palais-Royal
        Le Ruban (*The Ribbon*), Théâtre de l'Odéon
        L'Hôtel du libre échange (*Heart's Desire Hotel*), Théâtre des Nouveautés

1896   *Le Dindon* (*Sauce for the Goose*), Théâtre du Palais-Royal

	Les Pavés de l'ours (*A Little Bit To Fall Back On*), Théâtre Montpensier, Versailles
1897	*Séance de nuit* (*Night Session*), Théâtre du Palais-Royal
	Dormez, je le veux! (*Sleep, I insist!*), Théâtre de l'Eldorado
1899	*La Dame de chez Maxim* (*The Girl From Maxim's*), Théâtre des Nouveautés
1902	*La Duchesse des Folies-Bergères* (*The Duchess From the Folies-Bergères*), Théâtre des Nouveautés
1904	*La Main passe* (*She's All Yours*), Théâtre des Nouveautés
1905	*L'Age d'or* (*The Golden Age*), Théâtre des Variétés
1906	*Le Bourgeon* (*The Bud*), Théâtre du Vaudeville
1907	*La Puce à l'oreille* (*A Flea In Her Ear*), Théâtre des Nouveautés
1908	*Occupe-toi d'Amélie* (*Look after Lulu*), Théâtre des Nouveautés
	Feu la mère de Madame (*Madame's Late Mother*), Théâtre de la Comédie Royale
1909	Moved into the Hôtel Terminus, where he lived until 1919
	Le Circuit (*The Circuit*), Théâtre des Variétés
1910	*On purge bébé* (*Purging Baby*), Théâtre des Nouveautés
1911	*Cent millions qui tombent* (*A Hundred Million Falling*), Théâtre des Nouveautés
	Mais n'te promène donc pas toute nue! (*Don't Walk Around Naked!*), Théâtre Fémina
	Léonie est en avance (*Léonie Is Early*), Théâtre de la Comédie Royale
1913	*On va faire la cocotte* (*We're going to play cocotte*), Théâtre Michel
1914	Divorced
	Je ne trompe pas mon mari (*I'm Not Deceiving My Husband*), Théâtre de l'Athénée
1916	Suffered increasing bad health caused by syphilis
	Hortense a dit: 'Je m'en fous!' (*Hortense said: 'I don't care!'*), Théâtre du Palais-Royal
1919	Committed to a sanatorium by his family
1921	Died June 5

Introduction

Feydeau's father, Ernest Feydeau, was a stockbroker and novelist, a friend of Baudelaire, Flaubert and the Goncourt brothers – who mocked him in their *Journals* for an interest in ancient Egypt so passionate that it was 'a form of adultery with him'. He died when his son was eleven, and his wife and her second husband (the drama critic Henri Gouquier) sent the boy to boarding school. At about this time young Feydeau first became fascinated by theatre, and – like his near contemporary Alfred Jarry – wrote skits and sketches to amuse his schoolfriends.

From 1883 Feydeau worked as secretary to the Renaissance Theatre, and his first full-length play, *Tailleur pour dames* (1887), had a successful run there when he was twenty-five. At about the same time he met and married an heiress, and in 1892 he had a hit with *Monsieur chasse!* at the Palais-Royal, the theatre which had previously seen Labiche's greatest triumphs. In the same year, *Champignol malgré lui* opened at the Nouveautés, and it and *Tailleur pour dames* each ran for more than 1000 performances. Feydeau went on to write more than two dozen plays, ranging from one-act sketches to historical spectaculars, and including the *grands vaudevilles* for which he is best known outside France: these range from *Un Fil à la patte* in 1894 to his mature masterpieces *L'Hôtel du libre échange*, *Le Dindon*, *La Dame de chez Maxim* and *La Puce à l'oreille*.

Feydeau's public success was offset by private misery. He spent each afternoon writing or directing, each evening at the show and then at Maxim's (where he had a table permanently reserved); he returned home at three or four in the morning, and began again at noon the next day. His wife shared none of his interests, and eventually asked him to leave. He gambled on the stock exchange, and lost not only the fortune his plays earned but also his valuable art collection. In 1909 he moved to a suite in the Hôtel Terminus (near the Gare St Lazare), and spent ten years there, dividing his time between the theatre, Maxim's and a succession of whores, from one of whom he contracted syphilis. He stopped writing in 1916; in 1919 he announced that he was Napoleon III, and was committed to an asylum; he died in 1921.

This private anguish is occasionally reflected in the plays. A bitter or bilious note sometimes darkens the hilarity, and collapsing marriages and lonely bachelors are treated with more savagery than the plots seem to warrant. But it hardly impinged on his dazzling public success. He was the most successful dramatist of his generation in France, and regularly had two, three or even four plays running at the same time in Paris. He was an actor and a director whose stage business exactly matched the demonic ingenuity of his plotting and dialogue. By his death he was regarded as one of France's major comic dramatists, a worthy successor to Molière and Labiche, and his work is still performed cyclically at the Comédie Française, two different plays each year.

Feydeau's style

Feydeau was a highly self-conscious stylist. He learned his craft as a schoolboy by writing parodies and imitations of authors he admired, and in later life often wrote scenes and sketches simply as stylistic exercises. He analysed the work of his great forebears and successful contemporaries, borrowing – in a way which can easily be traced – a plot-inflexion here, a type of scene there, a turn of phrase or business somewhere else. Until the late 1890s he regularly worked with collaborators, in the manner favoured by all comic dramatists of the time – not so much sharing the actual writing, as honing ideas together before one or other set the results down on paper. (In Feydeau's case the writing is clearly his own. Each collaborator's role seems to have been mainly to give advice and approval, and in any case by the time of *Le Dindon* he was working, for preference, entirely on his own.)

Feydeau's main sources were Molière, and through him the *commedia dell'arte*, Plautus and Terence. These provided a repertoire of characters and situations, and above all an attitude to society and human nature, which are the basic stock of farce. His gulled husbands, scheming servants, pompous military men and vacuous idiots may wear the clothes and follow the social conventions of the *belle époque*, but they come directly from this tradition. From Molière, especially, he learned the power of farce to make barbed social comment: he particularly admired *Le Malade imaginaire* and *L'Avare*.

One of the most fertile strands in Molière's output, that of the *comédie-ballet*, had been devised initially as a court entertainment for Louis XIV. These works (*Le Bourgeois Gentilhomme* is typical) frame straightforward satirical farce with extravagant music numbers, often involving pantomime-like characters (such as genies and mad professors), and using an unlikely mixture of ballet skills and slapstick. This tradition was matched, in popular theatre, by the vaudeville, or *voix de ville*. This was satirical street entertainment, in which the manners and ideas of the pretentious were burlesqued in (often bawdy) verse set to popular tunes, and whose grotesque and slapstick action was sometimes – as in *commedia dell'arte* – totally unrelated to the words being said. In Britain, and later in the United States, the style evolved into 'music-hall' and 'vaudeville' respectively; the sketches were separated from the music-numbers (though both remained satirical) and the physical display was split between slapstick (for example drunk-scenes) in the sketches and displays of such skills as plate-spinning or eccentric dancing (and later, striptease) among the other items. In France, the vaudeville tradition was gentrified into a kind of pastoral opera with spoken dialogue (of which Rousseau, no less, wrote an early example), into operettas like those of Offenbach, and into farcical plays satirising the bourgeoisie, with interpolated songs set to popular tunes of the day.

Labiche was the great nineteenth-century master of this last form, and his *An Italian Straw Hat* (usually nowadays performed without the songs) is a characteristic example of the genre. He also perfected a kind of vaudeville without songs: plays using physical business and rapid crosstalk to satirise bourgeois manners of the time. They were called *grands vaudevilles*, and are the principal link between Molière and Feydeau, and the main influence on Feydeau's style. In his *grands vaudevilles*, Labiche worked consciously to develop character: the puppet-like figures of *An Italian Straw Hat* are the exception in his work. The comedy is motivated by each character's individuality as well as by the needs of the situation: obsession, irritation and obtuseness, and the misunderstandings they engender, motor every play.

Labiche's plots – and Feydeau's after him – were also crucially influenced by the then-current fashion for the 'well-made play'. In this, the plot (usually in three acts) begins with an exposition which tells us the background history of the characters and also that there is a secret whose discovery will change all their lives. It starts at normal pace, but gathers momentum irresistibly until the first-act curtain comes down on confusion (often caused by revelation of the secret in question). There follows a series of *quidproquos*: mistakes, ironies, deceptions, misunderstandings, which always lead to a reversal of the hero's situation, from heights to depths or vice versa. The third act then explores the way this reversal affects every other character, and tidies up loose ends. Thousands of serious 'well-made plays' were written in the late nineteenth century – Ibsen's prose tragedies are outstanding examples – and the style was a main theatrical form in France, seen at its best in the plays of Augier, Becque and Sardou and of course the farces of Labiche. It was particularly valuable to farce-writers, as its discipline corseted the raucousness of vaudeville, allowing slapstick and hilarity to co-exist with a sustained satirical assault on bourgeois morality and convention.

Although Feydeau's main debt is to Labiche, he also learned from three contemporaries in particular. Maurice Hennequin, in the 1870s and 1880s, had great success with lunatic-action farces, successions of non-sequitur dialogue and slapstick confrontation – the original 'doors' French farces and the models for many of Feydeau's second acts (such as that of *Le Dindon*). Henri Meilhac, 'the Marivaux of the boulevards', and his collaborator Louis Halévy, wrote, among other things, the books for Offenbach's mythological burlesques, and were masters of the difficult art of letting characters speak apparently airy, natural dialogue while actually articulating the most extravagant passions and bizarre ideas. Their scripts flow as evenly and seamlessly as Hennequin's are unpredictable, and their influence can be seen particularly in Feydeau's opening acts, and in the way he brings back dialogue-interest in his third acts, restoring a kind of urbanity which, while never less funny, produces a welcome change of pace from the breakneck slapstick of the second acts.

Feydeau's mastery of the conventions of the well-made play – not to mention his audience's familiarity with the form – allowed him to ironise and parody both it and its component parts, to deal easily and farcically with subjects which, handled by serious dramatists at the same period, evoked howls of outrage and embarrassment. Impotence, for example, is a subsidiary theme in Act Three of *Sauce for the Goose* (where it arises, if that is the word, from Redillon's sexual exhaustion) and it motivates the whole plot of *A Flea in Her Ear* (where, because Chandebise is impotent, his wife suspects – quite wrongly – that he is 'spending himself' with a lover). Another serious subject which runs through all the plays, to the point of obsession, is the status of women: their equality with men and their 'power' within society and especially within marriage and the household. Feydeau's plots may revolve around adulterous intrigues (or, rather, would-be or mistakenly-suspected-to-be adulterous intrigues), but the meat of the plays is often the way a wife takes control, asserts her individual dignity, even sanity, in a lunatic world. Invariably, he gives his women more richness of character than his men; the men bluster, scheme and flail, while the women change and grow. This gives his plays a dimension lacking in other farces – even in such masterpieces as (in English) *The Rivals* or *The Importance of Being Earnest* – and links them with such later writers as Orton, who explores what might be called the condition of psychological anarchy, or

Ayckbourn, in whose plays psychological inadequacy is a recurring theme. It is the essence of farce that such serious matters – indeed any serious matters – should not obtrude, that silliness should rule. But audiences leave a Feydeau play sated in a different way from most other farces, and I believe one of the main reasons is the way he touches on the darkness in human life and the unpredictable obsession not only at the surface but deep down in human character.

Each of the plays included in these two volumes shows a different aspect of Feydeau's art. *Jailbird* (*Gibier de potence*) is an early work, first performed in 1883, at a semi-private theatre club, organised by the twenty-one-year-old author and like-minded friends. It was one item in a miscellaneous programme of monologues, comic songs and daft poems; Feydeau himself directed and took the part of Plumard. The piece shows occasional apprentice touches: the inconsequentiality of some of the jokes, for example, climaxing in the very last line of all, suggests a group of students giggling together rather than a single-minded artist fully in control of his effects. But the themes of Feydeau's major works are all here, and the misunderstandings and dazzle of the dialogue show his mastery even at this early age. In particular, the 'unmasking' scene and the scene where Lemercier and Taupinier try to outboast one another as assassins stand with his most lunatic, most felicitous inventions.

Pig in a Poke (*Chat en poche*) was first performed in 1888, a year after Feydeau's first big 'hit', *Tailleur pour dames*. It is a masterpiece of construction, not so much an arch as continuous escalation of confusion – and the Meilhac/Halévy influence is especially noticeable, in that the characters' apparently ordinary dialogue (the kind of language you might have heard in any drawing room of the time) belies the astounding content of what the people are saying or the thoughts inside their heads. Examples of Feydeau's scintillating stagecraft in this play are his careful, almost Ibsenish control over the escalation of the daftness in the first act, the counterpointing in Act Two of the Winstanley/Julie story with the main plot, and the way he keeps back the play's major surprise, the Sistine Chapel business, until the last act, just when we might think that the comic possibilities of the situation had been exhausted. *Pig in a Poke* may be chamber music compared to the grand symphonic structures of *A Flea in Her Ear* or *The Girl from Maxim's*, but it is also one of his most accomplished works.

Now You See It (*Le Système Ribadier*, written in collaboration with Hennequin in 1892), a darker comedy altogether, subverts the vaudeville tradition, even as it follows it, letting the men's obsessions turn them into mechanistic puppets – in a manner English readers may associate with Orton's characters in *Loot* or *What the Butler Saw* – while the heroine's character and personality flower before our eyes. It has one of the smallest casts and tightest construction of any Feydeau farce. It was one of the author's own favourite plays and he revived it in 1909 under a new title, *Nothing Known*.

The One That Got Away (*Monsieur chasse!*, 1892) is a fine example of Feydeau's 'demented clockwork' style of plotting, an effect much heightened by the smallness of the cast. Act One sets up a dozen criss-crossing situations, and shows us a group of people each of whom has something to hide from at least two of the others. Act Two brings all these people together in a situation where they should never, ever, meet, and is a frenzy of mistaken identities, mock-tragic dialogue and slapstick action involving doors, a closet, a double-bed, a man in underwear and a police chase. (Feydeau, who directed his own plays, always made his actors perform the dialogue of such scenes with utmost seriousness, as if they were high tragedy; the action, by contrast, was speeded up, heightened and mechanistic. Dislocation between the two styles made for hilarity – a production-method still followed in France, where Feydeau's farces are performed in rotation at the Comédie Française, but curiously seldom observed in English-language productions, perhaps because our farce-traditions tend more towards the end of the pier in one direction or 'high comedy' in the other.) Act Three picks up all the dangling loose ends from Act Two, further twists them and then untangles them while at the same time resolving the 'serious' issues of the play: Duchotel's infidelity and the suspicions of Léontine which set the action spinning in Act One.

Sauce for the Goose (*Le Dindon*), which enjoyed a long run at the Théâtre du Palais-Royal in 1896, is a characteristic 'well-made' *grand vaudeville*, with a lunatic second act framed by gentler material. It is, however, driven by character. Each person is clearly individuated and the differences between Redillon and Potagnac or Lucienne and Clotilde make the point that two individuals can share the same approach to life, or the same response to unexpected events, but show it in entirely different ways. Both this play and *Heart's Desire Hotel* (*L'Hôtel du libre échange*), which dates from two years earlier, make use of the hotel setting in order to create a space situated half-way between the private and the public, a space where desires which cannot be spoken of in a polite bourgeois salon emerge and press for satisfaction. Both plays make hilarious use of rooms with several doors, some of which allow for escape, while others lead only into cupboards or bathrooms. And both plays benefit from the sense that hotel guests have of being constantly observed, even spied on, by people they hardly know. *Heart's Desire Hotel* is justly one of the most famous comedies of assumed identity in the repertoire; the fact that the only couple to achieve any satisfaction is the young Maxime and Victoire, while the older characters remain frightened and frustrated, is entirely in keeping with the traditions of farce going back to classical times.

In most of Feydeau's plays the characters are drawn from middle-class society, but the plot of *The Girl From Maxim's* (*La Dame de chez Maxim*, Théâtre des Nouveautés, 1899) turns on a liaison – or rather two liaisons – between representatives of the respectable middle classes and a show-girl named 'Shrimp' (*la môme crevette* in Feydeau's original). After a series of *quidproquo*s, all set off as usual by the terrified attempts of the respectable married man to find a way out of the embarrassing situation his sex drive, combined with a lot of drink, has landed him in, it is the show-girl who saves the day by her cool-headedness and lack of personal pretensions. In this respect, both this play and *She's All Yours* (*La Main passe*, Théâtre des Nouveautés, 1904) come close to the Naturalist plays of the period in which bourgeois hypocrisy, especially in sexual matters, was satirised in more serious dramatic form. The characters of *She's All Yours* are recognisable people, who might be part of a play by Galsworthy. They are trying to come to terms with the modern world (as the play opens Chanal is trying to record a message on a phonograph) and the dilemmas into which they get themselves are at least partly due to their chronic inability to communicate with one another that recalls Chekhov.

A Flea in Her Ear (*La Puce à l'oreille*) was one of Feydeau's greatest successes with the Paris public. It was first produced in 1907 at the Théâtre des Nouveautés, which had become the favourite venue for Feydeau's larger-scale plays. It attracted rave notices, critics commenting on its dazzle of speed and movement (particularly in Act Two), and calling it a classic. It had to be taken off when the character actor Torin, for whom Feydeau had specifically written the role of Camille, died unexpectedly. But it had a triumphant revival in 1915 and has since travelled the world, being considered one of the most perfectly constructed of all Feydeau's farces, a model for the form. Its handling of the theme of impotence with such consummate comic flair made it particularly successful in Britain, the USA and Scandinavia – perhaps the puritan inheritance makes sexual impotence an especially embarrassing topic in these countries – indeed this play has, somewhat unjustly, all but eclipsed Feydeau's other plays.

Translation
Translating farce is risky. We are dealing not just with a foreign country, whose customs and manners are only superficially like our own, but with foreign slang, foreign

preconceptions and foreign ideas of funniness. This is a major part of the appeal, but it can also give the plays, in translation, a kind of exotic, pseudo-literary gloss lacking in the original. Gogol's *The Government Inspector* is a case in point. Its humour depends on a clear view of Russian small-town society at a particular moment in time, and the attitudes of people of that place and time to each other, to visitors, dignitaries and servants, are vital to the jokes. But to go at it head-on, to assume that the audience will know, or pick up, every nuance, would be to produce a play in English whose oddness baffled as often as it seduced. The results might be funny, but would weight the play in a way quite different from the original: it would become first and foremost a literary work, a critique, rather than a piece of straightforward stage entertainment. I have seen foreign-language versions of Ben Travers which unwittingly give the same impression. An alternative method of translation, regularly followed in Britain until the 1960s, is to resite the farce in a local setting, to English it. (In 1896 *Now You See It* was performed in Drury Lane in a version resetting it among the English aristocracy; in 1959 Coward similarly reworked *Occupe-toi d'Amélie* as *Look after Lulu!*) This process of adaptation sanitises the foreignness, but it can also choke the original motor of the humour, replacing the original preconceptions and 'givens' with notions from entirely another place and time.

In this volume, I have treated each of the plays slightly differently, though my purpose has been the same each time: to try to recapture the effect I think Feydeau was aiming at, in a form instantly understandable by modern English-speaking audiences. The translation of *Sauce for the Goose* is ninety-eight per cent meticulous. The first exception is the title. *Le Dindon*, to a French audience, means not only 'the turkey' but also the standard farce fall-guy, the character on whom every indignity is dumped – including, in this case, the reversal of fortune on which a 'well-made' play depends. Potagnac's last line, in the original, is, 'It was written [in the stars]: I'm the dindon' – and so he is. The second exception is the characters of Brünnhilde and Soldignac. In the original they are English, and speak a kind of strangulated, invented English which must have been hilarious in 1890s France but doesn't work in 1990s Britain. I began by giving them the kind of plum-in-the-mouth English we are used to in farce, but found that this made them more complex than the simple 'volcanoes' Feydeau had in mind, overbalancing their scenes. In the end I made them German, or rather cod-German, as fake as Feydeau's original English.

Pig in a Poke combines farce and comedy of manners, and it seemed to me that a rigid but unspoken social framework ought to underlie the action. Although that of the original (bourgeois Paris of the *belle époque*) is remote from us, it is paralleled in Edwardian England, and I accordingly reset the play in Camberwell in 1909. Since this made nonsense of Pennyfeather's original home (southern France), I transposed him first of all to Wales and then, because this hardly seemed exotic enough, to South America. The play also depends, in part, on the absurdities and pretensions of 'polite language' (which is constantly undercut by the basic situation); for this reason I slightly formalised my English, leaning a little towards the style of Pinero, Grundy, or other farce-writers of the period. When I began work on *Now You See It*, I took notice of Shaw's criticism of the 1896 English production mentioned above. He said that the play would be strengthened if it were dovetailed from three acts to two, and if the action were 'rotated' so as to be seen from the wife's point of view rather than those of the husband or lover. When I tried this, I found that it highlighted Feydeau's exposition of her character, making its development central to the plot. I reinforced this by making Summersby (Ribadier in the original) not merely a pompous, hypocritical businessman but an MP working, officially at least, for female emancipation. I made Shaftesbury-Phipps (Thommereux in the original) come home from India, the British Empire, rather than from Batavia, the Dutch Empire. And finally, I replaced two tiny Feydeau characters, a maid and butler, with the invented character of Oriole. Satisfyingly, despite these shifts and redirections, it was possible to leave most of Feydeau's original dialogue intact.

Kenneth McLeish, June 1993
(with additional material by David Bradby)

Translator's note: the original French texts, prepared from the prompt script, were full of indications of the actors' moves in the first production ('he goes two steps up left'; 'she sits' and so on). I have pruned these to a minimum, keeping suggested blocking and business only when they seem integral to character or action.

Kenneth McLeish's great passion was for comedy, and he delighted in the skills it demanded from everyone involved. He intended that these plays should be dedicated to all those professionals and amateurs who worked with him over many years to make people laugh. Kenneth also wanted to thank David and Justin Bassett for technical advice in *The One That Got Away*. I am very grateful to David Bradby for his work in completing the introduction.

Valerie McLeish, 2000

Heart's Desire Hotel

L'Hôtel du libre échange

Characters

Pinglet, *an engineer*
Angélique, *his wife*
Paillardin, *an architect*
Marcelle, *his wife*
Maxime, *a student of philosophy*
Victoire, *the housemaid*
Mathieu, *a visitor*
His daughters
Bastien
Boulot
Ernest, *an acrobat*
Ernest's woman companion
Chervet, *an angry man*
Inspector Boucard
Constables
Porters

The action is set in Paris, in the 1890s. Acts One and Three take place in Pinglet's house, Act Two in Heart's Desire Hotel.

Act One

The studio of **Pinglet**'s *house in Passy, on the outskirts of Paris. Centre back, a large bay window, opening on the garden. R, the doors to* **Angélique**'s *bedroom and to the entrance hall; L, the door of* **Pinglet**'s *bedroom. Upstage C, an elegant drawing-board, flanked by a high stool and covered with papers, plans, pens, pencils, water-colours, rulers, a set-square and other draughtsman's tools, plus a city directory. Upstage L, a glass-doored sideboard filled with samples of tiles and different kinds of stone. Against the wall, a desk covered with books and scattered plans, a writing-set and a vase of flowers; above it on the wall, a mirror and above that a rack with still more plans. Down R, sofa, writing-desk; between the two doors, R, a wall-clock hung and a filing cabinet; bell-pull. Armchairs; chairs. The walls are hung with framed plans and plaster casts of mouldings, cornices and other architectural features.*

As the curtain rises, **Pinglet** *is working at his drawing-board. His back is to the audience, and he is humming and singing to himself.*

Pinglet   Hm, hm, hm, the sweet spring ... hm, hm, pretty birdies sing ... hm, hm, hm, bells ring ding-a-ling ...

Enter **Angélique**. *She is holding two samples of dress-material.*

Angélique (*sharply*)   Pinglet!

Pinglet (*without turning*)   My little cabbage?

Angélique   The dressmaker's arrived.

Pinglet (*over his shoulder*)   What of it, sweetness? (*He goes back to work.*)

Angélique   For heaven's sake pay attention when I'm talking.

Pinglet (*aside*)   Here we go again. (*Aloud.*) Light of my life, you don't understand. This is urgent work: the plans I'm doing with Paillardin. The new house.

Angélique   The house can wait.

Pinglet Whatever you say.

Angélique (*showing him the samples*) She wants me to choose. This one or that one.

Pinglet Hm. For curtains?

Angélique For an evening dress.

Pinglet I prefer ... that one.

Angélique Fine. I'll have the other.

Pinglet So kind of you to ask.

Angélique Don't be silly. I ask because I know you've no idea. It's foolproof. Whatever you choose, I choose the opposite.

Pinglet (*aside*) What *was* I thinking of?

Angélique Don't just stand there. Get on with your work.

Pinglet Yes, sweet one.

Angélique *makes a face at him and exit.*

Pinglet Slave-driver. (*To himself.*) Well, it's your own stupid fault. The whole family said 'No', and you said, 'I will, I love her so.' 'I love her so.' (*Back to his drawing-board.*) Twenty years. If we could see what they turn into after twenty years, we'd agree with our families. No, no, no. Too dark to work. (*At the window.*) It's pouring. (*Facing the audience.*) Well, *my* son's not getting married. Not if *I* say 'No'. (*Beat.*) If I ever have a son. And I won't. What, Angélique and I, we should ... ? No, no, no.

Knock at the door.

Come in!

Enter **Marcelle**. **Pinglet** *goes delightedly to greet her.*

Pinglet Madame Paillardin! Come in.

Marcelle (*flirting*) Tut, tut, Monsieur Pinglet. In a

dressing-gown, in front of a lady?

Pinglet (*full of good humour*) Not a lady: a friend, a neighbour. No need to stand on ceremony.

Marcelle Madame's gone out?

Pinglet Locked in conference with her dressmaker. How's Paillardin?

Marcelle Don't ask.

Pinglet (*taking her hands and looking into her eyes*) Something's wrong.

Marcelle No it's not.

Pinglet Yes it is. You've been crying.

Marcelle It's nothing. Same as always. An argument.

Pinglet Poor sweet girl. Did he . . . shout?

Marcelle If he'd shouted, it would have been all right. He never shouts. I mean less to him than a pair of old slippers. I don't want to talk about it. Where's Angélique?

Pinglet In there. Now don't you worry, I'll have a word with him.

Marcelle No. You'll make things worse. It'd be like . . . like teaching the violin to a one-armed man.

Exit.

Pinglet (*to himself, looking after her*) What a woman. Ah. (*To himself.*) Hah. Your wife says you're past it. And so you are, with her. Who wouldn't be? (*Going back to his drawing-board.*) That poor young girl. And him, that husband, that . . . cockroach of a man. (*Gazing out front, in a reverie.*) Paillardin, your oldest and dearest friend. If you can't call him a cockroach, who can? (*Back to work.*) If only he *wasn't* your oldest, dearest friend . . . and if only she . . . she . . . You mustn't. You're not a Red Indian. You can't do that to your oldest friend, just for a scalp. But what a scalp ... ! (*Spreading out a plan, hastily.*) Back to work. To work. What's Mr Cockroach suggesting? Sandstone. *Sandstone*? It's a load-bearing wall. He's joking ...

He unrolls and compares a plan of his own.

Head in the air. They're all the same. Fancy ideas, no grounding. No science. If we engineers weren't there to ...

He paces, pondering.

Sandstone! Load-bearing. (*Different tone.*) But what a wife. What a woman.

Enter **Paillardin**.

Paillardin   Morning, Pinglet. I'm not disturbing you ... ?

Pinglet   Not at all. In fact ... this plan ...

Paillardin   What about it?

Pinglet   You've suggested sandstone. Here, look. It's load-bearing.

Paillardin   So it is. What would you have used?

Pinglet   I don't know. Aggregate.

Paillardin (*shrugging*)   Aggregate. Bad for bonding.

Pinglet   Granite, then. Anything but sandstone.

Paillardin (*as before*)   Granite. Pricey.

Pinglet   Oh, for heaven's sake! Diorite, andesite, rhyolite, quartzite, basalt, gabbro –

Paillardin   You sound like an encyclopaedia.

Pinglet   I haven't finished. Portland, Parian, Carrara –

Paillardin   Now you sound like a gazetteer. What does it matter, so long as it takes the weight?

Pinglet Takes the weight! That's the whole point. You're such a dreamer. You're all dreamers. Architects. If it wasn't for us engineers . . .

Paillardin (*sitting on the sofa*) Yes, whatever you say. Have you seen Marcelle?

Pinglet Marcelle?

Paillardin My wife.

Pinglet I know she's your wife.

Paillardin But have you seen her?

Pinglet She's in there, with mine. That reminds me: what is it you've done to her?

Paillardin What did she say I've done?

Pinglet She didn't. You've only got to look at her.

Paillardin (*in a bored tone*) I don't know. I'm fed up with it. First one thing, then another. What does she want? I don't have affairs. I don't have a string of mistresses.

Pinglet A string of mistresses! There's more to marriage than that.

Paillardin So people keep telling me. I do my best. And she's still not satisfied. Says I'm not *nice* to her.

Pinglet Well, you aren't. Why aren't you?

Paillardin We have to be nice, as well as faithful? Huh! Are you nice to yours?

Pinglet Oh come on. Twenty years . . .

Paillardin They improve with age.

Pinglet Wines improve with age. Not wives. Mine's . . . corked.

Paillardin Well, mine isn't. Not after just five years. Mind you, it feels like a lifetime. *Nice*! If it's *nice* you want, get a mistress, not a wife.

Pinglet   Charming.

Paillardin   Look, I'm an architect, an artist. I work hard all day, drawing plans, visiting building-sites . . . I get home exhausted, I fall into bed, I sleep. I need it. But does she see that? Of course she doesn't. *Nice!*

Pinglet   Don't go on.

Paillardin   All that honeymoon stuff. I didn't get married for honeymoon stuff. It's not my style.

Pinglet   (*laughing*)   All right, all right. You've made your point. You're an iceberg.

Paillardin   So what are you? A tropical island?

Pinglet   Exactly. The molten core . . . the lava, pulsing, pulsing . . . the eruption! Well, I would if I had a crater.

Paillardin   You see. You're no volcano.

Pinglet   I'm a bigger one than you are.

Paillardin   What d'you mean?

Pinglet   You don't go in for lava. You said so.

Paillardin   So?

Pinglet   So a volcano without lava isn't a volcano. It's a . . . it's a . . . leaky mountain.

Paillardin   (*shrugging*)   Whatever you say. Look, I came round to ask . . . Can I borrow Victoire?

Pinglet   Victoire?

Paillardin   Your housemaid.

Pinglet   You don't need a housemaid.

Paillardin   She's not for me. She's for Maxime. My nephew, Maxime.

Pinglet   But he's a student.

Paillardin   That's why he needs Victoire.

Pinglet   Charming.

Paillardin   No, no, no, no, no. He's studying philosophy.

Pinglet   At his age? What'll he do when he grows up?

Paillardin (*patiently*)   His term starts tomorrow. He goes back tonight. To his lodgings. He needs someone to unpack for him. I gave all my staff the day off, weeks ago. So I need Victoire.

Pinglet   Why can't you unpack for him?

Paillardin   I'm far too busy. In any case, I'm sleeping in town tonight.

Pinglet   Ahah!

Paillardin   By myself.

Pinglet   Oh really?

Paillardin   Yes. Yes! In some ghastly little hotel. Haunted. Or so they say. Poltergeists.

Pinglet   No such thing.

Paillardin   Exactly. I don't believe in them. Show me a poltergeist, I don't believe in it. It's the pipes. Underground pipes. Knocking.

Pinglet   Obviously.

Paillardin   But the owner doesn't agree. Wants his rates lowered. The council won't budge. The court's called me. Expert witness. I'm to spend a night there, see what's going on.

Pinglet   Gas-pipes. Air-bubbles.

Paillardin   Could be.

He gets up to go.

Pinglet   Just a minute. This is what it's about. You and your wife.

Paillardin Don't remind me. She's been after me all day. 'You're always out. You're never in. You never spend time with me.' I'm an architect. We don't spend time with wives.

Pinglet Whatever you say. But be careful. Someone else might . . .

Paillardin Someone else might what?

Pinglet It's none of my business. But you're playing with fire. Wives . . . especially your wife . . . they like romance. I'm not suggesting that *you* . . . I'm just saying, don't be surprised if she finds someone else . . .

Paillardin You're joking. My wife? A lover? What d'you think this is, a Feydeau farce?

Pinglet Whatever you say.

Paillardin I *do* say.

Pinglet Your wife . . . a lover . . . what am I thinking of? (*Aside.*) What *am* I thinking of?

Knock at the door.

Come in!

Enter **Maxime,** *a studious lad holding a book.*

Paillardin Ah, Maxime.

Maxime Hello, Nunkie. Sorry if I'm –

Pinglet You aren't, you aren't.

Paillardin What's the matter?

Maxime The thing is, Monsieur Pinglet, I must have . . . I wonder if I . . . you haven't found it? . . . I bought it yesterday . . . a Russell.

Pinglet A rustle? My dear young man, what d'you mean, a rustle? Of what?

Maxime Pardon?

Pinglet You have to have a rustle of something. *Rustle of Spring*, perhaps?

Maxime Not rustle, Russell. The writer.

Pinglet Detective stories, of course. You should have said.

Maxime The philosopher.

Pinglet Philosophical detective stories. Exactly.

Maxime I don't understand.

Pinglet Like architects and engineers. (*With a look at* **Paillardin**.) *Some* of us can be both at once.

Maxime Did I leave it here?

Pinglet Oh. No.

Maxime I need it. Apparently it refutes Bergson's *On the Passions*. I'm doing that for an essay. (*He holds up the book he's reading.*)

Paillardin Passion, eh?

Pinglet You young rascal, hey?

Maxime (*huffily*) It isn't that at all.

He goes upstage.

Paillardin Now look what you've done.

Pinglet Me? I asked him a civil question. If you're learning billiards, you read a book called *On billiards*. So, if you're reading a book *On Passion* . . . Everyone has to learn.

Enter **Victoire**.

Victoire Monsieur . . .

Pinglet What is it?

Victoire Madame needs Monsieur.

Pinglet   There's always a first time.

Victoire   She's tried on her new dress, and she'd like Monsieur's opinion.

Pinglet (*to* **Paillardin**)   Damn nuisance. (*To* **Victoire**.) She never accepts it. You know that. She never . . . oh, all right.

Paillardin (*to* **Maxime**, *who is rooting about in drawers*) What are you *doing*?

Maxime   Looking for *Passion*, Nunkie.

Pinglet   Well you won't find it in there. Not in *my* drawers. Victoire, you haven't seen it, have you? A book. Hustle, bustle, some such name.

Maxime   Russell, Monsieur.

Pinglet   Well, Russell. Hustle, bustle, they're all the same.

Paillardin   He never could spell.

Victoire   I haven't seen it, Monsieur.

Maxime   I'll have to buy another one.

Pinglet   By the way, Victoire, I'd like you to go with Monsieur Maxime to his digs this evening.

Victoire   I'd love to, Monsieur.

Pinglet   Don't bother loving to, just go. What time, Maxime?

Maxime   We have to be in by nine.

Pinglet   Nine-ish, then. All right, Victoire?

Victoire   Oh yes, Monsieur.

She goes to tidy papers on the table. **Maxime** *reads.*

Paillardin   Thanks.

Pinglet   A pleasure.

Angélique (*off*) Are you coming or aren't you?

Pinglet My little temptress. (*Calling off.*) Coming,
beloved! (*To* **Paillardin**.) You come as well. Give her
your opinion. (*Pushing him off.*) Just keep your face straight.

Paillardin All right.

Exeunt.

Maxime (*reading*) 'Love is a sensation of the spirit
occasioned by the attraction of animal spirits to like-
minded and appropriate objects.' (*Fervently.*) That's so *good*!

Victoire (*leaning on the table*). Monsieur Maxime . . .

Maxime Yes?

Victoire What are you doing?

Maxime Learning about passion.

Victoire In that position? (*Aside.*) Isn't he divine? (*Aloud.*)
I'll help if you like.

Maxime You've studied passion?

Victoire Hasn't everyone?

Maxime You know Bergson?

Victoire Never met him.

Maxime You don't understand.

Victoire You don't want me to help you?

She strokes his knee.

Maxime You're distracting me.

Victoire Don't you like it?

Maxime I didn't say that. I said, you're distracting me.
(*Aside.*) What does she *want*?

Victoire It's rude to read when someone else is there.

Maxime I'm not reading. I'm studying. And how can I

study passion, if women keep distracting me?

He sits on the sofa.

Victoire   I never heard that before.

Maxime (*reading*)   'There are two kinds of passion, (a) protective and (b) predatory. The love of a father for his children in no way resembles that of a lover for his mistress. Their only point of resemblance is that both are forms of passion. However . . .'

He moves to the other end of the sofa from her.

'However, all emotion of the second kind is subsumed in category (b), and its entire object is predatory, that is to say, for possession . . .' (*To her.*) I say, that's rather nice.

Victoire (*who is stroking him*)   Really?

Maxime   Ra-ther. Don't stop. (*Reading.*) 'The first category, (a), by contrast, that of a father and his children, in no way involves the impulse for consummation by subsumption . . .'

Victoire   Isn't that lucky?

Maxime   'It involves, for example, the entire subsumption of their good in his good.'

Victoire (*stroking his hair*)   How sweet, how sweet, oh sweetikins.

Maxime   Please. Stroke, but don't talk.

Victoire   Monsieur Maxime, has anyone ever told you how . . . attractive you are?

Maxime   What? I don't think so. No, wait . . .

Victoire   Who?

Maxime   When I had my photo taken. I'd ordered a dozen prints. The chappie said, 'An attractive young fellow like yourself. An Adonis. You'll need three dozen.' So I took three dozen.

Victoire Photographers don't count.

She goes back to stroking his hair.

Maxime   Except when they're counting your cash.
(*Reading.*) 'In a certain sense, it's a purely mercantile
transaction.'

*She bursts out laughing, and stops stroking his hair. He notices, and
looks at her. She starts again. He reads again, or tries to.*

'Mercantile, that is, in the sense that it involves two beings
coming together for mutual benefit.'

Victoire   What do *you* think, Monsieur Maxime?

Maxime   About what?

Victoire   Things not in the book.

Maxime   Good grief, it doesn't tell me *everything*.

Victoire   Well, shut it, then.

She shuts it, enclosing his hands in hers.

A young man like you doesn't need books for love. When
you learn to swim, you don't sit on the bank, reading.
You dive straight in. So . . . dive.

She takes it and sits beside him.

Maxime (*aside*). What's she *doing*?

Victoire (*taking him by the shoulders*)   Let me look at you.
Look what the cat brought in.

She straightens his clothes.

Those horrible glasses.

She removes them.

Can't you see just as well without them?

Maxime   Better!

Victoire   And the way you brush your hair. Really,

when Nature makes a man so ... and he chooses to ...

She arranges his hair. He closes his eyes.

Maxime I say, that's really rather nice.

Victoire (*pushing him away*) Now, now.

Maxime The hair, I mean the hair.

Victoire So do I. (*Aside.*) I do! (*To him.*) There. Look in the mirror. Doesn't that look better?

Maxime Oh, yes. (*Admiring himself.*) Ohhh ... yessss.

Victoire There you are, then.

Maxime A great improvement.

Absent-mindedly, he puts his glasses back on, straightens his hair, sits down and takes up the book.

'It may even be a more caring relationship, in that it involves looking after others as if they were oneself.'

Victoire (*throwing up her hands*) Oh, for heaven's sake.

Maxime 'The objects can be totally unaware ...'

Victoire (*coldly*) Excuse me, Monsieur.

Maxime (*engrossed in the book*) Nine-ish.

Victoire Nine-ish.

Maxime (*looking up*) What's the matter?

Victoire Nothing. Nothing in all the world.

Exit. He's back in his book already.

Maxime 'In the same way, many human beings ...'

Noise, off. He puts his hands over his ears and tries again.

'Human beings ... feel affection of the (b) category as well as of the (a) ...'

Enter **Marcelle**, **Angélique**, **Paillardin** *and* **Pinglet**.

Marcelle *is furious.*

Marcelle   Oh! Oh!

Paillardin   Sweetheart, what's the matter?

Marcelle   I hate you, that's the matter.

Angélique   Ha! 'Sweetheart.' Wait till you've had twenty years of it, like me.

Pinglet   What d'you mean, like you? I've been so *nice* to you.

Paillardin (*to* **Marcelle**)   So have I.

The women (*each to her own husband*)   Nice! Huh! Nice!

The men   Pre-cisely.

The women   You call that nice?

The men   Ex-actly.

The women   Hah!

The row continues. **Maxime** *gets up, shouts above the racket.*

Maxime   Excuse me. I'm trying to read. I'm off.

Exit.

Marcelle   I was just saying . . . Oh, he's gone. I was just saying, why did I ever marry a husband who hasn't the faintest idea what a husband should have an idea . . . of.

Paillardin (*beside himself*)   Well, really!

Marcelle   He doesn't want a wife, he wants a housekeeper, a gardener, a pair of slippers. Nothing else. A chattel, that's what I am, a chattel.

Angélique   Poor darling. A chattel. There.

Paillardin   She's exaggerating. You don't understand.

Angélique   Don't understand? After twenty years of . . . Monsieur? Ha! If he'd ever tried that on me . . . If he'd just once tried . . .

Paillardin (*aside to* **Pinglet**)   Not even once?

Pinglet (*aside to him*)   *She's* exaggerating.

Paillardin (*to* **Marcelle**)   What is it you want? Tell me, what is it you want? I'm not to go tonight, is that it? My poltergeists?

Marcelle   Go, go, who's stopping you? Go, stay, it's all the same to me.

Paillardin   What is it you *want?*

Marcelle   A change. A proper relationship. Married to you, it's a miracle I've never . . .

Paillardin   What?

Pinglet   No, she's right, she hasn't.

Paillardin   You stay out of this.

Marcelle   I haven't, but I could. Any time I liked. Find someone . . . someone *nice* . . .

Paillardin   You?

Marcelle   You don't have to be pretty to find admirers.

Paillardin (*laughing*)   Just as well. Go on, then. Find one.

Marcelle   Don't encourage me. I know where to look.

Paillardin   Go on, then. Look. Who's stopping you?

Angélique   Stop annoying her.

Paillardin   Me? Tell her to stop annoying me. And tell her to find one. Someone *nice*. If she does, he can keep her.

Marcelle   Oh!

Pinglet (*to her*)   He's crazy. (*To him.*) You're crazy. (*To us all.*) He's crazy.

Marcelle Like that, is it. All right! All ... right!

Paillardin Go on, then. Go.

Angélique Come on, give her a kiss, make up.

Paillardin You're joking.

He stalks to the door. **Angélique** *goes after him.*

Angélique Monsieur Paillardin ...

Pinglet (*at the door*) You've gone too far, Henri. You've really gone too far.

But **Paillardin** *and* **Angélique** *have gone.* **Marcelle** *sits on the sofa, still furious.*

Marcelle You see how he treats me. How he talks to me. I've had enough of it.

Pinglet (*blurting it out*) Marcelle, Marcelle, I love you.

Marcelle Pardon?

Pinglet I can't keep it in a moment longer. You saw, just now ... I said all I could, I tried to warn him, I called him Henri ...

Marcelle I saw.

Pinglet I told him he'd gone too far. He wouldn't listen. He went. Fine. Let him go. You saw. And you saw what he said when you said you wanted to find someone nice ... 'Go on, then,' he said. 'Go on, then. Go!' He did!

Marcelle He did.

Pinglet You can't say there's no one. There's me. There's me.

Marcelle You mean you –

Pinglet With my own eyes, I saw him. He challenged you. Fine: I take up the challenge. 'Go on, find a lover,' he said. I accept the challenge. I'll do it. I'll be your lover.

Marcelle You mean you –

Pinglet Exactly! No one challenges a lady in front of me, and gets away with it. My best friend. It's appalling. But . . . chivalry must come first. A lady's good name . . . her honour . . . Marcelle, Marcelle, I love you.

He tries to embrace her.

Marcelle Monsieur Pinglet. No. My wifely duty –

Pinglet Wifely duty! Poor darling. A rose, a rose in a gilded cage. Marcelle, sweetness, there are moments in our journey through life, when we have to throw our duty out of the window.

Marcelle Really?

Pinglet Take me, for example. Take Madame Pinglet. Am I letting her stand in my way? Of course I'm not. There's duty, and there's . . . higher duty.

Marcelle You're right.

Pinglet He challenged us, and when a man's challenged, it's women and children first . . . no, devil take the hindmost . . . no, I mean . . . We must!

Marcelle We must.

Pinglet We must.

He takes her by the hand and tries to lead her out. She resists.

Marcelle Monsieur, I can't.

Pinglet You must. This is no time for pusi . . . pusillan . . . cowardice. *Courage, mon brave!* Have you forgotten, he challenged you? Here on this very hearthrug?

Marcelle How could he?

Pinglet How can you think of your scruples, at a time like this. Did he? His scruples? Did he think of those?

Marcelle He didn't.

Pinglet He cast them to the winds. And when he cast them, he cast yours too.

Marcelle That's right.

Pinglet (*taking her hands*) The most beautiful young woman in all the world, and he takes her scruples and ... tramples them!

Marcelle *cries. He wipes her eyes.*

Marcelle That's right. (*Taking her hanky from him.*) That's my hanky.

Pinglet He doesn't love you. He's never loved you. He isn't made for love.

Marcelle With a name like that! (*Seductively.*) Paillardin ... Paillardin ... (*Furious.*) Ha!

Pinglet (*in her ear*) He must be punished. Revenge must be taken. We must take it. And it must be huge.

Marcelle You're right. You know everything. Revenge. Huge revenge. Oh, yes.

Pinglet (*taking her in his arms*) There, there. I told you, I'm a man of honour. Not to mention tenderness ... devotion ... passion ...

Marcelle (*full of emotion*) You may be ugly, but you're beautiful inside.

Pinglet Oh, thank you.

Marcelle You say such lovely things. If you'd said them an hour ago, I'd have thrown my scruples, then.

Pinglet Ah! At the psychological moment, one waits, one speaks.

Marcelle So now, I say: it's now. This is the moment. Speak!

Pinglet (*hugging her again*)   Marcelle, my darling . . .

Angélique (*off*)   Pinglet! Pinglet!

Pinglet   Hooah! Reality, cold dawn . . . (*To* **Marcelle**, *who has broken free.*) Marcelle, my wife! It's now or never. Tonight, your husband's away, you're free. I'll make myself free as well . . .

Marcelle   Oh yes.

Pinglet   We'll go, together –

Marcelle   Where?

Pinglet   I don't know. I haven't decided. I'll tell you. Revenge. Don't forget, re – Shh! She's here.

They separate. Enter **Angélique**, *crossly.*

Angélique   Where have you been? I've been looking everywhere. What a charmer your friend is, your Paillardin.

Pinglet   Pardon, cabbage?

Angélique   What charming manners! All I did was try to calm him down, explain a few things, and what did he say? 'Keep out of it. When I want you to interfere, I'll tell you.'

Marcelle   That's him exactly.

Angélique   His very words.

Pinglet   To you?

Angélique   To me.

Pinglet   An older woman?

Angélique   That's not the point! (*To* **Marcelle**.) It's you I'm sorry for. What a husband.

Marcelle   Don't worry about me. I'm going to throw my –

Angélique What?

Marcelle Nothing.

Angélique If my husband ever so much as –

Pinglet Who, me? Beloved? Me?

Angélique No, you're right. You wouldn't.

Marcelle What would you do?

Angélique I'd take a lover.

Pinglet (*trying not to laugh*) I say, Angèlique. You wouldn't.

Angélique Of course I would.

Pinglet (*aside*) I can hardly wait.

Enter **Victoire**.

Victoire Madame, the postman's just come. He says he's left a parcel next door for Madame Marcelle.

Marcelle It'll be my new dress. You don't mind if I –

Angélique If you think dresses are the cure for a marriage in tatters. (*Kissing her cheek.*) Till later, then.

Marcelle Till later. (*To* **Pinglet**, *without inflexion.*) Till later.

Pinglet (*formally*) Till later. (*Then, urgently, aside to her.*) You do mean – ?

Marcelle Of course. (*Aside to the audience.*) He does like things clear.

Exit.

Victoire Madame, the post.

Angélique Bring it over here.

Pinglet Find somewhere. Quiet, discreet. Where? How do . . . ?

He knocks on the table as if to say, 'Got it!'

The street directory!

Angélique Don't make such a racket. I'm trying to read. Victoire, I won't be in to dinner.

Pinglet (*aside*) It's fate! (*Aloud.*) Not in to dinner? You'll be ... ah ... somewhere else?

Angélique I'll be in Ville d'Avray. With Marisette.

Pinglet Oh, Auntie.

Angélique She isn't well. See for yourself. (*She passes him the letter.*) I'll see how bad she is. I may have to stay the night. Have you got that? If I don't come back, I'm staying the night.

Pinglet Excellent. Excellent.

Angélique You understand, Victoire? Just one for dinner tonight: Monsieur.

Victoire Yes, Madame.

Exit. **Pinglet** *is thumbing through the street directory.*

Pinglet Hotels ... hotels ...

Angélique (*who has opened another letter*) Hm. Bill from the hatshop.

Pinglet (*triumphal shout*) Got it!

Angélique What d'you mean, Got it?

Pinglet Eh? Oh. I mean, 'Got it! The hatshop bill!'

Angélique *You* intend to pay it?

Pinglet No.

Angélique Then kindly don't shout about it.

Pinglet Whatever you say, beloved. (*To himself, reading.*) Hotel Thermidor ... no. Hotel King Penguin ... no.

Angélique (*who has opened yet another letter*)   Well, really!

Pinglet   What's the matter?

Angélique   Leaflets. Hotel leaflets. What do I want with hotels like these?

Pinglet   Hotels like what?

Angélique   Just listen. 'Discretion guaranteed. Heart's Desire Hotel, 220 rue de Provence. Speciality: parliamentarians and married couples, together or separately. Full Room Service.'

Pinglet   Full Room Service? Together or separately? It really says that?

Angélique   See for yourself. (*She gives him the leaflet.*)

Pinglet   So it does.

Angélique   We all know what goes on *there*.

Pinglet   Oh, we do. (*Aside.*) We do. (*Aloud, reading.*) 'Prices to fit every pocket.'

Angélique (*who is reading another leaflet*).   'Reductions for bulk purchase.' It's unbelievable.

Pinglet   Well, strenuous. (*Aside.*) I'll keep it. (*He pockets the leaflet.*)

Angélique   I'd like to give them a piece of my mind. Posting things like that.

Enter **Victoire**, *showing in* **Mathieu**.

Victoire   This way, Monsieur.

Pinglet   It's Mathieu. From last summer. Come in, come in.

Angélique   How lovely to see you.

Mathieu *kisses her.*

Pinglet   How very nice.

Angélique Do sit down.

Pinglet Give me your umbrella. Poor man, you're soaked.

Mathieu Thanks. I'm de ... de ...

Pinglet Pardon?

Mathieu I said I'm deedee, deedee ...

Angélique No: Mathieu, Mathieu ...

Mathieu No, no, I st ... I st ...

Pinglet Iced? What's he mean?

Mathieu You must be surprised to su ... su ... see me.

Pinglet What *is* the matter with him? My dear Mathieu, something dreadful's happened.

Mathieu Ha ... ha ... How?

Pinglet I mean, you can hardly speak.

Angélique You were perfectly all right when we stayed with you last summer.

Mathieu Last su .... su ... Ah! It's because of the su ... su ...

Pinglet Su-su?

Mathieu Let me f ... finish. Because of the su ... su ... (*Stamping his foot to get the word out, in a huge explosion.*) ... Nshine. Sunshine.

Pinglet I'm sorry?

Mathieu Because of the su ... su ...

He stamps again. This time **Pinglet** *does the explosion.*

Pinglet Nshine. You said that ...

Mathieu When there's su .... su ...

Pinglet (*prompting him*) ... Nshine ...

Mathieu I speak quite normally.

Angélique How interesting.

Mathieu But when it's po ... po ..., when it's po ... po ... po ...

Pinglet Post? Porcelain? Port? Any port in a storm?

Mathieu POURing ...

Pinglet Just as good. Go on.

Mathieu That's when my pa ... pa ..., my pa ... pa ..., my pa ... paHAH ... pa ...

Angélique Take your time.

Pinglet Your paHAH ... pa ...

Mathieu My pa-hah-ROBlems start.

Angélique How embarrassing.

Pinglet A human barometer.

Mathieu And as for li ... li ..., li ... li ... thunder-and-lightning – nothing.

Pinglet Nothing.

Mathieu Du ... du ...

Pinglet Dud?

Mathieu Dumb.

Pinglet No.

Mathieu Yes.

Pinglet Yes.

Mathieu A real ho ... ho ..., ho ... ho ...

Pinglet Very funny?

Mathieu Ho ... ho ... (*Stamping.*) OLDup in my profession.

Pinglet   Ah. OLDup. Naturally. (*To* **Angélique**.)
Holdup in his profession.

Angélique   Well, he *is* a barrister. My dear Monsieur
Mathieu, when it's raining, whatever do you do?

Mathieu   I ask for a def ... def ..., a de ... de ...
def ...

Pinglet   Deaf judge?

Mathieu   Def ... (*Stamping.*) ERRal.

Pinglet (*startled*)   Oof. Thank goodness you don't live in
India. You'd go out of business. Wet season.

Mathieu   No dou ... no dou ... (*Stamping.*) BTofit.

Pinglet   Well, anyway, it's wonderful to see you. After
all this time!

Mathieu   The pleasure's entirely my ... my ...

Pinglet   Mymy?

Angélique   Mine. The pleasure's entirely mine.

Pinglet   No, his.

Mathieu   That's right, my ... my ...

Pinglet   Such a silver tongue.

Mathieu   You said, last time we me ... me ... MET,
'If you're ever in Pa ... pa ... Paris, do come and see
us. Stay as long as you wa ... wa ... WANT.' So here I
am.

Pinglet   Ah.

Angélique   What a lovely surprise.

Pinglet   Stay as long as you want, of course. Two days
... three days ... you can squeeze in three days?

Mathieu   No.

Angélique   Oh, please.

Pinglet   I'm afraid you must.

Mathieu   No, no.

Pinglet   We'll have to insist.

Mathieu   Not three day ... day ... DAYS, four weeks.

Pinglet *and* **Angélique** (*not quite so warmly*)   Ah. Good. How nice.

Mathieu   If you can put up with me that long.

Angélique   Four weeks. A month.

Mathieu   Unless you –

Angélique   No, no. We wouldn't dream of ... Unless you ...

Mathieu   No, no, no, no, no.

Pinglet   Well, I'm glad that's settled.

Mathieu *takes off his raincoat. Meanwhile*:

Angélique (*aside to* **Pinglet**)   It's too long. You'll have to tell him. We only stayed two weeks.

Pinglet (*aside to her*)   But there were two of us. Two and two make four. (*To* **Mathieu**.) Mathieu! Ha, ha, ha.

Mathieu   You're sure it's no trou ... trou ...

Pinglet   Not the slightest trou-trou. We've plenty of room. I mean, you won't mind ... bachelor quarters ... just you, your one small suitcase ...

Mathieu   Aha. I've a little sur ... sur ... sur ... (*Stamping.*) PRISE for you.

Pinglet (*to* **Angélique**)   A little surprise for us.

Angélique   How nice.

Enter **Victoire**.

Victoire   Madame, there's a man with a trunk.

Mathieu   That's the one.

Enter **Porter***, with trunk. Exit* **Victoire***.*

Porter   Where d'you want it?

Mathieu   Why don't you pu ... pu ...

Porter   Poopoo. What's he saying?

Mathieu   Pu ... (*Stamping.*) TIT-there?

Porter   Tit-there?

Pinglet   Put it there. For heaven's sake. Don't you understand plain French?

Porter   Right.

Helped by **Pinglet***, he puts down the trunk.*

Mathieu   How much do I owe you?

Porter   Forty, mate.

Mathieu *pays.*

Angélique   It's the biggest trunk I've ever seen.

Pinglet   A portable bedroom. I mean, we'll put it in your bedroom.

Enter **Victoire***.*

Victoire   In here. Madame, the others are here.

Enter four more **Porters***, with luggage.*

Mathieu   They're mine.

Angélique   Four of them. Why four?

Mathieu   Because of the su ... su ... su ... (*Stamping.*) Rprise.

Pinglet   It's getting out of hand.

Angélique   Why all this luggage? Does your surprise

need all this luggage?

Pinglet Perhaps the luggage *is* the surprise.

Mathieu I say ... my dear fellow ... I wonder if you'd ... I've run out of change. For these good fe ... fe ... fe ...

Pinglet (*stamping and finishing – on* **Mathieu**'s *foot*) ELLows.

Mathieu Ow.

Pinglet Sorry. Right, you chaps. Here you are ... and you ... and you ... and you .... and you ... Now, go with this young woman, to the kitchen, and she'll find you each a beer.

Porters (*separately*) Right, mate. Thanks, mate. Cheers, mate.

Exeunt with **Victoire**.

Pinglet (*aside to* **Angélique**) One trunk, four suitcases. Quite a surprise. They do themselves well, down south.

Angélique We'll open them right away.

Mathieu Pardon?

Angélique For the surprise.

Mathieu No, no, no.

Angélique We're not to open them?

Mathieu The luggage is for la ... la ... (*Stamping.*) ATER.

Pinglet (*who has stamped as well, but too late*) Missed! This is ridiculous.

Angélique If you want us to wait, of course we'll wait. But it's only fair to warn you, we've seen the luggage.

Pinglet I mean, I've heard of generosity, but this is ri-di ... ri-di ... ri-di ...

Mathieu (*coldly and clearly*) Ridiculous.

Angélique Oh, well done!

Pinglet I do believe he's got it.

Mathieu I never have trouble with ridiculous.

Enter **Victoire**.

Victoire Madame, there's a carriage at the door. The young ladies . . .

Mathieu Ah. They're the ones. Bring them in.

Victoire Yes, Monsieur.

Exit.

Mathieu Ha, ha, ha! Your faces! *Now* you're surprised.

Pinglet *and* **Angélique** No, no . . .

Mathieu You didn't know, did you? When you stayed with me . . . you thought I was a bachelor. No, no, no, no. It's eight years now since Madame Mathieu pa . . . pa . . . PASSed on –

Pinglet Ah.

Mathieu I had my girls brought up in boarding school. But they've just had to close the school, because so many girls were having . . . ha . . . ha . . . having . . .

Pinglet We can guess what they were having.

Mathieu Mumps.

Pinglet Oh, mumps.

Mathieu So I thought, I'll take them to Paris. Monsieur and Madame Pinglet, they've never met them. It'll be such a surprise.

Pinglet *and* **Angélique** Of course.

Mathieu I left them at the station, and came on ahead.

Angélique   That's the surprise? You've daughters?

Mathieu (*dancing for joy*)   Yes! Yes!

Pinglet   Ha, ha, ha, ha. We thought it was the luggage.

Mathieu   The luggage is for the daughters!

Pinglet *and* **Angélique** (*stunned*)   You mean . . . ? Ah.

Mathieu   Here they are. Come in, come in!

Enter the **Daughters**, *in a giggling gaggle.*

Pinglet   Four of them.

Angélique   What a surprise.

Mathieu   In you come, dar . . . dar . . . , dar . . . dar . . .

Daughters (*in chorus*)   LINGS, Papa!

Mathieu   That's right. Say bonjour nicely to Monsieur and Madame Pan . . . pan . . . , Pan . . . pan . . .

Daughters   GLET, Papa!

Mathieu   That's right. Give them a great big kiss.

Daughters   Bonjour, Monsieur . . . Bonjour, Madame . . .

Pinglet *and* **Angélique** (*trying to fight them off*)   Yes. Thanks. Very nice. That's right.

Angélique   It's an invasion.

Pinglet   A locust-plague.

Angélique   We'd no idea you'd such a family.

Mathieu (*smugly*)   Aren't they darlings?

Pinglet   But what are you going to do with them? You're moving them to another school – today?

Mathieu   No, no. Quarantine. Till the mumps are over.

Pinglet   But where will you keep them?

Mathieu Here.

Angélique What?

Pinglet Here? Ah. No. Oh, no. No. Oh, no.

Mathieu But you clearly said . . .

Pinglet I know. 'Any time.' I said, 'Any time.' Everyone *says* that. It doesn't mean a thing.

Mathieu Pardon?

Pinglet You took it literally. You arrived. Fine. But you brought . . . you brought . . .

Mathieu What's the matter?

Pinglet This is a private house, not a youth hostel.

Mathieu Naturally. I wouldn't lodge my daughters in a you . . . you . . .

Pinglet THhostel! Of course you wouldn't. And you can't lodge them here. This is Paris. We don't go around in flocks, in Paris. This isn't the south, you know.

Angélique It's your fault. Your fault. Throwing invitations left, right and centre . . .

Pinglet Throwing invitations? Me? *You* said, *you* said, 'We have to ask him back. Two weeks' hospitality – no choice.'

Angélique I know what I said. You didn't have to listen.

Pinglet I can't help it if he accepted.

Angélique Of course you can help it. You could have said it lightly, tossed it off, ha, ha, ha. Instead, you made a thing of it. You went on, and on, and on, till he felt he had to. No other choice.

Pinglet Oh, take his side. (*To* **Mathieu**.) You were a witness. Was it my fault, or wasn't it?

Mathieu We'd better be going.

Pinglet You're certainly not staying.

Mathieu Come along, girls. Say merci beaucoup and au revoir to Monsieur and Madame Pinglet.

Daughters (*milling round, shaking hands*) Thank you, Monsieur. Au 'voir, Monsieur. Thank you, Madame. Au 'voir, Madame.

Pinglet It was nothing. Don't mention it. Angélique, d'you think those porters'll still be in the kitchen? To take the bags ... ?

Angélique I'll check.

Enter **Marcelle**.

Marcelle Good grief, whose are all these bags?

Angélique It's all right. They're leaving. Any minute.

Exit.

Mathieu (*going to shake* **Marcelle***'s hand*) Madame.

Pinglet Marcelle, my dear ... Monsieur Mathieu, an old, old friend. I must have mentioned him, and all his dynasty. Madame Paillardin ... (*Aside to her.*) I've found it. The very place. You still – ?

Marcelle Yes. Still.

Pinglet Meet me at eight o'clock on the corner of the avenue du Bois and the rue de la Pompe. In a carriage. Keep the blinds down.

Mathieu All this luggage. Where on earth can we stay?

Pinglet I'll be with you in a minute.

Mathieu If I only had an address.

Marcelle But where are we going?

Pinglet Heart's Desire Hotel, 220 rue de Provence.

Mathieu   Thanks. (*Writing it down.*) Heart's Desire Hotel, 220 Rue de Pro ... pro ..., Pro ... pro ...

Daughters   VENCE, Papa!

Mathieu   Say Au revoir then, and off we go.

The **Daughters** *start milling as before. Enter* **Angélique**.

Daughters   Madame.

Angélique   Mamzelles.

Daughters   Monsieur.

Pinglet   Mamzelles.

Mathieu (*to* **Marcelle**)   Madame.

Marcelle   Monsieur.

Mathieu   See you later.

Pinglet   Where?

Mathieu   At the hotel. Au 'voir.

Daughters   Au 'voir.

Pinglet   Don't start again.

He shoos them out. Exeunt all but **Pinglet** *and* **Marcelle**.

Pinglet   Marcelle! You don't know how happy you've made me.

Marcelle   Not now.

Pinglet   Has your husband left yet?

Marcelle   He didn't even say goodbye. So ... (*She makes a gesture of revenge.*)

Pinglet   Exactly. I'm by your side.

Marcelle   And I'm by yours.

Pinglet   If I'd ever dreamed ... dared hope ...
Marcelle, Angélique will be dining with her auntie. Shall

we . . . go out to dinner . . . together?

Marcelle   For revenge?

Pinglet   For revenge! Go and get ready. In half an hour, on the corner of the avenue du Bois and the rue de la Pompe.

Marcelle   At once!

She goes to the door. Enter **Angélique** *and* **Victoire**.

Angélique   Not leaving so soon?

Marcelle   A headache.

Angélique   Take care!

Exit **Marcelle**.

Angélique   Put it down there, Victoire.

Pinglet   Put what down?

Angélique   Your dinner. Victoire has to unpack for Maxime, at college.

Pinglet   My dinner?

Angélique   That's right. Thank you, Victoire.

Exit **Victoire**.

Pinglet   No, no, no, no, no. I won't hear of it. You're at Auntie's, I'm on my own. I'll have dinner in some little restaurant.

Angélique   You'll do no such thing.

Pinglet   Why not, sweetness?

Angélique   Because you're a husband. And husbands don't dine in restaurants without their wives.

Pinglet   Whyever not, dear one?

Angélique   Whatever would people think?

Pinglet   They'd think . . . What d'you want them to think?

Angélique The day you have dinner in a restaurant, you'll have it with me.

Pinglet They'd think I'd struck lucky.

Angélique That's enough of that. And tonight, you eat your dinner here.

Pinglet Can't you do anything but ... mollycoddle?

Angélique Mollycoddle?

Pinglet I will not be mollycoddled. I'm going to a restaurant, whether you like it or not.

Angélique You most certainly are not.

Pinglet I most certainly am.

Angélique You aren't.

Pinglet I am.

Angélique We'll see about that!

She pockets the door-key.

Pinglet Give me that. Give me that at once.

Angélique Let go.

Pinglet I order you. Give me that key.

Angélique I won't.

Pinglet You will.

Angélique I won't.

Pinglet You will.

Angélique Here!

She boxes his ears, and exit. Noise of the door being locked.

Pinglet Ow. Come back.

He goes and rattles the door.

She's locked it. She has. In here . . .

He runs into her room, then out again.

That one too.

He flails round the room, then stops, panting. Sudden inspiration.

Got it!

He flings up the window, fastens a rope ladder to a bar outside, and starts clambering out as the curtain falls.

Act Two

Heart's Desire Hotel – a cheap hotel, as the furnishings and fittings make clear. The stage is divided in three. Stage left, Room Number 10, visible to the audience. L, a table covered with a fringed cloth, the door to the bathroom, a fireplace whose mantelpiece contains a clock, two candleholders and two vases of artificial flowers and feathers; C, a curtained bed and a bedside table with water-carafe, sugar bowl and glass; R, door to the hall, chair. Centre stage, the reception hall. Upstage, a curving staircase (clearly visible to the audience) goes down to the cellar below and up to the floors above. Off this staircase, on the rear wall of the stage, about three steps up, the door of Number 9. On the hall wall, a board with hooks for keys, each with a room number; table covered with candleholders; a chair. Stage right, opening off the hall, Number 11. This is a large suite, with a window, a fireplace, a sofa, a big curtained bed and no less than four camp-beds. Night-table; door R to the bathroom. N.B. All doors should be functional and lockable. It is half-past eight in the evening, and the gas-lights are lit in the hall. **Bastien** *is sitting at the hall table, cutting candles in half. He speaks directly to the audience.*

Bastien   Look: one candle, two candles . . . snip, snip, four candles. Cheap trick, you think? If you'd been in this business as long as I have . . . fifteen years . . . the things I've seen! The things I've seen! . . . If you'd been in this business as long as I have, you'd know. This little candle trick alone, over fifteen years, adds up. Six thousand francs, give or take . . . And that's just one!

Enter **Boulot**, *falling down the stairs in total panic.*

Boulot   Oh my God. My God.

Bastien   Hey Boulot, quite an entrance. What's the matter?

Boulot   Oh Bastien, d'you know what I've just seen? My God, my God. It wasn't my fault. You told me to knock, so I knocked . . .

Bastien What did you see?

Boulot Number 32 rang, Bastien. I knocked, Bastien. They said 'Come in' – and there was a woman with nothing on, Bastien.

Bastien Yes? And – ?

Boulot No, I mean nothing on. Naked. Nude.

Bastien I know what it means.

Boulot She said, 'Ah, there you are. Fetch a pack of cards.' I didn't know what to do.

Bastien What you do is, you take a pack of cards.

Boulot But she was starkers.

Bastien What of it?

Boulot Naked. A woman.

Bastien Under their clothes, they all are.

Boulot Not where I come from.

Bastien Boulot, listen. This is Paris. The big city. Get used to it. Another fifteen years, you'll be unshockable. All you need is a blind eye and a thick skin. You'll manage. (*He goes back to cutting his candles.*) And you can start, if you wouldn't mind, by knocking up Number 9.

Boulot Number 9? Yes, Bastien. She won't be ... I mean, she won't be ...?

Bastien Of course she won't. And it's not an 'er, it's an 'im. That school caretaker Chervet. Hasn't paid his rent for weeks. Boss says we've to keep his bags and chuck him out. Get on with it.

Boulot Me?

Bastien Who d'you think?

Boulot Monsieur Chervet. He's the one that shouts. Says he'll box your ears.

Bastien   Words.

Boulot   But suppose he does?

Bastien   If he does, report him to me. Get on with it.

Boulot   Yes, Bastien. (*Muttering to himself.*) I don't like this at all.

He knocks timidly at Number 9. Huge shout from inside.

Chervet (*off*)   Come in!

Boulot (*recoiling*)   I wish it was her upstairs.

He goes into the room. **Bastien** *speaks to the audience.*

Bastien   They've all to start somewhere. Fifteen years, he'll get used to it.

Bell, off.

Guests. Ringing the bell. *They've* not been here before.

Enter **Ernest**, *with his* **Companion** *on his arm. She's veiled.*

Ernest   I say, you there.

Bastien   Yes, Monsieur? How can I help Monsieur ... Madame ... ?

Ernest   Do you by any chance have a room?

Bastien   A room, Monsieur? (*Honeyed voice.*) A nest, a nest made for two, a frame for a beautiful picture. I speak of Madame, Monsieur. What a charming lady. She does Monsieur great credit.

Ernest   I say, steady on.

Bastien   Of course, Monsieur. I know exactly what Monsieur requires. And by the purest good luck, we have it. Ready and waiting: Number 88.

Ernest   Two fat ladies? I don't think so.

Bastien   Unless Monsieur prefers Number 69.

Ernest Now look here. This lady is a . . . lady.

Bastien I saw that at once, Monsieur.

Ernest And I'm . . . I'm . . . You surely know who I am.

Bastien Ah, I –

Ernest Ernest. The Great Ernesto. His whip, his chair, his pride.

Bastien Pardon?

Ernest Lions, man, lions.

Bastien Ah, the Great Ernesto. Who doesn't know Monsieur? The talk of the town. Especially the ladies.

Ernest I say. What do they say? Hey, hey? (*To his* **Companion**.) Did you hear that? 'Especially the ladies.' (*To* **Bastien**.) This one's a Countess, don't you know.

Bastien Monsieur, congratulations. That's why I suggested Number 88. It was in that very room, Number 88, that Her Royal Highness the Princess Royal of Poland spent her wedding-night, with her first Groom of the Bedchamber. (*To the* **Companion**.) Only the very best is good enough, Madame . . .

Ernest (*jovially*) Absolutely! (*Aside to* **Bastien**.) Just a mo. The Princess Royal of Poland. Bit expensive, what?

Bastien What of it?

Ernest She's not paying, I am.

Bastien You are?

Ernest What did you think?

Noise, off.

What the devil's that?

Bastien Just a guest we're chucking out.

Enter **Boulot** *from Number 9, fast.*

Boulot Ow. No. I told you he would. I said he'd box my ears. He says he won't budge without his baggage.

Bastien Won't budge? He'll budge. (*Yelling.*) Chervet! Oi, Chervet! Here!

Chervet *appears at his door.*

Chervet What do you want, you?

Bastien See this line? Cross it. Out. Quick march.

Chervet I'm not budging without my baggage.

Bastien You'll get your baggage when you pay your bill.

Chervet Right, that does it. I've got a mate at police headquarters. You wait. You won't look so clever when the cops get here.

Ernest Cops? I say.

Chervet Yeah, cops. They'll be very interested in what goes on here. All I say is, check your bill.

Ernest What?

Bastien Oi. Have you quite finished?

Chervet I have with you. I'm talking to this gent here. (*To* **Ernest**.) Wait till you see the room. A dump. Creaking springs. Bedbugs.

Consternation of **Ernest** *and his* **Companion**.

Ernest Bedbugs?

Bastien We put down powder every morning.

Chervet Powder, huh! It guts the guests and breeds the bugs. In any case, the place is haunted.

Ernest Haunted?

Bastien (*to* **Chervet**) Shut up, will you? I said, shut up.

Chervet And I said haunted. Poltergeists. (*Pointing to Number 11.*) In there. Middle of the night. Knocking, banging, chucking stuff about. They used to sleep the staff in there. Not any more.

Ernest This is dreadful.

Bastien No it's not. It's rubbish.

Chervet Rubbish, is it? Have you or have you not got an expert coming this very night? A ghost expert?

Ernest That does it. You, fellow: you can keep Number 88.

Bastien You're not going?

Ernest What do you think? (*To his* **Companion**.) This way, your Grace.

Exeunt.

Bastien But Monsieur ... (*To* **Chervet**.) Now look what you've done.

Chervet See if I care. They've gone, and I'm going. And you know *where* I'm going. You wait. You'll see.

Exit.

Bastien (*shouting after him*). That's right, get out of it. Get lost. Get thrown out somewhere else.

Boulot Two clients lost, thanks to him.

Bastien Two clients. (*Shouting after them.*) They can get lost as well. (*To* **Boulot**.) Did you see that fraud? 'His whip, his chair, his pride.' Who did he think he was? 'This one's a countess, don't you know?' Ha! I'd have liked to see them at it.

Boulot You couldn't have done that.

Bastien Oh yeah? Why not?

Boulot They wouldn't have invited you.

Bastien   Idiot. Of course they wouldn't have invited me. But I'd still have seen.

Boulot   How?

Bastien   You know nothing. (*Showing a brace and bit.*) What d'you think this is for?

Boulot   Making holes.

Bastien   Exactly. When I want to see someone . . . (*Turning it.*) I see 'em.

Boulot   You mean . . . ?

Bastien   The fanciest women in Paris. I've seen 'em all.

Enter **Paillardin**, *with suitcase.*

Paillardin   Porter! Porter!

Bastien   This way, Monsieur. Monsieur's expecting company? I know just what Monsieur requires. A nest, a nest made just for two . . .

Paillardin   Monsieur wants nothing of the kind. Monsieur's on his own. Monsieur Paillardin, court-appointed expert. About the hauntings.

Bastien   The spook expert! You wait, Monsieur. You wait till you hear 'em.

Bell, off.

(*Honeyed voice.*) Excuse me just one moment. (*Yell.*) Boulot, someone's ringing. Get up there. (*Honeyed voice, to* **Paillardin**.) It's unbelievable, Monsieur. Every night, walls creaking, furniture leaping about . . .

Paillardin   Thank you, I'll see for myself. I don't need eye-witness accounts. Which room is it?

Bastien (*indicating Number 11*)   This one, Monsieur. I'll light Monsieur a candle.

Paillardin   Thanks. Let's have a look.

They go into the room.

Bastien I'm glad it's you, Monsieur, not me, who has to spend the night in here.

Paillardin Ha! If haunted rooms were all I had to face . . . H'm. It seems quiet enough, for a nest of poltergeists.

Bastien It's always quiet, this time of night.

Paillardin Of course. They'll be asleep . . . out shopping . . .

Bastien They start at midnight.

Paillardin Aha! Midnight poltergeists.

Bastien Joke if you like, Monsieur. You'll see.

Singing, overhead.

Paillardin Hang on. They're early tonight.

Bastien That's not them. Unversity students . . . and studentesses. I'll tell 'em.

He goes out into the lobby. **Paillardin** *starts unpacking.*

Paillardin Cigar-case . . . hairbrush . . .

Bastien (*yelling up the stairs*) Keep it down, up there!

Voice (*from upstairs*) Get stuffed.

Bastien Get stuffed, is it? I'm coming up.

Enter **Pinglet**, *suitcase in hand, enormous cigar in mouth.*

Pinglet Porter.

Bastien Right away, Monsieur. Don't go away, Monsieur.

He hurtles upstairs. Enter **Marcelle**.

Pinglet Right away, he says. Don't go away, he says. You can tell it's discreet.

Marcelle It's horrible. Where did you find it?

Pinglet   It doesn't look much. But that's the whole point. In a good hotel, someone might recognise us. But here? No chance.

Marcelle   That's true.

Paillardin (*sneezing, in Number 11*)   Atchoo!

Pinglet (*calling out, jokingly*)   *Gesundheit.*

Paillardin (*calling back*)   Thank you.

Pinglet   My pleasure. (*To* **Marcelle**.) In any case, all hotels look fine to me, when I'm with ... with ... (*Breaking off.*) Is that smell *drains*?

Paillardin *has gone into the bathroom of Number 11, taking his candle. It's pitch dark in Number 11 now.*

Pinglet   Ah, the porter.

Bastien (*coming down the stairs*)   Here I am, Monsieur. I know exactly what Monsieur requires. (*Honeyed voice.*) A nest, a nest made for two, a frame for a beautiful picture. I speak of Madame, Monsieur. What a charming lady. She does Monsieur great credit.

Pinglet   That's quite enough. This lady is my wife.

Bastien (*sure of himself*)   No she's not.

Pinglet   She is.

Bastien   Not.

Pinglet   Is.

Bastien   Can't be. If she was, she'd have come in first.

Pinglet   Ah. (*Aside.*) An expert. (*To him.*) Have you anything on this floor, here?

Bastien   Oh, yes, Monsieur. Number 10. Where Her Royal Highness the Princess Royal of Poland spent her wedding-night, with her first Groom of the Bedchamber.

Pinglet   Perfect. (*To* **Marcelle**.) Did you hear that? The

Princess Royal of Poland spent her . . . stayed in this room. They know how to treat their guests.

Bastien (*leading the way, with a candle*)   This way, Monsieur. As you can see: a fine room. Its own facilities. You'll have everything you need, Monsieur.

Pinglet   I'll take it.

Bastien   An excellent choice, Monsieur.

He goes to light the candles on the mantelpiece.

Pinglet   Oh, Marcelle.

Marcelle   Sh! The porter.

Pinglet   Ah. (*To* **Bastien**.) That's fine.

Bastien   Thank you, Monsieur. Good night, Monsieur, Madame . . .

Pinglet   Good night.

Bastien *goes into the hall, and* **Pinglet** *turns back to* **Marcelle**.

Pinglet   Marcelle.

Enter **Bastien**.

Bastien   The key, Monsieur. Good night, Monsieur.

He goes back into the hall, and meets **Paillardin** *coming out of Number 11.*

Bastien   Going out, Monsieur?

Paillardin (*handing him his candlestick*)   It's nowhere near my bedtime. There's a bar across the street. I'm going for a beer. Half an hour . . .

Bastien   That's right, Monsieur. Your candle will be waiting.

Exit **Paillardin**. **Bastien** *goes upstairs.*

Pinglet   Marcelle!

He embraces her.

Marcelle (*uneasy*)   Pinglet!

Pinglet   Not Pinglet. Never again, Pinglet. Call me . . .
Boniface-Benoît.

Marcelle   Boniface-Benoît?

She moves away.

Pinglet   Boniface-Benoît.

He pursues her, cigar still in mouth.

Oh Marcelle, it's time. Time for revenge.

He tries to hug her again.

Marcelle   Mind your cigar.

Pinglet   There. Marcelle, you're adorable!

He has her in his arms and the cigar in one hand.

Marcelle   You're singeing my dress, now.

Pinglet   Sorry.

Marcelle   Can't you put that thing out?

Pinglet   It cost twenty centimes. Every millimetre counts.

Marcelle (*pouting*)   Oh . . .

Pinglet   But what of that? (*He hurls it into the grate.*)
What's money compared to love? What a picture you are.

Marcelle   Does it suit me, this dress?

Pinglet   All dresses suit you.

Marcelle   It came this afternoon. This is the first time
I've worn it. You're the first person who's seen me in it.

Pinglet   Never mind the dress! The setting that
surrounds the jewel. All I see is you, my darling. I see no
dress, just you, just you. Oh come to me.

He hurls himself at her.

Marcelle What are you doing? Pinglet! Boniface-Benoît!

Pinglet I want you, I want you.

Marcelle What's wrong with you? Don't do that. What's the matter? You've had too much champagne.

Pinglet Champagne, huh! I'm happy, don't you see, happy? A gorgeous woman, a gorgeous dinner, gorgeous wine, liqueurs, a big cigar ... Angélique (my wife, you know) won't let me smoke cigars, drink wine ... Not good for me, she says. And she's right! She's right. Oh Marcelle, oh come to me.

He sits down, and tries to pull her on to his knees. The chair collapses.

Ow! That hurts.

Marcelle You do look silly.

Pinglet Silly? (*Aside.*) Me, silly?

Marcelle (*still laughing*) You haven't hurt yourself?

Pinglet Of course I haven't. I know how to fall. (*Getting up.*) Cheap chairs! You'd think, since there's only one, they'd have made it more ...

He hurls it out into the hall.

Out where you belong! (*To himself.*) Right, where were we? (*Chasing her as before.*) Marcelle!

Marcelle You should have seen yourself.

Pinglet (*huffily*) It wasn't all that funny.

Marcelle You looked so ... so ...

Pinglet There really is no need to ...

Marcelle (*biting her hanky*) You're right, of course.

Pinglet (*taking her in his arms*) My darling!

Out in the hall, **Boulot** *finds the chair.*

Boulot The chair from Number 10. I'd better . . .

He opens the door, goes in.

Ah!

Marcelle *and* **Pinglet** *(springing apart)* Ah-aah!

Boulot I'm sorry, Monsieur. I thought it was empty.
I've brought this chair.

Pinglet *(through his teeth, furious)* Thank you very much.
You've brought it in, and now you can take it out again.

Boulot I can't do that, Monsieur. It belongs here.

Pinglet And you don't. Out, out, out!

He pushes him out and slams the door.

Oh!

Boulot Nice bit of stuff. I wonder how they . . . ? Hang
on . . .

He fetches the brace and bit.

Bastien *(from upstairs)* Boulot! Boulot!

Boulot Coming!

He puts down the brace and bit and exit. In Number 10,
Pinglet *is feeling peculiar.*

Pinglet Oh. Ooh. Ooof.

Marcelle What's the matter?

Pinglet I don't know. Cold sweat – that is, perspiration.
Oh, emotion. It'll pass. Ha, ha, ha. *(Taking her in his arms.)*
Marcelle, my darling, alone at last. If you could only feel
my heart, my heart . . . *(Change of tone.)* Ooof, my heart.

Marcelle You've gone all white. Pinglet. Boniface-
Benoît.

Pinglet   I do feel odd.

Marcelle   Sit down.

Pinglet   He's taken the chair.

Marcelle   On the table. There.

Pinglet (*sitting on the coffee-table*)   Oh, Marcelle. I'm sorry. It won't take a ... I'll be quite ... Oof.

Marcelle   I'll get you some water. Sugar-water.

She goes to the bedside table to mix it.

Pinglet   It's the cigar. The champagne. I don't smoke. I never drink. Well, except water. Oh, ooh, ahh.

Marcelle   Drink this sugar-water.

Pinglet   If only Angélique was here.

Marcelle   Sit down. What are you doing?

Pinglet   Walking. Keep moving. Oh, I feel as if I'm going to ... I'm going to ...

Marcelle   Well, you *are* going to. We're both going to.

Pinglet   No, no. I feel as if I'm ... too hot, too hot ...

Marcelle   Take your jacket off.

Pinglet   Yes. Oh, oh.

Marcelle   It's all right.

Pinglet   Marcelle, I've just thought ... What if I ... die here?

Marcelle   Oh, don't do that.

She wets her hanky and wipes his forehead. **Boulot** *comes back downstairs and takes up the brace and bit again.*

Boulot   If Bastien can do it, Boulot can do it. (*Feeling the wall.*) Now, where's best ... ? A-ha!

He starts drilling. Inside, **Pinglet** *is moving about the room.*

Pinglet Thank you. You are kind.

He leans against the wall.

Boulot They won't notice a thing.

Marcelle How d'you feel now?

Pinglet Much better.

Boulot Nearly through.

Pinglet Ee-ow!

Marcelle What's the matter?

Pinglet A pinprick. Down here, on my ... I mean, in the lower back.

Marcelle That's good! The blood's left your brain. Less pressure.

Pinglet OW!

Marcelle What?

Pinglet Ah! Oh! Ooh!

He jumps away from the wall. **Boulot** *removes his drill.*

Boulot There we are.

Pinglet Oh my goodness. Oh my goodness.

Marcelle What?

Pinglet It was as if someone was ... was boring right into me, seeing –

Marcelle Seeing what?

Pinglet Seeing right inside.

Marcelle It's some kind of attack.

Boulot (*examining the end of his drill*) It's gone all wet and red. Huh! Rising damp!

Marcelle Call a doctor.

Pinglet   I'll be all right. Just let me breathe. And perhaps . . . a cup of tea?

Boulot (*on all fours, peering through the hole*)   Now then . . .

Pinglet *opens the door and shouts.*

Pinglet   Porter!

He falls over **Boulot**.

Pinglet   Now what are you doing?

Boulot   I was . . . er . . . Monsieur called, so I was . . . listening.

Pinglet   Fresh air. I need fresh air. Where's the balcony?

Boulot   Upstairs, Monsieur. Turn right, along the corridor . . .

Pinglet   Thanks.

Marcelle (*at the door*)   Fetch a kettle of boiling water.

Boulot   What?

Pinglet   A kettle of boiling water. Oh, oh, don't go, Marcelle. Wait for me.

He makes for the stairs.

Marcelle   Of course I'll wait.

Pinglet   Oh my goodness. Oh my goodness.

Exit up the stairs.

Marcelle   Well, don't just stand there. He wants a cup of tea.

Boulot   Tea. They're all shut. It's night. I know! Number 9. The one I threw out. He has tea. Just a minute, Madame.

He goes into Number 9.

Marcelle   What a night!

Boulot *comes out with kettle, spirit-stove and tea-caddy.*

Boulot   Here you are. Everything you need. I'll boil
some water. In there.

He goes into Number 10 to make the tea, and she goes after him.

Marcelle   Why did you tell him where the balcony is?
He'll catch his death of cold.

Boulot   Oh no, Madame. It's lovely out. Mind you, this
morning . . . did you *see* that rain? Not now though. Clear
sky, those little fleecy clouds, full moon . . .

Enter **Mathieu** *into the hall, followed by his* **Daughters**.

Mathieu   In here, darlings. Hurry.

Daughters   Yes, Papa. Yes, Papa.

Mathieu *(ranting)*   There's no porter. Why isn't there a
porter? What sort of hotel is this? There's always a porter.
Looking after you. Protecting you. No one. Not a single
soul. We could be cat-burglars, desperadoes, Vikings . . .
we could pillage the entire place, and there'd be none the
wiser. There was a bell. You saw the bell. I pressed the
bell. Nothing. No one. What's the point of having a bell
at all?

First daughter   Papa.

Mathieu   What?

First daughter   It's stopped raining, Papa. Listen to
yourself.

Mathieu   It's Pinglet's fault. All of it. He sent us here.
Why did he send us here? It's a dump. We'll stay one
night. But we won't unpack. At the crack of dawn, we're
leaving.

Second daughter   Waah! I don't like this hotel.

The other daughters *(one after another)*   I don't. I don't.
I don't.

Marcelle (*in Room 10*) All right, it's boiling. Fetch a teapot.

Boulot Yes, Madame. (*To himself as he steps out into the hall.*) Nice bit of stuff...

Daughters He's here, Papa.

Boulot My God, a school party.

Mathieu Ahem. Porter. We're here on the recommendation of Monsieur Pinglet.

Boulot Monsieur Pinglet? Of course, Monsieur. (*Aside.*) Never heard of him.

Mathieu We require rooms. My daughters and myself.

Boulot (*aside*) His daughters. All these? (*To him.*) Monsieur's daughters? (*Aside.*) What is he, a rabbit?

Mathieu Well? What have you got?

Boulot Ah, Monsieur, I'm sorry. We haven't that many rooms – (*To himself.*) Number 11! This could be it! (*To* **Mathieu**.) We may just be able to...

Mathieu Show me, then. Get on with it.

Boulot (*lighting and taking a candle*) This way, Monsieur. (*Showing him into Number 11.*) This big room here.

Mathieu It's a dormitory.

Boulot It's all there is, Monsieur. We're full up. One Monsieur, four Mamzelles ... five beds.

Mathieu I can't share a bedroom with my daughters.

Boulot Yes, Monsieur. Take the big bed. Go to bed first, pull the curtains, and then your daughters can go to bed. There are two dressing-rooms. Here, look ... here ...

Mathieu Well, beggars can't be choosers. Hotel is as hotel does.

He takes the candle. **Boulot** *hurriedly fetches another from the hall.*

Boulot Whatever you say, Monsieur.

Mathieu Does it cost a fortune?

Boulot Oh, no, Monsieur. Since Monsieur ...
Wotsname ... recommended you, how about seven francs
per night?

Mathieu Fair enough.

Marcelle (*in Number 10*) Where on earth is Pinglet?

Mathieu Fine, then, we'll take it.

He puts his candlestick down on **Paillardin***'s cigar-case.*

Boulot Thank you Monsieur. Good night, Monsieur.
Good night, Mamzelles.

Daughters Bonne nuit, Monsieur.

Boulot *goes into the hall.*

Marcelle Something's happened. I'd better –

She goes to the door of Number 10.

Mathieu We need another candle.

He goes to the door of Number 11.

Marcelle *and* **Mathieu** (*coming into the hall at the same
moment*) Porter!

Marcelle Monsieur Mathieu!

Mathieu Madame ... Paillardin!

Marcelle No, no. Oh, all right, yes.

Mathieu We met this afternoon. At Pinglet's.

Marcelle Yes.

Mathieu What a lovely surprise. Darlings ...

Marcelle (*trying to escape*) No, Monsieur, really ...

Mathieu No, no, they'll be so pleased. Darlings, it's Madame Paillardin.

Boulot (*passing into Number 10, with a teapot*) So that's her name.

The **Daughters** *foam into the hall.*

Daughters Madame Paillardin. It's Madame Paillardin. Bonsoir, Madame.

Marcelle (*aside*) I don't need this.

Boulot (*at the door of Number 10*) Madame Paillardin, tea's made.

Marcelle How does he know my name? (*To him.*) Thank you.

Mathieu Tea? You live here?

Marcelle No, you don't understand. My husband . . . we're moving house.

First daughter We're in this room here.

Boulot Madame Paillardin, it's stewing.

Marcelle (*aside*) I wish he'd stop calling me that.

Boulot Madame Paillardin . . .

Marcelle Yes, yes. Thank you. (*To* **Mathieu**.) I'm sorry, Monsieur . . . my tea . . . (*At the door.*) I'm sorry . . . I should've . . .

She goes in. He follows her.

Mathieu That's all right. We'd be delighted. Wouldn't we, darlings?

Daughters Tea, Papa. Yes, Papa. Please, Papa.

They mill about.

Marcelle (*to herself*) Pinglet's jacket!

She takes it into the dressing-room.

Mathieu (*leading his* **Daughters** *into Number 10*)   In here, darlings.

Marcelle   Do sit down.

Mathieu   Ah. No chairs.

Marcelle   Oh no. Ha, ha, ha. No chairs.

Boulot (*who has fetched cups*)   More cups. Seven.

Daughters   Hurray!

Mathieu   Never mind cups. Bring chairs.

Boulot   Right away, Monsieur.

Mathieu   Help him, darlings.

Boulot (*to the* **Daughters**)   We'll go to Number 9.

They go.

Marcelle (*aside*)   Why don't they go?

Mathieu   Now then . . . Shall I be mother . . . ?

Marcelle   Oh. Please.

Boulot   Here we are!

The **Daughters** *return with chairs.*

Marcelle (*aside*)   This is all his fault. This is Pinglet's fault.

Boulot   All comfy? I'll fetch a hot-water-bottle.

Marcelle   What for?

Boulot   For Madame's Monsieur.

Marcelle   Oh. Yes. Yes.

Exit **Boulot**.

Marcelle (*aside*)   What am I to do? (*Aloud.*) Is everybody . . . comfy . . . ?

Mathieu   Madame Paillardin, so sorry. Come on,

darlings, help Madame. Pour the tea!

The **Daughters** *see to this.*

Mathieu   Tell me, Madame, our good friend Pinglet.
D'you see him often?

Marcelle   Rarely. Very, very rarely. You know what it's
like in Paris. It's his wife I'm really friends with. That's
why I was there this after –

They continue their conversation. **Pinglet** *comes down the stairs
into the hall, very cheerful.*

Pinglet   I knew fresh air would do the trick. (*Breathing
deeply.*) Mff-hah! Mff-hah! Take in some air, get rid of the
dinner . . . Mff-ha! I really feel quite . . .

He sings to himself.

Sur le pont d'Avignon,
On y danse, on y danse . . .
Là chez soi, dans la maison,
On y danse tout en rond . . .

Mathieu   So you hardly know him at all?

Marcelle   No, that's right. Hardly at all. Ha, ha.

Pinglet *half dances, half walks into Room 10.*

Daughters   Monsieur Pinglet!

Pinglet (*stunned*)   I say!

Marcelle (*to him, aside*)   What next?

Pinglet (*to her*)   Where did they spring from?

Mathieu   Your ears must be burning. We were just
talking about you.

Daughters   That's right, Papa.

Pinglet   How kind of you. Ah, Madame Paillardin, how

are you? I was just passing . . . business, you understand
. . . I said to myself, 'I'll just pop round and say hello to
Madame Paillardin.'

Marcelle   What a lovely surprise.

Daughters   Lovely. Lovely.

Mathieu   Just a minute, you've lost your jacket.

Pinglet (*aside*)   Harg. (*Aloud.*) No, no, no, no, no, no. A
tiny tear, d'you see? I said, 'I'll take it to be mended, and
while they're doing that, I'll just pop round and say hello
to Madame Paillardin.'

Marcelle   Too kind.

Daughters   Too kind.

First daughter   A cup of tea, Monsieur?

Pinglet   Oh, thank you.

Second daughter   Sugar, Monsieur?

Pinglet   Sugar? Ah, sugar. Yes, yes, yes, yes, yes.

Third daughter   Monsieur does like sugar.

Pinglet (*continuing to ladle it in*)   Not really, no, no, no.

Fourth daughter   Monsieur is silly!

Mathieu (*drinking his tea*)   Well, Pinglet, apart from your
torn jacket, how's Paris?

Pinglet   Oh, you know . . . Paris . . .

He drinks his over-sweet tea.

Mathieu   Madame Pinglet's well?

Pinglet   You saw her this morning. And Madame
Mathieu?

Mathieu   Dead. Eight years ago. I told you.

Pinglet   Ah. So you did. Quite dead. (*To* **Marcelle**.)

They're like barnacles.

Marcelle (*to him*)   I know!

Enter **Boulot**.

Boulot   Monsieur's hot-water-bottle.

Marcelle (*aside*)   Oh no.

Pinglet (*snatching the hot-water-bottle*)   Not now! (*It's hot.*)
Yarg!

Mathieu   What d'you need a thing like that for?

Pinglet   Well, you know, this place is famous for them.
In any case, when I go out in the evening I always ...
My jacket, yes, my jacket ... Cold in the arms ...

He cradles the bottle like a baby. It's still hot.

Boulot   No, no, Monsieur, you said –

Pinglet   Yes, thank you very much. Good night.

Boulot (*as he is bundled out*)   Whatever you say, Monsieur.

Pinglet (*to* **Marcelle**)   Now, you really must be tired ...
(*All but in* **Mathieu**'s *ear.*) Exhausted ... I won't keep you
up a moment longer. I'll say good night, Madame.

Marcelle   Monsieur.

Mathieu   Exhausted? I should have noticed. Come on,
darlings ... bedtime ...

He picks up his chair and makes for the hall. The **Daughters**
follow suit.

Pinglet (*pretending to follow; aside to her*)   I thought that'd
do the trick.

Mathieu   Madame, good night. Good night.

Pinglet (*pushing him out*)   Yes, yes, yes. Mind all those
chairs. (*Aside to her.*) I'll get rid of them and come right
back. Don't go away.

Exit after the others. **Marcelle** *closes the door behind them.*

Marcelle   Whatever next?

Mathieu (*in the hall, shaking* **Pinglet**'s *hand*)   Good night, Monsieur. My compliments to Madame Pinglet.

Pinglet *contrives, in shaking his hand, to leave him with the chair he's been carrying.*

Pinglet   I will. Good night.

Exit. **Mathieu** *goes into Number 11 after his* **Daughters**.

Mathieu   Here we are!

Marcelle (*in Number 10*)   I've had enough. Never again. Oh, never again.

Daughters   Hello, Papa.

Mathieu   Shh. Get ready for bed. In there. Don't make such a noise, there are people trying to sleep.

He shoos the **Daughters** *into one of the dressing-rooms.*

Marcelle   I won't stay in this hotel another minute. It's accursed. As soon as Pinglet gets back . . .

She puts on her coat.

Mathieu   What a day! Can't wait to get to bed.

Marcelle   My hat. Where did I put my hat?

Mathieu   What a journey.

Marcelle   Did I hide it with Pinglet's jacket?

She takes a candle and goes into the dressing-room. Darkness.

Mathieu   It's not a bad room after all. Ordinary . . . comfortable . . . I like it.

He finds **Paillardin**'s *toilet things.*

I say! Combs, brushes, everything. That's what they mean by Full Room Service. And monogrammed, too. The

hotel initials. H.P. Hotel, yes ... but why P? Not HD?
Heart's Desire Hotel. Well, never mind.

He brushes his hair.

I don't know why I pack, if they provide everything.
They're cheap, but they'll do. Just a minute ... cigars? A
box of cigars? Oh, really. Regalias, best Havana ... What
a hotel! Seven francs a night, and Regalias. I'll smoke one
now, and take some for later.

He pockets some and lights one.

Pinglet was right. It's a fine hotel.

Marcelle (*coming out of her dressing-room into Number 10*)   It's
gone. It's a complete mystery.

Mathieu (*smoking his cigar, candlestick in hand*)   What a
cigar! How do they do it at these prices?

Marcelle (*opening her door and peering out*)   Where on earth
is Pinglet?

Mathieu (*who has found* **Paillardin**'s *nightshirt spread on the
bed*)   A nightshirt, too. Slippers.

He tries them on.

Magnificent! Mag-nifi-cent.

Pinglet, *candlestick in hand, creeps through the hall to Number
10.*

Marcelle   At last! There you are.

Pinglet   Not so loud.

Mathieu   They've forgotten just one thing. A hot-water-
bottle. I'll get them to fetch one.

Marcelle   Hurry up.

Mathieu *takes his candlestick and creeps out into the hall.*

Marcelle   Ah!

She slams her door.

Pinglet (*aside*)   Mathieu!

He freezes, but **Mathieu** *has seen him.* **Mathieu** *puts his candlestick on the hall table.*

Mathieu   You again.

Pinglet   No. Yes. No. I mean, it's for you. I suddenly remembered something I wanted to tell you.

Mathieu   Yes?

Pinglet   Yes? Oh, yes. Yes. Well, you know how it is ... I wasn't in a rush ... almost on the premises ...

Mathieu   Yes.

Pinglet   I thought, 'I'll just pop in ...' What it was ... these men ... this morning ... they were saying, you'll never believe this ... 'Hot, for the time of year' ...

Mathieu   Ah.

Pinglet   Not just *any* men, you understand. Er ... Councillors. In the council. Budget debate. Deadlock. Well, you can imagine ...

Mathieu   Yes.

Pinglet   What's the world coming to? Council collapsing, and all they can talk about is the weather. I said to myself at once, 'Mathieu should hear of this. Mathieu needs to know ...'

Mathieu   Why?

Pinglet   Oh, you don't? You don't need to ...? In that case, I'd better ... excuse me ... I'll just ...

Mathieu   No, no, no. It was kind of you to think of me. Thanks.

Pinglet   My pleasure. Ahem. Go back in. Go in.

Mathieu   I want a hot-water-bottle. You said the place

was famous for them.

Pinglet No problem. Here, take mine.

Mathieu I couldn't.

Pinglet I've done with it. (*Aside.*) In any case, it's cold now. (*Aloud.*) I'll get another on the way out.

Mathieu You're really too thoughtful.

Pinglet Oh, not at all. Go in, go in.

Mathieu Good night, then.

He leans against the doorpost of Number 11, smoking his cigar. Pause.

Pinglet Good night, then.

Mathieu Good night.

Pinglet Don't let me keep you up. Good night. Good night.

He has by now backed right out of sight, and disappears.

Mathieu (*going into his room*) Charming man. Tut! Forgotten my candle.

He goes out again and finds himself face to face with **Pinglet**.

Pinglet Eek! Ah! I forgot to shake your hand.

He shakes his hand and goes out. **Mathieu** *goes into his room, and* **Pinglet**, *as soon as the coast is clear, hurtles across the hall and into Room 10.*

Mathieu Time to get undressed.

He goes into the dressing-room not occupied by his **Daughters**.

Pinglet Oof!

Marcelle I thought you were never coming.

Pinglet Darling, I had to get rid of Mathieu and all his ... What a business.

Marcelle   I want to talk to you about Mathieu and all his . . .

Pinglet   Aren't they amazing? Out of all the hotels in Paris, they choose this one. D'you think we're cursed?

Marcelle   Of course we're cursed. Put on your jacket and your hat, let's get out of here.

Pinglet   Jacket, hat . . . where are they?

Marcelle   In there.

Pinglet   Right.

He goes into the dressing-room.

Marcelle   (*sharply – so that she sounds like* **Angélique**)   And while you're in there, bring my hat, would you?

Pinglet   (*reappearing; in the voice he uses to* **Angélique**) What, beloved? I mean, what?

Marcelle   What have you done with it?

Pinglet   It must be here somewhere.

Marcelle   Where? Where? Where?

Pinglet   (*panicking*)   I don't don't know where, where, where. Oh, yes I do. When I went upstairs to the balcony . . . I was holding it . . . I took it with me . . . and left it. Ha, ha, ha.

Marcelle   Oh, very funny! You steal it, you take it upstairs, you leave it. Go and get it. Now! I'll wait.

Pinglet   That's right. Wait.

Marcelle   Get on with it.

Pinglet   Get on with it . . . yes . . . right . . .

He rushes out, and bumps into **Bastien** *in the hall.*

Pinglet   Harg!

Bastien   Where the devil are you going?

Pinglet   Don't ask. Don't ask.

He rushes upstairs.

Bastien (*staring after him*)   Whatever you say.

Marcelle (*in her room*)   I've had enough. Enough.

She goes into her dressing-room. Bell, off.

Bastien   Someone else now.

Enter **Paillardin**, *tipsy.*

Bastien   Monsieur Ghost-hunter.

Paillardin   Thassright. Phew.

Bastien   Are you ready for bed, Monsieur Ghost-hunter?

Paillardin   If it's not too much to ask. My candlestick . . . ?

Bastien   Here, Monsieur Ghost-hunter.

Paillardin   No sign of my clients yet, Messieurs the ghosts?

Bastien   Not yet, Monsieur Ghost-hunter.

Paillardin   Oh, what a shame.

He goes into Number 11, lighting it with his candle. **Bastien** *follows him.*

Bastien (*aside*)   Big hero.

Paillardin   So this is a haunted room. You'd never guess. If you're listening, ghosts, please be kind enough to let me sleep.

Bastien   I hope they hear you, Monsieur Ghost-hunter.

Paillardin   Hey! My cigars!

Bastien   What about them?

Paillardin   They've gone. This box was full when I left. Now half are missing. Where did they go?

Bastien No idea, Monsieur.

Paillardin 'No idea, Monsieur.' They can't have gone on their own.

Bastien It'll be the ghosts, Monsieur.

Paillardin Ghosts. Smoking ghost cigars?

Bastien Monsieur, smoking. . .

Paillardin My combs! My brushes! What's going on?

Bastien I told you, Monsieur.

Paillardin Huh! I know the kind of ghosts you mean. Sticky-fingers, pretending to be ghosts.

Bastien (*aside*) He'll see. He'll see.

Paillardin All right. Go away. We'll settle this tomorrow.

Bastien Yes Monsieur. Good night, Monsieur.

Paillardin Good night.

Bastien (*in the hall, muttering*) I hope your ghosts give you a really good seeing-to.

Paillardin A thief. That's all it is. He's even left hairs in my comb.

Pinglet *comes down the stairs into the hall.*

Pinglet Gone! I searched everywhere. Where can it be?

Paillardin My nightshirt. My slippers. They've nabbed those too.

He goes to hang up his hat.

Pinglet Marcelle won't like this. But what else can I tell her? The truth.

He goes into Room 10.

Paillardin I'll sleep in my clothes. Then if anything

happens, I'm ready!

He stretches out on the bed and reads. In Room 10, **Marcelle** *comes out of the dressing-room.*

Marcelle   There you are. Where is it?

Pinglet   Marcelle ... cabbage ...

Marcelle   What is it?

Pinglet   It's gone. They've taken it.

Marcelle   Who's taken it?

Pinglet   They didn't leave a name.

Marcelle   Wonderful! Fortunately, I've a scarf I can wear. Come on. Now!

She veils herself in a scarf, and leads him out of the room.

Pinglet   I'm coming. I've had enough.

They disappear in the direction of the main door.

Paillardin (*yawning*)   I'm exhausted. My eyes are drooping. I've got to ...

He blows out the candle. Darkness. Re-enter **Marcelle** *and* **Pinglet**.

Marcelle   Hurry up! It's him!

Pinglet   Maxime. Your nephew – and my housemaid. Hurry!

They rush into Number 10.

Marcelle   Lock the door.

Pinglet   The key? Where's the key? I haven't got the key.

Marcelle   Just lock it.

Pinglet   How do I lock it without a key? Quick, in there! There's a bolt. Get in!

Marcelle   What a night!

They lock themselves in the dressing-room. **Victoire** *and*
Maxime *come into the hall, preceded by* **Bastien**.

Bastien   This way, Monsieur, Madame.

Maxime (*low to her*)   I say, you know: we shouldn't be
doing this.

Victoire   Don't keep on.

Bastien   I know exactly what Monsieur requires.
(*Honeyed voice.*) A nest, a nest made for two, a frame for a
beautiful picture. I speak of Madame, Monsieur. What a
charming lady. She does Monsieur great credit.

Maxime   Oh, er, yes. You think so?

Bastien   I suggest Number 9. It was in that very room,
Number 9, that Her Royal Highness the Princess Royal of
Poland spent her wedding-night, with her first Groom of
the Bedchamber. (*To* **Victoire**.) Only the very best is good
enough, Madame . . .

Victoire   A Princess Royal room!

Bastien   This hotel is *very* special.

Victoire   We know that. We read your leaflet. All right,
we'll take Number 9.

Bastien   Perfect choice.

Maxime (*low to her*)   He's laughing at me.

Victoire   Let him laugh.

Bastien (*lighting a candle*)   If Monsieur and Madame will
walk this way . . .

Maxime (*pulling back*)   Mamzelle, I'm not sure I . . .
What's going to happen?

Victoire   Don't worry. You'll like it.

Maxime (*as she pulls him into Number 9*)   Thank God I

finished my essay.

Bastien *follows them in. Darkness in the hall. In Number 11,*
Paillardin *is asleep in bed. The* **Daughters** *come into the*
room, in their nightdresses.

First daughter (*putting down her candle*)   I'll have this
one.

She goes to one of the small beds. The others follow suit.

Second daughter   I'll have this one.

Third daughter   I'll have this one.

Fourth daughter   I want that one.

Third daughter   You can't have it.

They argue, in a small way.

First daughter   Sh! Not so much noise. Papa said . . .

They sit on the beds and pull off their stockings.

Brr! It's cold. Papa's all right. All those blankets.

Second daughter   Well, *I'm* going to pluck my
eyebrows.

Fourth daughter   So am I.

Third daughter   So am I.

First daughter   So am I.

Bastien (*coming out of Number 9*)   'Night, Monsieur, 'night
Madame.

He goes upstairs.

First daughter   My turn for the candle.

Second daughter   No, mine.

Third daughter   No, mine.

Fourth daughter   No, mine.

In the struggle, it goes out.

First daughter   Now look what's happened.

Second daughter   Now see what you've done.

Third daughter   Light the nightlights.

They light the nightlights.

Fourth daughter   Look, shadows.

Third daughter   We look just like ghosts.

First daughter   Just like in the story.

They form a ring, dance and sing.

Daughters
Dance and sing,
Dance in a ring,
Howl and shriek,
Be bats and squeak:
Hee-hee, hee-hee, hee-hee!

Paillardin (*bolt upright in the bed*)   Ahaaaah. Spooks.

Daughters (*who haven't seen him*)
Howl and sing,
In a ghostly ring,
Dance and squeak,
Yowl and shriek:
Hee-hee, hee-hee, hee-hee!

Paillardin *jumps to his feet on the bed and shouts:*

Paillardin   Get back where you belong!

Daughters   Aaaaaaaah!

They rush into the dressing-room.

Paillardin (*beside himself, running into the hall*)   Ghosts!
Help! Ghosts!

Victoire *comes out of Number 9, followed by* **Maxime**.

Victoire   What's the matter?

Paillardin   Help! Ghosts! Help!

Victoire   Monsieur Paillardin!

Maxime   Uncle!

They take cover, **Maxime** *back in Number 9,* **Victoire** *in* **Paillardin**'s *bed in Number 11, with the curtains drawn.*

Paillardin   Ghosts! Help!

He disappears towards the street. Pause. **Mathieu** *comes out of his dressing-room, with a candlestick in one hand.*

Mathieu   What's all the shouting about? Was there a naughty man? Where is he? Ha-ha! He's hiding in the bed.

He draws the bed-curtains and sees **Victoire**.

Victoire   Aah!

Mathieu   Sorry, Madame. How silly. They thought it was a man. It was a lady. Sillies. Not a man, a lady.

He goes into the dressing-room. Darkness.

Daughters *(in the dressing-room)*   It was, Papa. A man. It was.

Maxime *comes gingerly out of Number 9.*

Maxime   He's gone. Uncle's gone. But where's Victoire? What's she playing at? Victoire?

Victoire *(from inside the drawn bed-curtains in Number 11)* Maxime, in here.

Maxime *goes to her, just as* **Mathieu** *and the* **Daughters** *come out of the dressing-room.* **Maxime** *and* **Victoire** *try to slip out unnoticed.*

Mathieu   Come and see for yourselves.

First daughter   Papa, it *was* a man.

Mathieu   You're joking. I saw what you saw. And at my age, we know the difference between a man and a woman.

Victoire *has now made it to the hall.*

Mathieu   And this was a woman. It was, I tell you.

Maxime *slips out. The* **Daughters** *see him.*

Daughters   Papa! A man!

Mathieu   A man *and* a woman.

Maxime   Come on, let's go.

He and **Victoire** *disappear towards the main door.*

Mathieu   I'll get to the bottom of this. Porter! Porter!

Enter **Boulot**.

Boulot   What now? What's all this shouting?

Mathieu   Porter, what's going on? This bedroom's full of people. Men, women . . . people.

Boulot   Oh, no, Monsieur. Aah! Monsieur must have seen . . .

Mathieu   Seen what?

Boulot   I didn't like to say before. The ghosts, Monsieur.

Daughters   Ghosts!

Paillardin *is coming gingerly into the hall from the street door.*

Boulot   This room's haunted, Monsieur. What you thought were men and women were . . . ghosts.

Daughters   Ghosts! Waaa!

They rush into the hall and up the stairs. **Paillardin** *sees them and flees ahead of them.*

Mathieu Come back. Get dressed. You can't go up there. Darlings.

He rushes after them.

Boulot What the devil are you doing?

He rushes upstairs too. When everyone's gone, **Pinglet** *and* **Marcelle** *come out of their dressing-room into Number 10.*

Pinglet Why's everyone shouting?

Marcelle There's something going on. I hate this place. I'm frightened. Let's go home.

Pinglet Home, yes. But ... carefully.

He opens the door, gingerly, and peeps out.

Marcelle I won't be happy till I'm away from here.

Pinglet There's no one. Hurry.

Marcelle (*joining him in the hall*) Thank goodness.

Paillardin *hurtles down the stairs.*

Paillardin Ghosts! Ghosts! They're after me!

Marcelle My God. In!

She goes into Number 10.

Pinglet What now?

Marcelle My husband.

Pinglet Oh.

He slams the door.

Paillardin More of them! (*Trying to open the door.*) Oh, no you don't. Open this door.

Pinglet (*from inside*) Go away.

Paillardin Open the door.

Marcelle Don't let him in.

Pinglet I can't hold him off for ever. He's stronger than I am.

Paillardin Open *up*, I said!

He forces the door open. **Pinglet** *staggers back into the fireplace.* **Marcelle** *rams* **Paillardin***'s hat on her head so that it hides her entire face.*

Paillardin Hey! My hat!

He tries to pull it off. She holds it by the rim.

Marcelle Help! Help!

Pinglet *surges out of the fireplace, face covered in soot.*

Paillardin A chimney-sweep.

Pinglet *punches him in the eye.*

Paillardin Ow!

Pinglet *kicks him into the hall.*

Paillardin Poltergeists! Help!

He rushes out to the main door.

Pinglet Oof. Marcelle, Marcelle, he's gone.

Marcelle (*coming out of the hat*) My God, a monkey now.

Pinglet No, no, it's me. Pinglet.

Marcelle This night'll be the death of me. My God, you're black.

Pinglet I know. What of it?

Marcelle What else can happen?

Pinglet Nothing. Nothing else. We can breathe freely now.

Marcelle Thank heavens.

Pinglet Whatever was going to happen has happened.

Voices, off.

What was that?

Marcelle There is something else.

Bastien (*off*) Police! A raid!

Pinglet A raid.

Bastien (*running in and hammering on the door of Number 11*) A raid! (*Rushing up the stairs.*) A raid!

Marcelle What's he mean, a raid?

Pinglet It's when the police arrive, and catch ... We're done for!

Marcelle Run for it!

They run into the hall, and meet **Boucard** *and his* **Constables**.

Marcelle Aah!

She runs into Number 10 and slams the door, leaving **Pinglet** *in the hall.*

Boucard There's one. Grab him.

Pinglet (*struggling*) You don't understand.

First constable Yeah, yeah. Later.

Boucard You. Open that door.

The **Second constable** *tries.*

Marcelle (*inside*) Keep out! Keep away!

Boucard Break it down.

The **Constable** *forces the door and bursts in.*

Marcelle I'm done for!

Constable Come on, lads.

Pinglet (*struggling with them*) Leave her alone.

Marcelle (*running out into the hall*) My God!

Boucard That's right. This way.

Marcelle Inspector, you don't understand. I'm a ... wife and mother.

Pinglet She is. A wife and mother. She is, she is.

Boucard Shut up, you. Constable, take him in there.

The **Constable** *tries to pull* **Pinglet** *into Number 11.*

Pinglet I ... will ... not ... go.

Constable Oh ... yes ... you ... will.

He wins.

Boucard Right, Madame. And let's have the truth this time. Name.

Marcelle Inspector, I don't understand. I came here with my husband.

Boucard Husband, is it?

Marcelle Well, of course. That gentleman your ... man has just dragged in there.

Boucard Oh yes. I'm so sorry. And your name is ...?

Marcelle I ... well, I ... (*Aside.*) Nothing for it. (*Aloud.*) Pinglet, inspector. Madame Pinglet.

Boucard Right. Constable, bring him out here.

Constable Come on, you.

Pinglet (*aside*) She hasn't told him her name!

Boucard All right, Monsieur. Your name, please.

Pinglet (*aside*) Nothing for it. (*Aloud.*) I don't quite follow, inspector. We came to this place quite innocently. And this lady is my lady wife.

Marcelle (*with a glint of hope*) Aah.

Boucard (*aside*)   Whoops. False arrest? Oh no. (*Aloud.*) I still need your name, Monsieur.

Pinglet   Surely Madame told you. It's Paillardin. Monsieur Paillardin.

Marcelle   Oh God.

Boucard   Thank you. Exactly as I suspected.

Marcelle (*aside*)   I'm done for.

Pinglet (*aside*)   That told him.

Enter, down the stairs, **Bastien**, **Boulot**, **Mathieu** *and* **Mathieu**'s **Daughters**, *more* **Constables** *in hot pursuit.*

Boucard   Round up all these people, and take them to the station.

All   The station?

Protestations, lamentations, mêlée as the curtain falls.

Act Three

The set is the same as for Act One, with the window open and the ladder dangling. Outside, it's dawn. The clock strikes seven.

Pinglet *climbs up the ladder and in through the window. His face is sooty from Act Two, and he is exhausted. He sits for a while on the window-sill, then pulls himself together, tiptoes to the door and checks that no one is about. Then he pulls up the ladder, puts it in a drawer, takes off his outdoor clothes and puts on a cardigan, a cravat and a foulard knotted round his head. Then he comes smugly downstage to talk to the audience.*

Pinglet There. She can come home when she likes. My wife. I've spent the night at home, I've just got up. Oh, what a night!

Knock at the door, off.

Already! No, she's got a key. She wouldn't knock. Who's there?

Victoire (*off*) It's me, Monsieur: Victoire.

Pinglet (*to himself*) Victoire, ha! Now what were you doing last night, at Heart's Desire Hotel? I can't ask her – I'd be giving myself away. (*Aloud.*) What is it?

Victoire (*off*) Morning chocolate, Monsieur.

Pinglet Bring it in, then.

Victoire (*off*) Someone's taken my key.

Pinglet (*aside, taking a key from his pocket*) I know! (*Aloud.*) It must have been Madame. Ask her.

Victoire (*off*) She isn't back yet, Monsieur.

Pinglet Of course she isn't back. Her auntie's not well. She's staying with her.

Victoire (*off*) What shall I do, Monsieur?

Pinglet Whatever you like. I haven't the key. Wait till

Madame comes home.

Victoire (*off*)   Yes, Monsieur.

Pinglet (*to the audience*)   What d'you mean, I could have opened it? And given myself away? Especially after last night. Raided. Like common criminals. Catnappers. Just because we . . . because Marcelle and I . . . None of their business. It's not as if Paillardin's complaining.

Knock, off.

What is it now?

Marcelle (*off*)   Pinglet. It's me.

Pinglet   Who's me?

Marcelle (*off*)   Marcelle.

Pinglet   Thank goodness. There's no one else?

Marcelle (*off*)   Open the door.

Pinglet   Just a minute.

He unlocks the door.

There's a latch on your side.

Marcelle (*off*)   There.

The door opens.

Pinglet   Be quick. Come in.

He shuts and locks the door behind her.

Oh, Marcelle! What a night! God, what a night!

Marcelle   Oh, Pinglet, what have you done to me?

She paces. He tries to keep up.

Pinglet   What have I done? All that happened was, we went to the same hotel. Two innocent people. We aren't riff-raff. Those raids are for riff-raff.

Marcelle   Not the raid. Today. There'll be statements, warrants, searches ... My husband'll find out. Oh Pinglet, what can we do?

She sits on the sofa. He hurries to kneel in front of her.

Pinglet   Heart's blood, angel, there there!

He kisses her.

Poor trembling little sparrow. There, there, there – (*Change of tone.*) You've soot on your face.

Marcelle   Soot? No, you've got soot. You did it.

She takes him to the mirror.

Look.

Pinglet   Good God! From the fireplace, last night. And I thought my wife would think I'd just got up. Oh, will it never end?

They wipe their faces.

Marcelle   Disaster! Utter disaster! (*Change of tone.*) Pass the water.

Pinglet   Not utter, no. They could have kept us all night, for questioning, the way they did the others. But I had a word with the inspector. Man of honour, woman of honour ... he let us go.

Marcelle   He saw who he was dealing with.

Pinglet   Exactly. Plus, I paid five hundred francs, for bail. (*Showing her his face.*) Have I got it all off?

Marcelle   A little bit there. Beside your nose. (*Grabbing his arm.*) You paid five hundred francs?

Pinglet   I offered him a choice: my word as a gentleman, or bail of five hundred francs. He chose the bail. We've to turn up this afternoon, with documents to prove our identity.

Marcelle   For heaven's sake! You don't have documents

proving you're Paillardin. You can't take them. So you can't go. And that means he'll come here.

Pinglet (*still wiping his face*) It's all right. I've been to the Chief Constable already.

Marcelle Chief Constable? When?

Pinglet Last night, after you went home to bed. To a good night's sleep.

Marcelle A good night's sleep? Ha!

Pinglet Sorry. I take that back. Anyway, I've been to him.

Marcelle What did he say?

Pinglet He wasn't in. Some dinner-dance ... I went back at half-past six.

Marcelle And what did he say?

Pinglet He was asleep. It's all right. I'll go this morning. We were at school together.

Marcelle Pardon?

Pinglet I'll tell him everything.

Marcelle You can't!

Pinglet They're sworn to silence. Like priests, the confessional. Mum.

Marcelle But I might meet him ... some dinner-dance.

Pinglet Don't worry. I won't name names. An affair of honour ... a lady's honour. He'll know what to do.

Marcelle Will he?

Pinglet Mum. You'll see.

Marcelle Why did we ever get into this? What a stupid idea, to tell them you're Paillardin when your name's quite obviously Pinglet.

Pinglet   No, the stupid idea was telling them you were Madame Pinglet when your name's quite obviously Madame Paillardin.

Marcelle   Excuse me. I said I was Madame Pinglet to make them think you were my husband.

Pinglet   Precisely. I said I was Monsieur Paillardin to make them think you were my wife.

Marcelle   Why should the inspector think your wife was called Madame Pinglet when he thought your name was Monsieur Paillardin?

Pinglet   For heaven's sake! When I told him I was Monsieur Paillardin, how was I to know you'd already told him you were Madame Pinglet?

Marcelle   If you didn't know, you should have kept your mouth shut.

Pinglet   Women!

Knock, off.

Who is it?

Paillardin (*off*)   Me. Paillardin.

Marcelle   My husband.

Pinglet   I know that. Sh! (*Through the door, to* **Paillardin**.) What d'you want?

Paillardin (*off*)   I've got to talk to you.

Pinglet   I can't open the door. My wife locked it and took the key.

Paillardin (*off*)   Oh, damn.

Pinglet   I know. Go into the garden, get a ladder from the shed, climb in the window.

Paillardin (*off*)   Charming. You've really let her lock you in, your wife?

Pinglet Ha, marriage . . .

Paillardin (*off*) Not *my* marriage. Mind you, *my* wife'd never try such a silly trick. She'd know I'd never put up with it.

Pinglet Oh.

Marcelle Huh!

Paillardin (*off*) Where did you say the ladder was?

Pinglet In the garden shed. (*To* **Marcelle**.) Simple.

Marcelle Open the door.

Pinglet Just a minute.

He listens. He looks out of the window.

He's down there.

He unlocks the door.

Hurry.

Marcelle What a night! God, what a night!

She's gone. He locks the door behind her, and crosses to the window.

Pinglet God, what a night! Exactly. (*To* **Paillardin**.) Did you find it?

Paillardin (*off*) I'm coming up.

Pinglet Be careful.

Paillardin *climbs in at the window. He has a black eye.*

Paillardin God, what a night!

Pinglet What happened to your eye?

Paillardin You wouldn't believe me if I told you. D'you believe in ghosts?

Pinglet Of course not.

Paillardin Neither did I. Until . . . They exist! I've seen them.

Pinglet (*flatly*) No.

Paillardin I have.

Pinglet You can't have.

Paillardin It's easy to mock. I mocked, yesterday. I went to that hotel, to mock. 'Knocking in the pipes,' I said. Well, it wasn't. I lay down in the haunted room . . . dropped off . . . and half an hour later the place was full of spooks, dancing, white as sheets, ghastly voices screeching, screeching . . . (*Sings.*) 'Howl and shriek, Be bats and shriek, Hee-hee, hee-hee, hee-hee!' It's nothing to laugh at. I wasn't laughing, I don't mind telling you. I picked up my stuff, I ran for it. And in another room, solid phantoms.

Pinglet (*without thinking*) What other room? Not 10?

Paillardin 10? What does it matter? Why should it be 10?

Pinglet (*struggling*) I don't know. Why shouldn't it be 10?

Paillardin All right, 10. I ran in. There was a female phantom . . . or something that looked like a female phantom . . . it had . . . you know, the usual . . . I couldn't see its face, because it rammed my hat over its head.

Pinglet Pardon?

Paillardin *I* don't know! There wasn't time to work it out. All I know is, it had a dress on, I'd recognise it instantly if I saw it again.

Pinglet (*aside*) Harg.

Paillardin Next thing . . . this proves ghosts exist . . . a phantom chimney-sweep came looming out of the fireplace. Why a sweep? I don't know. But it definitely *was* a sweep. About your size.

Pinglet (*without thinking*) No, no, no, much bigger.

Paillardin   What d'you mean, much bigger?

Pinglet (*hastily*)   Sweeps are always bigger.

Paillardin   Oh, it could have been. I didn't measure it. There wasn't time. It ran at me. *Poum*! Fist in the eye. *Blam*! Boot –

Pinglet   In the other eye?

Paillardin   Somewhere else entirely. I've had enough of it. Hotels, spooks. From now on, for me, no more poltergeists.

Pinglet (*aside*)   He knows what he saw. (*Aloud.*) And did Madame Paillardin believe all this, your spooks?

Paillardin   Of course she didn't. I haven't seen her. I couldn't find my key. I knocked at the door. No answer. Nothing.

Pinglet (*aside*)   Ahem..

Paillardin   She sleeps like a log. The servants were all away. I slept in the garden shed.

Maxime (*off, in the garden*)   Uncle! Uncle Paillardin!

Paillardin   Wasn't that Maxime?

They look out of the window.

Pinglet   What does *he* want?

Paillardin (*calling*)   I thought you were back at college.

Maxime (*off*)   I'll tell you.

Paillardin   Climb up the ladder.

Maxime (*off*)   Coming!

After a moment, he climbs into the room, nonchalantly, smoking a cigarette.

Maxime   Morning, Monsieur Pinglet. Morning, Uncle. What happened to your eye?

Paillardin   Never mind. What happened to you? And why aren't you at college?

Maxime   You'll never believe this. I forgot to wind my watch yesterday. It stopped. When I got to my digs, they were locked and bolted. I couldn't get in at all.

Paillardin   What have you been up to?

Maxime   Up to? Uncle, I'm a philosopher.

Pinglet (*aside*)   And we all saw you philosophising, at Heart's Desire Hotel.

Paillardin   Why didn't you come straight back here?

Maxime   It was so late. You weren't here ... I didn't want to disturb Auntie.

Paillardin   So where did you spend the night?

Maxime   At the YMCA.

Paillardin   What, really?

Maxime   Oh, Uncle.

Pinglet (*aside*)   He lies like a dentist. 'It won't hurt a bit ...'

Maxime   I went round to the digs this morning, and they wouldn't let me in. You have to write a note.

Paillardin   I'll do what I can.

Maxime (*aside*)   Thank God he didn't recognise me last night.

Marcelle (*off, at the main door*)   Henri! Henri!

Paillardin   Marcelle. (*To her, through the door.*) In here, darling.

Marcelle (*off*)   Open the door.

Paillardin   It's locked. Madame Pinglet has the key. I climbed in at the window. Pinglet's here.

Marcelle Is he?

Pinglet Good morning, Madame. Did you sleep well?

Marcelle (*off*) Fairly well, thank you. A few disturbances.

Pinglet I'm sorry to hear that.

Paillardin Talking of disturbances . . . you'll never guess what happened to me.

Marcelle (*off*) What?

Paillardin You know the Heart's Desire Hotel?

Marcelle (*off*) Never heard of it.

Pinglet Me neither. Never heard of it. Me neither.

Paillardin Of course you've never heard of it. It's one of *those* hotels. How could you possibly have heard of it?

The next three speeches very fast, overlapping.

Pinglet Well, yes. No. There you are, then.

Marcelle (*off*) Of course not. Ha, ha, ha.

Maxime Ha, ha, ha.

Paillardin Well, anyway. I went . . . Look, this is ridiculous. Shouting through a door. Wait there. I'll shin down the ladder and come round to you.

Marcelle (*off*) Right.

Paillardin All right, Pinglet? We had a sort of . . . row, yesterday. I'll just go round and patch things up.

Pinglet Be my guest.

Paillardin *goes to the window.* **Maxime** *is already on the ladder.*

Paillardin Get out of the way! Make room!

Maxime *disappears.*

Paillardin Are you coming, Pinglet?

Pinglet No thanks. I'm quite happy, here. (*Aside.*) Locked in, remember?

He unlocks the door, then runs back to the window.

Don't forget to put the ladder away.

Paillardin (*off*) Right!

Pinglet *hurries to* **Marcelle**, *who has crept in.*

Marcelle Has he gone?

Pinglet Yes.

Marcelle What did he say?

Pinglet It's all right. He's no idea.

Marcelle Thank God.

Pinglet There's one thing. Your dress. He saw it, he'll recognise it anywhere. Get rid of it. Burn it, give it away. Anything, just don't let him see it.

Marcelle Thank goodness you told me.

Pinglet He's coming. Quick, he mustn't see you.

He pushes her out, slams and locks the door.

I wish Angélique would hurry home. A sick aunt's one thing, but a locked-in husband's quite another.

Victoire (*off, outside the door*) Monsieur.

Pinglet Victoire. What is it?

Victoire (*off*) A telegram, Monsieur.

Pinglet Push it under the door.

Victoire (*off*) Yes, Monsieur.

She does.

Pinglet It'll be Angélique. No, it's from her sister.

'DEEPLY WORRIED STOP ANGÉLIQUE EXPECTED DINNER
STOP NOT HERE YET STOP WHAT MATTER STOP NOT
ILL SURELY STOP REPLY AT ONCE STOP' What? Missing?
She set off . . . she didn't get there . . . (*Sudden gleam of
hope.*) She's not been kidnapped, in broad daylight, on the
broad highway . . . No, no, such acts of heroism are rare
these days. Then . . . don't tell me she's having a . . .
What, *Angélique*? The man must be blind. And deaf.

Angélique (*off, outside the door, in a trembling voice*) Pinglet!
Pinglet!

Pinglet I knew it was too good to last. She *does* sound
upset. Time to stagger out of bed . . .

Exit into his room. The main door is unlocked from outside, and
Angélique *comes in. She has a black eye.*

Angélique Pinglet. Darling. Boniface-Benoît. Are you
there?

Pinglet (*off, yawning*) Hoo-ahh. What's the matter?

Angélique It's me. My darling. My patient one. It's all
right. I'm safe.

Pinglet (*off*) What a relief.

Angélique When I tell him . . . when he finds out what
happened . . . all I went through . . . while he was sleeping
here like a baby. (*Sharply.*) Boniface-Benoît!

Pinglet *comes to the door of his room.*

Pinglet What *is* the matter?

She falls into his arms.

Angélique Oh, Boniface-Benoît. Thank goodness you're
here.

Pinglet As you see. What is it?

Angélique God, what a night!

Pinglet (*aside*) Her as well? (*Aloud.*) What's happened?

What's wrong with your eye?

Angélique   Oh Pinglet. To think you . . . you nearly lost me.

Pinglet   I did? I mean, I did?

Angélique   Yes.

Pinglet   Ah.

Angélique   Isn't it awful?

Pinglet (*aside*)   Lost opportunity? Oh yes.

Angélique   A dreadful accident. It could have sundered us for ever.

Pinglet   Sundered us. Don't say that. You're breaking my heart.

Angélique   What a saint you are! I took a cab to the station. I always do. To start with, all went well. There we were, the three of us –

Pinglet   Three of you?

Angélique   The driver, the horse and me. We were nearly there, when a train whistled. The horse reared. Bolted . . .

Pinglet   No.

Angélique   The driver fought to control it. In vain! On we galloped . . . into the countryside . . . open fields. There was no one, no one! Oh Boniface-Benoît, it's at times like that, when you're dicing with death, that you realise how much you adore your husband. I could think of nothing else. Just you, that you were safe. I thought to myself, 'If only he was here, now, beside me.'

Pinglet   Oh, Angélique . . .

Angélique   Unfortunately, you weren't. I panicked. I lost my head. I opened the door. I jumped.

Pinglet (*still without emotion*) I say.

Angélique A heap of gravel.

Pinglet How terrible.

Angélique Everything went black. Next thing I knew, it was dawn, I was in a rude hut, a peasant abode, surrounded by peasants ... strangers ... How happy they were to see me stir! Such wonderful people. I only had a hundred francs. I wanted to give them everything we own.

Pinglet Far too much.

Angélique What d'you mean? They saved me!

Pinglet I know what I mean.

Angélique As soon as they saw I was fit to travel, they arranged transport ... a wheelbarrow, I think they called it ... took me to the Place de la Concorde. I hailed a cab, and here I am.

Pinglet (*still calm*) How dreadful.

Angélique Oh Pinglet, when I think ... when I remember ... Oh Pinglet, Pinglet ...

Pinglet No need to cry.

Angélique I can't help it. What if you'd lost me? Whatever would you have done?

Pinglet (*taking her in his arms*) I tell you one thing: I'd have learned my lesson. No more marrying. There, there.

He kisses her. Enter **Victoire**.

Victoire Madame, the post ...

Angélique Put it on the sofa.

Pinglet I'll go and get dressed.

He goes into his room.

Angélique Oh, I'm bruised all over. I need a hot bath.

She sits on the sofa.

Victoire   Madame. What happened to your eye? You've got a black eye.

Angélique   I know. And I need a bath. A hot bath, now.

Victoire   Yes, Madame.

Angélique   With bran.

Victoire   Yes, Madame. Oh, no, Madame. There was a cab-driver yesterday. At the kitchen door. His horse . . . I gave it all the bran.

Angélique   Is there nothing left?

Victoire   Just flour, Madame.

Angélique   Not for the horse, for me!

Victoire   Oh yes, Madame. Starch . . . ?

Angélique   Starch, then. A hot bath with starch.

Victoire   Yes, Madame.

Exit.

Angélique   Now, the post.

Pinglet (*singing, off*)   Spring, tra-la-la, the birdies on the wing . . .

Angélique   What on earth is this? 'Police Authority. By order.' What do they want? 'Madame, kindly present yourself at the station as soon as possible, with identification documents.' Why? 'Addressee: Madame Pinglet, discovered last night at Heart's Desire Hotel in the company of Monsieur Paillardin.' (*Stunned.*) Me? Heart's De . . . ? With Pai . . . ? Ridiculous. I can't have read it properly. Or else I'm going crazy.

Enter **Pinglet**, *shoe in hand.*

Pinglet   One of these laces is broken.

Angélique There you are. In the nick of time.

Pinglet Pardon?

Angélique I'm not mad, am I? I know how to read, don't I? And they . . . it's unbelievable. Here, you read it.

She hands him the letter. He reads it.

Pinglet (*aside*) A summons! That was quick!

Angélique Don't mutter. Read!

Pinglet (*aside*) Oh, really! (*Reads, aloud.*) 'Addressee: Madame Pinglet, discovered last night at Heart's Desire Hotel in the company of Monsieur Paillardin.'

Angélique There you are! Discovered. Last night. With Monsieur Paillardin.

Pinglet (*aside*) Thank you, God! (*Aloud.*) How embarrassing. You're admitting it?

Angélique What?

Pinglet (*getting crosser and crosser*) Being discovered, last night, with Paillardin?

He bangs his shoe on the sideboard.

Angélique He thinks it's true. It's rubbish.

Pinglet Rubbish, you say? What rubbish!

Angélique Pinglet!

Pinglet (*aside*) All's fair in love and war – and marriage. (*To her.*) And what, pray, were you up to with Paillardin? What, what indeed?

Angélique I keep telling you, it's rubbish.

Pinglet Nonsense. It's official. Madame Pinglet . . . woman . . . just exactly what were you and Paillardin up to?

Angélique Boniface-Benoît, I beg you . . .

Pinglet   Answer!

Angélique   You surely don't want me to lie to you.

Pinglet (*waving his shoe about*)   Haah, haah!

Angélique (*on her knees*)   Boniface-Benoît!

Enter **Victoire**.

Victoire   Did you ring, Monsieur?

Pinglet (*charm personified*)   I did indeed, my dear. One of
the laces has broken in this shoe. See if you can find
another. Would you?

Victoire   Yes, Monsieur.

Pinglet   Thanks so much. (*Changed tone, as soon as she's
gone.*) Now then, Jezebel . . . The wife I trusted, the wife
of my bosom . . . People said to me: 'She's a shrew, a
crab, a fright' – and I answered: 'Yes, but faithful.' Now I
see that . . . despite your age . . . you aren't.

Angélique   You're making a serious mistake.

Pinglet   Now I see why you locked me in. To give you
free scope, you and that snake in the grass, Paillardin, my
best, my oldest friend.

Angélique   You don't know what you're saying.

Pinglet   And where do you choose for this . . . for this
. . . ? Heart's Desire Hotel, a knocking-shop in the rue de
Provence.

Angélique   I've never heard of the rue de Provence.
Just a minute: how do you know it's in the rue de
Provence?

Pinglet   It's written down here, in black and white.
(*Reading.*) Oh. No it isn't.

Angélique   I told you what happened. The horse . . .
the train-whistle . . . the dear, dear peasants . . .

Pinglet   Ah yes, these peasants. Where exactly were they?

Angélique   In their rude huts. I told you.

Pinglet   Rude huts. You have the addresses, naturally?

Angélique   No! I completely forgot. The knock on the head . . . Just a minute: Paillardin's name is in that summons, as well as mine. Perhaps he can explain.

Pinglet   Maybe he can, and maybe he can't. (*Looking out of the window.*) My goodness, here he comes, quite by chance, across the garden. Paillardin! Paillardin!

Paillardin (*off*)   What is it?

Pinglet   Come up here. I want a word with you.

Paillardin (*off*)   What about?

Pinglet   Come up and see. And you, Madame, when your accomplice is talking, not a word, not a movement, silence! Silence in court!

Angélique   God help us all.

Enter **Paillardin**.

Paillardin   What's all the fuss about?

Pinglet (*solemnly*)   Approach, Monsieur.

Paillardin   What d'you mean, approach?

Angélique   The thing is, Paillardin –

Pinglet   Not a word, Madame. Leave this to me. (*To* **Paillardin**.) Where did you say you were last night?

Paillardin   Heart's Desire Hotel: I told you.

Angélique (*stunned*)   What?

Paillardin   220 rue de Provence.

Angélique   I have gone mad. That knock on the head. I must have . . . No, I can't have . . .

Paillardin (*aside*)   What's wrong with them both?

Pinglet   And with whom did you visit Heart's Desire Hotel? I ask again: with whom?

Paillardin   With myself. I mean, alone.

Pinglet   Don't play games with me. You were with . . . Madame!

Paillardin   Pardon?

Pinglet (*huge*)   I know everything, Monsieur. You and my wife . . . are lovers!

Paillardin   We are not.

Angélique   I *told* you.

Pinglet   Be quiet, Madame.

Paillardin   It's a practical joke. A game.

Pinglet   A *game*? Read this! (*Aside.*) It's hard work, but it's working.

Paillardin   'Addressee: Madame Pinglet, discovered last night at Heart's Desire Hotel in the company of Monsieur Paillardin.' Ha, ha, ha. Very clever. Very funny.

Pinglet   Funny? You think this is funny?

Angélique   You don't understand. My husband thinks that I . . . that you . . . that you and I are . . .

Paillardin   He doesn't. You . . . and me . . . ? Now that *is* funny.

Pinglet   How dare you – laugh?

Paillardin   What? Oh. You mean it. You really do think that I . . . Sometimes you really are a fool.

Pinglet   Impertinence won't help you.

Paillardin   But me . . . she and I are . . . (*Taking him aside.*) My dear chap, I don't want to annoy you, but look at her. Look at her.

Pinglet That's right, now spurn her. Spurn my lady
wife.

Angélique Spurn me?

Pinglet Yes, my sweet one! First he puts you on a
pedestal, and then he spurns you. Throws you on the
compost heap like a . . . like a squeezed lemon.

Paillardin Now you *are* being a fool.

Pinglet Never mind all that. How d'you explain this
summons?

Paillardin Some practical joke, some idiot . . . I'll prove
it. If I'm so guilty, if I'm an accomplice, why didn't I get
one? Well? I didn't. And until I do, I deny everything.
Innocent till summonsed.

Enter **Victoire**.

Victoire Monsieur, they've just sent this round from
next door. A letter from the police for Monsieur
Paillardin.

Paillardin (*snatching it*) Let me see.

Pinglet Not a letter, a summons.

Paillardin 'Addressee: Monsieur Paillardin, discovered
last night at Heart's Desire Hotel in the company of
Madame Pinglet.'

Pinglet Get out of that.

Paillardin (*stunned*) What is all this?

Angélique It's some kind of evil spirit.

Pinglet Well, do you still deny it? Both of you? Either
of you?

Paillardin I don't understand. Am I going mad?

Victoire (*giving* **Pinglet** *his shoe*) I found a lace,
Monsieur.

Pinglet (*charming*)   Thank you so much. (*Broken-hearted; betrayed.*) Infamy! Infamy, infamy!

Victoire   Sorry, Monsieur?

Pinglet (*charming*)   Not you, my dear.

Victoire   Oh. Thank you, Monsieur.

Exit. At the door she shows in **Marcelle**.

Paillardin   Marcelle!

Pinglet   Madame. You couldn't have come at a better moment. You see this man?

Marcelle   My husband!

Pinglet   Exactly – and the lover of my wife.

Marcelle   What?

Paillardin *and* **Angélique**   Oh God!

Pinglet (*aside to* **Marcelle**)   Go along with it. Fall into my arms.

Marcelle   Aah!

She falls into his arms.

Oh!

Paillardin   It isn't true. I'm not. We're not. (*To* **Pinglet**.) What are you playing at? (*To* **Marcelle**.) Marcelle! Marcelle! (*Tapping her wrists, as you do.*) Smelling salts!

Angélique   I've got some. In here.

She goes into her room. **Paillardin** *hovers at the door. Meanwhile, aside:*

Marcelle   What's going on?

Pinglet   They've seen the summons. This is a blind.

Marcelle A what?

Pinglet A blind.

Marcelle Oh. Right.

Pinglet They're coming. Faint!

Marcelle *goes limp again as they return with smelling salts. Almost speechless with fury,* **Paillardin** *brandishes the bottle at* **Pinglet** *as if it were a revolver.*

Paillardin Monsieur, what you've done . . . what you've done . . . you cad!

Pinglet Don't you take that tone with me, Monsieur. (*Different tone.*) And stop waving those about like that. They sting. Oh here, let me.

He snatches the bottle.

Paillardin (*backing hastily away*) My God, what a scene! Bring some water!

Pinglet (*aside to* **Marcelle**) That's good. Now come round.

Marcelle Right. Ah, ah, ah . . .

Angélique She's coming round.

Paillardin Marcelle, Marcelle, please don't believe a word of this.

Angélique The whole thing's rubbish.

Pinglet Including the hotel, the police raid, the two of them?

Marcelle (*weakly*) How dreadful. (*To him, aside.*) Should I faint again?

Pinglet (*aside to her*) No, you've done that. Be furious.

Marcelle Right. (*Roaring at* **Paillardin**.) Haargh!

Angélique (*astounded*) Eek!

Paillardin   Marcelle, darling, I beg you. Don't believe that summons. It's a joke, a practical joke.

Marcelle   Leave me alone! (*Acting hard.*) Ghosts! Ha! Ghosts, you said! And I believed you!

Pinglet   They're as bad as each other. He had ghosts, she had a runaway horse. But they've both got black eyes. Black eyes, in the bosom of their families. And they have the gall to claim they got them from ghosts and horses, not struggling with police.

Marcelle   Outrageous.

Paillardin   This is ridiculous! Why are we trying to defend ourselves? You won't be told. You've got it into your heads we were arrested in a raid.

Pinglet   That's right.

Paillardin   It's perfectly simple. We'll go down to the station, ask the inspector, see if he recognises us.

Pinglet *and* **Marcelle** (*hastily*)   Ah. No.

Angélique   That's right. The inspector. He'll sort this out.

All four hold hands, pulling each other different ways.

Pinglet *and* **Marcelle** (*resisting*)   No, no.

Paillardin   Yes, yes. You've made your charges. The inspector will sort it out. Come on.

Victoire *shows in* **Mathieu**, *then goes.*

Victoire   Monsieur Mathieu.

Pinglet *and* **Marcelle**   Not him, now!

Mathieu   God, what a night!

Pinglet *and* **Marcelle**   Here we go again.

Mathieu   Ah, Pinglet . . .

Pinglet (*pushing him to the side room*)   Good morning. Wonderful to see you. Wait in there, will you. I won't be a moment.

Mathieu   Morning, Madame Paillardin. Morning, Madame Pinglet. What happened to your eye?

Angélique   Nothing, nothing.

Mathieu (*as he is pushed towards the door of* **Pinglet**'s *room*)   You won't *believe* what happened to me last night.

Pinglet   Tell me later.

Mathieu   We spent most of the night in a cell –

Pinglet (*quickly*)   -ar. In a cellar! (*To the others.*) It's his old trouble. Stammering.

Mathieu   I'm not stammering.

Pinglet (*aside*)   Why doesn't it *rain*?

Mathieu (*taking his chance and coming into the centre of the room*)   Fortunately, when we showed them our papers this morning, they let us go.

Pinglet (*rushing to push him out again*)   Well, wasn't that lucky? In there! In there!

Mathieu   I've had enough of Paris. I'm going –

Pinglet   In there. You're going in there.

Mathieu   I don't want to.

Pinglet   Oh yes you do.

He forces him in and shuts the door.

Paillardin   Boy, that was close.

Mathieu (*surging out again*)   That reminds me. What happened to the rest of you, last night?

Pinglet   It's all right. Thank you.

Mathieu   Pardon?

Pinglet   In!

He pushes him in and shuts the door, as before.

Angélique   What did he mean, 'What happened to the rest of you, last night?'

Pinglet   It's how they talk down south. Up here, we say, 'Did you get a good rest last night?' Down south they say, 'What happened to the rest of you, last night?'

Angélique   Do they?

Paillardin   Come on. The inspector.

They hold hands and start pulling again, as before.

Pinglet *and* **Marcelle**   No, no.

Victoire *shows in* **Boucard**.

Victoire   Inspector Boucard.

All   The inspector!

Paillardin   The very man.

Pinglet   He's all we need.

He turns his back so that **Boucard** *won't recognise him.*

Paillardin *and* **Angélique**   Good morning. Do come in.

Boucard   Monsieur Paillardin. Which one of you's Monsieur Paillardin?

Angélique   We are.

Paillardin   She means, I am.

Boucard   Of course you are. I should have recognised you at once. But of course, last time I saw you you were covered in all that soot.

Paillardin   Pardon?

Boucard   I recognise you now, though. Perfectly.

Paillardin *and* **Angélique**   What's going on?

Pinglet (*aside to* **Marcelle**)   He thinks it's him. So far, so –

Paillardin   You've seen me before?

Boucard   Of course I have. Last night, with Madame Pinglet, at Heart's Desire Hotel.

Angélique   Me? You really saw me?

Paillardin   With me?

Boucard   You're Madame Pinglet. Pleased to meet you.

Angélique   Of course I'm Madame Pinglet.

Boucard   I'm sorry. Last night, you were wearing that veil . . .

Angélique   Me?

Boucard   But now I can see it's you.

All   Oh.

Boucard (*aside to* **Paillardin**)   She was better, veiled.

Angélique   You recognise me.

Pinglet (*aside to* **Marcelle**)   He does, he does.

Paillardin   Inspector, this is impossible. You can't have seen us before, at Heart's Desire Hotel, for the simple reason you didn't arrest us at Heart's Desire Hotel.

Boucard   Of course I didn't arrest you. I took you in for questioning. Then I let you go, on bail.

Paillardin   You can't have. It was someone else. Impostors. Jokers.

Boucard   Well, it doesn't matter now.

Paillardin *and* **Angélique**   Doesn't matter?

Boucard   That's right. We won't be going any further. A mistake. There shouldn't have been a summons. One of my sergeants, too quick off the mark. I knew it as soon as

I saw your name this morning. Monsieur Paillardin, architect, court expert. You are Monsieur Paillardin the court expert?

Paillardin That's irrelevant.

Boucard Maybe for you. But not for me. I need an expert, an architect. And where do you find one?

Paillardin Inspector –

Boucard You've no idea how glad I am to meet you. It's just a little thing. I bought a cottage in the country, for when I retire, and –

Paillardin Never mind your cottage. We're talking about last night.

Boucard Don't worry about last night. You've identified yourself, your name, your address . . . the police are satisfied.

Paillardin It's not the police I'm trying to satisfy. It's Monsieur and Madame.

He gestures at **Pinglet** *and* **Marcelle**.

Boucard (*politely*) Monsieur . . . Madame . . .

They acknowledge his greeting without turning towards him.

Paillardin My wife, this lady's husband. Because of your summons, they think that we . . . well, never mind. Since it's all over, since it's all a mistake, I want you to tell them, loud and clear, that you've never seen us before in your life.

Boucard I said so just now.

Paillardin Excuse me, you said you didn't see our faces. Which is quite true, you didn't. But you still said it was us you arrested.

Boucard I didn't arrest you –

Paillardin And it wasn't us. Try to remember. Think

who it might have been.

Angélique You didn't see the lady's face. But you must have noticed her shape . . . her height . . .

Pinglet *hides* **Marcelle** *so that* **Boucard** *can't see her.*

Boucard Well, it's true she looked . . . a bit less, ahem, *imposing* . . . than Madame. But it might have been an optical illusion. The ceiling in my office is very high . . . makes people look smaller than they are.

Angélique Really?

Boucard I do remember one thing. She wore a very distinctive dress. Puce, for a start.

Angélique I haven't got one.

Marcelle (*quickly*) Neither have I.

Pinglet (*aside to her*) Sh!

Paillardin He didn't mean you.

Boucard It's all too vague. I can't be sure.

Paillardin Fine. Hold an inquiry.

Boucard What d'you mean?

Paillardin Isn't that what you do?

Pinglet (*aside*) Now he's an expert in police work.

Boucard I want to talk about my cottage.

Paillardin Later. You arrested all kinds of people last night. Interrogate them. See if any of them knows who we are. Who are they, anyway?

Boucard I made a list.

Paillardin Give it here. (*Reading.*) 'Aeneas Bloomfontein . . . never heard of him. Adèle Dufausset, also known as Flirtatious Flossie . . . Bastien Gueule-de-Bois . . . Aristide Mathieu and his four daughters . . .'

Angélique   Mathieu? We've got a Mathieu, in there.

Pinglet (*aside*)   Damn.

Boucard   Here, in the house?

Angélique   Exactly. *And* he has four daughters.

Paillardin   He said he spent last night in a cell −

Pinglet   -ar! Cellar! He said it was a cellar.

Paillardin   No, you said 'ar'. All he said was 'cell'.

Boucard   That proves it, then.

Angélique   Now we're getting somewhere. Mathieu! Mathieu!

Marcelle (*aside to* **Pinglet**)   I think I'm going to −

Pinglet   Not now!

Angélique (*opening the door of the side room*)   Mathieu!

Paillardin   Monsieur Mathieu!

Enter **Mathieu**.

Mathieu   What is it?

Paillardin (*pulling him into the room*)   In here.

Mathieu   The inspector. No!

He tries to get away. Mêlée.

Paillardin   You're the only one who can help us.

Angélique   Tell the truth. It's the only way.

Boucard   Take your time. Try to remember every detail.

Mathieu (*shouting above the noise*)   One at a time!

Silence.

I'm sorry. One at a time. What is it you want me to remember?

Pinglet (*aside*) Oh God, he's grassing. And he isn't stammering.

Paillardin You were at Heart's Desire Hotel last night?

Mathieu Until I was arrested, yes. Utterly innocent! God, what a night!

Paillardin That's not important. The important thing is, did you see *us* there: Madame Pinglet and me?

Mathieu Of course I didn't.

Angélique (*to* **Boucard**) There, you see?

Mathieu When I think of my poor darling daughters, arrested, dragged off with their papa and dumped in a cell . . .

Paillardin Oh, don't keep on. You didn't see us. Did you see *anyone*?

Mathieu Of course I did.

Boucard, **Paillardin**, **Angélique** Who?

Mathieu No need to shout. I'll tell you.

Pinglet *and* **Marcelle** (*aside*) We're done for!

Mathieu (*to* **Pinglet**, *very man-of-the-world*) D'you hear, Pinglet? They want me to tell them who I saw.

Pinglet Ha, ha.

Mathieu I'll tell you who I saw. (*To* **Pinglet**, *who is pulling his coat*.) What are you doing? (*To* **Angélique**.) You won't believe it. I saw –

Thunder, lightning, hail on the window.

Bo, bo . . . Bo, bo . . . [i.e. 'both of you']

Angélique Bobo?

Marcelle (*aside*) His trouble!

Pinglet (*on his knees on a chair, praying*) Thank you. Thank you for raining. Thank you.

Boucard Come on, spit it out. Who did you see?

Mathieu I saw bo, bo . . . In the ho, ho . . . bo, bo
. . . , ho, ho . . .

Paillardin We haven't got all day.

Pinglet (*aside*) It's no good shouting at him.

Angélique You're doing this on purpose.

Mathieu Bo, bo, bo, bo . . .

Paillardin It's hopeless.

Boucard (*sudden inspiration*) No it's not!

All What d'you mean?

Boucard He can write it down.

Paillardin *and* **Angélique** Yes!

Pinglet *and* **Marcelle** No!

Boucard Sit down there, Monsieur. Write down
everything you remember.

Mathieu About the ho, ho . . . the ho, ho . . . [i.e.
'hotel']

Boucard About the hoho, exactly.

Marcelle (*aside to* **Pinglet**) Now what do we do?

Paillardin, **Angélique**, **Boucard** Go on, then, write!

Enter **Maxime**.

Maxime Everyone's here. Including him! The man
from last night. My God, if he sees me, he'll tell.

He picks up the sooty towel with which **Pinglet** *wiped his face,
puts it over his head and rams his hat on top of it. Then he tries to
open the window and get out.*

Mathieu (*pointing at him*) Loo, loo, loo . . .

Paillardin   A burglar!

Pinglet   A Bedouin!

Boucard   Leave this to me. Halt, in the name of the law.

He and **Paillardin** *grab* **Maxime***, who struggles.*

Boucard   Take off that towel.

Maxime   Let go.

Paillardin   Take it off.

Maxime   I won't. I –

He is detowelled.

All   Maxime!

Boucard   It was him, last night.

All   Eh?

Boucard   The sooty man last night. It was him.

All   Maxime.

Paillardin   What the devil are you playing at? You?

Maxime   What's wrong with you all?

Boucard   Were you, or weren't you, at Heart's Desire Hotel last night?

Maxime   My God, you know!

Pinglet (*to* **Boucard**)   He admits everything.

Mathieu   He, he ... he, he ...

Pinglet (*to him*)   Yes, yes. Thank you.

Angélique   And who were you there with? If you don't mind telling us. You're not suggesting you were there with ... me?

Maxime (*horrified*)   Good God, no.

Boucard   Who, then? We know it was a woman. Her name?

All   Her name?

Maxime   Well, I ... Victoire.

All   Victoire?

Paillardin   Where is she? Don't dilly-dally, boy. Where is she?

Maxime   Upstairs. Changing. She said she'd something to show me ...

Pinglet   We'll soon settle this. (*At the door, calling.*) Victoire!

Mathieu   It was su, su ... su, su, su ... [i.e. 'someone else']

Pinglet   Not now!

Mathieu   Right.

He writes, feverishly.

Pinglet (*at the door*)   Be quick. We need you.

Victoire (*off*)   I was changing my dress, Monsieur.

Paillardin   Never mind that. Come in here, now.

He brings her into the room.

All   The puce dress!

Angélique   I didn't know you had a puce dress.

Victoire   I was just trying it on. Someone gave it me.

Pinglet   Yes, yes, yes, yes. We won't go into that.

Paillardin   You were at Heart's Desire Hotel last night.

Victoire   How d'you know that, Monsieur?

Angélique   And you used my name.

Victoire   I didn't.

Pinglet   We don't need to go into all that. Victoire, thank you.

Victoire   But Monsieur, I –

Pinglet   Thank you!

He tries to shoo her out.

Angélique   Just a minute . . .

Pinglet   It's all right. Leave this to me. (*To* **Victoire**.) Go on.

Victoire (*as she goes*)   What's wrong with them all?

Pinglet   What a business!

Mathieu (*who has finished writing, to* **Boucard**)   Here you are. My e, e . . . my e, e, e . . . [i.e. 'evidence']

Pinglet   Your e-e? We don't need that. Now we know everything. No need for your e-e. No need at all.

He tears it up.

Mathieu   Oh.

Pinglet (*looking at his watch*)   Good heavens, is that the time? Your train! You'll miss your train!

Mathieu   But I –

All   You'll miss your train.

Mathieu   But it's rai, rai . . . rai, rai . . . it's pouring with rai, rai . . .

Pinglet   But not in the south. Bye bye.

All   Bye bye.

Mathieu *is bundled out.*

Pinglet   Oof.

Boucard (*to* **Maxime**)   Now, young fella-me-lad, as you know, we're not taking this any further. So these five hundred francs are yours.

Maxime   Pardon?

Pinglet (*aside*)   What was that?

Maxime   Five hundred francs? Why mine?

Boucard   Because you were at Heart's Desire Hotel.

Maxime   They *pay* you to stay there?

He breaks downstage with his money.

Pinglet (*also going downstage*)   It'd be cheaper at the Ritz. What a hotel!

Maxime   What a hotel! I'll go there again.

Pinglet   I won't.

Final curtain.

Sauce for the Goose

Le Dindon

Characters

Lucienne Vatelin
Vatelin, *her husband*
Pontagnac
Clotilde, *his wife*
Redillon
Brünnhilde, *from Hamburg*
Soldignac, *her husband*
Jean, *manservant*
Armandine, *a lady of the night*
Victor, *a pageboy*
The manager
Clara, *maid*
Doctor Pinchard, *an elderly army doctor*
Madame Pinchard, *his wife*
Guests
Police inspector
Constables
Gérôme, *manservant*

The action takes place in Paris: Act One in Vatelin's house, Act Two at the Hotel Ultimus, Act Three in Redillon's apartment.

Act One

The elegant salon of **Vatelin**'s *house in Paris. Upstage C, door; L, two doors; R, two doors. As the curtain rises, the stage is empty for a moment. Then we hear noises off, and* **Lucienne**, *in outdoor clothes and furious temper, explodes onstage. She tries to slam the door, but someone outside blocks it with a walking stick.*

Lucienne For heaven's sake. No. Go away. Go . . . away!

Pontagnac (*trying to push in*) Madame. Please, Madame.

Lucienne I said no. What are you playing at? Jean! Augustine! Where are they?

Pontagnac It's quite all right.

Lucienne No, I said no.

Pontagnac *pushes in.*

Pontagnac I just want to talk to you.

Lucienne How dare you? Out. Get out.

Pontagnac There's no harm in it. What I have in mind . . . No harm in it at all.

He advances on her.

Lucienne You're out of your mind.

Pontagnac (*chasing her*) Exactly. Out of my mind . . . with passion. For you, Madame, you. You'll say, 'You can't do this.' I say, *pif, paf,* I can, I shall, I must.

Lucienne Oh, no you mustn't. Out.

Pontagnac Never! Never, I say. I need you, need you, need you. (*Chasing again.*) Ever since the moment I first saw you, I've needed you. It was like a thunderclap. I've needed you, and pursued you. Well, surely you noticed.

Lucienne Noticed, no.

Pontagnac You must have. When women are needed, they notice.

Lucienne Don't be ridiculous.

Pontagnac It's scientific fact.

Lucienne You're a total stranger.

Pontagnac We can soon put a stop to that. Oh, Madame . . .

Lucienne That's enough.

Pontagnac Oh, Marguerite . . .

Lucienne (*forgetting herself*) My name's Lucienne.

Pontagnac Ah, thanks. Oh, Lucienne . . .

Lucienne Who said you could call me Lucienne?

Pontagnac You did. 'My name's Lucienne,' you said.

Lucienne I'm a respectable woman.

Pontagnac Ex-actly!

Lucienne I'm warning you. If you don't go, now, I'll call my husband.

Pontagnac Good God, you're married.

Lucienne Entirely.

Pontagnac Fine. Ignore him. He's an idiot.

Lucienne My husband.

Pontagnac My rival. An idiot.

Lucienne I'm warning you . . . Well, are you going?

Pontagnac Of course I'm not going.

Lucienne In that case . . . (*Calling, off.*) Crépin!

Pontagnac What an idiotic name.

Lucienne Crépin!

Enter **Vatelin**.

Vatelin Yes, darling?

Pontagnac (*aside*) Him!

Vatelin My dear Pontagnac. How are you?

Lucienne What?

Pontagnac My dear old Vatelin.

Lucienne (*aside*) He knows him.

Pontagnac Well, well, well, well, well. Fancy finding you here.

Vatelin No, no. I live here. If you come here, I'm here.

Pontagnac I meant, fancy me finding you here.

Vatelin Oh, I see.

Lucienne This is ridiculous. D'you know this . . . gentleman?

Vatelin Well, of course I –

Pontagnac (*to himself, in a panic*) Do something, fast.

He takes a coin from his pocket and presses it into **Lucienne**'*s hand.*

Pontagnac Take it. Mum. Keep mum.

Lucienne Ten francs.

Vatelin (*who has seen none of this*) Well, well, well. How are you?

Pontagnac What d'you mean? How d'you think I am?

Lucienne (*aside to him*) Take this back. I don't want ten francs.

Pontagnac I'm sorry. (*Writhing, aside.*) That's torn it.

Vatelin My dear old chap. What a pleasure . . . D'you

know, I'd almost given you up. All the times you've been saying . . .

Lucienne   You wait till you hear what he's been saying.

Pontagnac *writhes some more.*

Vatelin   I said so, too. We must get together one day. Soon. That's what I said. But I never expected this.

Lucienne   I don't expect you did.

Pontagnac   My dear old chap . . . Madame . . . (*Aside.*) What's she going to say?

Vatelin   Oh, I'm sorry. You've haven't met. Lucienne, darling . . . Monsieur Pontagnac, my dear old friend. My dear Pontagnac . . . my wife.

Pontagnac   Madame.

Vatelin   Mind you, I don't know how safe it is to introduce him.

Pontagnac   What?

Vatelin   He's such a devil. Can't see a woman without . . . pursuing her. Chases anything in skirts.

Lucienne   Ah. Anything . . .

Pontagnac   He's making this up, Madame. (*Aside.*) Why this? Why me?

Lucienne   You mean, a poor unfortunate woman thinks she's the only one, and then finds there's a queue?

Pontagnac   He's exaggerating . . .

Lucienne   All I can say is, I never queue. (*Change of tone.*) Please do sit down.

Pontagnac (*aside*)   She's taking this too seriously.

Vatelin   D'you know, I think she's taking this too seriously.

Pontagnac Really?

Lucienne Of course I'm taking this seriously. The way you treat us, some of you. Dalliance, courtship, flirting, that shows respect. But chasing us down the street . . .

Pontagnac (*aside*) I knew it.

Vatelin No one chases women down the street. Well, cads . . . bounders . . . imbeciles . . .

Lucienne (*sweetly, to* **Pontagnac**) You choose.

Pontagnac I don't know what you mean.

Vatelin She means as a general rule.

Lucienne Well, of course I do.

Pontagnac Ah. (*Aside.*) Some people just don't know when to stop.

Lucienne I don't know about you, but if I was a man, I'd find some other way. Only two things can happen – either she turns you down, and you're exactly where you started, or she says yes, and you don't respect her.

Pontagnac Ah. Hum. (*Aside.*) What is this? A sermon?

Lucienne But obviously men don't think like that. At least, he doesn't seem to, the one who keeps chasing after me.

Pontagnac (*aside*) Isn't it hot in here?

Vatelin A man keeps chasing you?

Lucienne All the time.

Pontagnac Ahem. Please let's change the subject.

Vatelin Don't be silly, old man. There's a man chasing my wife.

Pontagnac But discreetly. Discreetly.

Vatelin They always are. (*To* **Lucienne**.) Why didn't you tell me sooner?

Lucienne I didn't take him seriously.

Pontagnac (*aside*) Oh, thanks.

Vatelin But why didn't you shake him off? To be followed everywhere . . . so irritating.

Lucienne The very word.

Vatelin I'd have . . . I don't know . . . taken a taxi, gone into a shop . . .

Lucienne Oh, I did that. A cake shop. He followed me.

Vatelin When someone's after you, never choose a cake shop. A jeweller's. You should have tried a jeweller's.

Lucienne I did. He waited outside.

Pontagnac (*aside*) Anyone would've.

Vatelin They're like limpets. Never give up. (*To* **Pontagnac**.) There are some real bounders walking the streets in Paris.

Pontagnac Bounders, yes. Do let's change the subject.

Vatelin A man can't let his wife go out alone without her being pestered by some . . . leering buffoon.

Pontagnac (*furiously*) Vatelin!

Vatelin What?

Pontagnac You can't say things like that.

Vatelin If I ever lay hands on him . . .

Lucienne That's easy. Isn't it, Monsieur Pontagnac?

Pontagnac Goodness, is that the time?

Vatelin You mean, he knows him?

Lucienne No one better. Go on, Monsieur Pontagnac: tell us his name.

Pontagnac   You're joking.

Lucienne   It's not hard. Try. With me. Pon ... Ta ... Go on.

Pontagnac   Pontago-on. Could be.

Lucienne   Pontagnac.

Vatelin   You?

Pontagnac (*laughing hard*)   Me. Hahahahaha. Me. Heeheeheeheehee.

Vatelin   You are a fool.

Pontagnac   I knew who she was. I knew it was Madame Vatelin. I thought, 'I'll play a joke. A practical joke. I'll pretend I'm after her ...'

Lucienne (*aside*)   Pretend!

Pontagnac   ' ... and then when we meet one day at her husband's, won't she be surprised?'

Vatelin   You thought nothing of the kind. You'll never learn. You were unlucky this time ... a friend's wife. That'll teach you.

Pontagnac   Oh, yes, yes, yes. You're not angry ... ?

Vatelin   Of course I'm not angry. You're my friend. But I am annoyed. I trust my wife – absolutely – but this sort of thing makes me feel such a fool. Someone chases my wife. I think, 'He knows who she is. Every time he meets me, he'll think, that's her husband, the cuckold ...' But not this time. Not now it's you. I mean, you know I know. And I know you know I know. We both know we both know we both know. So how can I look a fool?

Pontagnac (*looking at him*)   Yerss ...

Vatelin   In fact, if anyone looks a fool, it's you.

Pontagnac   Me?

Vatelin   You've really done it this time.

Pontagnac   No. No. It brought me here . . . your lovely home . . .

Vatelin   How kind.

Pontagnac   My pleasure.

Vatelin   Entirely mine.

Lucienne (*aside*)   Don't they break your heart? (*Aloud.*) I'm so happy to have brought you two together.

Vatelin   All you have to do, is beg her pardon.

Pontagnac   My dear Madame, how can I ever – ?

Lucienne   It's time you got married.

Vatelin   He is married.

Lucienne   No.

Vatelin   Yes.

Lucienne   You're married.

Pontagnac   Er . . . a bit.

Lucienne   It's disgusting.

Pontagnac   Pardon?

Lucienne   How did it happen?

Pontagnac   Oh, you know. Lovely afternoon . . . register office . . . they ask questions, you answer 'Yes', the way you do . . . place full of people . . . off they all go, and *peef*! You're married. For life.

Lucienne   It's disgusting.

Pontagnac   Getting married?

Lucienne   Chasing women afterwards. What does she think – your wife?

Pontagnac   I never tell her.

Lucienne You never tell her. How dare you?

Pontagnac Pardon?

Lucienne You promise to love and honour her. You promise to share everything. And that's exactly what you do. You go up to every woman you meet and share, share, share.

Pontagnac If one has a generous nature . . .

Lucienne What?

Pontagnac Look at Rothschild. Charity . . . endless charity.

Lucienne Well, you're not Rothschild. Or not after today, you're not.

Pontagnac You can't do this.

Vatelin (*standing shoulder to shoulder with her*) Oh, yes she can.

Lucienne From now on, keep it all for her. No sharing.

Pontagnac I never touched the capital. It was only the interest. At least let me reinvest the interest.

Lucienne No reinvesting.

Pontagnac You sound just like my bank manager.

Lucienne Suppose she started? Suppose she reinvested too?

Pontagnac It's completely different.

Lucienne Of course it's not. You're all the same. Men! It would serve you right if she auctioned the house, the furniture, the fittings, and started reinvesting right there in the street outside.

Vatelin Steady on, Lucienne. You're upsetting him.

Lucienne What do I care about him? Upsetting him? It's you I'm warning. If I ever catch you following his footsteps –

Vatelin Me?

Lucienne If I ever do, it won't be long.

Vatelin The auction. Reinvesting.

Lucienne Going, going, gone.

Pontagnac (*sigh of relief that the subject's shifted from him*) . Well, my goodness.

Vatelin You're enjoying this.

Pontagnac No, no, no. I didn't mean ... 'My goodness', I meant (*Stern tone.*) 'My goodness'.

Lucienne It's Madame Pontagnac I'm really sorry for.

Pontagnac Oh, so am I. I'm sorry for her ... every single time.

Vatelin I hope one of these days, when you're passing, the two of you, you'll pay us a visit. We'd love to meet her ... the two of us.

Pontagnac (*aside*) Not likely. (*Aloud.*) We'd be delighted, of course. Unfortunately, it's out of the question.

Lucienne Why?

Pontagnac Her ... problem. She's a martyr to it.

Vatelin Really.

Pontagnac Hardly ever leaves the house. In a little cart. With an attendant.

Vatelin An attendant?

Pontagnac An attendant.

Vatelin We'd no idea.

Lucienne So sad.

Pontagnac A tragedy.

Vatelin   Never mind. We'll come to see her at your house.

Pontagnac   Oh. What? Yes.

Vatelin   What's the address?

Pontagnac   Geneva. In the Alps.

Vatelin   Quite a way.

Pontagnac   Nonsense. There's a through train. It's her problem . . . she needs the hills. She must have height.

Vatelin   It is a bit far.

Lucienne   Unfortunately.

Enter **Jean**.

Jean   Monsieur, the man from the art shop.

Vatelin   My Corot! I bought a Corot, yesterday.

Pontagnac   Really?

Vatelin   Six hundred francs.

Pontagnac   For a Corot? Signed, is it?

Vatelin   Well, it's signed Poitevin. But the shopman explained: the signature's a fake.

Pontagnac   That's a relief.

Vatelin   I scratch out Poitevin, and I've got my Corot. (*To* **Jean**.) Put it in the study. (*To the others*.) Excuse me a moment. I'll set it up, and then . . . Pontagnac, I'll show you all my pictures. You're bound to like them, a man of the world like you . . .

Pontagnac   Of course.

Exeunt **Vatelin** *and* **Jean**.

Lucienne   Sit down.

Pontagnac   I've stopped scaring you.

Lucienne   You've stopped.

Pontagnac   You think I'm pathetic.

Lucienne   Do I?

Pontagnac   You're laughing at me.

Lucienne   Well, what did you expect? All that hullabaloo.

Pontagnac   When a man pursues a woman he doesn't know, he hopes for ... you know what he hopes for.

Lucienne   At least you're honest.

Pontagnac   If I said I'd been pursuing you to ask what you think of Voltaire, I don't think you'd believe me.

Lucienne   You mean ... what you do ... it works? There are women who ... ?

Pontagnac   Thirty-three point three per cent. Recurring.

Lucienne   Unfortunately, today you picked one of the other sixty-six point six per cent. Recurring.

Pontagnac   If you knew how I'm haunted by it ... harried –

Lucienne   Not to mention married.

Pontagnac   It's bigger than I am. Genetic. Some men crave alcohol, tobacco. I crave wives.

Lucienne   You've got one.

Pontagnac   I don't mean mine. I've read that book too often.

Lucienne   She's a book, now? Missing pages ...

Pontagnac   Pardon?

Lucienne   Her problem.

Pontagnac   What problem?

Lucienne   You told us.

Pontagnac (*quickly*)   Oh, that problem. Geneva, the Alps, that's right.

Lucienne   Exactly.

Pontagnac   So I'm hardly to blame. I'm walking along, and suddenly, out of a clear blue sky, heaven strews my path with beauty – strews it . . .

Lucienne   I thought you wanted to change the subject.

Pontagnac   You've got another lover.

Lucienne   You never stop. Have you never heard of faithful wives? Anyone who refuses you, must have another lover. What sort of women do you know?

Pontagnac   Promise me . . . what I tell you . . . you'll never breathe a word to a living soul.

Lucienne   Not even my husband.

Pontagnac   Just as well. Because what I want to tell you is . . . I don't think you're in love with him.

He edges closer.

Lucienne   What nonsense. Keep your distance.

He tries again.

Lucienne   I said, keep your distance.

Pontagnac   I mean, he's a charming fellow. I really like him.

Lucienne   That was obvious from the start.

Pontagnac   But let's admit it, hardly a man to inspire . . . passion.

Lucienne   He is my husband.

Pontagnac   You see, you agree with me.

Lucienne   I don't.

Pontagnac   Of course you do. If you loved him – really loved him – you wouldn't need reasons. You'd say things like, 'I love him, I adore him', not 'He is my husband'. Love is champagne, fine champagne to be sipped from frosted, fluted glasses. You make it sound like soda water.

Lucienne   You sound like a barman.

Pontagnac   What's so wonderful about husbands? Anyone can be a husband. The parents agree, the registrar . . . registrars. That's all. No exams, no aptitude tests. But lovers . . . that takes passion, artistry, devotion. A lover's a Bayeux tapestry, a ceiling by Michelangelo. A husband's a tablemat.

Lucienne   Now we're back to art.

Pontagnac   The art of love.

Lucienne   In that case, let me tell you, Monsieur, when it comes to love, my husband's a Bayeux tapestry, not a tablemat.

Pontagnac   What a rare specimen.

Lucienne   Unique. And mine. And so long as he stays that way –

Pontagnac   You mean, so long as he never –

Lucienne   Nothing else would ever – But that – [i.e. 'would change things entirely'] On that, I'm passionate.

Pontagnac   I see . . .

Lucienne   You see nothing. I was saying so just yesterday to – to –

Pontagnac (*prompting*)   Yes?

Lucienne   To my aunt. My aunt, yes. We were discussing it. Auntie.

Pontagnac   Auntie.

Enter **Jean**, *ushering in* **Redillon**.

Jean Monsieur Redillon.

Lucienne Come in. You can help me with Monsieur. (*Introducing them.*) Monsieur Ernest Redillon, Monsieur de Pontagnac. Friend of my husband . . . another friend. Now, tell him. You know me well. I'm the faithfullest wife in Paris, and I won't deceive my husband unless he goes first.

Redillon What brought this up?

Lucienne He brought it up. Monsieur.

Redillon (*thinly*) Ah. Monsieur brought up – ? I came at the wrong moment, obviously.

Lucienne You came just in the nick of time. To rescue me.

Pontagnac We were joking.

Redillon Joking. Monsieur's an old friend, is he? One it just so happens I've never seen before?

Lucienne I've known him for twenty minutes.

Redillon Fine. My dear, I'm sorry. There are some matters a gentleman never discusses with ladies present. I must absolutely decline to comment.

Pontagnac (*aside*) Who does he think he is?

Redillon Your husband's at home?

Lucienne In the study. With Corot. I'll fetch him. You wait here . . . talk to Monsieur.

Exit. The two men have nothing to say to one another.

Pontagnac (*aside*) This must be Auntie.

The two men are at opposite sides of the stage. In step, they move abstractedly about, gazing at the pictures, admiring the furniture. From time to time their eyes meet, but they refuse to speak. Finally **Redillon** *sits in an armchair and starts whistling through his teeth.*

Pontagnac   Beg pardon?

Redillon   Pardon?

Pontagnac   I thought you said something.

Redillon   No.

Pontagnac   Terribly sorry.

Redillon   Quite all right.

He whistles again. After a moment, **Pontagnac** *hums a different tune.*

Pontagnac   Hoom, hoom, hoom, hoom, hoom.

Redillon *takes a newspaper, ostentatiously turns his back on* **Pontagnac** *and starts to read.* **Pontagnac** *does the same. Pause. Enter* **Lucienne**.

Lucienne   I'm sorry to interrupt –

The two men close their reading matter and snap to attention.

It's my husband. Monsieur Pontagnac, he says if you go in now, he'll show you his collection.

Pontagnac   How thoughtful.

Lucienne   Through there, first on the right.

Pontagnac (*unenthusiastically*)   On the right, you say?

Lucienne   Go on. Go on.

Pontagnac *dithers for a bit.*

Pontagnac   Aren't you coming?

Redillon   Who? Me?

Lucienne   He hates fine art.

Pontagnac   Of course he does. (*Aside as he goes.*) And we all know what he likes!

Exit. **Redillon** *paces nervously.*

Lucienne   Do sit down, darling.

Redillon   I came by cab. I need to pace.

Lucienne   What's wrong with you?

Redillon   Do I look as if something's wrong?

Lucienne   You look like a tiger in a cage. I know what it is: it's Pontagnac.

Redillon   Ha! Pontagnac! Why should I care a straw for Pontagnac?

Lucienne   That's right.

Redillon   Who exactly is he?

Lucienne   I thought you didn't care.

Redillon   Oh, pardon me for asking.

Lucienne   That's quite all right.

Redillon   Thank you. (*Pause.*) Is he ... pursuing you?

Lucienne   Yes.

Redillon   Ha!

Lucienne   You demand exclusive rights?

Redillon   I love you, dammit.

Lucienne   So does he. He says.

Redillon   You've only known him for ten minutes.

Lucienne   Twenty.

Redillon   For heaven's sake, who's counting?

Lucienne   We've only spoken for twenty minutes. I've known him by sight for ages. Eight days. He's been following me about.

Redillon   He hasn't.

Lucienne   He has.

Redillon   The bounder.

Lucienne   Exactly.

Redillon   And now your husband introduces you. They must do it on purpose, husbands – to make their lives more interesting.

Lucienne   Now, now.

Redillon   I mean it. And then when ... something happens, they take it personally. What's Vatelin playing at, filling this house with men? Aren't there enough already? We were so cosy, the three of us. Him, me, you – how many more does he want? Stop laughing. It makes me so cross, when men start following you like poodles. What d'you want me to do? I can hardly tell your husband.

Lucienne   Darling, darling ...

Redillon   (*beside himself*)   I knew today would be absolutely foul. I dreamt, my teeth. They all fell out. Forty-five of them. When I dream about my teeth, something foul always happens. Last time, last time, someone stole my pet chihuahua. This time they're trying to steal my mistress.

Lucienne   I'm not your mistress.

Redillon   In my heart you're my mistress, and no one can stop me.

Lucienne   Oh, thank you.

Redillon   Swear you don't love him. Monsieur.

Lucienne   Monsieur? I hardly know him. How can I love him?

Redillon   I thought not. You've only got to look at him. Ugly. Did you see his nose? How can a man be a lover, with a nose like that?

Lucienne   H'm.

Redillon   Now my nose ... a nose of noses ... a
Cyrano of a nose ... a lover's nose.

Lucienne   How d'you know?

Redillon   People tell me.

Lucienne   I won't argue.

Redillon   Darling, you did say you'd have no other
lovers except me. You promised.

Lucienne   'If I ever have a lover, it'll be you,' I said.
Things have to happen first.

Redillon (*defeated*)   I know. Your husband has to take a
mistress. Hahhhhh. (*Aside.*) What's the matter with the
man? No style, no ... (*Aloud.*) You're torturing me. Can't
you see that? A man dying of hunger, and fed every day
on crumbs.

Lucienne   Find another restaurant.

Redillon   Don't say that. I'm flesh and blood. And I'm
starving, starving.

Lucienne   When you say 'starving', your face goes just
like a baby's.

Redillon   Thanks.

Lucienne   What d'you want me to do? Burst into tears?
Especially after the liberties you're taking.

Redillon   Liberties. Ha! You can have them. And if you
don't want them, give them to anyone you like.

Lucienne   They'll enjoy that.

Redillon   They most certainly will.

Lucienne   The great lover speaks, the nose of noses
speaks.

Redillon   It's not my fault if part of being a lover is
being ... an animal.

Lucienne   I thought we'd get round to that. Kill it. The animal. Kill it.

Redillon   I was brought up to be kind to animals.

Lucienne   All right, then, keep it on a lead.

Redillon   That's all I ever do. The trouble is, it's bigger than I am, stronger. Takes me walkies. But what can I do? What else can I do?

Lucienne   Poor darling Ernest. What's her name?

Redillon   Whose name?

Lucienne   The one you take for walkies.

Redillon   Fifi. Short for Fifinette.

Lucienne   How sweet.

Redillon   But the heart has its reasons. The heart, the head. What do I care for Fifi? On every altar I sacrifice to my beloved, the beloved's name is yours.

Lucienne   Too kind.

Redillon   I may be walking with Fifi, but my heart's with you. I hold her in my arms – Fifi – and I make believe it's you. Cuddling me, kissing me. I tell her, 'Shh! Don't say a word.' I shut my eyes and call her Lucienne. Lu-ci-en-ne.

Lucienne   Impersonation, now. What does she do while this is going on?

Redillon   She does the same. Shuts her eyes and calls me Bigboy.

Lucienne   It's understudies' benefit.

Redillon (*oblivious*)   Oh Lucienne, how long, Lucienne, how long? Unceasing torment! When will you fold me in your arms and cry, 'Take me! Take me!'?

Lucienne   Steady.

Redillon (*on his knees*) I adore you, Lucienne, Lucienne.

Lucienne Get up. If my husband comes in ... He's caught you twice like this already.

Redillon I don't care. Let him come! Let him see!

Lucienne Don't be so silly. I won't. I won't!

She breaks free, making him collapse on the floor.

Redillon Hard-hearted one!

Enter **Vatelin** *followed by* **Pontagnac**.

Vatelin Hello! Down there again?

Redillon Yes. Eugh. How are you?

Vatelin Fine, thank you. You really do prefer it, don't you? (*To* **Pontagnac**.) It's Redillon. A friend of mine. (*Introducing them.*) Monsieur Redillon, Monsieur Pontagnac.

Pontagnac We've met.

Vatelin He spends a lot of time down there. Every time he calls, in fact. It's not that we're short of chairs. I come in, and there he is.

Pontagnac Really.

Redillon I'll explain. You know how when you're a baby ... on a bearskin rug? Well, I've never lost the habit. It just comes over me.

Vatelin Amazing. And there was I thinking, 'Lead shot in the longjohns'.

Redillon (*as he gets up*) Hahahaha. Brilliant. Lead shot in the ... Hahahaha.

Pontagnac (*through his teeth*) That's not all in the longjohns.

Lucienne Monsieur Pontagnac, did you enjoy my husband's collection?

Vatelin Of course he did. He was overwhelmed. He said, 'You don't see paintings like this in museums.' Didn't you?

Pontagnac Of course I did. (*Aside.*) Thank God.

Bell, off.

Vatelin I've plenty more. Through here –

Pontagnac Not today, thanks. The mind can just take so much. Some other time.

Vatelin Such a shame about Madame Pontagnac. Her . . . problem. I'd have loved to show her my collection.

Pontagnac Well . . . Geneva . . . the little cart . . .

Vatelin Poor, poor lady.

All Ahhhh.

Enter **Jean**.

Jean Madame Pontagnac.

All Uh?

Pontagnac (*aside*) It's her.

All Your wife.

Pontagnac Yes. No. No, yes.

Lucienne I thought she was in Geneva.

Vatelin She needs the height.

Pontagnac She's cured. A miracle cure. (*To* **Jean**.) We're out. Tell her we're out.

Lucienne No, no, no, no. Show her in.

Pontagnac Oh. Yes. Show her in. Haha. Hahaha.

All (*aside*) What's wrong with him?

Redillon (*aside*) Lead in the longjohns?

Pontagnac (*aside*) It's the only way. (*Aloud.*)
Hahahahaaaa. Ladies and gentlemen, please. If my wife
... I can't explain ... Later ... If she ... whatever she
asks, just say what I say. What I say ... er ... say it.

Enter **Clotilde**.

Clotilde Excuse me. Madame ... Monsieur ...
Monsieur ...

Pontagnac (*running to her*) Darling, there you are. What
a lovely surprise. I was on my way. Really. Say goodbye
to Madame ... Monsieur ... Monsieur. We really must
go. We really must go.

All Unh?

Clotilde What d'you mean, go? Ridiculous.

Pontagnac We can't stay.

Clotilde We can.

Lucienne Of course you can.

Pontagnac Oh. Right. Right. (*Aside.*) My Go-o-o-o-od.

Clotilde I'm sorry to call unexpectedly. A complete
stranger, after all.

Lucienne It's quite all right.

Vatelin No problem.

Clotilde It's just that my husband's told me so much
about you. I seem to know you all so well ...

Vatelin Good old Pontagnac.

Clotilde I just suddenly decided: 'This is ridiculous. It
can't go on. The husbands such good friends, and the
wives have never even met.'

Lucienne *and* **Vatelin** Good friends?

Clotilde That's right. I was getting rather jealous.
'Where are you going tonight?' 'To Vatelin's.' 'Where will

you be tomorrow?' 'At Vatelin's.'

Vatelin   At Vatelin's.

Pontagnac   That's right. Why's everyone so surprised?
You haven't seen his collection, have you? His Corot. Let
me show you his Corot.

He tries to urge her out.

Clotilde   Stop it. What are you doing?

Pontagnac   Me? What d'you think I'm doing?

Vatelin   What is going on?

Redillon   Don't stop them.

Clotilde   You do seem upset. You haven't – ?

Pontagnac   Of course I haven't. What did you have to
tell them that for? That I said I'd been coming here day
after day?

Lucienne (*aside*)   Haha!

Vatelin (*aside*)   I see!

Pontagnac (*making frantic signs to* **Vatelin**)   I have, I
have. Vatelin, haven't I?

Vatelin   Oh. Yes. Yes. Yes.

Pontagnac   You see?

Redillon   I've never seen him here.

Pontagnac   What? Thanks.

Redillon   Don't mention it.

Pontagnac   Never mind that. You see? You see?

Clotilde   Well, I think I –

Pontagnac   For heaven's sake . . .

Vatelin (*aside*)   I can't bear to watch. (*To him.*) Psst. I'll
see to it.

Pontagnac   Ah. Thanks.

Vatelin   My dear Madame, you can't imagine. Your name, never off his lips. Every time he calls. Every single time.

Clotilde   Oh, really?

Pontagnac (*aside to him*)   Keep going.

Vatelin   The number of times I've said to him, 'We'll drop in and visit, the very next time we're in Geneva.'

Clotilde   Geneva?

Pontagnac (*aside*)   Storm brewing. (*Aloud.*) No, no, no, no, no. Geneva? Whoever mentioned Geneva?

Vatelin   You did.

Pontagnac   Geneva? Me?

Vatelin   You mentioned Geneva. So naturally, I said . . .

Pontagnac   Not Geneva. Not.

Vatelin   Not.

Pontagnac   Distinctly not. (*Aside to him.*) For God's sake, shut up.

Vatelin   I'm completely lost.

Redillon (*aside*)   Thin ice . . .

Clotilde (*aside*)   I thought something was going on. (*Aloud.*) Monsieur Vatelin, no need to make excuses. I never expected you to visit, after what my husband told me.

Pontagnac (*aside*)   Here we go again.

Vatelin   What did he tell you?

Clotilde   About . . . the problem.

Vatelin   Ah, your –

Clotilde   No, your. The little cart.

Vatelin   But that was you.

Clotilde   Excuse me: you.

Pontagnac (*going to him*)   My God, not you as well!
(*Dragging him clear.*) Your other collection, my dear chap.
I'd like to see your other collection. Now.

Vatelin   What a good idea. My other collection.

Clotilde   Edmond, stay where you are.

Pontagnac   We'll be right back.

Vatelin   Right back, right back.

Exeunt.

Clotilde   What is going on? Do you know, Madame?
Are they playing tricks on me?

Lucienne   Of course they are. If the men are ganging
up, we'll do the same. Yes, they're playing tricks on you.

Clotilde   I knew it.

Lucienne   Our husbands hardly know each other. They
work in the same office, that's all. Today's the first time
he's ever been here – and he didn't come to visit a
friend. He was following a woman.

Clotilde   You're joking.

Lucienne   Me.

Clotilde   You're not joking.

Lucienne   For days he's been sticking to me in the
street like . . . like . . .

Redillon (*from his armchair*)   Sticking plaster.

Clotilde   Has he?

Lucienne   He wasn't delighted to find that the woman
he was chasing was a colleague's wife. Unlucky, that.

Anyway, he was lying to you. Every time he told you he
was coming here, he was with one of his . . . one of
his . . .

Clotilde   Oh, don't go on.

Redillon   No, don't.

Lucienne   I'm sorry. You did ask me to be frank.

Clotilde   That's all right.

Lucienne   And if you ever find out that my husband –

Redillon (*glumly*)   Fat chance of that.

Lucienne   Thank goodness.

Clotilde   Right. That's all I was waiting for. I'm on to
you now, Pontagnac. I'm on your track. I'll be watching
every step you take, and the minute I catch you, I'll . . .
I'll . . . (*She picks up a chair.*)

Lucienne   Heavens!

Clotilde (*putting it down again*)   Watch out, that's all.

Lucienne   Sauce for the goose?

Clotilde   Exactly.

Redillon   One for all –

Lucienne (*carried away*)   And all for one. I mean, if my
husband so much as –

Redillon   Oh please, please.

Clotilde   I mean I'm young, I'm pretty . . .

Lucienne   We both are.

Clotilde   This is no time for hanging back.

Lucienne   It's a time for revenge.

Clotilde   Plenty of men would find me attractive.

Redillon   I'll say.

Lucienne   Pardon?

Redillon   You too, naturally.

Clotilde   I shan't even waste time choosing. Revenge must be swift and sweet. I'll take the first idiot who comes along.

Redillon   Well said.

Clotilde   You, if you like.

Redillon   Ah. You see, I –

Lucienne   Me too. Me too.

Redillon   Oh, Lucienne!

Clotilde   Don't waste time. Your name? Your address?

Redillon   Redillon. 17 rue Caumartin.

Clotilde   Redillon, 17 rue Caumartin. Thank you, Monsieur Redillon. The moment I catch my husband in the . . . in the . . . I'll come to you crying 'Take me, Monsieur Redillon, take me. I'm yours!'

She throws herself into his arms.

Lucienne   And so will I. 'Monsieur Redillon, I'm yours, I'm yours!'

Same business. He is now supporting both of them.

Redillon   Madame . . . Madame . . . (*Aside.*) From famine to glut. This is ridiculous.

Voices, off.

Clotilde   They're coming! Shh!

Vatelin and **Pontagnac** *hover in the doorway.*

Clotilde   Come in, come in. What's the matter with you?

Vatelin   Nothing. We're fine.

Clotilde   Did you see them all? Did you gaze your fill?

Pontagnac   They're wonderful! (*Aside.*) She hasn't told her! (*Aloud.*) You should see them. Almost great masters, every one of them.

Vatelin   I told you.

Pontagnac   'Son of Rembrandt.' 'Great-grandfather of Toulouse-Lautrec.' Who needs the real ones?

Vatelin   The relatives take far more trouble.

Redillon   And cost far less.

Clotilde   Well, while you've been doing your art appreciation, Madame Vatelin and I have become great friends. We've had so much to talk about. (*To* **Pontagnac**.) You, especially.

Pontagnac   Ah . . .

Clotilde   This gentleman said you were an old acquaintance. He knew you very well.

Pontagnac   He did? Oh, he did. (*To* **Redillon**.) I say, old man . . . (*Aside.*) How embarrassing. (*Aloud.*) Let me introduce you. Monsieur . . . Durillon.

Redillon   Red . . . Red . . .

Pontagnac   Hahaha! Red, Dur . . . Monsieur Redillon, Madame Pontagnac.

Clotilde   We've met.

Pontagnac   Oh. Right. Good. Hahaha. (*To* **Redillon**.) My dear fellow, we have open house every Wednesday . . . if you're ever in the neighbourhood . . .

Redillon   Count on it! (*Aside.*) When he's a lover, he's showery. When he's a husband, he's sunny. He's not a man, he's a weatherhouse.

Enter **Jean**.

Jean   There's a lady asking for Monsieur.

Vatelin   Me? Who?

Jean   No idea.

Lucienne   What can she want?

Vatelin (*with an expansive gesture*)   Who can tell? (*To* **Jean**.)
Why didn't you ask who she was?

Lucienne   Is she pretty?

Jean (*grimacing*)   Pflutt.

Vatelin   It's no good asking him. In any case, she's my
visitor: I'll decide. (*To* **Jean**.) You said I was in?

Jean   I asked her to wait.

Vatelin   Five minutes. I'll see her then.

Exit **Jean**.

Clotilde   Monsieur Vatelin, you've got company. We
mustn't keep you. Especially for a lady.

Vatelin   That's all right. Some client. They see me as a
lawyer, not as a man.

Lucienne   I should hope they do.

Clotilde   Au revoir, Madame. Monsieur ... uh ...

Pontagnac   Redillon!

Redillon   17 rue Caumartin.

Clotilde (*to* **Pontagnac**)   Remember that, darling.

Redillon   No need. I'm in the book.

Pontagnac   I'll remember it anyway.

Redillon   In any case, I'll come with you now. I've
things to do. (*To* **Lucienne**, *aloud*.) Au revoir, Madame.
(*Aside to her*.) All for one, eh? All for one? (*To* **Vatelin**.)

Au revoir, old friend...

Pontagnac We'd best be off. (*Shaking hands.*) Monsieur ... Madame ... (*Aside to her.*) I'll get rid of the wife and hurry back.

Clotilde Are you coming?

Pontagnac I'm coming.

Clotilde (*aside*) Just watch your step, that's all.

Exeunt all but **Lucienne** *and* **Vatelin**, *who rings.*

Vatelin Five minutes, darling. I'll soon get rid of her.

Lucienne Five minutes, darling.

Exit. Enter **Jean**.

Jean Yes, sir?

Vatelin Bring her in, please.

He sits at the table and pretends to be busy. **Jean** *brings in* **Brünnhilde**, *and exit. Still feigning busyness,* **Vatelin** *doesn't look at her.*

Vatelin Please sit down, Madame.

Brünnhilde *goes up behind him, takes his head in her hands and kisses him.*

Brünnhilde (*strong German accent*) Vatzi!

Vatelin Heuggggh! Brünnhilde! Brünnhilde Soldignac!

Brünnhilde Vatzi, Schatzi.

Vatelin What are you doing here? You're crazy.

Brünnhilde What d'you mean?

Vatelin You're in Hamburg.

Brünnhilde No, no, no, I'm here.

Vatelin What about your husband?

Brünnhilde He's here too. Meetings.

Vatelin But won't you be bored?

Brünnhilde Bored? Oh Vatzi, you ask if I'll be bored? Mein Vatzi-Schatzi, the man I adore, my shining light, the master of my heart –

Vatelin (*anxiously listening for* **Lucienne**) Ah. Yes. Good. Fine.

Brünnhilde I took a cab, I caught the train, I took another cab, and all for you, my Vatzi, my little Schatzi-Vatzi, my lovely one. And you ask if I'll be bored.

Vatelin You didn't understand. It sounds different in French. I didn't mean 'bored', I meant (*Different inflexion.*) 'bored'. Whatever will you find to do?

Brünnhilde Oh, liebchen. I'll be with you, you, you.

Vatelin Me, me, me?

Brünnhilde I luff you. I took cabs and trains. So travelsick I was.

Vatelin No need to go into details.

Brünnhilde And all for luff. For luff. I'll be eight days here.

Vatelin That's more than a week.

Brünnhilde And all of them with you. Tell me you luff me. My briefchen, why d'you never answer my briefchen? Oh, Vatzi, Vatzi, say you luff me.

Vatelin Of course I luff you.

Brünnhilde As soon as I arrived, I wrote a briefchen. But then I thought, 'Nein, nein, nein. Not another briefchen. Suppose he doesn't answer?' I threw it from me, the wastebasket, HA! I call a cab, what d'you call it, a fi-AH-cre. Very awkward. The driver hardly spoke French at all, at all.

Vatelin (*aside*) Good for him.

Brünnhilde I say him, 'Rue Thremol. He say me, 'Never-erdovit.' 'Never-erdovit.'

Vatelin You should have said, rue la Trémoille.

Brünnhilde So I did. Rue Thremol.

Vatelin Very clear.

Brünnhilde Darling Vatzi, you will come this evening?

Vatelin The thing is –

Brünnhilde Don't say no. I found just the place, this morning. I told you, in my briefchen. 48 roo Rocky-pain.

Vatelin You're staying in the rue Roquépine?

Brünnhilde No, no, no. With my husband. Hotel Donner und Blitzen. This other place, I found it this morning. Just for you and me. The two of us.

Vatelin Oh, no. No.

Brünnhilde Why d'you say so, no?

Vatelin It's out of the question, that's why. I've got a wife. I'm married.

Brünnhilde Married?

Vatelin What did you think I was?

Brünnhilde In Hamburg, you said you were fencyfri.

Vatelin Pardon? Oh, fancy-free.

Brünnhilde Exactly.

Vatelin Well, there you are. Fencyfri, free – not the same at all.

Brünnhilde You told me.

Vatelin I was fancy-free in Hamburg because my wife was in Paris. Now I'm in Paris, it's not the same at all.

Brünnhilde   You mean ... all ist over between us?

Vatelin   What can I say ...?

Brünnhilde   You'll never luff me again?

Vatelin   Next time I come to Hamburg.

Brünnhilde (*sobbing*)   Oh, Vatzi, Vatzi.

Vatelin   Do keep it down. My wife'll hear.

Brünnhilde   Dein weibchen. Why should I care?

Vatelin   But I must. I do. Please. Be sensible. I mean, I'm flattered, but that was Hamburg, not for ever. I met you on the train, you were travelsick, I was travelsick, a bond in common, our hearts beat as one, I saw you to your hotel, I met your husband, we got on like a house on fire, and ... what happened, happened. A beautiful memory. One must never go back. In any case, this is Paris. Things are different in Hamburg. In Paris, we're ... [i.e. 'far more strait-laced'.] And over there, there's all Germany between my wife and me. Not here. Do as I do. Renounce. That's it, renounce me. Hamburg's full of handsome devils.

Brünnhilde   I can't, I can't. I believe in being ... faithful.

Vatelin   What about your husband?

Brünnhilde   Oh, ja, ja, ja. One husband, one luffer. Vaithful.

Vatelin   I think I understand.

Brünnhilde   So the answer's nein?

Vatelin   Put yourself in my place.

Brünnhilde   Very well. Vatzi, auf wiedersehen.

Vatelin (*melodramatically opening the door for her*)   Adieu, my dear, adieu.

She collapses into a chair.

Brünnhilde I knew this would happen. When you didn't answer my briefchen. There's only one way now. I've written him a briefchen. Mein husband. Listen. (*She reads.*) 'Liebling, me to forget do try. You I betrayed altogether have. It all away I've thrown. An affair I've had, with Herr Vattelinn, 28 Thremol Street. Now I forsaken am, and it all I mean to end.'

Vatelin Fine. Post it. It's gibberish.

Brünnhilde I translate. 'Goodbye. I'm a fallen woman. I'm going to kill myself.'

Vatelin What?

Brünnhilde 'I've been having an affair. Monsieur Vatelin, 28 rue Thremol ...'

Vatelin You gave him the address?

Brünnhilde 'He's just ... just ...' What you say in French ...? 'Dumped me. I'll kill myself.'

Vatelin You can't send him that.

Brünnhilde Oh, ja.

Vatelin Killing yourself ...! Giving him my address ...! 28 rue –

Brünnhilde Thremol.

Vatelin Thremol. Oh, Brünnhilde ...

Brünnhilde After today, liebling, no more Brünnhilde.

Vatelin It's crazy. You mustn't.

Brünnhilde All right. This evening, 48 roo Rockypain.

Vatelin I told you, I can't. What can I tell my wife?

Brünnhilde I'll kill myself.

Vatelin Oh, God. All right. I'll come.

Brünnhilde   Oh, Vatzi, say you luff me still.

Vatelin   I luff you still. (*Aside, furious.*) Aaaaaargh!

Brünnhilde   Vatzi, liebling, Schatzi ...

Bell, off.

Vatelin (*aside*)   Why didn't you stay in Hamburg?

Enter **Jean**.

Jean   There's a gentleman, Monsieur.

Vatelin   What's his name?

Jean   Monsieur Soldignac.

Brünnhilde   Mein husband!

Vatelin   Here! (*To* **Jean**.) Tell him I won't be a moment.

Exit **Jean**.

Vatelin   What does he want?

Brünnhilde   A social call.

Vatelin   He mustn't find you here. Quick, this way.

He hustles her out by another door.

Brünnhilde   Till this evening.

Vatelin   Yes, yes, yes.

Brünnhilde   48 roo Rocky-pain.

Vatelin   Roo Rocky-pain, yes. Come on.

Brünnhilde   Oh, Schatzi ...

Exit.

Vatelin   If I'd only known ...! One lapse, one, after fifteen years of marriage ... the whole of Germany ... if I'd only known!

Enter **Lucienne**.

Lucienne She's gone, your visitor?

Vatelin What? Oh. Yes.

Lucienne Who was that at the door?

Vatelin Just someone I met in Hamburg.

Jean *ushers in* **Soldignac**.

Jean Monsieur Soldignac.

Soldignac (*German accent*) Good day for you.

Vatelin How nice to see you. Darling, this is Herr Soldignac.

Lucienne Monsieur.

Soldignac Dear lady. Good day for you. My dear man, a moment I have only. An instant. Meetings, all day meetings. One evening, soon. Dinner, in eveningtime, I've time. But for now, hupzi pupzi. To shake hands I come, and for my wifechen.

Vatelin She's well, your wifechen?

Soldignac Well, you say? Well. Too well. What I'm saying is: other man.

Vatelin Ozzerman? Oh, other man.

Lucienne Excuse me. I think you ought to be alone. The two of you.

Soldignac Dear lady, no. Philosophy, ja? It shames me not. In any case, no time. This morning ... this morning, in the wastebasket, this I find.

Vatelin (*aside*) My God, the briefchen. Not my name, not my name ...

Soldignac (*reading*) Schatzi –

Vatelin (*aside*) Schatzi. Thank God. Not Vatzi, Schatzi.

Soldignac (*reading*) 'I'm here, in Paris. I have to see you.' You hear me what I say?

Vatelin   Yes.

Soldignac   'Siegfried, my husband' – is I – 'will be out this evening. Business. Meet me at 48 roo Rocky-pain. Your Brünnhildechen.' How you like?

Vatelin   There's probably some simple explanation.

Soldignac   Soon we know. To the police I go. This evening they descending, roo Rocky-pain. My Brünnhildechen, her Schatzi, in the act they catching.

Vatelin (*aside*)   Thanks for the warning.

Soldignac   So grieving it iss, Madame.

Lucienne   Oh. Yes.

Soldignac   They catching; I divorcing.

Vatelin   Divorcing?

Soldignac   Oh ja. Such a Valkyrie she is. For a busy man, too much, too rushings. So to you I come. You handle.

Vatelin   Me?

Soldignac   My lawyer, ja.

Vatelin   Paris lawyer. Not Hamburg lawyer.

Soldignac   A-HA! Mistake you make. Is easy done. You think I'm German. No, no, no. French. Like you, quite French.

Vatelin *and* **Lucienne**   Pardon?

Soldignac   What you think, is Soldignac a German name? No, no, no. Is French. Bordeaux. To school in Hamburg, *gymnasium*, *universität*. But French. Entirely French. Married here, in Paris.

Vatelin   So now you –

Soldignac Divorcings, yes. You handle.

Vatelin Thank you. (*Aside.*) I don't believe this.

Soldignac Is good. So now I go. Hupzi pupzi, meeting.

Vatelin There's just one thing. I'll handle it, but first you must catch them together, your wife and her . . .

Soldignac No problem is. Tonight, roo Rocky-pain.

Vatelin (*aside*) Don't count on it.

Soldignac First I catching, then I teaching him.

Vatelin Pardon? Teaching him what?

Soldignac The duel. The sabre. My wife she boxing. But I sabre. All the time. Hamburger champion.

Vatelin A duel.

Soldignac Oh, not for death. A scar, here, here. For honour, scar. Now, excusings, please. Hupzi pupzi. Ha!

He goes to the door, making feints and passes, and bumps into **Pontagnac**.

Pontagnac Sorry.

Soldignac Many excusings.

Vatelin Darling, will you show Monsieur Soldignac out? I must have a word with Pontagnac.

Lucienne Of course.

Exit with **Soldignac**.

Pontagnac Who's that . . . volcano?

Vatelin He's a Hamburger. From Bordeaux. Listen, I want to ask you a favour.

Pontagnac Me?

Vatelin A . . . personal favour. This evening, I've

arranged to meet a woman.

Pontagnac   HahahaHA. You dog.

Vatelin   Precisely.

Pontagnac   You're having an affair.

Vatelin (*as if it explains everything*)   I *am* married.

Pontagnac (*aside, overjoyed*)   An affair. And he comes to tell me! Oh, Lucienne!

Vatelin   The point is, the place we arranged isn't quite ... it's a bit too ... You're used to these things. Can't you recommend somewhere? Some hotel, where we could – ?

Pontagnac   Let me think. The Imperial ...? The Grand ...? I know. The Ultimus. Hotel Ultimus. Personally recommended. Ideal: dozens of escape routes. Just book in advance, that's all.

Vatelin   Thanks. I'll send a telegram. 'A double room tonight, for Monsieur Vatelin' – that kind of thing?

Pontagnac   That's it. Your wife ... she won't suspect?

Vatelin   That's easy. I'm a lawyer. I'm often out of town. A will to read, a farm to sell ... I'll think of something.

Pontagnac   Brilliant.

Vatelin   I'll go and send that telegram.

Exit.

Pontagnac   He's having an affair. At last!

Enter **Lucienne**.

Lucienne   What a peculiar man.

Pontagnac   Lucienne. No: Madame. Quick. Now.

Lucienne   What is it?

Pontagnac   I . . . I . . . no, I can't.

Lucienne   Can't what?

Pontagnac (*aside*)   Don't be silly, of course I can.

Lucienne   What is it?

Pontagnac   You said, didn't you, 'I'll never betray my husband, unless he betrays me first.'

Lucienne   Of course I did. You heard me.

Pontagnac   Sauce for the goose, you said. All you needed was proof.

Lucienne   That's right.

Pontagnac   Ohhh! Ahhh! Tonight. Hotel Ultimus. Your husband. A woman.

Lucienne   You're making this up.

Pontagnac   Any minute now, he'll come in here, he'll say, 'Darling, urgent business, out of town. A will to read, a farm to sell, that kind of thing.'

Lucienne   Who, Crépin?

Pontagnac   That's an idiotic name.

Lucienne   You mean, he'd . . . ? Oh, if I ever catch him –

Pontagnac   Tonight. As soon as he leaves the house, I'll fetch you, take you to the Hotel Ultimus, and there, and there –

Lucienne   I'll be ready.

Pontagnac   So will I!

Enter **Vatelin**.

Vatelin   Ah, there you are, darling. Something's come up.

Lucienne   Oh, really?

Pontagnac (*aside*)   Out of his own mouth . . .

Vatelin   Urgent business. Tonight. The eight o'clock train.

Lucienne (*aside*)   I don't believe this.

Vatelin   The reading of a will. In Amiens.

Lucienne   Can't you send one of the clerks?

Vatelin   No, no. In person. They insist, in person.

Lucienne   Fine. Hupzi pupzi, as your Hamburger keeps saying.

Vatelin   It's a perfect nuisance.

Lucienne   Of course it isn't. Go on, go on.

Vatelin   I'll go and pack.

Exit.

Pontagnac   You see?

Lucienne   Ohhhhhh! That paragon, that jewel, that . . . husband! Fine, Monsieur Pontagnac. This evening, I'll be waiting, and as soon as I see with my own eyes, I swear to you I'll . . . I'll –

Pontagnac   Thanks very much. (*Aside.*) What d'you mean, underhand? Sauce for the goose, all's fair in love and – oh, for heaven's sake, you know what I mean. (*Aloud.*) Till this evening.

Lucienne   I'll be waiting.

Exeunt. The curtain falls.

Act Two

Hotel Ultimus, Room 39. Evening. A large, comfortably furnished hotel room. Upstage, bed in an alcove. In the middle of the room, a table. Downstage L, door to the corridor. Centre L, connecting door to Room 38. Upstage of this, a fireplace. Upstage L, door to the bathroom.

As the curtain rises, **Armandine** *is fastening a travelling bag. Knock, off.*

Armandine Come in.

Enter **Victor**.

Armandine Ah. Have you done it?

Victor Yes, Madame. The manager said he'd be here right away.

Armandine You told him I wanted a different room?

Victor Yes, Madame. He knew already. The maid told him.

Armandine Thanks. (*Aside.*) What a pretty boy. (*Aloud.*) Come here.

Victor Yes, Madame.

Armandine How old are you?

Victor Seventeen. [*Translator's note: for the present time fourteen or fifteen might play better.*]

Armandine Seventeen. You're very good-looking.

Victor Oh, Madame.

Armandine You're blushing. Don't you like being called good-looking?

Victor Oh, Madame.

Armandine Well anyway, you are.

She strokes his face. As her hand reaches his lips, he seizes it and kisses it avidly.

Good heavens!

Victor   Oh, I'm sorry, Madame.

Armandine   I don't mind.

Victor   I don't know what came over me. I didn't hurt you?

Armandine   Hurt me? No, you didn't . . . hurt me.

Victor   Don't tell the manager. He'll kick me out.

Armandine (*teasing*)   We'll have to see.

Victor   It's just that . . . when I felt your hand on my cheek, so soft, so warm . . . I felt . . . I began to . . . Ever since I was seventeen [fourteen/fifteen], I've begun to . . . And then there are spots, spots everywhere. Look, Madame, here on my neck. I showed it to a doctor who was leaving this morning, and he said, 'What you've got, my boy, is a bad case of puberty.'

Armandine   Puberty. Is that serious?

Victor   I don't know, Madame. All I know is, it makes me want to . . . It's as if the sap keeps rising . . .

Armandine   I know what you mean.

Victor   So when you . . . when you . . . You're not cross, Madame?

Armandine   Of course I'm not cross. Here.

Victor (*hot with embarrassment*)   Three francs.

Armandine   Something for yourself.

Victor   I can't, Madame.

Armandine   Why not?

Victor   Not from you, Madame.

Armandine What d'you mean?

Victor I'd have given all three of them, and seven more, to have . . . to have . . .

Armandine To have what?

Victor (*overcome*) Oh, Madame . . . (*Abrupt change of tone.*) The manager!

Armandine Poor darling.

Victor *flattens himself against the wall to let the* **Manager** *come in, and exit.*

Manager You wanted to see me, Madame?

Armandine The room, Monsieur. I wondered what arrangements . . .

Manager No problem, Madame. There's one free on the front.

Armandine Thank you. It's stuffy here. And since I'm staying a fortnight. As soon as it's ready . . .

Manager Yes, Madame.

Armandine You're sure it's no trouble?

Manager It might have been, Madame, at this hour. But as it happened, we were able to let this room right away.

Armandine How lucky. And lucky for someone else, too. Who was it?

Manager A Monsieur Vatelin sent a telegram this afternoon. I've let it to him.

Armandine Vatelin. Vatelin. Never heard of him. Ah, well.

Manager Your new room's Number 17, Madame. Facing the street.

Armandine Fine. So long as it's big enough. I may be

entertaining a friend later. A friend who may want to stay overnight . . .

Manager   Ah. In that case, I'll put you in 23, Madame. Twin beds.

Armandine   Twin beds? Whatever for?

Manager   Beg pardon?

Armandine   I'm not taking in paying guests.

Manager   But Madame's friend . . .

Armandine   A bed of his own. What would he do with it? I'll stick to 17.

Manager   Yes, Madame.

Armandine   Have them move my bags.

Manager   Of course, Madame.

He goes out, but stops in the doorway to talk to someone off.

Monsieur? Can I help you? Oh. Along here, Monsieur . . .

Armandine   Who is it?

Manager   A gentleman.

Armandine   What gentleman?

Manager   For you, Madame.

Armandine   What's his name?

Manager   I don't know, Madame.

Armandine   Oh well, show him in anyway.

Manager   This way, Monsieur.

He presses himself against the wall to admit **Redillon***, and exit.*

Redillon   Evening.

Armandine   You!

Redillon   That's right.

He goes to put his hat on the chimney breast.

Armandine   Make yourself at home.

Redillon   Thanks.

Armandine   How are you?

Redillon   Fine, thanks. Excuse me . . .

Armandine   What?

He puckers his lips for a kiss.

Armandine   Oh.

She kisses him.

Redillon   Jolly good.

Armandine   You love me, then?

Redillon   Adore you.

Armandine   You're not very tall. What's your name?

Redillon   Ernest.

Armandine   Ernest what? You have got a family name? You did have a family?

Redillon   Don't be silly. Redillon.

Armandine   What an ugly name.

Redillon   It goes with the family.

Armandine   Ah well, it's the man that matters, not the family. You're not bad-looking, are you?

Redillon *makes a face.*

Armandine   D'you know what?

Redillon   What?

Armandine   You look just like my other gentleman.

Redillon   Pardon?

Armandine Has no one ever told you?

Redillon Of course not. What other gentleman?

Armandine Schmitz-Mayer.

Redillon The jockey?

Armandine That's right. Sister married a baronet. Reservist. Foreign Legion.

Redillon Fascinating. I didn't come here for a family history.

Armandine He's on manoeuvres. All weekend. That's why he isn't here.

Redillon Well, that's a relief. Come on, then.

Armandine What d'you mean?

He puckers as before.

Armandine Oh.

She kisses him.

I could tell right away you fancied me. At the theatre, the other night.

Redillon And you were right.

Armandine Wasn't that Fifi with you?

Redillon D'you know her?

Armandine By sight. We've never actually met. But classy. That's what I thought. 'She's classy. I fancy him.' That's why I waved. I don't normally wave at strange men, in the theatre.

Redillon You don't?

Armandine Much less send them a note with my address.

Redillon So all this is thanks to Fifi?

Armandine   Don't breathe a word to her.

Redillon   You're joking.

Armandine   Or it's all off. We do have our standards.

Redillon   It's all right. I say, you aren't half ... It is all real ... ?

Armandine   Every bit of it.

Redillon   And all for me.

He takes her in his arms.

Armandine   Don't be greedy. I want it back again.

Redillon   Of course you do.

Armandine   For Schmitz-Mayer.

Redillon   Him again!

Armandine   I told you, he's my other gentleman. He says, 'I love you, little monkey.' Little monkey! Do you think I'm a little monkey?

Redillon   Oh, Armandine ...

He grabs her again.

Armandine   Oof. Oh, er ... er ...

Redillon   Ernest.

Armandine   Oh, Ernest.

Redillon   Sit on my lap.

Armandine   Cheeky.

Redillon   Lucienne, Lucienne.

Armandine   No. Armandine.

Redillon   Oh, what's it matter? Let me call you Lucienne. Oh, Lucienne.

Armandine   You are silly. I had a friend once –

Redillon   Don't talk. Just kiss me. Lucienne, at last, tell me it's you at last.

Armandine   I keep telling you I'm not –

Redillon   I didn't say answer, did I? Kiss me, I said. Just kiss me. Oh Lucienne, tell me it's you at last.

Knock at the door. He is too carried away to hear.

My darling. My sweet. My own.

Armandine   My God, you do go on. There's someone at the door. (*Loud.*) Who is it?

Victor (*off*)   Victor, Madame.

Armandine   Come in.

Victor (*as he comes in*)   Is it all right if I – ? Oh! Oh . . .

Armandine   What's the matter?

Victor (*tenderly*)   The bags, Madame. Can I move the bags?

Armandine   Over there.

Redillon   What bags?

Victor (*sharply*)   These bags. Here. Don't ask silly questions.

Redillon (*getting up*)   Hang on, hang on. Who d'you think you're talking to?

Armandine   Oh, don't be horrid to him.

Redillon   I'll box his ears.

Armandine   No, no. Give him a franc.

Redillon   A franc? Did you hear how he spoke to me?

Armandine   Well, if you won't give him a franc when I ask you . . .

She sulks.

Redillon   Oh, for heaven's sake. (*To* **Victor**.) Here. And this is the last time.

Victor (*curtly*)   Thanks. (*Aside*.) Pig.

Redillon (*who hasn't heard*)   That's right, and don't forget it.

Victor (*tenderly*)   Madame, I'll just fetch the maid. To help me with your bags.

Armandine   Off you go, then.

Exit **Victor**.

Redillon   I don't think he'll talk to me like that again.

Armandine   You have to make allowances. The poor boy's sick.

Redillon   What if he is? Why should I care?

Armandine   You would if you had what he's got.

Redillon   What has he got?

Armandine   Puberty.

Redillon   What d'you mean, puberty?

Armandine   Since this morning. A doctor told him.

Redillon   So he's got puberty. I'll see the manager.

Armandine   It isn't serious?

Redillon   Oh yes it is.

Armandine   It'll get worse?

Redillon   Unfortunately, not. If it did, and I could predict it, I'd make a fortune.

Victor *returns with* **Clara**.

Victor   In here. That one, there. Room 17. I'll bring the little one.

Exeunt.

Redillon   You're not leaving?

Armandine   Changing rooms. I want one facing the street.

Redillon   Facing the street. Perfect. Off we go, then.

He goes for his hat.

Armandine   Pardon?

Redillon   No time to waste.

Armandine   Till what?

Redillon   Haha. You know very well till what.

Armandine   No, no, no, no. Not tonight.

Redillon   Hey.

Armandine   Never mind 'hey'. I'm sorry.

Redillon   Sorry! You've got a nerve. You can't ... You can't lead a horse to water –

Armandine   I'm sorry. There's someone else. Eleven o'clock. He'll be here any minute.

Redillon   Oh, he will, will he? And what's his name, this someone else?

Armandine   You won't know him. He's from Hamburg. Soldignac. Every time he comes to Paris –

Redillon   That's disgusting.

Armandine   That's life. So, if you don't mind –

Redillon   Don't be here. Come home with me.

Armandine   Home with you?

Redillon   Yes. Home with me. I've got a home. What d'you think I do, doss in the park?

Armandine   But what can I tell him?

Redillon   Tell him ... sick mother, that's it. She's very old, and very sick.

Armandine   That's not very nice.

Redillon   It's nice. It's nice. Get your hat and come along.

Armandine   I must say I'm tempted.

She goes for her hat. Knock, off.

Redillon *and* **Armandine**   Come in.

Enter **Manager**.

Manager   Excuse me, Monsieur, Madame. But the people who booked this room are here.

Armandine   You want us to move.

Manager   I'm sorry to trouble you.

Armandine   It's all right. I'll just put on my hat. Ask Monsieur – Monsieur –

Manager   Vatelin.

Redillon   Vatelin?

Armandine   – to wait a moment.

Redillon   Vatelin, here? That's wonderful. Bring him in. I'd love to meet him.

Armandine   You know him?

Redillon   Do I know him . . . !

Manager   This way, Monsieur.

Redillon   He's one of my oldest, dearest –

Enter **Pinchard** *(in uniform) and* **Madame Pinchard**.

Redillon   Oh. Someone else entirely.

Pinchard   Terribly sorry to disturb you. My dear chap . . . my dear young lady . . . (*Aside.*) I say, what a filly! What? (*Aloud.*) We wrote for a room, some time ago, and they wrote back saying 'Room 39'. As soon as we decabbed, they brought us here.

Armandine   That's right, General. We're just leaving.

Pinchard   Don't rush on our account, my dear. If there's room for two, there's room for four.

Armandine   What a charming man.

Pinchard   Oh, Madame. (*To* **Redillon**.) I say, old chap, what a delightful little wife you have. I don't suppose you'd swap for mine?

Redillon *and* **Armandine** *gaze at* **Madame Pinchard**, *who has been occupied since she came in at making nervous, birdlike gestures.*

Redillon   Steady on.

Pinchard   It's all right. You can say what you like.

Redillon   She doesn't mind?

Pinchard   She's doesn't hear. Deaf as a post.

Redillon *and* **Armandine**   Ah.

Madame Pinchard   Please don't take trouble on our account.

Armandine   Your husband was just saying the same.

Madame Pinchard   Oh, always on Thursdays.

Pinchard   You see what she means?

Redillon   Not exactly.

Pinchard   You always get an answer, but not always the one you were expecting.

Madame Pinchard   Just what I always say.

Pinchard   Twenty-five years. This is our anniversary. That's why we're here. I'm taking her to the opera.

Redillon   In her condition? Wouldn't ballet be better?

In any case, tonight ... (*He looks at his watch.*)

Pinchard I know it's late. But we only ever go for the curtain calls. She adores the curtain calls. Don't you, Folifoline?

Madame Pinchard What d'you say?

Pinchard I said you only enjoy the curtain calls.

Madame Pinchard Quite better, thanks. It was just the movement of the train.

Pinchard You see, that's another thing. Liver. She's a martyr to her liver. Aren't you? Well, you know what they say: for better or worse ...

Armandine Well, if you'll excuse us. Are you ready, Ernest?

Pinchard Pleased to meet you. Delighted.

Redillon You know, it's amazing.

Pinchard Oh, yes?

Redillon My best friend's called Vatelin.

Pinchard Really?

Redillon Really.

Pinchard Well, well, well. Mine's called Piedlouche.

Redillon Astonishing.

Pinchard Isn't it?

Redillon Isn't it? (*Aside.*) Why?

Pinchard Well, delighted to meet yer.

Redillon Charmed.

Pinchard Folifoline. Say goodbye to the lady and gentleman.

Madame Pinchard What d'you say?

Pinchard (*loud*)   Say goodbye to the lady and gentleman.

Madame Pinchard   Not really.

Pinchard   No, no. Watch my lips. (*Articulating, in total silence.*) Say goodbye to the lady and gentleman.

Madame Pinchard   Oh. Goodbye, Monsieur. Goodbye, Madame.

Redillon   Amazing.

Pinchard   Never fails.

Armandine   Come on, Ernest.

Redillon   Coming.

Knock, off.

All *except* **Madame Pinchard**   Come in.

Enter **Victor**.

Victor   Can I carry anything else for you, Madame?

Armandine   No, thanks. Oh, but you could tell them downstairs that if a gentleman calls for me, I've had to leave suddenly. My poor, sick old mother. You know what I mean?

Victor   Yes, Madame.

Armandine   Go on, then. And I hope you're better soon.

Victor   Thanks, Madame.

Pinchard   What's wrong with him?

Armandine   Spots. (*To* **Victor**.) Look after yourself, darling. (*To* **Redillon**, *as she goes.*) My other bag.

Redillon (*to* **Victor**)   Her bag.

Victor   Her bag.

He takes the **Pinchards'** *bag, and gives it to* **Redillon**.
Exeunt **Redillon** *and* **Armandine**. **Victor** *gazes after her.*
The **Pinchards** *are engrossed in conversation and see none of this.*

Madame Pinchard   We mustn't be late.

She goes into the bathroom.

Pinchard   That's what I said! (*To* **Victor**.) Don't just stand there, boy.

Victor   Sergeant?

Pinchard   Come over here. Spots, you say?

Victor   Yes, Sergeant. Just little ones.

Pinchard   Ha! Don't tell me about spots. Cavalry surgeon, thirty years, I know all there is to know about spots. Turn round.

Victor   You see, I caught them –

Pinchard   Speak when spoken to! Trousers ... down!

Madame Pinchard *returns.*

Victor   Sergeant?

Pinchard   What's the matter with you, man? Take your trousers down.

Victor   But Sergeant –

Pinchard   My wife, you mean? Don't mind her. She's deaf.

Victor   Ah.

Pinchard   Well, what now?

Victor   I'll take them down if you say so, Sergeant. But the spots are on my neck.

Pinchard   Neck, eh? Neck? Why didn't you say so? That's not going to keep you off your horse. Don't you try those tricks with me. Back to your post: request denied.

Victor   But Sergeant . . .

Pinchard   Hup, hup, hup!

Victor   Yes, Sergeant. (*Aside, as he goes.*) Pig.

Exit.

Pinchard (*to his wife*)   Any excuse! They always try it on.

Madame Pinchard   That's right, half past ten.

Pinchard   I didn't mean that. I didn't mean that.

Madame Pinchard   No, you've got the tickets.

Pinchard   Oh, never mind. Where's the bag?

Madame Pinchard   What d'you say?

Pinchard (*loud*)   The bag! (*Articulating silently.*) Where's the bag?

Madame Pinchard   You had it last.

Pinchard (*loud*)   What d'you mean, I – (*Articulating silently.*) What d'you mean, I had it last?

Madame Pinchard   You must have put it somewhere.

Pinchard   She's right.

He starts searching. Knock, off.

Come in.

Enter **Clara**.

Clara   I just want to turn the bed down. Monsieur, Madame . . . have you lost something?

Pinchard (*without looking at her*)   Travelling bag. Where the devil can I have put it?

Madame Pinchard   It may be next door. In 38.

Pinchard   Right. Just a moment . . .

Exit into the next room.

Clara   Madame, shall I plump the pillows up, or leave them?

No answer.

Madame, shall I plump the pillows up, or leave them?

No answer.

What's wrong with her?

She goes and stands in front of her.

Madame –

Madame Pinchard   Good evening, my dear.

Clara   Good evening. Er. I was –

Enter **Pinchard**.

Pinchard   Don't talk to her. You're wasting your – I say! What a handsome filly!

Clara   Shall I plump the pillows up, or leave them?

Pinchard   Well, well, well, well. You are a pretty little girlie, what?

Clara   Shall I plump them up, or leave them?

Pinchard   Well, little girlie, that's rather up to you, don't you know?

Clara   Monsieur!

Pinchard   What's little girlie's name?

Clara   Dirty old man.

Pinchard   I say.

Clara   You called me girlie.

Pinchard   No, no, no. I don't mind in the least. Let me plump your pillow. Ha hey, ha hey.

He pinches her bottom.

Clara   Ow. Madame! Madame!

Pinchard   You're wasting your time.

Clara   Madame, please tell Monsieur to stop.

Madame Pinchard   Six hours on the train, that's right.

Clara   She can't hear.

Pinchard   That's right. (*Pinching again.*) Ha-hey!

Clara   Mon-sieur!

She slaps him.

Pinchard   Ouch.

Madame Pinchard   You've got it?

Pinchard (*rubbing his cheek*)   I certainly have.

Clara   Anything else, Monsieur?

Pinchard   What? Er, no, no. (*Aside.*) Once is quite
enough.

Madame Pinchard   Have you got toothache?

Pinchard   Not toothache. (*To* **Clara**, *warily.*) It must be
in the lobby. Get them to send it up.

Clara   Yes, Monsieur.

She goes to turn down the bed.

Pinchard   Come on, Folifoline. (*Articulating, silently.*) Don't
want to be late.

Madame Pinchard   I'm ready.

Pinchard   Curtain down any moment. (*Silently.*) Any
moment.

Madame Pinchard   Come along, then.

Pinchard Yes, dear.

Exeunt.

Clara (*to herself*) That cooled him down. Plump up my pillows. Ha!

Pontagnac *sticks his head round the door.*

Pontagnac No sign of him. Vatelin. Good. Time to get to work.

He creeps in. He is carrying a parcel.

Clara Can I help you, Monsieur?

Pontagnac Aee! (*Aside.*) The maid.

Clara Were you looking for something, Monsieur?

Pontagnac Looking? Ah. Yes. I. Looking.

Clara Yes, Monsieur.

Pontagnac You haven't seen him?

Clara Who, Monsieur?

Pontagnac The King of Belgium.

Clara He's not here, Monsieur.

Pontagnac Ah. I didn't think he was. Well, there you are.

Clara Yes, Monsieur.

Pontagnac This is Room 39. But is this the hotel? A-ha! It's the wrong hotel.

Clara An easy mistake, Monsieur.

Pontagnac It's incredible. 'Room 39,' he said, 'Hotel Ultimus, Room 39.' At least, I think he said Ultimus. Belgian accent – you know. He may have said 'Continental'.

Clara Are you in the government, Monsieur?

Pontagnac   Oh, yes. Minister Without ... ha, importance. I booked Room 38, to be next door to His Majesty. This one, is it?

Clara   Oh, yes, Monsieur.

Pontagnac (*trying to pocket the key of the connecting door to Room 38*)   This one. Haha. Room 38.

Clara   That's right, Monsieur.

Pontagnac (*aside*)   Got it! (*Aloud.*) Well, that's settled, then. That's entirely ... settled.

Exit, humming.

Clara   Bye, Monsieur. Now, towels ...

Exit into the corridor. At once, the key turns in the connecting door to Room 38, and enter **Pontagnac** *and* **Lucienne**.

Pontagnac   It's all right. It's empty.

Lucienne   This is it?

Pontagnac   This is it.

Lucienne   Here?

Pontagnac   Room 39.

Lucienne   It's disgusting. You mean, in this room ... this delightful room ... my husband, and another person –

Pontagnac   A woman, yes.

Lucienne   In this delightful room, he'll give her my kisses, the kisses that belong to me, my hugs, my sweet nothings ... and she'll give him – I don't know what she'll give him. It's disgusting. How can you let it happen? How can you stay so calm?

Pontagnac   Technique.

Lucienne   I can almost see them ... I can't bear it ... see him ... her ... I can't bear it... (*She covers her eyes, then uncovers them quickly.*) No, no, that's even worse.

Pontagnac   For heaven's sake calm down.

Lucienne   I hate this room. These walls have ears, this chair has eyes, this table ... No, no, no. Where's the bell? The bell?

Pontagnac   What d'you want the bell for?

Lucienne   I want them to get rid of the bed.

Pontagnac   You mustn't. D'you want to catch him at it, yes or no?

Lucienne   Oh, yes.

Pontagnac   Well, if you want to catch him at it, you've got to leave him somewhere to ... be at it.

Lucienne   I can't bear it.

Pontagnac   We won't stretch it out.

Lucienne   No.

Pontagnac   We'll burst in as soon as ... as soon as ... at the proper time.

Lucienne   Sooner.

Pontagnac   I don't mean ... After the orchestra tunes up, but before the –

Lucienne   Before the symphony.

Pontagnac   Exactly.

Lucienne   But how will we know?

Pontagnac   Ah! I've thought of that.

He unwraps his parcel and takes out two discs, one larger, one smaller.

Lucienne   What are those?

Pontagnac I used to go fishing a lot. Boring, fishing. I used to doze off a lot. So I tied a bell to the end of the line. I'm dozing, fish bites, bell rings, bam! That's what these will do with Vatelin.

Lucienne Fish bites, bell rings, bam!

Pontagnac That's it. They'll tip us the wink themselves, your husband and his . . .

Lucienne But where's the fishing line?

Pontagnac The beauty of this is, you don't need line. (*At the bed.*) Which side does your husband sleep?

Lucienne Next to the wall.

Pontagnac That won't work here: he'd be on the pillows. This side? Right. I take the two bells. This one's for him . . . (*He activates the big disc: bass ring.*) This is for her . . . (*The smaller disc: soprano ring.*) I put them together . . . (*Double ring.*) Perfect. Monsieur goes in here (*Sliding it under the bedclothes.*), Madame goes in here (*Same business.*), and there we are.

Lucienne Where are we?

Pontagnac Going fishing.

Lucienne That's it, is it?

Pontagnac We go next door, and listen. One of them gets into bed, one bell rings, we stay where we are. The other one gets into bed, the other bell rings, we stay where we are. They . . . move . . . both bells ring, and bam!

Lucienne You're a genius.

Pontagnac (*modestly*) I wouldn't say that . . .

Voices, off.

They're coming.

Lucienne I'll tear their eyes out.

Pontagnac (*struggling with her*)   No, no, no. They haven't even got here. Save it for later.

Lucienne (*to the imagined* **Vatelin**, *off*)   You wait. You wait.

Pontagnac *takes her out by the connecting door, and we hear the key in the lock. At the same moment,* **Clara** *comes in by the main door, carrying towels and followed by* **Brünnhilde**.

Brünnhilde   This is his room? Herr Vatelinn?

Clara   I'm sorry, Madame, but you can't come in. No one's allowed in a room booked by someone, except with the permission of the someone who booked the room.

Brünnhilde   This I know. He booked it, Herr Vatelinn. He sent me this briefchen. Read, please.

Clara   Briefchen?

Brünnhilde   Read, read, read.

Clara   Oh, yah.

Brünnhilde   'Ja'? You speak German?

Clara   Oh no, Madame. (*Reading.*) 'Your husband knows everything. He found the note.'

Brünnhilde   Not that bit. This bit. (*Reading.*) 'Meet me at the Hotel Ultimus.' This bit.

Clara (*reading*)   'Ask for the room booked for Vatelin, and if I'm not there yet, wait for me there.'

Brünnhilde   Ist gut?

Clara   Er, Madame.

Brünnhilde   Now I take off my hat. I arrange my hair. And while I do so, you fetch tea. And don't forget the schlagobermefistofelesentörten.

She takes her bag and goes into the bathroom.

Clara   Yes, Madame. Tea, after dinner. Ugh!

Victor *ushers in* **Vatelin**.

Victor   This way, Monsieur.

Vatelin   Thank you.

Clara   You can't show Monsieur in here. This is Monsieur Vatelin's room.

Vatelin   And I'm Monsieur Vatelin.

Clara   But . . . the lady and gentleman who were here before?

Vatelin   Ah. They were a mistake. At the desk, downstairs. They wrote to book 59, and your manager couldn't read the writing, so he gave them 39. As soon as they come back, he'll put them right.

Clara   Yes, Monsieur.

Vatelin (*to* **Victor**)   Thanks, young man. Oh, if anyone asks for me downstairs, tell them it's Room 39 and send them right up.

Victor   Yes, Monsieur.

Exit.

Clara   Monsieur means a lady?

Vatelin   No thanks, I've got one.

Clara   I mean, a lady came asking for Monsieur. Just now.

Vatelin   My God, she's prompt.

Clara   Shall I tell her?

Vatelin   No, no. She's better where she is.

Clara   Yes, Monsieur. I'll fetch the tea.

Exit.

Vatelin   Far better where she is. Wherever that is. I don't want to see her. Why did I come?

We hear **Brünnhilde** *humming, off.*

Vatelin She's in there!

Enter **Brünnhilde**.

Vatelin She's in here!

Brünnhilde Vatzi. Schatzi.

Vatelin (*coldly*) There is such a thing as being on time.

Brünnhilde Oh but is me wait for you. Ten minutes.

Vatelin Fah.

Brünnhilde Vatzi, I'm so happy. What's wrong? You look like a stenderd lemp.

Vatelin What?

Brünnhilde A stenderd lemp.

Vatelin Oh, a standard lamp.

Brünnhilde Oh, Vatzi . . .

She runs to hug him. He evades her.

Brünnhilde What is it you have?

Vatelin I don't have anything. You wanted me to come, I came. I didn't want a scene. But . . . it's finished. We can't just start again.

Brünnhilde Vatzi, mein Vatzi, why must you be so shtern?

Vatelin What d'you mean, shtern?

Brünnhilde So shtrict. You were once so kind, so shweet. So different from Siegfried.

Vatelin Siegfried?

Brünnhilde My husband. Such a yentleman you were.

Vatelin Ah, that's where you're wrong. I'm tough, me, tough. No yentleman here. If it's trouble you're looking for, you've found it. Hopla. Hopla. (*He shadow-boxes ineptly.*)

Brünnhilde   So silly man.

Vatelin   Now I'm silly! You just don't know me at all. I may have seemed like a yentleman. But that was in Hamburg. This is Paris, and in Paris I'm tough, I'm rough.

Brünnhilde   You aren't.

Vatelin   I am. A giant, an ogre. Grrrr!

Brünnhilde (*laughing*)   Oh, Vatzi...

Vatelin   Don't Vatzi me, or I'll ... I'll...

Brünnhilde (*playing along*)   Yes. What?

Vatelin   Well, I'll...

He pats her away gently on the upper arm.

Brünnhilde   A-HA! So you do want to box. On guard! One, two, haha, take that, and that...

She shadow-boxes, expertly. He falls back into a chair.

Vatelin   No, it's all right, really...

Brünnhilde   Take that, and that ... (*Falling on his neck.*) Oh Vatzi, Schatzi...

Knock, off. She disengages.

Come in.

Vatelin (*aside*)   Saved by the bell.

Enter **Clara** *with a tray.*

Clara   The tea, Madame.

Brünnhilde   Put it down there.

Exit **Clara**. **Brünnhilde** *starts seeing to the tea.*

Brünnhilde   Poor Vatzi. You do look downcast. Is that what it means to be rough and tough?

Vatelin You didn't have to –

Brünnhilde You'll be a yentleman to Brünnchen now?

Vatelin Will nothing get it into your head? Your husband's picked something up.

Brünnhilde What was this he dropped?

Vatelin Picked up about us! Didn't you get my note? Can't you behave? Well, if you can't, I can. I've had enough. I'm going home.

Brünnhilde Vatzi, nein.

Vatelin I'm going.

Brünnhilde You can't.

Vatelin I can.

Brünnhilde I kill myself.

Vatelin Fine, fine. Kill yourself. Just leave me alone.

Brünnhilde I drink this tea, and *pleep*.

Vatelin *Pleep*? Oh, pleep.

Brünnhilde You too?

Vatelin What?

Brünnhilde A cup of tea?

Vatelin Whatever you say.

She pours and passes.

Brünnhilde Sugar?

Vatelin Four.

Brünnhilde Too many.

Vatelin (*stirring the tea*) Pfffoh.

Brünnhilde (*taking out a phial*) One drop? Two?

Vatelin I don't know. A spoonful.

Brünnhilde　Too much.

Vatelin (*holding out his spoon*)　I like my . . . what is it?

Brünnhilde　A spoonful would kill a regiment.

Vatelin　What is it?

Brünnhilde　Strichnine.

She lifts the phial to her lips.

Vatelin　Put that down!

Brünnhilde　Don't shtop me. I drink, and pleep.

Vatelin (*struggling with her*)　Brünnhilde!

Brünnhilde (*struggling*)　Vatzi!

The struggle involves a few waltz-steps.

Vatelin　Oh, Brünnhilde, whatever you like. Just say it, I'll do it.

Brünnhilde　You mean this?

Vatelin　I mean it.

Brünnhilde　With trueness of heart?

Vatelin　Yes, yes. Trueness.

Brünnhilde　Sehr schön.

She puts the phial away.

Vatelin (*aside, meanwhile*)　It's the only way. Get it over with. (*Aloud.*) You're right! It's bigger than both of us. Oh, Brünnhilde, darling, I love you. Come here to me, be mine. (*He tries to pull her to the bed.*)

Brünnhilde　Vatzi! So hasty you are!

Vatelin　I said I was rough and tough.

Brünnhilde　Oh, Vatzi.

She advances.

Vatelin Don't try to stop me.

Brünnhilde Oh Schatzi, my love, my own . . .

Vatelin Come to me, come to me.

Brünnhilde One moment.

Vatelin Now where are you going?

Brünnhilde Undressings. Shtrippings.

Vatelin Can't you do it here?

Brünnhilde Donner und blitzen, in front of you?

Vatelin Oh . . . Hurry up.

Exit **Brünnhilde** *into the bathroom.*

Vatelin This is marvellous. In at the deep end. I wish
I'd never heard of Hamburg.

He sits on the bed. The bell rings, and rings, and rings.

You'd think, in a hotel like this, they'd have quieter bells.

As he sits there, and the bell goes on ringing, **Lucienne** *opens the
connecting door and comes up behind him, hands out to throttle him.
Just in time,* **Pontagnac** *pulls her back into Room 38 and shuts
the door.* **Vatelin** *has seen nothing. But he gets up, suspiciously,
and the bell stops.*

Vatelin What was that? Haunted? Burglars?

He tries the connecting door.

Locked. I'm hearing things. Feeling things, too. Draught
on the neck. It's a nightmare. That stuff she nearly made
me drink. They can come and take it away. Dreaming.
Having nightmares. (*He picks up the information card beside the
bed.*) Room Service, two rings . . .

*He pulls the bell-pull twice. Immediately there is a knock at the
door.*

That was quick. Come in.

Enter **Soldignac.**

Soldignac   Good night for you.

Vatelin   Haha! (*Aside.*) It's him. (*Aloud.*) It's you.

Soldignac   Is I, ja.

Vatelin   Well, well, well. Fancy. Fancy you, here.

Soldignac   I surprising you.

Vatelin   Not in the least. No, no. (*Aside.*) Not yet, at least.

Soldignac   Downstairs I was, in lobby. I hear them say, if anyone want Vatelin, to Room 39 they come.

Vatelin (*aside*)   I knew it.

He edges towards the bathroom door, to block it. But **Soldignac** *is anxious to talk to him, keeps going to him, taking him by the arms and plucking him downstage.*

Soldignac   I surprising you. To this hotel I come, for rendezvous. Lady is here, but waiting not. Going she is. Excuse she send.

Vatelin (*his mind elsewhere*)   Good, good.

Soldignac   To zickbed she goes. Old mother. Zick. (*After a pause.*) You care what I say?

Vatelin   Oh! yes! Zick, you said. Zick. Where does it hurt?

Soldignac   Who zick?

Vatelin   You zick.

Soldignac   Not me zick, she zick.

Vatelin   Seasick?

Soldignac   She zick. Mother zick.

Vatelin   Your mother's sick. Well, of course you must go to her, right away.

Soldignac   Why you say me, you go now?

Vatelin   No, no, no, it's quite all right. Off you go. I'll be quite all right.

Soldignac   You yoking.

Vatelin   Yoking? Ha! (*Aside.*) I wish I was. (*Aloud.*) It's just that, you always seem to have so little time. Hupzi pupzi . . .

Soldignac   In daytime, hupzi. In evening time, I've time.

He stretches out in the chair.

Vatelin (*aside*)   What fun.

Soldignac   Here staying I must. Police inspector I tell to meet me here.

Vatelin   What police inspector?

Soldignac   I tell you. My wife he catch. This night.

Vatelin   Oh, yes. (*Aside.*) He knows! (*Aloud.*) Not here, not here.

Soldignac   This I know. At roo Rocky-pain she is.

Vatelin   Right. Right. (*Aside.*) He doesn't know.

Soldignac   Inspector he catch her now, this minute.

Vatelin (*abstracted, edging to the bathroom door again*)   Good, good, good, good.

Soldignac   On her tracks he was, all afternoon. (*After a pause.*) You care what I say?

Vatelin (*hastily, going to him*)   Yes. Yes. Zick. You said she was zick.

Soldignac   Not now.

Vatelin   She's dead? A bit final.

Soldignac   My wife I talk.

Vatelin   Your wife's sick?

Soldignac   Not zick.

Vatelin   Your wife.

Soldignac   My wife.

Vatelin   She's in there . . .

Soldignac   What is this you say?

Vatelin   In there, er, there. Rue Roquépine . . . in there. Haha. There.

Soldignac   Yah. On her tracks he follow.

Vatelin   You mean she's gone already? Hahaha! Left?

Soldignac   The inspector he report here to me.

Vatelin   Fine. Fine.

Soldignac   What it is you have?

Vatelin   Pardon?

Soldignac   You nervings? Why you yump like this?

Vatelin   Nervings? Yump?

Soldignac   Is zick you are?

Vatelin   Oh, sick. Yes, a little. Sick.

Soldignac   You butterflies.

Vatelin   Pardon? Oh, in the stomach.

Soldignac   Is no problem.

Vatelin   No problem. No. Eughhhhhhhh!

This because **Brünnhilde** *has reached one arm through the bathroom door, to hang her coat over the back of a chair.* **Soldignac** *has also seen.*

Soldignac   A-HA! Now I see. I understand. So pretty she is, this arm. Whose arm she is?

Vatelin   Well, I . . . I don't know. Not mine. Just an

arm. Some . . . arm. Next door, it must be for next door.

Soldignac   Sly dog. Is arm your wife.

Vatelin   That's it. Your wife . . . my wife. Is arm my
wife. Wife arm. Arm wife. Haha.

*He hurries to pick up the coat. Just as he gathers it, the arm
reappears with a dress.* **Vatelin** *grabs it and stuffs it and the coat
under the bed.*

Soldignac   Where you are?

Vatelin   Here. Here.

Soldignac   Zit down, please.

Vatelin   There. Zitting.

Soldignac   Such a charming arm. So sweet.

Out of his line of vision, **Brünnhilde** *comes out of the bathroom,
in her chemise. She sees him, squeaks and rushes back in again.*
Soldignac *turns his head to the sound, but* **Vatelin** *grabs him
and twists it round.*

Soldignac   What you do?

Vatelin   I'm sorry. My wife. She wasn't . . . she hadn't
. . . I couldn't . . .

Soldignac   I understand. Excuse, please.

He gets up, takes his hat. **Vatelin***, aside, shrugs at the audience.*

Soldignac   I go now. Embarrass Madame, no.

Vatelin   That's right. You go. I stay.

Soldignac   I go.

Vatelin   I stay.

Soldignac   Is good.

Knock, off.

Be coming in.

Vatelin (*aside*) I booked this room . . .

Enter **Redillon**, *carrying the bag he took out earlier.*

Redillon I really am sorry –

Vatelin (*aside*) It's Redillon!

Redillon I picked up the wrong bag just now. Eh? Vatelin? You here?

He puts the bag on the chair by the table.

Vatelin Eugh, yes. Missed the train. Explain later. Take this gentleman downstairs and play snooker.

Redillon I don't know him.

Vatelin Monsieur Soldignac . . . Monsieur Redillon. Take him and play snooker.

Redillon I don't know how to.

Vatelin He does. He'll show you.

Redillon I won't. I can't. There's someone waiting.

He sits.

Vatelin Don't sit down, in that case. We're going.

Redillon Oh, right. You'll never guess –

Vatelin That's right. Not now. No time. Where's my hat?

Redillon (*aside*) What is going on? I'm exhausted.

He goes to drink one of the cups of tea.

Vatelin (*putting on his hat*) Got it. (*Snatching the cup.*) Put that down. No time.

Knock, off.

Soldignac Be coming in.

Vatelin Who does he think he is? 'Be coming in'?

Enter **Clara**.

Clara   Monsieur rang the bell?

Vatelin   Yes. Half an hour ago. Take away the tea.

He takes the cup from **Redillon**, *who has lifted it to his lips again, and puts it on the tray. He passes the tray to* **Clara**.

Clara   Thanks, Monsieur.

Exit.

Vatelin   Come on.

Redillon   I can't do that. I came for my bag.

Vatelin *hands him the bag he (***Redillon***) just brought.*

Vatelin   Here. Come on.

Redillon   It isn't that one. I just brought that.

Vatelin   This one, then.

He gives him **Brünnhilde**'s *bag.*

Redillon   I don't know. This isn't yours?

Vatelin   Of course it isn't.

He puts **Pinchard**'s *bag on the table, in place of* **Brünnhilde**'s.

Redillon   This must be it. Come on.

Soldignac   Come on.

Vatelin   That's it. You two go on. I'll catch you up.

Exeunt **Redillon** *and* **Soldignac**. *He rushes to the bathroom door.*

Vatelin   Hurry up.

Enter **Brünnhilde**.

Brünnhilde   They are now awaying?

Vatelin   Oh yes. Awaying downstairs. Snooker. We've

all got to play snooker now. With your husband. And
while we're doing that, you stay here. Don't leave this
room. I'll lock the door. You'll be safer that way. In any
case, if anyone comes, lock yourself in the bathroom and
don't come out till I say so. All right?

Brünnhilde   Oh, ja.

Soldignac (*off*)   Vatelin!

Vatelin   Hide!

Brünnhilde *presses herself up against the bed.*

Soldignac (*at the door*)   Be coming. Hupzi pupzi,
schnooker, hop!

Vatelin   I'm hopping, I'm hopping.

He goes and locks the door.

Brünnhilde   What now shall I do? My husband I see,
my courage she flees me. Flees me. I dress, I go. My
dress. Where it is, my dress?

Voices, off.

Mein gott, again they come.

She runs into the bathroom.

Pinchard (*off*)   Someone's locked the blasted door. You,
boy. You.

Victor (*off*)   Monsieur?

Pinchard (*off*)   Unlock this blasted door.

The door is unlocked, and **Victor** *shows in the* **Pinchards**.

Pinchard   Thank you.

Victor   Monsieur.

He goes and shuts the door. **Pinchard** *is supporting his wife.*

Pinchard   This way, old girl. That's right. Sit down,
you'll feel better.

He steers her to a chair. She looks soulfully at him.

Damn nuisance, these attacks. Always in the stalls, don't know why. We're hardly in before we're out. We'll try a box next time. Ah, the bag. They have brought it up. How d'you feel now? (*In a silent whisper, as before – and all that follows is the same.*) How d'you feel now?

She moves her head slightly.

Still bad, eh?

She nods, slightly.

Put out your tongue.

She does.

Looks all right to me.

She shakes her head, tongue out, as if to say 'It feels terrible'.

You'd better go straight to bed.

She looks enquiring at him.

No, bed.

She signals 'Good night'.

Yes, good night.

She goes towards the bed, then comes back and kisses him.

Me too. Happy anniversary.

She goes to the bed, and starts to undress.

(*Still in a whisper.*) I'll make her . . . (*Aloud.*) I'll make her a sleeping draught.

He takes a candle from the mantelpiece, goes to the table, and starts rummaging in the bag.

Where's that damn bottle? Ah, my slippers. (*He tosses them out, takes out another pair.*) Hers. Folifoline . . .

He takes them to her.

Madame Pinchard   Thank you.

Pinchard (*at the bag*)   Ahem, a ... whatjemacallit. (*He has taken out a lacy nightie.*) Folifoline. Whatjemacallit.

Madame Pinchard   Thank you.

She takes it and goes to put it on. He returns to the bag.

Pinchard   Here we are. Sleeping drops. Just the ticket.

Madame Pinchard (*from the bedside*)   Is my hairbrush there?

Pinchard   Hairbrush. Hairbrush. Here, brush. (*He passes it to her. He finds the glass beside the bed.*) This'll do.

He starts mixing a sleeping draught. **Madame Pinchard** *sits on the bed to brush her hair. At once, the bell starts ringing. She doesn't hear it, and* **Pinchard** *is preoccupied, counting drops.*

One ... two ... three ... Who the devil's that, ringing like that at this time of night? Four ... five ... six ... (*He puts the glass on the table, and gets up crossly.*) How's a chap supposed to concentrate?

He opens the door and shouts down the corridor.

How's a chap supposed to concentrate?

Voice (*off*)   Just what I say.

Pinchard   Just what I say. (*Shouting.*) We're trying to sleep in here!

Madame Pinchard *comes downstage. The bell stops.*

Madame Pinchard   What's the matter?

Pinchard (*to the other person, off*)   It's stopped.

Voice (*off*)   About time, too. Good night, Monsieur.

Pinchard   Good night to yer.

He comes in and shuts the door.

Madame Pinchard   What's the matter?

Pinchard   It's all right. (*Steering her to the bed.*) Some fool ringing, that's all. Lie down.

He takes off his uniform jacket and hangs it up. **Madame Pinchard** *sits on the bed again, and the bell starts ringing.*

My God, he's at it again. Some people have no consideration.

He sits on the bed to take off his boots. The other bell starts ringing.

What is this, a bell-ringers' conference?

He has his back to the door to the adjoining room. It now bursts open to admit **Lucienne***, followed by* **Pontagnac***.*

Lucienne   So there you are, you swine!

She grabs **Pinchard** *by the shoulders. He jumps up and staggers about, one boot on and one off. He doesn't see them.*

Lucienne *and* **Pontagnac**   It's someone else!

They rush back into their room and shut the door. **Pinchard** *recovers his balance and stumps about the room, one foot booted, one bare, trying to find them.*

Pinchard   Where are you? Who are you? Come out this instant.

Enter **Victor***.*

Victor   Monsieur, what's the matter?

Pinchard (*putting on one slipper*)   What d'you mean, what's the matter?

Enter **Clara***.*

Clara   Your bell, Monsieur.

Pinchard   My bell?

Enter **Manager***.*

Manager   Please stop ringing, Monsieur. You'll wake

the whole hotel.

Pinchard   What're you talking about?

*Enter a **Guest**, in dressing-gown and nightcap.*

Guest   For heaven's sake. You're disturbing my wife.

*Enter many more **Guests**.*

Guests   It's too much. What's going on? Stop it, d'you hear me, stop it.

Pinchard   Who are all these people? Get out of here. Out, out.

Manager   We'll go when you stop ringing.

Guests   That's right.

Pinchard   Me, ringing? What d'you mean, ringing?

Manager   Listen to it, Monsieur.

Pinchard   This is some kind of joke. Get out of here. All of you. Now.

All (*advancing on him*)   Will you stop that ringing?

Pinchard (*furious*)   I ... tell ... you ... it ... isn't ... me!

*With each syllable, he thumps the bed. Each time, the bell gives a single shrill ring. **Pinchard**, amazed, tries it again – a controlled experiment.*

My God, it's the bed. It's in the bed.

He takes out the bell from his side.

Look. Some damn fool, playing practical jokes.

Manager   It hasn't stopped.

Pinchard   There's another one. This side.

*They all surge round to **Madame Pinchard**'s side. She's amazed.*

Madame Pinchard   What is it? Who are you? Help!

Pinchard   It's all right.

Manager   Excuse me, Madame. (*He fishes out the other bell.*) Here we are.

Pinchard (*taking it*)   Told yer. Well, I'd like to know what you think you're playing at.

Manager   Me, Monsieur?

Pinchard   Yes, you. Damnfool tricks, last thing at night. Practical jokes . . .

Manager   Monsieur, I –

Pinchard   Take it. And the other one. Out. All of you, out. Hup, hup, hup!

He shoos them all out, and shuts the door.

What a performance!

Madame Pinchard (*kneeling up in bed, clutching a pillow*)   What's happening?

Pinchard   She didn't hear a thing. Oh, Folifoline . . .

Madame Pinchard   What did they want?

Pinchard (*shrugging*)   Nothing. Nothing at all.

He takes off his second boot.

Madame Pinchard   Just when I was feeling a little better . . .

Pinchard   I'll get them to bring a poultice.

Madame Pinchard   Pardon?

Pinchard (*silently*)   Would you like a poultice?

Madame Pinchard   I can't see what you're saying.

Pinchard (*holding the candle to light his face*)   Poultice, poultice.

Madame Pinchard Oh, please.

Pinchard Just a minute.

He rings. Enter **Victor**.

Victor Monsieur?

Pinchard Yes, it was me this time. Bring Madame a poultice.

Victor But Monsieur, there's no one in the kitchen.

Pinchard Of course there isn't. They're all up here, rushing into people's rooms in the middle of the night. Oh, give me my jacket. I'll make it myself.

Victor Yes, Monsieur. The thing is, Monsieur –

Pinchard Thing is? Thing is? Quick march!

He shoos him out, then takes the candle and whispers to **Madame Pinchard**.

Pinchard I'm going to the kitchen to make a poultice. You try to rest.

Madame Pinchard Oh, don't be long!

She turns to the wall. Exeunt **Pinchard** *and* **Victor**. *Pause. Enter* **Brünnhilde** *from the bathroom.*

Brünnhilde No noise now is. No Vatzi is. I dress, I go. My dress, where it is, my dress?

She searches, sees **Madame Pinchard***'s back in the bed, screams and runs out into the bathroom. Pause. Enter* **Vatelin**.

Vatelin Thank God. What a game! What on earth is 'Snookered again, old chap' in German? I'm coming, Brünnhilde.

Snore from the bed.

Ah. She got tired waiting. What a woman. Ah, well, ah, well.

He opens his bag and starts getting ready for bed.

All to the good, really. If she's asleep . . . better not disturb her. Slip in beside her. Doze off . . . wake up next morning, breakfast . . . home . . .

*He falls over **Pinchard**'s boots.*

My God, they've got big feet in Hamburg. Thirsty . . . I'm thirsty . . . Ah.

He sees the glass on the table, and drains it.

Perfect. Now then . . . trousers folded, over here . . . nightshirt on . . . (*Yawning.*) Heugggh. What a day. What an evening. Slip in beside her . . . gently . . . don't wake her up. Move over a bit. No, no, mustn't push . . . Silly really, sharing a bed with one's lady-friend . . . so tired, heugggh, so tired. Funny water, that. What was it, arsenic . . . strychnine . . .

*He's asleep. Pause. Enter **Victor** with the candle, followed by **Pinchard** with a poultice. **Victor** puts the candle on the mantelpiece.*

Pinchard   That's right. Dismiss.

*Exit **Victor**.*

Pinchard   Now then, Folifoline. Here we are. Careful, it's hot. Are you ready?

*He applies the poultice to **Vatelin**.*

Vatelin   Eeeowww!

Pinchard   I say.

Vatelin   Help!

Pinchard   You're a man.

Madame Pinchard (*waking up*)   What is it?

*She sees **Vatelin**, and screams loudly.*

Vatelin   Who is this woman?

Pinchard (*leaping on him*)   You swine, you filthy swine.

Vatelin   Leave me alone.

All three   Help! Help!

Pinchard   Get out of there!

Vatelin   Stop doing that!

Lucienne and **Pontagnac** *burst out of the adjoining room.*

Lucienne   My husband!

Vatelin   My wife!

He grabs his clothes, and the chair, and rushes out.

Pinchard   You saw him, Madame. You're a witness. In
bed with Folifoline.

Lucienne   Oh, I saw him.

Pinchard (*rushing to the door*)   Stop him! Adulterer! In bed
with Folifoline!

Madame Pinchard (*going after him*)   Where are you
going? What's happening?

They're gone.

Pontagnac   Now d'you believe me?

Lucienne   Oh yes. The swine.

Pontagnac   Was I right to make you stay, or wasn't I?

Lucienne   Oh yes. You were right. I stayed, and here I
stay.

Pontagnac   I hope you haven't forgotten ... your
revenge.

Lucienne   Oh no. My revenge. Oh no.

Pontagnac   You do remember your promise. 'If I ever
find out that my husband's ... then I'll ...'

Lucienne   Then I'll ... Oh yes.

Pontagnac Jolly good.

Lucienne I swore I'd take a lover. Fine. I'll take one.

Pontagnac Jolly good.

Lucienne If my husband ever asks if I've a lover, and who it is, tell him.

Pontagnac No need to go too far ...

Lucienne Tell him it's ... Redillon.

Pontagnac Pardon?

Lucienne His best friend. Redillon. Oh yes. Excuse me, now.

Exit into the adjoining room.

Pontagnac Lucienne!

He rushes to the door, but it's locked.

Now what?

He goes to the main door, to be met by the **Police inspector**, *a* **Constable** *and* **Soldignac**. **Soldignac** *has a snooker cue.*

Inspector Stop! In the name of the law.

Pontagnac I beg your pardon.

Soldignac Is him. The man of affairs, is him. (*He holds out the snooker cue like a rapier.*) En garde ...

Inspector Don't try to get away. We know everything. You were here, the pair of you.

Pontagnac Pair of us?

Inspector You, Monsieur, and this gentleman's lady wife.

Pontagnac I beg your pardon ... I ...

Inspector Your accomplice, my friend? Where's she lurking?

Pontagnac   What accomplice?

Inspector (*to the* **Constable**)   Search the premises.

Pontagnac (*aside*)   What is all this?

The **Constable** *brings* **Brünnhilde** *from the bathroom.*

Constable   Here we are, then.

Brünnhilde   Mein mann!

Soldignac   Mein weib!

Pontagnac   Frankly, I'm amazed.

Enter **Second constable**, *followed by* **Clotilde**.

Second constable   Hello, hello, hello.

Pontagnac   Another of them. My God, my wife.

Clotilde   Constable, arrest that man.

Exit.

Pontagnac   Clotilde, I can expl –

Soldignac *bars his path.*

Soldignac   First to me, ja? First to me.

Mêlée. Enter **Redillon**, *with* **Brünnhilde**'s *bag.*

Redillon   Here we are, then!

Silence. All gaze at him.

Terribly sorry, I took the wrong bag.

He puts down the bag, grabs the right one and exit hurriedly. The mêlée resumes, as the curtain falls.

Act Three

Redillon's apartment. Enter **Gérôme**. *Over his arm he has some folded clothes, a man's and a woman's, and he is holding two pairs of shoes which he has been polishing.*

Gérôme   Another skirt. Every day another skirt. What does he do with them? Young people today ... Rush, rush, rush. Why can't they all be like me?

He knocks at the door upstage R.

Redillon (*off*)   What is it?

Gérôme   It's me, Gérôme.

Redillon (*sticking his head out*)   Well? What?

Gérôme   It's eleven o'clock.

Redillon   Fine.

He shuts the door, hard.

Gérôme   Thanks very much. Door in the face, now. You bring them up, you dandle them on your knee, give them the best years of your life, and what do you get? Skirts to fold, boots to polish, and the door in your face.

Voices, off, in **Redillon**'s *bedroom. The door opens.*

Gérôme   At last!

Exit into the kitchen. **Armandine** *comes out of the bedroom. Her hair is down, and she is wearing* **Redillon**'s *dressing-gown. He follows her, crossly.*

Armandine   Your dressing-gown's too big.

Redillon   Too big for you. Not too big for me.

Armandine (*putting up her hair*)   Who's wearing it? Whose fault is it anyway? You bring me every bag in the hotel, except my own.

Redillon   How was I to know which was yours?

Armandine   There were so many, you might have hit on it by chance.

Redillon (*yawning*)   Ah, well ...

Armandine   What exactly do you mean, ah well?

Redillon   What's the matter?

Armandine   Exactly: what's the matter?

Redillon   The matter is, I'm exhausted.

Armandine   You've been in bed for eleven hours.

Enter **Gérôme** *with a feather duster.*

Redillon   But I haven't been asleep for eleven hours.

Gérôme   Rush, rush, rush.

Redillon   What's wrong with you?

Gérôme   Nothing.

Redillon   What are you looking at me like that for?

Gérôme   Tut, tut, tut.

Redillon   I beg your pardon?

Gérôme   It'll end in tears.

Redillon   Who asked you?

Gérôme   You mark my words.

Redillon   Out! Out!

Gérôme   Hah!

Redillon   Hah!

Exit **Gérôme**.

Redillon   I'm sorry. He dandled me on his knee.

Armandine   I'm delighted to hear it.

Redillon (*yawning*)   God, I'm worn out.

Armandine   Poor Ernest. You're just not used to this.

Redillon   I'm used to it. I'm just not the national champion, that's all.

Armandine   You're doing very nicely. (*Kissing him.*) It isn't me you're tired of?

Redillon (*without conviction*)   No, no, no.

Armandine   I knew it.

Redillon   I'm not. I mean, I'm tired, that's all.

Armandine   Men! You're all useless in the morning.

Redillon   Especially after the night before.

Armandine   This is a lovely flat. What's that painting?

Redillon   Prize pig.

Armandine   Amazing.

Redillon   What d'you mean, amazing?

Armandine   Just something Soldignac said. You know, Soldignac.

Redillon   Yes, yes. What?

Armandine   He kept on and on ... I don't know ... something about me saving the bacon.

Redillon   You?

Armandine   I don't even know him.

Redillon   Well, then –

Armandine   He wouldn't stop thanking me. Said they should give me a medal. Hey, d'you think he's got a ... a ... sweetheart?

Redillon   Oh yes. And you, what about you?

Armandine   Oh, sweetheart!

She kisses him. Enter **Gérôme**, *with a glass on a tray.*

Gérôme   Not again. Please, Madame, oh please.

Armandine   Please what?

She sits on the table.

Gérôme   Look at him.

Redillon   I'll throw you out.

Gérôme   I won't go. Here, drink this.

Redillon   I won't.

Gérôme   You will.

Redillon   Oh, give me strength.

He drinks.

Armandine   What is it?

Gérôme   Tonic.

Armandine   Pardon?

Gérôme   Nerve tonic. To build him up. (*Aside to her.*)
Please, Madame. He's a child, a stripling. He's only thirty-
two. Now, if it was me . . .

Redillon   What are you whispering?

Gérôme   Nothing.

Armandine   Secrets.

Gérôme   None of your business.

Redillon   I do beg your pardon. Here. (*He gives him the
glass.*) Any callers?

Gérôme   First, Fifi.

Armandine   Fifi?

Gérôme   Demanded to see you.

Redillon   What did you tell her?

Gérôme 'He's at his mother's,' I said. 'I'll wait,' she said. 'All right,' I said, 'but when he goes to his mother's, it's usually a week.'

Armandine Well done. If she'd found me here . . .

Gérôme Then Monsieur Mondor came.

Armandine Mondor? Mondor?

Redillon You won't know him. He's past all that.

Armandine Ah.

Redillon Antique dealer. Lives opposite. Pops in and out.

Armandine That's a relief. I thought he said Condor. Condor, my South American. Eyes like a hawk.

Redillon There you are, then. (*To* **Gérôme**.) What did he want, Monsieur Condor?

Gérôme Mondor.

Redillon I'm not myself this morning.

Gérôme He said something had come in. He thought it might interest you. Fourteenth something. Chastity belt.

Redillon Ah.

Armandine Fourteenth what?

Gérôme I don't know. Lady-friend?

Redillon Century.

Gérôme Century.

Redillon Anyone else?

Gérôme Not a soul.

Bell, off.

I'll get that.

Redillon I'm in, and I'm not going out. Unless it's a

woman, in which case, I'm out already.

Gérôme   I know. I know.

Exit.

Armandine   It's bound to be Fifi. And it's bound to be trouble.

Redillon   Where are you going?

Armandine   To get dressed, of course.

Gérôme (*off*)   He's out, Madame. I'm sorry, out.

He sticks his head round the door, and hisses:

It's a woman. Vanish!

Redillon   Come on.

He and **Armandine** *go into the bedroom.*

Gérôme (*opening the main door*)   Look for yourself, if you don't believe me.

Enter **Lucienne**.

Lucienne   Nobody.

Gérôme   I told you, he's out.

Lucienne   Tell him Madame Vatelin wants to talk to him.

Gérôme   Madame Vatelin. The wife of Monsieur Vatelin? Monsieur Vatelin, his friend?

Lucienne   Precisely.

Gérôme   Oh, in that case ... I'm sorry, Madame, I thought you were a ... woman.

Lucienne   Pardon?

Gérôme   Ernest, it's Madame Vatelin.

Redillon (*off*)   Who?

Gérôme Madame Vatelin. (*To* **Lucienne**.)   See?

Redillon (*hurrying in*) Fancy seeing you. Well, well, well, well . . .

Lucienne You're surprised? Well, so am I.

Redillon (*aside to* **Gérôme**) Tell . . . her . . . I'm sorry, I've been called away. Urgent business. And as soon as she's dressed, get rid of her.

Gérôme Of course.

He knocks at the bedroom door.

Armandine (*off*) You can't come in.

Gérôme Thank you.

He goes in.

Redillon You, here.

Lucienne You must know why.

Redillon No.

Lucienne Of course you do. If I come here, you must know why.

Redillon I don't.

Lucienne Last night, I caught my husband, in the act.

Redillon What act? Oh, that act. And now you've come to –

Lucienne To keep my promise.

Redillon Oh, Lucienne! I'm overwhelmed. Delighted. Take me. I'm yours.

Lucienne Just a minute. I should say that.

Redillon That's what I mean.

Gérôme *appears at the bedroom door.*

Gérôme Psst!

Redillon   Erk?

Gérôme *signs to him to distract* **Lucienne**.

Redillon   Right.

He gets between her and the bedroom door.

Lucienne   What is it?

Redillon   Someone going out. Hide behind me. They mustn't see you.

Lucienne *makes herself small behind his back.* **Gérôme** *leads* **Armandine** *on tiptoe out of the bedroom. She is now dressed. He shows her to the main door, where she turns and blows* **Redillon** *a kiss, then exit.*

Lucienne   Has she gone?

Redillon   Shh! Just a minute.

Gérôme *comes back, signs 'All clear' and exit.*

Redillon   All right.

Lucienne   Ah.

Redillon   Sit down.

Lucienne   Can you believe that man?

Redillon   What man?

Lucienne   My husband.

Redillon   Oh. Right. Sorry. Miles away.

Lucienne   And to think, all these years . . . I was faithful . . . I repulsed my poor, dear Redillon.

Redillon   Poor, dear Redillon.

Lucienne   Things are different now. Revenge. Revenge.

Redillon   Oh, Lucienne.

Gérôme (*sticking his head round the door*)   I'm going to the butcher's. Chops again?

Redillon   Chops. Chops, at a time like this. Oh, Lucienne . . .

He runs after **Gérôme**.

Redillon   Don't forget the peas.

Gérôme (*off*)   I won't.

Redillon (*returning*)   Sorry. He has a thing about string beans. I do apologise. He dandled me on his knee.

Lucienne   I understand.

Redillon   What was I saying?

Lucienne   'He has a thing about string beans.'

Redillon   Before that.

Lucienne   Something like, 'Oh, Lucienne . . .'

Redillon (*as if trying to remember the line*)   Oh, Lucienne . . . Oh, Lucienne . . . (*He gets it.*) Oh, Lucienne, Lucienne. You're mine? You're really mine?

Lucienne   I'm yours, I'm yours.

Redillon   What joy!

Lucienne   Ah yes. One person's pain is another's joy.

Redillon   Poor darling. Put your dear head here, no here.

Lucienne   I'll take off my hat.

Redillon   Let me.

He holds it out in one hand, embracing her.

Let me swim, darling, swim in your beautiful hair.

Lucienne   Have you put it down somewhere, carefully?

Redillon   Just a minute.

He puts the hat on the sideboard, and goes back to her.

Oh, Lucienne, Lucienne . . .

Lucienne   Revenge.

Redillon   Revenge.

Lucienne   From today, I'm his wife no longer. I'm yours, I'm yours.

Redillon   You're mine, you're mine.

Lucienne   How I loved that man. How I gave him everything: my devotion, my duty, my . . . girlish honour.

Redillon   Don't think of it. Don't think of him. Think only of me, of us. Oh, Lucienne . . .

He goes down on his knees. Enter **Gérôme**.

Gérôme   I'm back.

Redillon   Go away.

Gérôme   What are you doing?

Redillon   Never mind. Go away.

Gérôme   Whatever you say.

Redillon   And shut the door.

Gérôme   You're in a draught.

Redillon   Just do it. And stay out till I tell you.

Gérôme *sighs theatrically. False exit.*

Gérôme   They didn't have peas.

Redillon   What of it?

Gérôme   I bought string beans.

Exit.

Redillon   I'm so sorry. He did dandle me. (*Still on his knees.*) Oh, Lucienne . . .

Lucienne You do love me?

Redillon Love you? Of course I ... Just a minute. If I could just ... move up a little ...

He sits on the sofa next to her.

That's better. Now then ...

He crushes her to him.

Lucienne That fortune-teller was right after all.

Redillon (*eyes half-closed with rapture*) What fortune-teller?

Lucienne She said two passionate affairs would light up my life. One at twenty-five, the other at fifty-eight. Well ... I was twenty-five last week.

Redillon And I'm lighting up your life. At least ... just a minute ... if I ... perhaps if we ...

He stretches out on the sofa.

Lucienne What are you doing?

Redillon I want to see you better. Hold you closer. Lucienne, Lucienne ...

Lucienne (*sitting bolt upright, sighing romantically*) Ah.

Behind her back, **Redillon** *suddenly registers extreme dismay. He caresses her hand, but clearly his brain is racing. She turns to look at him, and immediately he grins.*

Lucienne Well?

Redillon Well, what?

Lucienne Is that all?

Redillon What, all? Oh, Lucienne ... (*Aside, in dismay.*) Oh, why did I ask Armandine back last night? (*As she looks at him.*) Lucienne, Lucienne ...

Lucienne (*getting up*) Can't you say anything else? 'Lucienne, Lucienne ...'

Redillon (*sitting up*)   The thing is . . . how can I put it?
. . . This has never happened before, I promise you.

Lucienne   Promises. 'Lucienne, Lucienne . . .'

Redillon (*getting up*)   I love you so much . . . I was taken
aback . . . that's it, joy, joy, I'm surprised by joy. And also
. . . how can I put this . . . I am his best friend, your
husband. A scruple, I admit. It'll be gone in a moment.
In any case, that swine! Just let me get used to it . . .

Lucienne   This is no time for doubts.

Redillon   No, no, no, no. I just need time. Not much
time. Come back tomorrow . . . this evening.

Lucienne   Tomorrow? This evening? He'll be here any
minute.

Redillon   Who will?

Lucienne   My husband. And by the time he arrives, I
want my revenge to be complete.

Redillon   What's he coming here for?

Lucienne   I told him. 'You cheated me, I'm cheating
you. At Redillon's, tomorrow morning, eleven thirty. If
you don't believe me, come and see for yourself.'

Redillon   Oh, fine. Thanks very much. I just can't wait.

Gérôme (*off*)   No, Madame, you can't go in.

Clotilde (*off*)   Oh yes I can.

Redillon   Now what?

Clotilde (*pushing past* **Gérôme**)   Excuse me!

Redillon   Madame Pontagnac!

Lucienne   Clotilde!

Clotilde   It's all right. I know you weren't expecting me.
Quite so soon, anyway. Dear Monsieur Redillon, you
remember what I told you, yesterday. 'Show me proof

that my husband's been unfaithful, and I'll take my revenge.'

Lucienne   What?

Clotilde   (*throwing herself on the sofa*)   I'm yours, all yours.

Redillon   Not her as well.

Lucienne   I beg your pardon.

Redillon   Nothing, nothing. Just thinking . . .

He goes upstage.

Lucienne   My dear Clotilde, 'Revenge! I'm yours, I'm yours' – you can't say things like that.

Clotilde   It's all right. Monsieur Redillon and I arranged it.

Lucienne   I'm terribly sorry, Madame, but I was here first.

Clotilde   I'm devastated, Madame, but yesterday, I booked him.

Lucienne   Booked him? Hah!

Clotilde   Hah?

Lucienne   Hah.

Redillon   (*interposing himself*)   Ladies, please! I am here, you know.

Lucienne   You certainly are. Well?

Clotilde   Well?

Redillon   Well? Ah. Ha. It's amazing, that's what it is, amazing. You want revenge, you both want revenge, and it's me who's supposed to . . . What am I, some kind of instrument?

Lucienne   Never mind that. Choose.

Clotilde   Choose.

Redillon   All right, I will. Neither of you.

The women   Pardon?

Redillon   You heard. Please leave.

The women   Well, really!

Gérôme *runs in.*

Gérôme   It's Fifi now.

Redillon   What d'you mean, Fifi?

Gérôme   She's here. Insists on seeing you.

Redillon   That's all I need. Tell her I'm . . . dead.

Gérôme   Dead. Right.

Exit.

Lucienne   Redillon . . .

Clotilde   Monsieur Redillon . . .

Redillon   No thanks!

He storms into his bedroom and slams the door. They rush to it.

Lucienne *and* **Clotilde**   Locked!

Clotilde   This is all your fault.

Lucienne   My fault? Your fault.

Clotilde   How can you say that? If you knew what this . . . this adventure is costing me. What agony.

Lucienne   I'm not enjoying it much myself.

Clotilde   All I ask is revenge.

Lucienne   Me too.

Clotilde   Life is so hard.

Lucienne   Husbands.

Clotilde   Husbands.

Gérôme *sticks his head round the door.*

Gérôme   Madame, there's a young gentleman. Madame Vatelin . . .

Lucienne   For me? A young gentleman? What's his name?

Gérôme   Monsieur Pontagnac.

Lucienne   Young?

Gérôme   They're all young to me, Madame. I could have dandled him.

Clotilde   What does my husband want?

Lucienne   Never mind. It couldn't be better. I wanted revenge, and I needed an instrument.

Clotilde   You surely don't –

Lucienne   My husband has earned it. It's not as if I loved Monsieur Pontagnac.

Clotilde   Oh, in that case –

Lucienne   Permission granted?

Clotilde   It'll give me something else to blame him for.

Lucienne   Good. Wait in there. In the kitchen. I won't be long.

She guides her out through the kitchen door.

Gérôme, show him in.

Gérôme   Yes, Madame. (*Aside as he goes.*) This place is a madhouse.

He shows in **Pontagnac** *and exit.*

Pontagnac   At last!

Lucienne   You did want me?

Pontagnac   Have you been here long?

Lucienne Just arrived.

Pontagnac And Redillon?

Lucienne Any minute.

Pontagnac Thank God, I made it in time.

Lucienne But what do you want?

Pontagnac I want to stop you. Doing something you'll regret. I want to throw myself between you and Redillon. Snatch you away from him.

Lucienne You can't do that.

Pontagnac You're joking. After all I've been through since yesterday? Have you any idea what's happened to me since yesterday? The slightest idea? Caught in the act, twice, except that there wasn't any act. Caught by a husband I'd never seen in my life before . . . with a wife I'd never seen before. Caught by my own wife . . . for this other wife, the one I'd never seen before. Divorce hanging over me: my wife. Another divorce hanging over me – the wife I'd never seen before and the husband I'd never seen before. She calls round this morning – the wife I'd never seen before – tells me in German that I must 'pay ze price'. Then her husband – the husband I'd never seen before – challenges me to a duel with sabres. Trials, divorces, duels, I'm plucked, I'm dressed, I'm stuffed, I feel like a Christmas turkey – and you say I 'can't do that'!

Lucienne (*aside*) Got you! (*Aloud.*) Life! Can you imagine, just as you came I was thinking, 'No, no, it's not fair. Not Redillon. It was Monsieur Pontagnac after all, Monsieur Pontagnac who lifted the scales from my eyes, showed me what my husband was up to.'

Pontagnac Pre-cisely.

Lucienne So if anyone should be my instrument of revenge, it's him.

Pontagnac   You're joking.

Lucienne   So if I asked very nicely . . .

Pontagnac   Asked? Nicely? I'd be . . . I'd be . . .

Lucienne   Of course you would. In that case, dear Monsieur Pontagnac, please be my instrument.

Pontagnac   You mean it?

Lucienne   I mean it.

Pontagnac   And under Durillon's own roof, er, Redillon's own roof! That's really rich.

He goes to close the curtains. She takes off her coat, revealing herself in a low-cut evening gown fastened with a diamond brooch. She lets down her hair.

Lucienne   My husband always says like this I'm adorable. Am I? Adorable?

Pontagnac (*taking off his gloves*)   Adorable. Yes. Adorable. Sheherazade.

Lucienne   That's right! I was reading it just this morning.

Pontagnac   Whatever for?

Lucienne   Ideas. I've never taken revenge before. (*Changed tone.*) My darling, do you love me?

Pontagnac (*taking her in his arms*)   How can you doubt me?

Lucienne (*aside*)   He's read it too. (*Aloud.*) For ever and a day?

Pontagnac   For ever and a day.

Lucienne (*breaking free*)   Good. Sit over here.

Pontagnac   Sit? What d'you mean, sit?

Lucienne   Sit.

Pontagnac   But I thought –

Lucienne   Of course you did. But not so fast. Slowly. I want to be wooed, to be carried away to ecstasy . . . I want my lover to lie at my feet, obedient to my every waking whim. (*Different tone.*) I said, sit.

Pontagnac   Oh, sorry.

He sits.

Lucienne   Thank you.

Pontagnac   Your waking whim.

Lucienne   Take off your jacket.

Pontagnac   I'm sorry?

Lucienne   It reminds me of . . . him, of him.

Pontagnac   Oh, right. If you're sure . . .

Lucienne   I'm sure.

Pontagnac   What next?

Lucienne   Sit down here, next to me.

Pontagnac   Sit down . . . here.

Lucienne   That's right.

Pause.

Pontagnac   What are we waiting for?

Lucienne   The right moment.

Pontagnac   Ah.

Lucienne   Take off your waistcoat. You look like a bartender.

Pontagnac   Take off my –

Lucienne   Do it! Now, sit.

Pontagnac   Don't you think this is a bit – ? Don't I

look a bit – ?

Lucienne Don't worry about that. (*She undoes one of his braces.*) Where did you buy these? They're horrible. And your hair. Who cut your hair? You look like a snooker ball.

Pontagnac (*struggling with his braces*) H'mmmm.

Lucienne Turn your head. (*She fluffs up his hair.*) That's better.

Pontagnac (*forgetting himself*) Oh, Lucienne, Lucienne ...

Lucienne That's enough.

Pontagnac Sorry.

Lucienne Please control yourself. It's not as if anyone was here.

Pontagnac I'm not made of stone, you know.

Lucienne All right. You'll do.

Pontagnac Phew.

Lucienne *takes a magazine from the table, and reads. Pause.*

Pontagnac Are you looking for more tips? (*He looks at it.*) Racing Weekly.

Lucienne There's a meeting at Longchamps this afternoon.

Pontagnac Really?

Lucienne Will you be going?

Pontagnac No.

Lucienne Mm.

She goes on reading. He whistles, gets up, stretches, walks up and down with his hands behind his back, looking at the furniture and fittings.

Lucienne Oh, do sit down.

Pontagnac   Sorry.

He sits. Pause.

What are we waiting for? Must I be a good boy to get a sweetie –

Lucienne   Shh!

Voices, off.

Pontagnac   Someone's coming.

Lucienne   (*getting to her feet, bundling up the paper; aside*)   At last. (*Aloud.*) Let them come. What do we care. Who d'you think it is? My husband, perhaps?

Pontagnac   My God, your husband.

Lucienne   Time for my revenge.

Police inspector (*off*)   Open, in the name of the law.

Pontagnac   It's them. Quick, hide.

Lucienne   Why should I hide? Don't you love me enough to fight for me?

Pontagnac   Well, of course, but –

Inspector (*off*)   Open this door.

Lucienne   Good. Take me, then, take me. I'm yours!

Pontagnac   What did you say?

Lucienne   It's now or never.

Pontagnac (*retreating fast*)   No, no, no.

Inspector (*off*)   Open up, or I'll break it down.

Lucienne   You heard him. Open up, or he'll break it down.

Pontagnac   Oh. Yes.

He hurries to open the door. She throws herself in a defiant posture, sprawled on the sofa, with a glare of scorn ready for her husband.

Enter **Vatelin** *and the* **Inspector**.

Vatelin She was!

Inspector Stay exactly where you are.

Vatelin It was true.

Pontagnac Oh, look, Chief Constable . . .

Inspector Stay exactly where you are. Is it always you?

Pontagnac An innocent house-call . . .

Inspector Put your jacket on.

Pontagnac *puts on his jacket, forgetting to fasten his braces.*
Redillon *comes out of the bedroom.*

Redillon All right, what's going on?

Inspector Madame, I'm here at the request of your
husband, a Monsieur Crépin Vatelin, of –

Redillon Excuse me. This is my house. What's going
on? (*Aside.*) Pontagnac!

Lucienne It's all right, Inspector. Monsieur Pontagnac
can tell you whatever story he likes, to protect my
honour. His duty as a gentleman. But I want everyone to
know the truth. (*Defiantly, staring straight at* **Vatelin**.) I came
here this morning of my own free will, because I wanted
to, I chose to. And the reason I came was to meet
Monsieur Pontagnac, my lover.

Vatelin She admits it.

Lucienne Please take all that down, Inspector, and use
it in evidence.

Vatelin Oh.

Clotilde (*appearing from the kitchen*) And now it's my turn.

Pontagnac Heeuggggh!

Clotilde Please take this down, Inspector. I, Clotilde

Pontagnac, the lawfully wedded wife of ... my husband
... came here, here where you found me, to meet ... my
lover.

Pontagnac   What did you say?

Clotilde   Goodbye for ever.

Exit into the kitchen.

Pontagnac   Wait!

He starts after her, his braces flapping.

Inspector   One moment, Monsieur.

Pontagnac   You heard what she said. Her lover. What
lover? Where is he? I'll wring his neck.

Gérôme (*aside*)   Oh dear. That must be young Master
Ernest.

Pontagnac   Where is he, that's all I want to know,
where is the swine?

Gérôme   Here I am.

Pontagnac   Eughhh!

Gérôme (*aside to* **Redillon**)   Don't say a word.

Pontagnac   In that case, Monsieur, name your seconds.

Gérôme   I haven't got any. I work for Master Ernest.
(*Fondly looking at* **Redillon**.) I dandled him ...

Pontagnac   Dandled him?

Inspector   Don't you see what's going on? (*Taking him
downstage.*) Don't you see what's going on? They've
planned this. Planned it in advance. It's not a husband's
little peccadillo, as we say in the force, it's a wife's
revenge.

Pontagnac   We'll see about that.

He starts for the kitchen again.

Inspector   Not yet, Monsieur, if you don't mind.
Statements. (*To* **Redillon**.) A pen, Monsieur? Some
paper?

Redillon   In there, Inspector.

Inspector   Thank you, Monsieur. (*To* **Pontagnac**.) If
you'd be kind enough, Monsieur, Madame . . . please walk
this way.

Lucienne   Oh yes. I'll walk that way.

She goes upstage, her face fixed on **Vatelin**. *As she passes him,
still in total silence, her face crumples and she mouths to the
company: 'My husband! The man I loved!'* **Vatelin** *turns
haughtily away, and she recovers her icy calm.*

Lucienne   Inspector, lead the way.

Exeunt all but **Redillon** *and* **Vatelin**. *The door to the hall is
left open, and during what follows we can see* **Lucienne** *and*
Pontagnac *making statements to the* **Inspector**, *who sits at a
writing-desk.*

Redillon   What a mess this is.

Vatelin *has slumped in a chair, head in hands, and is sobbing
silently.*

Redillon   I say, old chap . . .

Vatelin   Don't you understand, it hurts me here . . .
here . . .

Redillon   It's nothing.

Vatelin   Oh thank you. Nothing for you, perhaps. If it
had been anyone else's wife . . . But mine! I loved her, I
trusted her, and . . . and . . . It hurts me here.

Redillon   My dear chap, can I be brutally frank?

Vatelin   Oh, please.

Redillon   You really are a clown.

Vatelin   Really?

Redillon   Really.

Vatelin   A broken-hearted clown.

Redillon   No, no, no, no, no. If that's what you think, you are a clown. Don't you remember her note? 'Go to Redillon's. I'll be in my lover's arms.' That should have told you everything. A woman who's having an affair doesn't issue invitations.

Vatelin   I don't understand.

Redillon   She was trying to make you jealous. Look at the evidence. The darkened room . . .

Vatelin   Yes.

Redillon   The dress . . .

Vatelin   Yes.

Redillon   The sofa.

Vatelin   Yes.

Redillon   And Pontagnac – a man she'd never even met till yesterday.

Vatelin   Yes!

Redillon   And how do I know all this? Because she came to ask me first. Of course, I had to refuse . . . We won't go into the reasons.

Vatelin   My dear chap. My dear, dear chap.

Redillon   And you fell right into it. What a clown you are.

Vatelin   All I know is law.

Redillon   That's all there is to it.

Vatelin   Oh Redillon, I'm so happy. (*Sobbing again.*) So . . . happy.

Redillon Anyone can see that.

Lucienne *comes in, and stops astounded.* **Redillon** *signs to her to keep quiet and listen.*

Vatelin I'm so happy, waaaah.

Redillon Try not to let it show.

Vatelin Please, please ... find her ... tell her I love her ... tell her the truth ... I'm hers, I'm hers for ever.

Redillon But what about last night?

Vatelin Last night! Ha! If you'd only been there, last night.

Redillon That would never have done. At all.

Vatelin That mad Hamburger. Did you see her feet? No, of course you didn't. Her boots! I've never so much as ... well, once ... it was a business trip, I'm not made of stone. But once is all. Except that she ... she didn't think so. She hunted me down, like a bloodhound, a bloodhound. She said if I didn't ... she'd ... she'd ... I couldn't have Lucienne upset, so I ... so I ...

Redillon What a shame she can't hear you now. Lucienne.

Vatelin Oh yes. I'd explain, she'd believe me, I'd go on my knees, she'd gaze into my eyes, see the love in my eyes, I'd hold out my hand, she'd take my hand, I'd hear her dear voice saying, 'Darling Crépin, I forgive you –'

Redillon *has taken his hand and joined it to* **Lucienne**'s.

Lucienne Darling Crépin, I forgive you.

Vatelin Aah! Darling ...

He runs into her arms.

Darling ...

Lucienne   Darling . . .

Vatelin   I love you, darling . . .

Lucienne   I love you, darling . . .

Redillon   Oh God, I love you both.

They embrace him, too.

Vatelin   Dear friend . . .

Lucienne   Dear friend . . .

All three   Aaah . . .

Enter **Inspector**.

Inspector   Your statement, Madame. If you'd like to come through and sign . . .

Vatelin   Statement? What statement? We're tearing it up.

Inspector   Now just a moment –

Vatelin   Tearing it up, d'you hear me, tearing it up!

Exit.

Inspector   That's government property . . .

Exit after him.

Redillon   So there we are.

Lucienne   So there we are.

Redillon   All over.

Lucienne   All over.

Redillon   You and me, too?

Lucienne   Ah. The fortune-teller said two adventures. One now – I've just had that – the other when I'm fifty-eight. You will wait?

Redillon   H'm. Fifty-eight.

Lucienne   You don't need to think about it!

Redillon It's not that. You'll still be as charming as ever. But I might be . . . a little . . . worn.

Lucienne Let's wait and see.

Enter **Vatelin** *and the others.*

Vatelin That's that, then. My dear Pontagnac, I ought to wring your neck. But I won't. Why should I? We have open house next Monday. Be there.

Pontagnac Pardon?

Vatelin It's perfectly safe. My wife'll be at her mother's. In fact, come every Monday. I insist. I'll show you my collection.

Pontagnac Ah. (*Aside.*) Something to look forward to.

Redillon (*aside to* **Lucienne**) And if any time in the years to come, you feel like . . . feel like . . . please warn me the day before.

Gérôme (*at the kitchen door*) How many for lunch?

Redillon Count for yourself.

They all go upstage, except for **Pontagnac***.*

Pontagnac (*to the audience*) Well, there you are, then. Sauce for the goose. All's fair in love and war. You're joking!

He joins the others, as the curtain falls.

The One That Got Away

Monsieur chasse!

Characters

Duchotel
Léontine, *his wife*
Doctor Moricet, *his friend*
Gontran, *his nephew*
Cassagne, *a visitor to Paris*
Madame Latour, *concierge*
Babet, *the maid*
Inspector Bridois
Two constables

Acts One and Three take place in Duchotel's house in Paris. Act Two takes place in a love-nest rented by Moricet.

The play can be performed by seven actors only, if the parts of Babet and Madame Latour are doubled, and the parts of the Constables and Bridois are combined.

Note *The One That Got Away (Monsieur chasse!)* was first performed at Feydeau's favourite theatre, the Palais-Royal, in 1892, and was his first success for several years. The cast included members of his 'stock company' (Saint-Germain as Duchotel; Raimond as Moricet) and also two newcomers, Berthe Cerny as Léontine and the very young Marcel Simon as Gontran. (Simon, especially, went on to greater things, creating many leading roles in later Feydeau, and having a distinguished career in films.) In the original, Duchotel goes hunting, not fishing; I changed this because hunting gives the wrong kind of resonance to the English ear.

Act One

The parlour of **Duchotel***'s house in Paris. Centre back, main door leading to the hall. Downstage L, fireplace crowned by a mantelpiece and mirror. On the mantelpiece, an ornamental clock and candlesticks, a small candleholder and some matches. R of the mantelpiece, a bell-pull. Centre L, door to* **Léontine***'s sitting room. Downstage R, door to* **Duchotel***'s study. Between this door and the proscenium arch, a small writing-desk one of whose legs has been propped up with a book. In the desk are writing-materials. Centre-stage, a largish oval table with a chair on each side. On the table are all the implements required for fishing: bait-boxes, lead weights, floats, lures, spinners, and so on. An expensive wicker fishing-basket is on the floor beside the table. By the writing-desk R, a wing-chair; between the table and the fireplace, L, a pouffe. On each side of the main door, centre back, a whatnot with a vase of flowers; between each of these whatnots and the side-doors to L and R, an armchair. On the armchair R, a man's hat; leaning against the sideboard L, a walking-stick. A fire burns in the fireplace.*

As the curtain rises, **Léontine** *and* **Moricet** *are sitting at the table, sorting the fishing gear.* **Léontine** *works on, ignoring the sheep's eyes* **Moricet** *keeps throwing her, and the fact that he is trying to nerve himself to speak. At last:*

Moricet (*imploring*) Léontine!

Léontine (*briskly*) No.

She passes him a handful of weights and spinners.

Sort these for me, please.

Moricet Of course. (*Pause.*) But why not?

Léontine I said no, and I meant no.

Moricet The first little proof of love!

Léontine You mean, the last.

Moricet That's not what I meant. (*Warming to his theme.*)

It's simple, it's beautiful, it's natural ... Two people are very close ... The husband of one of them goes off on a fishing trip ... His best friend asks his wife to share his evening ...

Léontine   Yes, and his breakfast.

Moricet   Oh, no. I breakfast very early. I have to take surgery at eight.

Léontine   You'll let me sleep in. How kind!

Moricet   Léontine, trust me.

Léontine   Even if I agreed to ... what you suggest, what about my reputation? Have you forgotten my reputation? What would the servants say, the porter, if I stayed out all night? What *wouldn't* they say?

Moricet   You'll find some explanation. Women always do.

Léontine   Thanks very much. Pass me the lures.

Moricet   Pardon?

Léontine   The lures. Pass me the lures.

Moricet   Oh. Here. You must have an elderly relative, out of town somewhere.

Léontine   Of course I do. Great-Aunt Eugénie.

Moricet   There you are, then. Your husband's away, you go to stay with Great-Aunt Eugénie.

Léontine   And on the way I stop off for the night at 40 rue d'Athènes. The Moricet love-nest.

Moricet (*eagerly*)   Oh, yes!

Léontine   You see me visiting your love-nest ... climbing the stairs ...

Moricet   Oh, yes!

Léontine   It's going too far.

Moricet It's just round the corner.

Léontine Very funny.

Moricet In any case, you chose it for me. I told you I
was thinking of taking ... somewhere, I couldn't decide
where. I asked your advice, not a word to your husband
– and you said, '40 rue d'Athènes. We'll be so close.'
Green light! Home and dry! It was occupied already.
Mamzelle Fifi. Charming woman. But she owed six weeks'
rent. So I had her evicted, and there we are. All
arranged. Not very *nice*? Not *gentlemanly*? What did I care?
You said, 'We'll be so close', and that was enough for me.

Léontine I don't know what you mean.

Moricet That's because you're a woman and I'm a
man. As soon as you said, 'We'll be so close', I *knew*.

Léontine That's what you think I do? Go to
gentlemen's love-nests?

Moricet No, no, no. God forbid.

Léontine Is there a box of maggots there?

Moricet In the kitchen. You don't understand. When I
said, 'Come to my love-nest', I didn't mean you go to
gentlemen's love-nests. I meant, well, it's like *family*. I
didn't mean you were a ... were a ...

Léontine It comes to the same thing.

Moricet It isn't what I meant.

Léontine It isn't? Fine. Let's not talk about it. Let's
forget it.

Moricet Right. We'll forget it. Won't mention it again.
I'm sorry I brought it up in the first place.

Léontine Good. Now ring the bell and ask them to
bring the maggots.

Moricet Women! Ha! Women!

Léontine   You don't want to touch them?

Moricet   After this, not with a bargepole. A bargepole!

Léontine   I was talking about the maggots.

Moricet   Maggots! Ha! I won't be seen dead with them. Have you any idea what it costs me, my pride, to sit here sorting weights and sorting maggots for His Lordship your husband? I put you on a pedestal, and you kick me down. Fine, fine. I see you now. Through and through. The naked truth.

Léontine   I beg your pardon?

Moricet   It was a metaphor.

Léontine   Thank goodness.

Enter **Duchotel** *from his study. He is holding the pieces of a fishing-rod, which he is trying, in a useless sort of way, to fit together.*

Duchotel   Everything all right?

Moricet (*sarcastically*)   Couldn't be better.

Duchotel   What's the matter?

Moricet   Everything.

Léontine   Nothing at all.

Moricet   From *your* point of view. But what about me? Hot-blooded, passionate – and getting nowhere.

Duchotel   It's your own fault. One should always sort maggots calmly. Just hold your horses.

Moricet   Maggots, horses! I'm blazing!

Duchotel   I'll stay and help if you like.

Moricet   No. No, no, no, no, no. You'd get in the way.

Duchotel   Just what I told myself, in there just now. 'He's got my wife, he doesn't need me.'

Moricet Oh. Yes.

Duchotel So, calm down. Eh?

Moricet Thanks very much. (*To* **Léontine**.) So kind of him.

Duchotel It's absurd to let these things get on top of you. Look at me: my rod, do I let it get on top of me? I can't get it together, and do I worry?

Moricet You haven't the slightest idea . . .

Duchotel I haven't?

Moricet You haven't.

Duchotel All right, if you're so clever, how would *you* get it up?

Moricet I'd take it to the rod-shop.

Duchotel Rod-shop?

Moricet Rod-shop.

Duchotel What a good idea.

Léontine The weights are sorted.

She starts packing the fishing-gear in the basket.

Moricet (*huffily*) I don't know how people can *bring* themselves to fish.

Duchotel Don't start again.

Moricet Dumb animals, suffering . . . I wouldn't hurt a fly.

Duchotel Oh, come on, you're a doctor.

Moricet You're going fishing with Cassagne? Slaughtering dumb animals, with Cassagne?

Duchotel I always go fishing with Cassagne.

Moricet You always go *there*. He never comes *here*.

Léontine   That's right.

Duchotel   He lives up north, for heaven's sake. How could we fish in Paris?

Moricet   It would be in the Seine.

Duchotel   Exactly. Oh.

Moricet   I suppose he goes fishing to drown his sorrows.

Duchotel   What? Oh, yes. No, nothing serious. He's left his wife, that's all.

Moricet   She did have a lover.

Duchotel   No one ever proved that.

Moricet   But everyone knew. It's the same thing. They do things differently up north. (*To* **Léontine**, *with meaning.*) She did have a lover . . .

Léontine *turns away, pretending not to understand.*

Duchotel (*puzzled*)   You sound as if you approve. 'She did have a lover . . .'

Moricet   You weren't listening. I didn't say, 'She did have a lover', I said, (*Different inflexion.*) 'She did have a lover'. It's completely different.

Duchotel   I still don't get it.

Moricet   Well, you wouldn't, would you?

Duchotel   How do *you* know, anyway? 'She did have a lover.' How do *you* know?

Léontine   Yes. How *do* you know?

Duchotel   Because her husband said so? How did *he* know? Husbands are always the last to know. They suspect, but they seldom *know*. That's what really gets up his nose, Cassagne. He hasn't any proof – and until he gets some, he can't get divorced.

Léontine   What a good Catholic.

Duchotel   No, she'd stop his allowance.

Moricet   A practical Catholic.

Duchotel (*still fiddling with his rod*)   Stupid thing! I'll do what you suggest. Send it to the rod-shop. Babet, Babet . . .

Exit. Pause. **Léontine** *goes on packing the basket.* **Moricet** *paces.* [*Feydeau's note: Moricet must play the following scene with absolute, passionate sincerity. The humour is in the sincerity.*]

Moricet   You're not going to change your mind.

Léontine   Oh dear. Please leave it.

Moricet   Fine. I'll leave it. You've just admitted you love me. 'Oh dear,' you said. But I'll still leave it. (*He looks for a response, and gets none.*) You said what you said. You can't deny it.

Pause.

You remember the parrot? The one that died. The one that used to put its head on one side and say, 'Give us a quick one, don't be shy.' It snuffed it, and there we were, the three of us: you, me, the dear departed. Your husband was out. D'you remember how you cried? How I held you? Your head on my breast. You cried, I held. Oh, how I held! I was intoxicated, adrift on a sea of . . . our tears mingled together, yours, mine . . . I moved the parrot, laid it out on the pouffe . . . You were carried away, carried to the true soul of your being, and what did you say, what did you say? 'Oh, love!' 'Oh, love!' – that's where all this started. I was just about to dance for joy, when your husband came in. Just time to grab the parrot. We stood there, all three of us. Floods of tears. Don't tell me you don't remember. 'Oh, love!' The beginning of the end.

Léontine   I wasn't myself. I'd had a tragic loss.

Moricet   Of course you were yourself. Who else could

you have been? It's at moments like that, when a woman lets down her guard, says what she really thinks –

Léontine   'Oh, love!' That's all I said. 'Oh, love!' You took it the wrong way.

Moricet   I know what it really means, 'Oh, love!' Every man on earth knows what it really means.

Léontine   You mean – Oh!

Moricet   That's right. A pact. Unspoken. A debt of honour. Not negotiable.

Léontine   Thank goodness for that.

Moricet   People can't just blurt out 'Oh, love!' to people. It's not enough. Proof is what's needed. And I'm ready to accept your proof. Any time you say.

Léontine   You may have a long wait. It's a misunderstanding, don't you understand? 'Oh, love!' You say I said it. I believe you.

Moricet   You see!

Léontine   I'm very fond of you. Of course I am. Compared to some of the other men in Paris.

Moricet   You don't know any other men.

Léontine   That's just what I mean. You're charming, write poetry – how many doctors write poetry? Poetry! What woman wouldn't respond to that?

Moricet (*formally*)   How kind. Have you by any chance had time to glance at my latest slim volume, *Tears of the Heart?*

Léontine   Oh. No. My husband's still got it. (*Back to previous tone.*) It's hardly surprising you found ... what you found ... in my heart, my soul. The heart, it's full, it's all-embracing. But just because a woman's heart embraces everything, that doesn't mean she does the same. Especially if she's married.

Moricet I knew it. It's all *his* fault.

Léontine He is your best friend.

Moricet Of course he is. Absolute trust. Which is more than you have.

Léontine And this is how you repay him?

Moricet Well, naturally. I wouldn't do it for everyone. I love that man. I mean, I love you too, but I really love that man.

Léontine What an odd way of showing it.

Moricet What d'you mean? Oh, I see what you mean.

Léontine We married people, Dr Moricet – we promise to forsake all others and cleave only unto our husbands, our wives. It's a solemn vow.

Moricet You do it to please the priest.

Léontine We still *do* it. And so long as my husband keeps his vow, I won't break mine.

Moricet It takes two to polka.

Léontine Precisely. But the moment I hear that he's broken his vow, he's visiting a lover, you'll be the first person I'll turn to. I promise. 'Moricet, avenge my honour!' That's what I'll say.

Moricet Oh, Léontine!

Léontine It's all right. It'll never happen.

Moricet Of course not. He's not the lover type. Not of women. Fishing, canoeing . . . not women.

Léontine Precisely.

Moricet You hear of husbands who go fishing. 'I'm just off fishing,' they say – and slip round the corner to their lovers. But not him, not him.

Léontine He wouldn't.

Moricet I mean, I have wondered. Often. 'Dear old Duchotel,' I've said to myself. 'I wonder if . . . No, no.' In any case, when he comes back from a fishing trip, you can see from his face that his conscience is clear.

Léontine You can, you can.

Moricet It's just that . . . I've said this to myself. Often. 'If his conscience *wasn't* clear, there are one or two *little* things . . .'

Léontine What little things?

Moricet Nothing at all. Last week, for example, he brought back a hamper of trout and lobster.

Léontine What of it?

Moricet Trout, lobster. Where you get trout, you don't get lobster, and where you get lobster, you don't get trout. Everyone knows that.

Léontine (*taken aback*) How do they know?

Moricet Zoology. There's only one place you can get the two together.

Léontine Perhaps that's where he got them.

Moricet Exactly: the fish shop.

Léontine My God! Why didn't you tell me sooner? I thought you were my friend. You let me go on believing, go on believing . . .

She goes to the door.

Where is he? I'll demand an explanation.

Moricet No, no, no. You mustn't. I told you: I trust him, implicitly. Duchotel, my oldest friend. If I hadn't trusted him, implicitly, I'd never have suggested . . .

Léontine Well you did, and . . . you did.

Moricet Léontine, please.

Léontine It's all right. He's coming. We'll have a little talk.

Moricet You're not going to tell him – ?

Léontine Everything.

Moricet You can't. You mustn't. Léontine.

Duchotel *appears at the door, R.*

Moricet I'm off.

Duchotel You going?

Moricet No, I, yes. How are you?

Duchotel 'How am I?' You saw me ten minutes ago.

Moricet That was then, this is . . . I've got to go.

He goes to pick up his stick.

Duchotel Just a minute. It's pouring with rain. D'you want an umbrella?

Moricet No thanks, no. I've got my stick.

Exit.

Duchotel What's wrong with him? Has he seen a ghost? And what's wrong with you? What's wrong with you both?

Léontine I've just had a lesson. In zoology. It's pulled the scales from my eyes.

Duchotel I don't follow.

Léontine I've learned a lesson every wife on earth should learn.

Duchotel And whatever's that?

Léontine Where you get lobster, you don't get trout, and where you get trout, you don't get lobster.

Duchotel Thank goodness that's settled.

Léontine Don't try to pretend *you* knew. If you had, you wouldn't have filled the same hamper with trout and lobsters.

Duchotel Me?

Léontine Just because I didn't know. Just because I thought, 'Trout, lobsters, they're both water-creatures, they come from the same place.' How was I to know? I went to a convent school. Fortunately, Moricet was here to enlighten me. A man of science.

Duchotel You mean, *Moricet* –

Léontine It just slipped out. He didn't mean to.

Duchotel Thanks, Moricet.

Léontine You do well to thank him. Pulling the scales from my eyes. Showing me exactly what my husband gets up to.

Duchotel Just a minute. All this zoology proves nothing.

Léontine Proves nothing? Prove it!

Duchotel It's perfectly simple.

Léontine I'm listening.

Duchotel You know your friend Madame Chardet? And your other friend, Madame de Fontenac? The ones that don't speak to each other?

Léontine Don't change the subject.

Duchotel Just a minute. The ones that don't speak to each other.

Léontine (*tight-lipped*) Yes.

Duchotel They never meet?

Léontine Of course they don't.

Duchotel And when you see them, what do you do?

Léontine   What d'you think I do? I visit them.

Duchotel   There you are. You visit them.

Léontine   We're talking about trout and lobsters.

Duchotel   This *is* trout and lobsters. When you visit Madame Chardet, you go where Madame Chardet is, and when you visit Madame de Fontenac, you go where Madame de Fontenac is.

Léontine   What of it?

Duchotel   It's obvious. My lobsters are Madame Chardet, and my trout are Madame de Fontenac.

Léontine   My friends are fish?

Duchotel   When I want to get lobster, I go where lobster are. And when I want to get trout . . .

Léontine (*getting it*)   You go to Madame de Fontenac.

Duchotel   Every time.

Léontine   Oh, darling. I thought you were –

Duchotel   There, there. Silly little goose. (*Hugging her.*) Suspecting your own husband . . .

Léontine (*overcome*)   Oh.

Duchotel   Your own sweet, innocent, wronged husband . . .

Léontine   It's Moricet's fault. This was his idea.

Duchotel   He's an idiot. I mean, he's just run out into the pouring rain. Without his hat.

He picks up the hat from the chair.

Léontine   What a fool!

Duchotel   He'll catch his death of cold. Oh, darling, put it out of your mind. Kiss me.

They hug again.

Now, bring a light, and I'll show you my new fishing trousers.

Léontine *lights the candle on the mantelpiece. Doorbell, off.*

Léontine   There's someone at the door. Moricet.

Duchotel   He'll have noticed he forgot his hat.

Enter **Moricet**, *wet and embarrassed.*

Moricet   It's me. I forgot my hat.

Duchotel   You noticed, then?

Moricet   Not exactly. A boy shouted, 'Oi stupid, pawned your lid?'

Duchotel   How kind of him. And how kind of *you*, telling my wife what you've been telling my wife.

Moricet   What d'you mean?

Duchotel   Lobsters, trout: what you really meant was, other women.

Moricet (*hopping about in embarrassment*)   Oh, that's what you mean. She thought . . . No, no, no . . . Quite the opposite. I tried . . . if you'd seen her . . . you think I . . . ? Quite the opposite . . . I was on your side.

Duchotel   Funny way to show it.

Léontine   Stand still. My husband's explained exactly.

Moricet   Good . . . ah . . . the point is . . . 'Lobsters and trout,' you said . . . You should have seen her. 'Lobsters and trout!' *I* said, 'What does it prove, lobsters and trout, what does it prove?' You know how ladies are . . .

Léontine   There's a perfectly simple explanation. The trout are Madame de Fontenac.

Moricet   There, you see?

Léontine   And the lobsters are Madame Chardet.

Moricet Obviously. The trout are Madame de . . .

Léontine Fontenac.

Moricet Fontenac, and the lobsters are Madame . . .

Léontine Chardet.

Moricet Exactly. Simple. Thank goodness I was there.

Duchotel Now that's settled, pass me the candle. And next time, if it involves upsetting my entire family, keep your zoology to yourself.

Moricet (*fetching the candleholder*) How was I to know?

Léontine (*to* **Duchotel**, *as he's about to take the candleholder*) You aren't still cross?

Duchotel (*pushing away the candleholder*) Cross, darling, cross? Come here.

He hugs her at length. **Moricet** *stands glumly with the candleholder.*

Moricet I do feel a fool.

Duchotel (*to him, at length*) Well, are you going to hand over that candle or aren't you?

Moricet I was waiting till you'd finished.

Duchotel You look like Wee Willie Winkie.

Enter **Babet**.

Babet Monsieur's new clothes have come.

Duchotel Oh, good. They can put them in there.

Babet Yes, Monsieur.

Duchotel (*as she goes*) Just a minute. Any news of my fishing-rod?

Babet It's back.

Exit.

Duchotel   Wait till you see my new clothes. The trousers! The waistcoat! A new boutique: 'Chic Alors, Tailors to the Chic'. Gontran recommended them. My nephew, Gontran.

Moricet   Gontran! If he spent as much time on schoolwork as he does on clothes . . .

Duchotel   With schoolwork, he takes his time. He's also an idiot. Nice boy, though.

Moricet   A nice idiot. What a combination.

Duchotel   Unusual.

Léontine   Let's see this waistcoat.

Exit R, taking the fishing-basket.

Duchotel   Just coming. (*To* **Moricet**.) Wait here. If you get bored waiting, read a book.

Moricet   Thanks!

Duchotel   Oh, by the way, I forgot to say thanks for your latest book of poems. *Beers of the Tart.* Fascinating title.

Moricet   *Tears of the Heart.*

Duchotel   Well, almost the same. I haven't read it yet, but it *is* out.

Moricet   I know it's out.

Duchotel   I meant, out, in a vital position, here in this room. If anyone gets bored, they pick it up, and *poof!* – they see your name.

Moricet   Good. Thanks.

Exit **Duchotel**.

Moricet   *Beers of the Tart.* Philistine! (*Pacing.*) Why ever did she *tell* him? Trout and lobster. You try to help someone, and that's what happens.

He leans on the writing-desk, which wobbles.

What's wrong with this? Ha! One leg wobbly. Propped on
a book... (*He fishes out the book.*) *Tears of the Heart.* I might
have guessed. 'In a vital position, here in this room.'
Thanks very much. (*He reads the title page affectionately.*) '*Tears
of the Heart.* Sonnets and other occasional verses. By
Gustave Moricet, Doctor of Medicine, etc., etc.' Fancy
propping furniture, with *this*!

Enter **Duchotel** *in a fancy waistcoat and trousers. He goes to
preen in the mirror over the fireplace.*

Duchotel   What d'you think of these, then?

Moricet (*offhand, not looking*)   Very nice.

Duchotel   Very *nice*? They're the same as he made only
yesterday, for Gontran.

Moricet   No doubt. Thanks for putting my poems in
such a vital position.

Duchotel   Think nothing of it.

Moricet   Propping up furniture. I don't.

Duchotel   The leg was wobbly. It was the first thing
that came to hand. Books aren't entirely useless after all.
Eh? Eh?

Moricet   We don't write them to prop up furniture. I
even dedicated one of the poems to you.

Duchotel   You didn't!

Moricet   I needn't have bothered.

Duchotel   To me?

Moricet   If you'd opened the book, you'd have noticed.
Here. Page 91. 'Heartbreak'.

Duchotel   Pardon?

Moricet   The poem. 'Heartbreak. A Sonnet. To

Justinien Duchotel.'

Duchotel *shakes his hand, with emotion.*

Duchotel   Thank you.

Moricet *reads, pointing the metre as poets do.*

Moricet
'Dear friend, believe me, life is bleak and tough.
I see you laughing, heedless, ha, ha, ha,
I think, "Enjoy yourself, make merry, stuff
Yourself with joy. You'll find what sorrows are."'

Duchotel   Charming.

Moricet   Sh! (*Continuing.*)

'I look in the glass. I see myself, all bent
With grief, all twisted. Sorrow wrings my heart.
I look at you, I think, "Dear friend, by heaven sent,
Where would I be, if you and I did part?"'

Duchotel   Oh, come on. What is all this?

Moricet   'It's fate.'

Duchotel   No it isn't.

Moricet   'It's fate.'

Duchotel   It isn't.

Moricet   It is. That's how the line starts. (*Reading.*)

'It's fate, that's what it is, it's fatal fate
Must sunder us. And yet I dream, I know,
We'll meet again, some happy, future date,
A happy land, a garden, sunset glow.'

Duchotel   Er . . . much more, is there?

Moricet   It's a sonnet.

Duchotel   You told me. But is there much more? The tailor's waiting.

Moricet   Oh, go. I'd hate to keep him waiting.

Duchotel It is late. Thanks.

He goes to the door, then comes back.

Oh, and . . . thanks.

Moricet Don't mention it.

Duchotel *goes to the door, then comes back again.*

Duchotel What d'you really think? These trousers?

Moricet Poetry on legs! (*Aside.*) What a connoisseur!

Duchotel (*to someone off, as he goes*) I still think the left leg's shorter than the right leg.

Moricet Trouser-legs! Beers and tart and trouser-legs! (*He sulks briefly, then finishes reading his poem, with great emotion.*)

'Mysterious it is. A darkened room.
We'll enter it. We'll understand. The tomb.'

Straight to the heart. Experience, expressed. Not just because I wrote it. *Beers of the Tart.* No soul, some people. I didn't expect him to read it, but he might have put it *on* the table, not under it.

He slumps crossly in a chair. Enter **Gontran***, wearing clothes identical to those* **Duchotel** *has just tried on.*

Gontran Doctor Moricet!

Moricet Gontran. No school today?

Gontran Bank holiday. The bug-house rests.

Moricet Pardon?

Gontran School's closed. The bug-house rests.

Moricet The bug-house. In my day we called it the loonybin.

Gontran How odd.

He seems preoccupied, looks round the room a bit.

Nunkie not here?

Moricet   Nunkie? Oh, your uncle. In there, trying on your trousers.

Gontran   My trousers?

Moricet   Identical.

Gontran   He knows a good thing when he sees one. (*He taps himself idiotically on the knee.*) A-one stuff, hey?

Moricet (*mocking*)   A-one, A-one. (*Not mocking.*) He's in there, anyway. If you really want him.

Gontran   Oh, I can't wait. No hurry, mind.

Moricet   Pardon?

Gontran   Come to touch the old fruit.

Moricet (*not following*)   Ah. You touch your relatives.

Gontran   Five hundred francs.

Moricet   Got it! Touch him! Got it!

Gontran   Trouble is, I'm into him for six already.

Moricet   Six hundred already. Haha! This is about women.

Gontran   Well, naturally.

Moricet   You can't be.

Gontran (*eagerly*)   She's a pip, Doctor Moricet, a peacherino. And no one's ... I'll be the ...

Moricet   She told you?

Gontran   There is the sugar-daddy. Grand-daddy, more like. But no one cares about him.

Moricet   Naturally.

Gontran   He's rolling. That's vital, don't you know, in affairs like this. She told me, she told me: 'If the old baboon comes back unexpectedly, hide in the wardrobe.' Larks! He thinks he's the only one. What larks!

Moricet   And where did you meet her, this . . . peacherino?

Gontran (*after a conspiratorial look round*)   At the pawnshop. She was pawning her necklace, I was pawning my fountain-pen. Twin souls! No wonder our hearts beat as one. We saw at once, we were made for each other.

Moricet   Romeo and Juliet.

Gontran   She gave me her heart, and her apartment key. I go there every Sunday. Unless I'm in detention.

Moricet   Ah.

Gontran   Like I was last Sunday, for example. Crikey! That reminds me, my note. Saying I'll be there tonight. (*He hunts through his pockets.*) She'll be glossified! A whole fortnight . . . I mean, the old fool can't . . . (*He fishes out his wallet.*) Ah, here it is. No. Guarantee for Nunkie, in case he slips me that rhino.

Moricet   Pardon?

Gontran   The rhino, the tin, the dibs, the bread, the five hundred.

Moricet   Ah. You give guarantees.

Gontran   Always with me, just in case.

Moricet (*reading the guarantee*)   'On the day I come of age, I herewith undersigned guarantee to hand over five hundred francs, or currency in lieu.' Some guarantee.

Gontran (*stuffing it back in his wallet*)   Isn't it, though? Cash in the bank. (*He puts away his wallet, and finds his note.*) Aha. The note. I'll get Babet to send it.

He rings the bell, then says seriously to **Moricet**.

Deuced embarrassing. Touching Nunkie. If there was only some other . . . I say, you wouldn't care to lend a fellow half a bundle, what?

Moricet   What?

Gontran   Five hundred.

Moricet   No thanks.

Gontran   I'd give you a guarantee.

Moricet   No thanks.

Gontran   Didn't think you would. Still, worth a try, eh? Eh?

Enter **Babet**.

Babet   Sir rang?

Moricet   No. Sir did.

Gontran   He means me. Could you get the porter to deliver this note for a chap?

Babet (*reading the envelope*)   'Mamzelle Fifi, 40 rue d'Athènes ...'

Gontran   Don't read it, just take it to the porter.

Babet   Yes, sir.

Gontran   Oh, and give him ... this for going. (*He hands her a small coin.*)

Babet (*aside*)   He'll be living it up tonight, that porter.

Exit.

Moricet   He's coming. Duchotel. You can ask him, now.

Gontran   Oh crikey.

Enter **Duchotel** *and* **Léontine**, **Duchotel** *in the new trousers.*

Duchotel   How about these, then?

Léontine   Gontran.

Gontran   Hello, Auntie. Nunkie. I say, those *are* my trousers.

He and **Duchotel** *hold out their legs, comparing trousers.*

Duchotel   Two peas in a pod.

Gontran (*aside*)   I'll never wear these again.

He starts fawning on **Duchotel**, *tweaking the creases straight, smoothing the line, and so on. Meanwhile:*

Moricet (*to* **Léontine**)   Thanks very much. Telling your husband . . .

Léontine   No trouble.

Moricet   I'll never speak to you again.

Duchotel   Crikey, I have to send a note.

He makes for the writing-desk. **Gontran** *is still holding his trouser-leg, so that he almost falls.*

Duchotel   Let go, for heaven's sake.

He gets to the writing-desk, and finds it wobbly.

Who's taken the . . . Ah!

He takes **Moricet**'s *book of poems, and props the writing-desk with it.*

Moricet (*crossly*)   Why not Shakespeare while you're at it?

Duchotel   You're thinner. Don't fuss.

He sits to write.

What time is it?

Moricet (*looking at his watch*)   Five past five.

Duchotel   It can't be.

Léontine   Of course it can't. (*Looking at her watch.*) It's ten past.

Duchotel (*to* **Gontran**)   What does yours say?

Gontran (*looking at a cheap watch*)   Half past nine.

Duchotel   It must have stopped.

Gontran (*forced laughter*)   Ha ha ha. That's good, Nunkie. That's very good.

He plucks up his courage. Meanwhile, **Duchotel** *starts to write.*

Duchotel (*loudly, for* **Léontine**'s *benefit*)   No time to waste, if I want to catch the six-fifteen.

Léontine   That note's for Cassagne?

Duchotel (*hiding the note quickly*)   Oh yes. He needs to know when to meet me. At the station. Could you ask Babet to bring my things?

Léontine   I'll get them.

Exit.

Duchotel (*busy with his note*)   Madame Cassagne, 40 rue d'Athènes.

Moricet (*meanwhile, to* **Gontran**)   Get on with it.

Gontran   Not now. He's writing.

Duchotel   'Six o'clock, at Maxim's. Don't be late. Monsieur Zizi.'

He folds the note and pockets it. **Gontran**, *encouraged by* **Moricet**, *gingerly approaches.*

Gontran   Nunkie . . .

Duchotel (*not concentrating*)   What? (*Fishing in his pocket.*) I've got enough cash . . . (*He takes out his wallet and counts the banknotes.*)

Moricet (*aside to* **Gontran**)   Go on. He's loaded.

Gontran (*nerving himself*)   Nunkie, how amazing to see you counting rhino. You couldn't see your way to slipping a chap five hundred?

Moricet (*aside*)   He did it!

Duchotel   Me? Oh no. You owe me six hundred already.

Gontran (*aside*)   Skinflint. (*Aloud.*) Dear old Nunkie, ha, ha, ha! You didn't think I meant, a present? Good heavens, no. Exchange, fair exchange, that's what I meant. You give me five hundreds, I give you one five hundred.

Duchotel   Oh, change. That's different. Here.

He counts out notes. He drops one more, unnoticed, and **Gontran** *niftily catches it in his hat, whipping it on his head with a flourish.*

Duchotel   One, two, three, four, five. Here.

Gontran *stuffs the notes in his wallet.*

Gontran   Thanks, Nunkie. And this is yours.

He hands him the guarantee.

Duchotel   Just a minute. 'On the day I come of age . . .'?

Gontran   Cash in the bank.

Duchotel   You're joking. Give me my hundreds. Now.

He chases him round the table.

Gontran   But Nunkie, you agreed. Five hundreds, one five hundred. 'Yes,' you said.

Duchotel   I did no such thing.

Gontran   Bye, Nunkie. Thanks!

Exit.

Duchotel   Gontran! (*Coming back.*) Missed him.

Moricet   You always do.

Enter **Léontine**, *with* **Duchotel**'s *coat and hat.*

Léontine   What's wrong with Gontran? You'd think it was sports day.

Duchotel It was. And I was the sport. Five hundred francs.

Léontine He didn't . . .

Moricet He gave you his guarantee.

Duchotel 'Cash in the bank.' You can have it. One franc, it's yours. No, I'm robbing you. He'll pay for this.

Léontine (*handing him his coat and hat*) You'll need to hurry, if you want that train.

Duchotel Oh. Yes.

Doorbell, off.

Who can that be?

Enter **Babet**, *with the fishing-rod and basket.*

Babet Monsieur, there's a gentleman. I put him in the parlour.

Duchotel Not now. No time. Who is he?

Babet He didn't say.

Duchotel Too bad, then. Léontine, you see him. I'm off. Babet, did you get my suitcase?

Babet I'll bring it, Monsieur.

Exit L. **Duchotel** *makes passes with the rod.*

Duchotel Fine. They've fixed it. Till tomorrow, darling.

Léontine Till tomorrow. Don't do anything I wouldn't do.

They hug, to **Moricet**'s *disgust.*

Duchotel You coming, Moricet?

Moricet I'll see you to the cab.

He goes for his hat and stick.

Duchotel Must rush. Darling, listen for the clock. When it strikes seven, you'll know, 'He's there, my darling, the train's arrived, Cassagne's meeting him at the station now.'

Exit.

Léontine   Byebye, darling.

Moricet (*at the door*)   Léontine . . .

Léontine   Yes?

Moricet   Well?

Léontine   No.

Moricet   Ah.

Exit. Enter **Babet**.

Babet   That gentleman in the parlour. Shall I show him in?

Léontine   Yes, please.

Babet   Yes, Madame.

She ushers in **Cassagne**.

Babet   Monsieur Cassagne.

Léontine   What?

Exit **Babet**. *Enter* **Cassagne**, *very cheerful. He has a northern accent and a natty walking-stick.*

Cassagne   By, lass, it's grand to see you. How's your husband?

Léontine (*aside*)   Him? Here?

Cassagne   Out, is he?

Léontine   Oh. Ah. No. You wanted to see him?

Cassagne   I've not clapped eyes on him for months.

Léontine (*aside*)   For months. (*Aloud.*) Really?

Cassagne   Personal matter. Man to man. I'll tell you,

shall I?

He puts his top hat on the table.

It's the wife, d'you see. I expect you know, we're apart.
We live apart. I'm hoping for a divorce.

Léontine (*who has other questions on her mind*)   Very nice,
yes.

Cassagne (*pursuing his own train of thought*)   Trouble is,
you have to have grounds. That's what I came to see
Monsieur about. To tell him. I've got 'em. I think I've
got 'em. Tonight, tonight I hope to catch her at it.
Adultery, dear lady. She's got a lover, and I've got proof.

Léontine (*who hasn't taken in a word*)   How kind.

Cassagne   Monsieur Zizi, his name is.

Léontine (*as before*)   Congratulations. Er ... you said it's
been months since you saw my husband?

Cassagne   Nay, I've not been counting. Five, six months.

Léontine   Six months!

Cassagne   He's a right scallywag.

Léontine   You haven't been fishing?

Cassagne   Nay, lass. Against my religion.

Léontine   You mean you ... ?

She chokes for a moment, then starts uttering harsh cries which take
Cassagne *completely by surprise.*

Léontine   Harg, harg, harg, harg, harg, harg.

Cassagne   Hey up.

Léontine   Swine! Hargggg, swine!

Cassagne   What have I done? (*Aside.*) What?

He retreats. She advances.

Léontine   You told me you were going fishing.

Cassagne   I never . . .

Léontine *opens the door R and shouts through it.*

Léontine   Play tricks, would you? Butter wouldn't melt? We'll see about that.

Cassagne   Who mentioned butter?

He retreats. She advances.

Léontine   I see it all. Now I see it all. No hiding now. No hiding place.

Cassagne   No, Madame.

He is by the table, holding on. She picks up his stick and raps the table and his knuckles.

Léontine   Be quiet!

Cassagne   Ow!

Léontine (*pacing, waving the stick*)   I should have guessed. I should have known from the start. Well, now I do.

Cassagne (*aside*)   You have to humour them . . . (*Aloud, going to her.*) Madame . . .

Léontine (*brandishing the stick*)   We'll see who laughs last.

She sits at the table, and puts down the stick.

Cassagne (*aside*)   Now's my chance.

He creeps up to retrieve the stick.

Léontine (*more calmly*)   To think I believed. Every word . . .

Cassagne (*soothingly*)   Whatever you say, Madame.

Léontine   I was so calm, at peace . . . (*With each word, calmly, she crushes his top hat.*)

Cassagne   My hat.

She throws it away.

Cassagne Hey.

She has jumped up and is hitting the table with the stick.

Léontine I've been such a fool. A fool.

Cassagne (*once again rapped on the knuckles*) Ow.

Léontine But it's my turn now. You've seen nothing yet. Oh no, Monsieur. Now I demand . . . revenge!

Cassagne (*trying to rebuild his hat*) Yes, yes, Madame.

Léontine You think you can do as you please. One household not enough for you. Well, two can play that game.

She rings the bell.

I'll write to Moricet.

Enter **Babet**.

Babet Madame rang?

Léontine Pack a suitcase. I'm going out of town for a couple of days. To stay with Great-Aunt Eugénie.

Babet Yes, Madame. (*Aside to* **Cassagne**.) What's wrong with her?

Cassagne (*aside to her*) Summat bad, lass, summat big and bad . . .

Exit **Babet**.

Léontine Revenge. That's it. Revenge. I'll show him! (*In her fury she snaps the stick and hurls it from her.*) Haraaaaagh!

Exit.

Cassagne Nay, lass! My stick!

He scrabbles for the pieces, as the curtain falls.

Act Two

Moricet's *love-nest. An apartment furnished in up-to-the-minute style. Downstage L, a piano against the wall, covered with sheet music and ornaments; its lid is open and there is music on the music-rest. Centre L, the door to an inner room — a door with a prominent lock and key. Upstage L, facing the audience, an elegant boudoir, with colourful hangings representing the Triumph of Venus, is swathed and curtained in silk. In the alcove, a bed whose covers (duvet, white linen coverlet and sheet) are drawn back ready for the occupant(s). By the head of the bed (L), a bedside table with a candleholder and matches; at its feet, a pair of slippers. At the foot of the bed, a chair; on the floor, a bearskin rug. Upstage L, R of the bed, a window, with Venetian blinds and drapes like those of the alcove, gives on to a balcony, and beyond that a moonlit street. Centre R, a lockable door like that centre L; downstage R, the door of a large built-in closet. Between the two doors, a fireplace with a bright fire; on the mantelpiece a candleholder, two candlesticks, matches, a hand-mirror, a statuette; above it, an elegant oval looking-glass. The room is furnished with a sofa well stocked with cushions, and a dining table set for two, with matching chairs. On the table are a lamp with a large lace shade, a bowl of radishes in water, a partridge, a 'nest' of shrimps, a bottle of Bordeaux in a basket, etc. Pictures, ornaments, statuettes ad lib.*

As the curtain rises, **Madame Latour** *is discovered at the window with a perfume atomiser, spraying perfume on the curtains.*

Madame Latour   There, that's the curtains. Time for the sofa. The sofa ... that's where everything starts ... vital ... the first crucial skirmishes. Plenty for the sofa. (*Spraying vigorously.*) Leave nothing to chance. (*Going to the bed.*) Here, too? No. By the time they get here ... No, well, an offering to Venus. (*Spraying lightly.*) There we are. I hope he's satisfied, Doctor Moricet. Nights of Old Russia, nearly a whole bottleful, at sixteen francs. That's the kind of man for me. The kind of lover. Spare no expense! (*Spraying herself, as she crosses to put the vaporiser on the* *piano.*) Expense, for the women they love? Never! What a blessed sex we are. That's the kind of lover I should have had. The Countess Latour du Nord, crème de la crème. That's the kind of lover I should have had. Not a circus act.

She sits on the sofa.

That kind of husband would never have abandoned me. I'd never have ended up here. A concierge.

She stretches out on the sofa.

Happy days, ah, happy days. That perfume ... ah, that perfume, those happy days ... (*Declaiming.*) 'A flask of wine, a book of verse, and – some manly man or other ...'

Duchotel (*off*)   Madame Latour!

Madame Latour (*sitting up*)   A manly man!

Enter **Duchotel**, *in his new clothes and carrying his fishing-rod.*

Duchotel   Madame Latour! Oh, you're in here.

Madame Latour   Monsieur Zizi!

Duchotel   I've been shouting for twenty minutes. What a stink in here. You haven't bought a cat?

Madame Latour   Nights of Old Russia.

Duchotel   Nights of Old Cabbage. Foo! I've been knocking for twenty minutes. The apartment across the hall. Madame Cassagne, she's out?

Madame Latour (*cast down*)   Yes, Monsieur.

Duchotel   Charming. I was expecting her at Maxim's. Dinner for two. I had to eat them both. Didn't she get my note?

Madame Latour   Oh yes, Monsieur. She told me, 'Uncle Zizi's coming.'

Duchotel   There you are.

Madame Latour   'Uncle Zizi, up from the country, just as usual. Without any warning, just as usual. Tell him, if I'd had his note in time, I'd have stayed in. But I've arranged my evening. Give him my key and ask him to wait.' (*She takes a key from her pocket.*)

Duchotel   'Arranged her evening.' What's that supposed to mean?

Madame Latour (*handing over the key*)   Signed, sealed and delivered. Well, Monsieur Zizi, how's everything in Sainte-Olive-sur-Marne?

Duchotel (*baffled*)   Sainte-Olive-sur-Marne?

Madame Latour   Exactly.

Duchotel   How should I know?

Madame Latour   Ah. I was sure Madame Cassagne said the reason you visited her was that you came from the same village, Sainte-Olive-sur-Marne.

Duchotel   No, I . . . Oh! Sainte-Olive-sur-Marne!

Madame Latour   Don't you find it rather dull?

Duchotel   *Dull?* With a bowling green, a silver band?

Madame Latour   In any case, you spend a lot of time in Paris. Why do you always bring your fishing-rod when you come to Paris?

Duchotel (*glibly*)   Not a fishing-rod, a riding-whip. Latest style. (*Looking round the room.*) H'm, not bad. She does herself well, the floozie who rents this apartment.

Madame Latour   Floozie? Oh, Mamzelle Fifi. She doesn't live here, Monsieur Zizi. We were obliged to let her go.

Duchotel   You're joking.

Madame Latour   We can't allow tenants of that kind,

Monsieur Zizi. They lower the whole tone. I mean –
high-school boys . . . That reminds me, I must get the key
back from her last little scallywag. They were hardly in
long trousers before she . . . began taking them in hand,
teaching them everything she knew. And I had to open
the door for them. With this hand, that shook the hand of
princes!

Duchotel   You're pitiless, your Grace.

Madame Latour   With floozies, we have to be. Sordid
little escapades: we simply can't tolerate such behaviour.
Fortunately, since that . . . person left, the tone of the
establishment is beyond reproach. Everyone here is
married – and several to each other.

Duchotel   Just what's needed: running water, gas, and a
wife in every room. Your new tenants here, are they
married?

Madame Latour   He isn't. But she is. He hasn't told
me her name, but he blushes when he says she's coming
– I can always tell.

Duchotel   What a gay dog! What's he do?

Madame Latour   He's a doctor.

Duchotel   A doctor, and someone else's wife! Some fool
of a husband, blind, deaf, a dormouse! Ah well, excuse
me, your Grace, I'll see if Madame Cassagne's back yet.

Madame Latour (*at the door*)   That's right, Monsieur
Zizi.

She half opens the door, then shuts it again.

Just a minute, someone's coming. (*Peeping out.*) The new
tenants! They mustn't find you here.

Duchotel   Let me past, then.

Madame Latour   No. You'll meet them.

She takes him to the closet door.

Wait in there. I'll tell them you're a relative. The hall porter.

She pushes him into the closet.

Duchotel Just a minute . . .

Madame Latour Don't come out till I tell you.

Duchotel It stinks of mothballs.

Madame Latour What d'you expect, it's a closet. Get inside.

She closes the door, and leans against it.

Foof! Just in time.

Enter **Moricet**, *ushering in* **Léontine**, *who is veiled.*

Moricet It's all right. We're here. We're safe.

Léontine I daren't. I'm scared.

Moricet Why? There's no one here.

Léontine I think someone's watching.

Madame Latour (*aside*) At her age, we were all the same.

Léontine A woman!

Moricet Where? (*Seeing* **Madame Latour**.) Oh, her.

Madame Latour Pardon?

Moricet (*introducing her*) Her Grace the Countess of Latour du Nord.

Madame Latour *curtsies to the astounded* **Léontine**.

Léontine I . . . er . . . your Grace . . .

Moricet The concierge.

Léontine The concierge?

Madame Latour Alas, yes, Madame. How are the

mighty fallen.

Moricet (*pointedly, to her*)   They can fall a little lower. Your own flat, your Grace. Downstairs. We've . . . everything we need.

Madame Latour *makes to leave. Sneeze from the closet.*

Léontine   What was that?

Moricet   The closet sneezed.

Madame Latour (*quickly*)   It's all right, Monsieur. A relative. The hall porter.

Moricet   What's he doing in there?

Madame Latour   Tidying . . .

Moricet (*crossly*)   At this hour? Does he really need to, now?

Madame Latour (*conspiratorially*)   Monsieur, if you don't want him to see Madame, show her in there a moment. That door, there. As soon as she's inside, I'll get rid of him.

Moricet   Hurry up, then. Oh, and give him this for his trouble.

Madame Latour   Twenty centimes. How kind, Monsieur.

Moricet   Get on with it. (*Ushering* **Léontine** *into the room, R.*) This way, darling. Nothing to be afraid of.

Exeunt. **Madame Latour** *flings open the closet door.*

Madame Latour   Monsieur Zizi, quick!

Duchotel (*emerging*)   I stink of mothballs. At a time like this!

Madame Latour (*trying to hurry him out*)   Yes, yes, it's awkward. Here. This is for you.

Duchotel   Twenty centimes?

Madame Latour From the doctor. For tidying the closet.

Duchotel Ah. Hall porter. You keep it. After all, I am your relative.

Madame Latour Thanks. Now –

She's still trying to hurry him out.

Duchotel Yes.

He stops by the alcove.

I say . . .

Madame Latour What?

Duchotel (*pointing to the door R*) In there, are they?

Madame Latour Who?

Duchotel Him . . . and her. The wife.

Madame Latour (*gaily*) Well, of course they're in there. Ha, ha, ha.

Duchotel Of course they are. Ha, ha, ha, ha.

Madame Latour Why are you laughing?

Duchotel I don't know. You said, 'Of course they're in there', and it struck me, in an hour or so they'll be . . . they'll be . . . Tra, la, la, la, la. It tickled my fancy, that's all.

Madame Latour It isn't funny. That poor young girl. I don't think she's ever . . .

Duchotel No! (*Solemnly, removing his hat.*) One more for the human race.

He blows ironic kisses towards the door, R.

Night, night, little lovebirds. Sleep tight, mind the bugs don't bite. Ha, ha, ha, ha. Now then: Madame Cassagne! Tallyho!

Madame Latour   Across the corridor.

Duchotel   I know. Good night!

Exit. **Madame Latour** *shuts the door behind him.*

Madame Latour   I thought he'd never go.

She opens the door to **Moricet** *and* **Léontine**.

Madame Latour   You can come out now.

Moricet   Not before time.

Madame Latour   Is there anything else I can do, Doctor?

Moricet   No thanks, your Grace.

Madame Latour   I'll say good night then, Monsieur, Madame.

She hovers.

Moricet   Yes. Thank you.

Madame Latour (*sighing*)   Ah.

Exit.

Moricet   Léontine . . .

Enter **Madame Latour** *like a jack-in-the-box.*

Madame Latour   If you need anything at all, just ring. The bell goes straight to my sitting-room.

Moricet   Please: do the same.

He shuts the door on her and locks it.

Léontine.

Léontine   Moricet?

Moricet (*clasping her to his bosom*)   Alone at last.

Léontine   I can't believe I'm doing this.

Moricet (*holding out his hands to her*)   I hardly believe it

either. Let me look at you ... Ah. Let me hold you ...
Ah. Let me –

He makes to kiss her. She puts her hand over his mouth.

Léontine   Ah, no.

Moricet   Ah, no? But you said ... So many lonely
hours ...

Léontine (*breaking away*)   Pardon?

Moricet   I've longed for you. So many hours, well, days,
well days *and* nights ...

Léontine   Tell me it's right. Tell me it's not the silliest
thing I've ever done.

Moricet   Silly? Which part of it?

Léontine   All of it! A respectable married woman, till
now – and then tomorrow ...

Moricet   You'll be just the same.

Léontine   You think so?

Moricet   Well, naturally. Unless you tell people.

Léontine   Never!

Moricet (*with passionate conviction*)   Well, then.
Respectability – it's what other people think. And how
can they think anything, unless they know?

Léontine   Oh, philosophy.

Moricet   Philosophy, yes. What stops you being
respectable just because you give yourself to the man you
love? Society – the society that says, 'Love no one but the
man I give you, by law: that is, your husband.' Society
invented husbands: functionaries. But natural justice,
Léontine, true justice, true marriage, what is it but the
union of two hearts that beat as one? A woman's true
husband is her lover. She marries a functionary in law,
and a lover, a soul-mate, deep in her heart.

Léontine An assistant husband.

Moricet Exactly. A kind of second mate. Like on a ship. They do all the work. But never mind, forget all this. What else matters? We love each other! Don't tell me you've forgotten the note you wrote, so warm, so loving, so open-hearted . . .

Léontine I was furious.

Moricet So furiously open-hearted. What a note! My gateway to Paradise!

Léontine You kept it?

Moricet Kept it? (*Beating his chest.*) Crushed it to my heart!

Léontine (*flirting*) Show me.

Moricet *Voi-LÀ!*

With a flourish, he produces the note, from the back pocket of his trousers.

Léontine (*smothering a laugh by feigning a blush*) Is *that* your heart?

Moricet My heart is everywhere, everywhere. Oh, this note, your note, your dear, dear note, the note you wrote . . .

Léontine That's the one.

Moricet The language of love. So fine, so pure. From the heart, from here, from here . . . (*He thumps his chest again.*)

Léontine (*meaningfully*) Or there.

Moricet (*reading*) 'Dear friend . . .' (*He kisses the note.*) 'What can I say? Nothing stands between us . . .' You see? You remember? So fine, so pure, so . . .

Léontine Fine.

Moricet Exactly. (*Reading again.*) 'If it was up to me, you'd have my heart.' There. That says it all.

He starts to fold the note.

Léontine No it doesn't. There's another sentence.

Moricet A trifle! A bagatelle.

Léontine (*reading over his shoulder*) 'If it was up to me, you'd have my heart. But it belongs to another.' (*Firmly.*) 'It belongs to another': look.

Moricet Oh, you had to put that in. Women always do.

Léontine Do we?

Moricet (*repocketing the note*) How could anyone say 'No' after such a note? Léontine, look round, look round. The night, the silence, this place, all whisper 'Yes! Yes! Yes!' The very air seduces us, caresses our nostrils, swooning, swooning . . .

Léontine There *is* a funny smell.

Moricet (*guiding her gently, as if in an ecstatic dance*) Look: a table. Set for two. An intimate dinner, sweet nothings . . .

Léontine (*clapping her hands like a little girl*) Partridge! Shrimps! Justinien's favourites!

Moricet (*matter-of-fact*) He's not getting them. (*Lyrically.*) Lights low, just low enough to glow on our love, a little lower, lower . . .

Still clasping her, he turns the lamp down with his free hand.

Léontine What are you doing?

Moricet (*matter-of-fact*) Scene-setting. (*Lyrically.*) Look, darling, look: the window. And through the window, the moon. Look how she smiles, on lovers, how she smiles.

Léontine Very pretty.

Moricet Oh star of eve –

Léontine (*opening the window*) Oh look, there's a little balcony.

Moricet That's right! It goes all the way round the building. A balcony, darling! You be Juliet, I'll be your Romeo.

Léontine But he was outside.

Moricet It's the middle of winter.

He guides her as before, towards the bed. They leave the window ajar.

Look, darling, here in this alcove of Venus –

Léontine Ah!

She breaks free.

Moricet Now what?

Léontine Not that!

Moricet But that's the whole point –

Léontine I can't. I won't.

Moricet Of course you won't. Of course not. (*Aside.*) Slow down a bit. (*To her.*) Léontine ... Oh, Léontine ...

Léontine (*blushing*) Oh, Moricet ...

Moricet What is it? Trembling ... Do I see tears?

Léontine (*overcome*) It's just like my wedding night!

She bursts into tears and runs into his arms for comfort.

Moricet (*taken by surprise*) Oof.

Léontine He was there, just like you, on our wedding night. He held me, stroked me ...

Moricet (*stroking her*) There, there ...

Léontine Whispered sweet nothings ...

She pushes him away.

And next thing I knew, the bed!

Moricet   Oh, really! It's too much. My own best friend.

Léontine   If only he was. Still was. We'd not be here.

Moricet   Léontine, please, can we forget your husband, just for a moment? Or if you must remember him, remember him this morning.

Léontine   Don't remind me.

Moricet   I most certainly will. The way he behaved! And the way he's behaving now, this minute, making someone else the promises he should have kept to you.

Léontine   Pardon? Oh. The swine!

Moricet   And still you have scruples?

Léontine   No scruples.

Moricet   He's taken a lover.

Léontine (*throwing her arms round his neck*)   Well, so have I.

Moricet   You see! (*Holding her.*) That swine . . . he's holding her . . . (*Stroking her.*) Stroking her . . . Crushing her to his bosom . . .

Léontine (*hammering his chest in a fury*)   Crush me, crush me.

Moricet (*crushing her*)   Like this. And then, like this.

Léontine (*raging*)   Oh!

She gestures to him to kiss her.

Get on with it!

Moricet   Right. (*Kissing her.*) How sordid!

Both (*furiously – she genuinely, him feigned*)   How sordid!

Moricet   Something else. Worse. She's kissing him back. Showering him with kisses.

Léontine (*beside herself with rage*)   Showering him? Like this? Like this? Like this? (*She showers him with kisses.*)

Moricet (*in ecstasy*)   Oh, Léontine . . .

Léontine *collapses exhausted into a chair.*

Léontine   Gosh, I'm thirsty.

Moricet (*overwhelmed with rapture at everything she does*)   Thirsty! What can I get you?

Léontine   Anything. Champagne would be nice.

Moricet (*searching feverishly*)   Champagne . . . That stupid woman . . . Where's she left the champagne? (*Pacing in a fury.*) She's forgotten it.

Léontine   Aren't you thirsty?

Moricet (*rushing to dandle her*)   Oh thirsty, yes, oh yes, thirsty for you, for you. (*Declaiming.*) 'A flask of wine, a book of verse, and thou . . .'

Léontine (*enraptured*)   My wild one, my poet! Go on, go on.

Moricet   I don't know any more.

Léontine (*holding out her hands to him from the chair*)   When you talk in poetry, I can refuse you nothing.

Moricet   Ah. Aha!

He falls on his knees and rolls his head ecstatically in her hands, on her lap. Knock at the door. He and **Léontine** *spring apart.*

Moricet   Who is it?

Madame Latour (*off*)   It's only me.

Moricet (*reassuringly to* **Léontine**)   It's only her.

He turns up the lamp and opens the door.

Come in!

Enter **Madame Latour**.

Moricet   Now what are you thinking of, your Grace? A dinner-party, tête-à-tête – and no champagne?

Madame Latour   You told me, 'Do what you'd do at home.' I never drink champagne. It gives me indigestion.

Moricet   Oh, a medical problem ... I suppose the wine's all right?

Madame Latour   If you really want champagne, there are two bottles in the other room, top shelf.

Moricet   Perfect.

Madame Latour   I'll fetch them.

Moricet   No, no. You're not tall enough. I'll go. Stay and talk to Madame.

Madame Latour   Certainly, Doctor.

Moricet (*as he goes*)   'A flask of wine, a book of verse, and thou ...'

Exit.

Madame Latour (*gazing after him*)   What a fine man. A gentleman.

Léontine   You think so?

Madame Latour   The kind of man a ... lady could really fall for.

Léontine   Which lady had you in mind?

Madame Latour (*quickly*)   None in particular. Me, if you like. Except it's too late for me. I chose my man ... from a different rung entirely.

Léontine   A rung?

Madame Latour (*sighing with mortification*)   Alas, yes. And they drummed me out for it. Lapses they understood, but scandal ...! Banned from the Four Hundred, cast out by my husband. As you see me now: that's what became of me.

Léontine   Oh, your Grace! Who was this man?

Madame Latour   A circus act. A lion-tamer.

Léontine   A lion-tamer.

Madame Latour   You should have seen him! I remember the day I saw him for the first time ... a matinée, I was in the front row with my husband ... Oh, what thighs!

Léontine   Your husband?

Madame Latour   My husband had chicken legs. The lion-tamer. (*Roars.*) Rrraaagh. There he was, in his cage, dominating those vicious wild beasts ... 'Just look,' I said to myself, 'every woman's dream. Rrrraaaaaagh.'

Léontine   I'm sure I don't know what you mean.

Madame Latour   That's all right, my dear. One has to be a connoisseur. Two weeks, that's all it took – and there we were, tamer and tamed, in a love-nest not unlike this one.

Léontine   Not bad for a lion-tamer.

Madame Latour   Not bad for a countess. I rented it, I furnished it.

Léontine   Ah.

By now she is sitting on the (revolving) piano stool.

Madame Latour   Whatever you do, Madame, never surrender your heart to a circus act.

Léontine   I'll try to remember.

Madame Latour   Especially when you've made such a noble choice already: Doctor Moricet.

Léontine (*shortly*) I'm sure I've done nothing of the kind.

Madame Latour I do beg your pardon.

Awkward silence, broken when **Léontine** *opens the sheet music on the piano and tries over a bar or two.*

Madame Latour No, no, *piano, più piano.* (*Catching herself up.*) Rubinstein always took it *piano.*

Léontine You knew Rubinstein?

Madame Latour (*preening herself a little*) Well, you know, we played the odd duet . . .

Léontine When?

Madame Latour *Before.*

Léontine Ah.

Madame Latour (*drawing herself up*) Never now. Monsieur Rubinstein disdains this house.

Another awkward pause. **Léontine** *starts playing again, not to* **Madame Latour***'s satisfaction.*

Madame Latour No, no, no. It's a duet. You need four hands.

Léontine *moves the piano stool along, and beckons her.*

Léontine Perhaps, your Grace . . . ?

Madame Latour Thank you.

She takes over a chair and settles herself.

Four beats for nothing?

Léontine Four beats for nothing.

Both One, two, three, four . . .

They start to play. **Moricet** *comes back with two bottles of champagne.*

Moricet   That shelf *is* high. Good lord! What on earth are you doing?

Léontine (*above the music*)   Playing a duet.

Madame Latour *is singing as well as playing.*

Moricet   How sweet. Your Grace . . . (*Louder.*) Your Grace . . .

Madame Latour (*turning towards him, still playing and singing*)   La, la, la, la, la, yes?

Moricet   La, yes? Oh, la, yes. (*Shouting over the music.*) I found the champagne. Now I need a corkscrew.

Madame Latour (*over her shoulder as she plays*)   Top drawer, under the table napkins.

Moricet   Thank you. Don't let me disturb you.

He makes to go out again.

Madame Latour (*jumping up*)   I'm sorry. I was carried away. Do let me fetch it.

Moricet   It's quite all right. I can manage. Don't stop. Don't stop.

Madame Latour   Why, thank you, Doctor.

Exit **Moricet**. *She goes back to the piano.*

Madame Latour   From the top of page four, my dear?

Léontine   No, I've got all these runny bits.

Madame Latour *puts her chair back at the table.* **Léontine** *is at a loss. She plays a chord or two, then asks slightly wildly:*

Léontine   Was it long ago . . . the lion-tamer?

Madame Latour   Twelve years. The eighth of December. The Feast of the Immaculate Conception.

Léontine (*sitting on her stool like a little child*)   It must have seemed very strange.

Madame Latour   It wasn't that. It was the way he caught me.

Léontine   Who caught you?

Madame Latour   My husband. The oldest trick in the world. The husband says he's going on a fishing trip.

Léontine   A-hah!

Madame Latour   You've heard of it?

Léontine   Oh yes. The oldest trick in the book.

Madame Latour   He doesn't go fishing at all.

Léontine   Exactly. He goes to see his mistress.

Madame Latour   Exactly. No! Not at all. When he's visiting his mistress, a husband says he's going to his club. When he says he's going fishing –

Léontine   He hasn't got a mistress?

Madame Latour   Exactly. He suspects his wife and he's out to catch her.

Léontine (*jumping up*)   Oh no!

Madame Latour   What's wrong?

Léontine   I see it all. Now I see it all.

Madame Latour   See what, Madame?

Léontine   Suppose . . . your Grace, suppose he *often* goes on fishing trips?

Madame Latour   That's obvious. He doesn't get enough evidence the first time, so he keeps on trying.

Léontine   Oh no! And I thought . . .

She runs to the door and shouts:

Moricet!

Madame Latour   What is it?

Léontine   Moricet! Come now!

Enter **Moricet** *with a corkscrew.*

Moricet (*cheerfully*)   Found it! (*Change of tone.*) What's the matter?

Léontine   My hat, my cape. Be quick.

Moricet   What?

Léontine   I won't stay here a moment longer.

Moricet   Whatever's the matter?

Léontine   The matter is, you *told* me things. No proof, and you *told* me things.

Moricet   Ah.

Léontine   It doesn't matter. I've done nothing wrong. I've been true to him.

Moricet   That again.

Léontine   And he's been true to me, poor darling.

Moricet   You're joking. He says he's going fishing, he runs to his mistress . . .

Léontine (*putting on her hat*)   Oh, really. You know if a man's going to his mistress, he doesn't say he's going fishing, he says he's going to his club.

Moricet   Beg pardon?

Léontine   If he says he's going fishing, it's because he suspects his wife and wants to catch her.

Moricet   Whoever told you that?

Léontine (*checking her hat in the mirror*)   Ask her Grace if you don't believe me.

Moricet   A-ha!

He advances on **Madame Latour**, *who retreats.*

Moricet You told her this.

Madame Latour I said it sometimes happens . . . often . . .

Moricet (*beside himself*) It's none of your business!

He makes fists and advances on her, quite incandescent.

Put 'em up! Don't just stand there. Put 'em up!

Léontine Leave her Grace alone. It's nothing to do with her. I'm going home. That's all. Going home.

She starts to put on her cape.

Moricet You most certainly are not. (*To* **Madame Latour**.) You! Go! Shoo!

Madame Latour Yes, Doctor. Right away, Doctor.

Exit.

Moricet (*at the door*) HA!

He slams the door behind her.

Léontine, you're playing a game. You're playing.

Léontine You'll soon see. Playing!

Moricet I just don't understand. When I went in there, you were happy –

Léontine Yes.

Moricet Calm –

Léontine Yes.

Moricet Agreed –

Léontine Yes. (*Drawing herself up.*) No.

Moricet I go for a corkscrew, I come back with a corkscrew, and *bam*! Total change. You're hopping mad, you're leaving . . .

Léontine Pre-cisely.

Moricet   But whatever for?

Léontine   Whatever for? I don't have to say whatever for. If I want to go, I go. I'm allowed.

She tries to get to the door. He blocks her way. She puts the sofa between them.

Moricet   You certainly are not allowed. You gave me your word, your sacred word . . .

Léontine   Never mind my word!

She circles the sofa, trying to catch him offguard. He watches her.

Moricet   Revenge – have you forgotten why we're here? Revenge. When I take on a case, I solve it, whatever the cost.

Léontine   You're not a detective.

Moricet   I'm a chartered physician.

Léontine   And what you had in mind – that's your case, your cure, your revenge?

She makes a break for it, but he blocks her way again.

Moricet   Léontine, stop torturing me. I love you.

Léontine   Ha!

Moricet   I love you! (*At the top of his voice.*) 'A flask of wine, a book of verse, and thou – '

Léontine   Oh no. Not now.

Moricet (*deflated*)   Oh.

Léontine   Not if you knew *all* the verses.

Moricet   You said you couldn't resist poetry.

Léontine   That was then. And this is now.

She makes a break for the door. He catches her, and they execute an awkward dance-step or two before he pushes her on to the sofa.

Moricet Now stay there!

Léontine Violence!

Moricet If necessary!

Léontine Oh!!

Moricet When you stepped under this roof, my roof, you put yourself in my hands, under my protection. Fine. I'll protect you, even against yourself.

Léontine Now what are you talking about?

Moricet Your family, the servants, everyone – they think you're in the country, staying with Great-Aunt Eugénie. You may want the whole world to know that Great-Aunt Eugénie's nothing but a blind – but I won't let you hurt yourself that way.

Léontine For the last time, will you let me PAST?

Moricet No, no, NO.

Léontine All right, I'll spend the night here, on this sofa.

She takes her hat and cape off, and sits bolt upright, blazing with rage.

Moricet All right, and so will I, on this chair.

He sits on the chair, in the same attitude.

Léontine It's up to you.

They ignore each other. She picks at the cushions in her fury, punching them back into shape now and then. He mutters indistinguishably, and drums with his hands along the back of the chair, across the table – and into the radish bowl. Furious, he dries his fingers on a table napkin.

Moricet I'll never forget tonight.

Léontine Neither will I.

Moricet A lovers' tryst, her on one piece of furniture, him on another.

Léontine   Oh, don't put yourself out on my account. Your bed's over there. Use it.

Moricet   And what about you?

Léontine   I'll go through there. There'll be something. A kitchen chair, a stool . . .

Moricet   I won't hear of it. I'll sleep in there. You'll sleep in here.

Léontine   In *your* bed? Never!

Moricet   I won't be there.

Léontine   You certainly will not.

Moricet   Well, then.

Léontine   Whether you're there or not, it comes to the same thing.

Moricet   Hardly. From my point of view . . .

Léontine *is at the mantelpiece, trying to light the candle.*

Léontine   I'll find something through there and sleep on that, or not sleep at all. That can be my penance.

Moricet   Penance, now. Oh, that concierge!

Léontine *has at last lit the candle.*

Léontine   I suppose you *can* spare a blanket.

Moricet   Of course.

He picks up the coverlet and drops it within range.

You'll be sorry.

Léontine   What exactly do you mean?

Moricet   It's like an igloo in there.

Léontine   I'll light a fire.

Moricet That concierge!

Léontine Don't start again.

She goes into the next room and slams the door.

Moricet *picks up the coverlet by one corner and drags it downstage, tangling it in his feet and almost tripping himself up. As he speaks he folds it neatly.*

Moricet What a performance. What's she thinking about? First she promises, then she . . . I won't make a fuss. But if there's any more of this, there are plenty of others.

He goes upstage, then returns as if to announce an afterthought.

She's not all that delightful.

He goes upstage.

Well, round three any minute . . .

Knock at the door.

What now?

He puts down the coverlet and opens the door.

Madame Latour (*nervously, half in half out*) Oh Doctor, it's only me.

Moricet (*blocking her path*) Not again! Go away. I've seen enough of you.

Madame Latour Oh Doctor, it's the tenant across the landing. He sent me.

Moricet Not interested.

Same business.

Madame Latour It's his niece. She isn't feeling well. And you being a doctor, Doctor . . .

Moricet I'm a day doctor, not a night doctor. Go away. Things are complicated enough.

He pushes her out.

Madame Latour (*as she goes*) I'll tell him, Doctor. Thank you.

Moricet *locks the door, goes to the table, puts one foot after another on a chair and starts unfastening his boots.*

Moricet What a cheek! Who does he think he is? 'It's his niece. She isn't feeling well.' What's that to do with me?

Enter **Léontine**.

Moricet What do you want?

Léontine (*going to the mantelpiece; curtly*) Matches. To light a fire.

Moricet On the mantelpiece.

Léontine I know. I'm not blind.

She takes the box and exit.

Moricet A shrew. That's what she is, a shrew. It's her husband I pity. He puts up with it, day in, day out . . .

Knock at the door.

What now?

Duchotel (*off*) It's me, from across the landing.

Moricet I'll break his neck! (*Flinging open the door.*) What is it now?

Duchotel (*who hasn't taken in who he is*) Oh, come on, Doctor . . .

Moricet (*aside*) Duchotel! (*Aloud.*) You can't come in.

He pushes the door hard, trapping **Duchotel**'s *arm.*

Duchotel Ow!

Moricet (*aside*) She'll hear him!

He leans against the door.

Duchotel (*from outside*)   You're hurting me.

Moricet   You can't come in.

Duchotel *pushes the door open so hard that he sends* **Moricet** *flying centre-stage.*

Duchotel   For heaven's sake!

Moricet (*cannoning into the sofa*)   Ow!

Duchotel (*recognising him; jumping in amazement*)   Moricet!

Moricet   Duchotel! Well, well, well. What a surprise.

Duchotel (*rubbing his arm*)   This is your apartment?

Moricet   Oh, didn't I tell you?

Duchotel   No.

Moricet   I've only just rented it.

Duchotel   You're the doctor?

Moricet   The doctor? Yes. I'm the doctor. Ha, ha, ha. (*Aside.*) She'll come back in!

Duchotel   What's wrong with you?

Moricet   Nothing.

Crash from the inner room.

Duchotel   What on earth is that?

Moricet   Chimney-sweeps.

Duchotel   It's the middle of the night.

Moricet   Night-shift. They work night-shifts now. (*Hastily locking the door to the inner room; aside.*) She mustn't get out . . .

Duchotel   What are you doing that for?

Moricet   The soot. We don't want soot in here.

Duchotel   You can't fool me. You've got a woman in there.

Moricet   Who, me?

Duchotel   Don't try and deny it. Look: two dinners.

Moricet   They came with the apartment. It was fully furnished.

Duchotel   Why all the mystery? I know it's a woman.

Moricet   Who told you?

Duchotel   Madame Latour, the concierge.

Moricet   That concierge! Oh, all right, I have got a lady friend.

Duchotel   Told you. And ... who is the lucky little charmer?

Moricet   I can't tell you.

Duchotel   Your best friend?

Moricet   Exactly.

Duchotel   Afraid I'll tell?

Moricet   Oh, I'm sure you wouldn't.

Duchotel   Well, then?

Moricet   Oh, all right. It's ...

Duchotel   Yes?

Moricet (*playing for time*)   It's ... er ... (*Sudden inspiration.*) Madame Cassagne!

Duchotel (*laughing*)   Oh, no it isn't.

Moricet   It is.

Duchotel   It isn't. (*Savouring his moment.*) She's over there, with me.

Moricet   What?

Duchotel It's all right. If you don't want to share your secrets ... The point is, you're a doctor and I need you, now.

He takes him by the arm to lead him out.

Moricet What for?

Duchotel To see to Madame Cassagne. Across the landing. She's having an attack.

Moricet Ah. You ... She ... I ... (*Aside.*) What about Léontine?

Duchotel Come on, it's opposite. I'll send the concierge to the chemist and come right back.

He goes to the door. At this moment **Léontine** *tries to turn the handle of her door from inside. Finding it locked, she begins furiously shaking it.*

Moricet It's an earthquake.

Duchotel Your chimney-sweep wants out.

Moricet Well, he can't come out.

The shaking continues. Pounding on the door.

(*Aside.*) She's going to shout. I know it. She's going to shout.

Léontine, *off, begins shouting 'Moricet, Moricet!' To hide her voice, he starts singing the Marseillaise at the top of his voice.*

Duchotel Now what are you doing?

Moricet It's all right. (*He sings even louder.*) Join in.

Duchotel If you say so.

He joins in. They sing for a bit, then he breaks away. The noise has subsided from inside. **Moricet** *goes on humming, ready to raise his voice at the slightest sound from* **Léontine**.

Duchotel I didn't come here for a concert. I'm going to the chemist's. You go to Madame Cassagne. (*Loudly to*

Moricet, *who is suddenly singing again*.) I said ... Did you hear what I said?

Still singing, **Moricet** *signals 'Yes'.*

Duchotel I won't be long.

Exit. **Moricet** *locks the door behind him, and leans on it.*

Moricet What a performance!

Furious banging from **Léontine** *at her door.*

Léontine (*off*) Open this door.

Moricet All right.

He opens it. She bursts in, beside herself with rage.

Léontine What are you doing? Locking me in. Howling and yelling.

Moricet (*stung*) Yelling! (*Urgently.*) Never mind that now. Listen: I have to go out. Five minutes. Don't go away, and don't let anyone see you. It's vital.

Léontine What are you talking about?

Moricet I can't explain now. If anyone knocks, don't answer. I'll come straight back.

Exit, fast.

Léontine He's gone completely mad. I'll get my cape. I'll go. That's all I have to do. What a night. What a night.

Exit into the room R, closing the door behind her. Pause. Enter **Duchotel** *by the main door. He is holding a bottle of smelling salts.*

Duchotel I got some smelling salts. You can – Oh, he's gone.

Crash from **Léontine** *offstage.*

Duchotel He's in there. (*Knocking.*) Hurry up, for

heaven's sake.

He moves downstage, back to the door, as **Léontine** *opens it.*

Léontine   My God, my husband!

She doesn't know what to do. Then she sees the bed-cover on the back of the sofa, snatches it up and drapes it over her head, completely hiding her so that she looks like a ghost. At this moment, **Duchotel** *turns round.*

Duchotel (*startled*)   Eugh! What is it?

Pause. **Léontine** *starts edging towards the door.*

Duchotel   It's alive. Ah! She's pretending to be a ghost. (*To* **Léontine**, *who can't see what she's doing and is about to bump into the fireplace.*) Careful, Madame. You don't want to go up in smoke. (*Aside.*) Moricet's little charmer! (*Aloud to her.*) Don't worry, Madame. Your secret's safe with me.

Under the bed-cover, **Léontine** *bows acknowledgement.*

Duchotel   I was looking for Doctor Moricet. He isn't here.

Léontine *shakes her head vigorously under the cover.*

Duchotel   He's gone.

Léontine *nods vigorously under the cover.*

Duchotel   Thanks, Madame. That's all I wanted to know.

He bows low, mockingly. She bows back.

Duchotel   Sorry to have disturbed you.

He goes to the door, and meets **Moricet**, *who is hurrying back in.*

Duchotel   Aha!

Moricet   Still here . . .

Duchotel   Still here.

Léontine, *still covered, sits on the sofa.*

Moricet (*aside*) Eugh!

He hurries to screen her from **Duchotel**.

Duchotel Now what are you doing?

Moricet Nothing.

Duchotel (*pointing to* **Léontine**) Ha, ha, ha.

Moricet (*forcing himself to do the same*) Ha, ha, ha. (*Aside.*)
That was close.

Duchotel Well, did you see her?

Moricet (*at a loss*) What? Eugh. Yes. No. Yes.

Duchotel Well, which? Did you or didn't you?

Moricet Yes. I took her temperature.

Duchotel She hasn't got a temperature.

Moricet I was in a hurry. And so are you. She's
waiting.

He tries to push him out.

Duchotel All right, all right. I understand. You can't
wait. She is a charmer. A bit overdressed, perhaps . . .

Moricet Medical reasons.

Duchotel Ah. I'll leave you to it.

Moricet (*opening the door for him*) Bye.

Duchotel *exits, then changes his mind, comes in again and goes
to bow with great solemnity to* **Léontine**.

Duchotel Madame.

Léontine bows back. **Duchotel** *goes upstage.*

Duchotel (*roguishly to* **Moricet**) Ha-hey! Eh? Ha . . .
HEY!

Exit.

Moricet Thanks.

He tries to shut the door, but **Duchotel** *returns.*

Duchotel And mine. Ha-hey! And mine.

Moricet Oh, yes. Ha-hey.

Exit **Duchotel**.

Moricet Phew.

He locks the door and leans against it. **Léontine** *takes off the bed-cover.*

Léontine I'm freezing. My feet are like blocks of ice.

Moricet What a performance! What a performance!

Léontine (*mechanically rolling the bed-cover into a ball*) What now? Whatever now? Go home, I suppose.

Moricet Certainly not!

Léontine You want me to stay here, when my husband's . . . my husband's . . .

Moricet If we go out there, he'll see us. If we stay in here, we're safe. The door's locked. Look: I'm putting the key on the bedside table. No one can get in now.

Léontine (*exhausted, clutching the balled-up bed-cover*) I can't take much more of this.

She rests her head on the cover, as if it's a pillow.

Moricet It's all right. The danger's past. Nothing else can happen. All we have to do is get some sleep. Tomorrow morning you can go home as if you'd come back from a delightful stay with Great-Aunt Eugénie. But now, we must try to get some sleep.

He makes for the bed.

Léontine You don't really think I'll sleep . . .

She makes for the door, R.

Moricet   Try, just try. And so will I. Try.

He lays his jacket on the chair by the bed.

Léontine   Good night. (*Sudden rage.*) I'll never forgive you, never.

Exit, with bed-cover.

Moricet   Oh, fttt!

Léontine (*returning sharply*)   Pardon?

Moricet (*injured*)   Nothing. I just said, 'Oh, my foot'. Foot gone to sleep.

Léontine   It's lucky.

She goes into the room and closes the door.

Moricet   This is ridiculous.

He takes off his waistcoat and unshoulders his braces.

A hornets' nest.

He lights a candle.

She'll hate it in there. She won't be comfortable. (*Philosophically.*) But I'll be all right.

He puts the candle on the bedside table, and goes to put out the lamp.

Women! I never do remember.

He goes to check the door.

Securely locked. Well, time for bed.

He takes off trousers, shirt and boots, and slides into bed, then sits up.

It's ridiculous. A night of passion? Me here, her there? Oh, go to sleep. Stop fussing.

He blows out the candle. Pitch darkness.

I'm exhausted. Frazzled.

He snuggles down in bed, yawns.

Night of passion. Ha!

Pause. Enter **Léontine**, *with candle. She is going to the sofa.*

Léontine   You've gone to bed.

Moricet (*sitting up*)   Thanks to you, there was nothing else to do.

Léontine (*nervously, plumping the cushions to choose the softest*)   So long as you're comfortable. That's all that matters. So long as you sleep well.

Moricet   You came back in here to tell me to sleep well?

Léontine   I came for a cushion to rest my head.

Moricet   I do hope you found one.

Léontine   I found one. Not that you care. Tucked up so cosily . . .

Moricet   Don't start again.

Léontine   Don't worry about me. My kitchen chair. Don't trouble your beauty sleep for me.

Moricet (*crossly, turning over and putting the blankets over his head*)   Oh . . . foh!

Léontine   That's right. An honest woman, a loving wife, trusting – that's what I was, despite my devil-may-care exterior, ha, ha, ha – and you ruin me. I'm found in your room. Discovered. My fault, the guilty one, the other woman. And you claim to be a gentleman! (*Going to the bed-end.*) Don't deny it, a gentleman!

Moricet *snores.*

Léontine   Oh!

She makes as if to throw the cushion at him, but restrains herself, goes back into her room and slams the door. Darkness. **Moricet** *sleeps on. After a while, we hear a key turning in the main door and* **Gontran** *comes in.*

Gontran   I say, it's dark. I haven't any matches.

He tiptoes to the table, and sticks his hand in the radish-dish. He wipes it dry, whispering towards the bed:

It's all right, Fifi darling. It's only me. Gontran. (*To himself.*) No answer. She's fast asleep.

He tiptoes to the main door, locks it with a key on a ring and pockets the ring.

Thank goodness I had my own key. A chap can come and go as he pleases. I say, won't she be glossified to see me?

Moricet snores.

Gortan   She's asleep, all right. That's how they breathe when they're asleep. A chap just knows.

Louder snore.

I say, she has got a cold. Unless she's terrified. Terrified, yes. I'll wake her with a kiss. If you kiss them, they know you come in peace.

He goes to the bed. Loud snores from **Moricet**.

Gotran   She has got a cold.

He kisses **Moricet**, *who mutters in his sleep.*

Gotran   She's fast asleep.

He climbs on the bed and embraces **Moricet**.

Moricet   What now?

Gontran   A man!

Moricet   Oh, Léontine!

He flings his arms round **Gontran**.

Gontran (*terrified*)   I say!

Enormous struggle: pillows flying, legs, arms, panting. It ends with
Gontran *on the floor in the gap between bed and wall.*
Moricet *leaps out of bed and feels all round.*

Moricet Who is it? A man! My God! Where are the
matches? He's in there now. With Léontine. Just a
minute. Where are my slippers?

He puts on his slippers.

Léontine . . .

He rushes into the inner room.

Léontine (*off*) What d'you want now?

Gontran It's the old man. The baboon. The sugar-
daddy. Hide!

He slides under the bed, across the room and into the closet. Pause,
then **Moricet** *returns, backwards, pursued by* **Léontine** *who is*
carrying a candle and in a fury.

Moricet There is. A man. I'm telling you.

Léontine Where? Show me.

They search.

Moricet Keep looking. Keep looking.

Léontine You're scaring me to death. Where was he?

Moricet There. In the bed. My bed. He kissed me.

He lies flat on the floor to look under the sofa.

Léontine You had a nightmare.

Moricet I tell you he kissed me.

Léontine The door's shut and locked. How did he get
in? Through the keyhole?

Moricet How d'you mean, it's locked?

Léontine Look for yourself.

Moricet That's very odd. I wasn't dreaming. I felt it: here.

Léontine I tell you it was a nightmare.

Moricet You really think so?

Léontine I've had enough of this. I really can't take any more of this.

Moricet Léontine, darling, I swear. It was. (*Change of tone.*) In any case, I'm having such fun.

Léontine (*raging*) Well, I'm not. My God, what a night! My God!

Moricet Exactly. What a night! My God!

Impasse. Pause. Three loud knocks at the door.

Léontine (*terrified*) Aee! Someone's there.

Moricet (*the same*) That's right.

Bridois (*off*) Open, in the name of the law.

Moricet *and* **Léontine** The police!

They scatter. More knocking.

Léontine What now?

Moricet (*rushing about like a headless chicken*) Hide, hide, hide.

Léontine Where? Where?

Bridois (*off*) Open up, or I break it down.

Léontine The bed!

Moricet (*restraining her*) Not there. Not now.

Léontine All right, the window!

Moricet (*restraining her*) We're two floors up.

Léontine Where, then? Help me. Where?

Moricet How should I know? Get on with it.

Bridois (*off*) Escape is useless. We know you're in there.

Moricet (*furiously, in the direction of the door*) All right, all right! (*To* **Léontine**.) We'll just have to brazen it out.

He puts on his jacket, forgetting he's in underwear and slippers.

Calm.

He buttons the jacket.

Dignity. My hat, my hat!

She passes it, he puts it on.

Now, whatever I say, go along with it.

Bridois (*off*) For the last time, are you going to open, or do we break it down?

Moricet (*opening the door*) Good evening, Inspector.

Bridois (*bursting in, calling off*) Wait there, lads.

Moricet (*putting on his gloves with a flourish*) You do have a warrant for this intrusion?

Bridois Of course we've got a – (*Change of tone.*) I'm sorry. Monsieur, Madame, good evening. The public servant does his unpleasant duty, the gentleman says (*Bowing.*), What a charming evening.

Moricet Get on with it.

He and **Léontine** *are hand in hand, like babes in the wood.*

Bridois The cause of this, ah, intrusion, is a request from Monsieur your husband, Madame, a request for proof. Of the presence of Monsieur here. In your house here, Madame.

Moricet I don't understand at all, Monsieur. I'm a married man, and Madame's my . . . wife.

Bridois   Ho, ho. Nice try, Monsieur. They all say that. The gentleman approves your little lie, but the public servant . . . (*Taking out his notebook.*) Name?

Moricet   Doctor Moricet.

Bridois   And your name, Madame?

Léontine   My name?

Moricet   Madame Moricet.

Bridois   Come, come, come, come, come. We know very well that Madame is not Madame Moricet.

Léontine *and* **Moricet** (*aside*)   They know!

Bridois   Madame Cassagne, good evening.

Moricet *and* **Léontine**   Madame Cassagne?

Moricet   Madame Cassagne. He called you . . . you called her . . . Madame Cassagne.

Léontine (*radiant*)   Madame Cassagne. That's right.

Moricet *goes beaming towards* **Bridois**.

Moricet   Inspector, Inspector . . . (*Change of tone.*) Madame Cassagne's across the landing.

Bridois   Pardon?

Moricet   You heard, Inspector.

Bridois (*with his back to the audience*)   Excuse me. The concierge said 'Second floor, first on the right.' This is my right hand, I think you'll agree.

Moricet (*turning him through 180 degrees*)   But the staircase is on this side.

Bridois   Ah. I see what's happened. I've got the wrong room.

Moricet   How kind of you to wake us up to tell us.

Bridois   What can I say, Monsieur? Madame . . . (*As*

Moricet *ushers him to the door.*) Do carry on. Don't let me interrupt you. Carry on.

Moricet   I've been trying to carry on all night.

Bridois (*as he goes out*)   Across the landing, this door – (*As **Moricet** shuts the door in his face.*) Oof.

Léontine (*collapsing on the sofa arm*)   I just can't go on. I can't.

Moricet (*piteously, collapsing in a chair*)   Léontine . . .

Léontine   What?

Moricet   I can't go on.

Léontine   I've just said that.

Moricet   I didn't hear you.

Léontine   The police. What else have you up your sleeve?

Moricet   It's not my fault. They wanted Madame Cassagne. I sent them to Madame Cassagne.

Léontine (*furious*)   That's no excuse.

Moricet (*suddenly*)   My God!

Léontine   What now?

Moricet   He's with her! They'll arrest him there!

Léontine   What d'you mean? Who's there?

Moricet   Never mind. Poor devil!

*To indicate **Duchotel**'s dilemma, he does a dumbshow which involves shaking both hands, clicking his fingers, lifting one leg and then the other, like a bear dancing.*

Léontine   You're enjoying this. You're having a wonderful time.

Moricet   What d'you mean?

Léontine   Dancing! Dancing!

She flounces out, R.

Moricet   Léontine!

He hurries after her, slamming the door. At that precise moment, **Duchotel** *opens the window fully and jumps in. He is in his underwear, with his jacket and waistcoat half on, half off, and he's carrying his fishing-rod. He rushes about the room like a trapped animal, seeking a way out, finds the main door, and is about to dash out when he realises he's in his underwear.*

Duchotel   My God, my trousers! I can't escape without them. (*He sees* **Moricet**'s *trousers.*) Ah! Moricet's trousers. Saved!

He puts them on, leaving the braces dangling.

Just in the nick of time!

He runs to the door. At that exact moment, **Gontran** *bursts out of the closet.*

Gontran   Nunkie!

Duchotel   Gontran!

Gontran *rushes back into the wardrobe, and* **Duchotel** *opens the main door and runs for it. Enter* **Moricet**, *still in his underwear.*

Moricet   What's going on now?

The **Police constables** *leap in at the window.*

First constable   There he is!

Moricet   What are you doing?

Second constable   Got you!

Moricet   What is it?

Mêlée. The **Constables** *chase* **Moricet** *round the room, before finally catching him.*

Constables   Got you!

Moricet   Will ... you ... put ... me ... DOWN?

First constable   Running along balconies in your underwear. You've had it this time.

Moricet (*struggling; lifted bodily off the floor*)   Help! Put me down! You're mad.

Second constable   You can put it in writing at the station.

They cart him off. Enter **Léontine**.

Léontine   What on earth's going on?

Gontran bursts out of the closet.

Gontran   Auntie!

Léontine   Gontran!

She runs for it, as the curtain falls.

Act Three

Set as for Act One. When the curtain rises, the stage is empty. A bell rings, off, and a moment later the main door is opened and **Babet** *ushers in* **Moricet**.

Moricet Is she here, Madame?

Babet Yes, Doctor. Madame took the first train home from the country.

Moricet The first train. Yes. And Monsieur?

Babet Monsieur's not back yet.

Moricet Splendid. Please tell Madame I'm here.

Léontine *enters L.*

Babet Doctor's here, Madame.

Léontine So I see. Thank you.

Babet Yes, Madame.

Exit.

Léontine At last!

Moricet I waited on purpose, to stop anyone suspecting. Oh, Léontine, you don't know what it's been like all morning. What happened to you last night?

Léontine A horrible dream, a nightmare. You gone, the house in an uproar, the window wide open, Gontran looming out of wardrobes. Why *Gontran*? I thought I'd gone crazy. I ran for my life. I was in the street. No coat, no hat.

Moricet No hat!

Léontine Anyone could have seen me. I walked and walked. I'd still be walking, if a young idiot hadn't stopped me and said, 'Madame, I've got five francs.' (*Pause.*) Five francs – why tell me he had five francs?

Moricet   Perhaps he wanted change.

Léontine   I couldn't stay walking the streets all night. I couldn't come home. I couldn't go to a hotel. I called a cab. If you can call it a cab. 'Drive round the Place de la Concorde,' I said. 'Round and round, I'll pay by the hour.' He must have thought I was a lunatic. Round and round, round and round, till daybreak. I know every cobblestone by heart, in the Place de la Concorde.

Moricet   Oh Léontine! (*Change of tone.*) You did get my note, explaining?

Léontine   Explaining my husband's behaviour, yes. To think you tried to tell me that when a man goes fishing he's not visiting his mistress!

Moricet   Me? Oh, thanks.

Léontine   That's exactly where he was, with Madame Cassagne.

Moricet   And I'm the one who suffers. He goes fishing without a licence, and I get the summons.

Léontine   Ah, well, that *was* your fault. The inspector had just seen you in the room across the landing. You'd only to explain.

Moricet   D'you think I didn't try? The inspector! You think it's as easy as that, with that inspector? 'As man of the world, I understand exactly what you mean; as public servant I'm only interested in facts. A man was in here with Madame; a man without trousers ran out of here along the balcony; a man without trousers was arrested; that man was you. Those are the facts. You can give your explanations to the jury.'

Léontine   You should have been firm with him.

Moricet   I couldn't. He was dashing off. A party.

Léontine   What party?

Moricet   A Coming-out Party. The local prison.

Léontine   Oh.

Moricet   Well, I won't stand for it. I'm going right round there this morning. He can summons Duchotel, and they can sort it out between them.

Léontine   Exactly.

Moricet   Why should I take the blame? If you and I were caught red-handed, would he take the blame for me?

Léontine   Of course he wouldn't.

Moricet   Well, then.

Léontine   You do that, then. I'll get on with the divorce.

Moricet   What?

Léontine   Why shouldn't I? No one knows what I was doing yesterday. I'm the injured party. Just one thing: I need to destroy every shred of evidence of my ... of my ... I need my letter back.

Moricet   Your letter? *That* letter? You need it ... ?

Léontine (*briskly*)   Right now.

Moricet *starts feeling in all his pockets.*

Moricet   All I ever had from you ... Ah well ... Just a minute, where the devil ... ? Oh my God!

Léontine   What is it?

Moricet   My God, my God!

Léontine   Tell me.

Moricet   It's in my trousers pocket.

Léontine   Pardon?

Moricet   It's in my trousers. And so's your husband!

Léontine   You're joking.

Moricet   What can we do?

Léontine   You're doing this on purpose. You don't want to give it back.

Moricet   How was I to know he'd take my trousers?

Léontine   You should have thought of that. You never think of anything. What if he's found the letter, read it?

Moricet   He wouldn't! Read someone else's trousers!

Léontine   You're sure he wouldn't?

Moricet   All right, you think of an explanation. You *are* a woman.

Léontine   What sort of explanation?

Moricet   Well, it was a . . . or perhaps a . . .

Léontine (*shaking his hand*)   Brilliant!

Moricet   Something along those lines.

Léontine   Oh, go away. You're useless.

Moricet   Whatever you say. I've an appointment with the inspector, in any case.

Léontine   Go, go, go.

Moricet   If he's away from the Coming-out Ball, that is . . .

Exit. **Léontine** *paces.*

Léontine   He never thinks of anything. A woman sends you a note, a compromising note, you don't keep it in your trousers. It's not hard! You say to yourself, 'Suppose the husband puts on these trousers?' What's hard about that? He never thinks of anything. 'You think of an explanation. Perhaps a . . . or perhaps a . . .' Not good enough! Just when I was the injured party. When everything was going so well.

Enter **Babet**.

Babet   Madame, Monsieur's in a cab, outside.

Léontine   Monsieur! Open the door, then.

Exit **Babet**.

Léontine   We'll soon see if he's read it. And if he hasn't, we're going to enjoy ourselves. He's going to flounder, and we're going to enjoy ourselves.

Enter **Duchotel**. *He's wearing his fancy costume from Act One, except that he has on* **Moricet***'s trousers from Act Two. He carries his fishing-rod and a huge hamper, tied with string.*

Duchotel   Madame, where's Madame?

Léontine   Darling! Aren't you early?

Duchotel   Oh, Léontine!

He runs to her and kisses her.

Léontine (*aside*)   He doesn't know.

Duchotel (*aside, as he goes to put down his rod*)   She doesn't know.

Léontine   You must be worn out. All that fishing.

Duchotel   No, no, no. Refreshed.

Léontine   I'm so glad.

Duchotel   It was magnificent!

Léontine   Really?

Duchotel   Picture the scene. Up with the lark . . .

Babet   You didn't catch cold, Monsieur?

Duchotel (*without thinking*)   No, I was hot, hot.

Léontine   Hot-hot, darling?

Duchotel (*quickly*)   In my fishing clothes. Hot, hot, hot. And hot to hurry home. Darling, to you! Cassagne wanted me to stay.

Léontine   Oh, did he?

Duchotel   But I insisted. I said, 'We've been here long enough. I must be going home, home to the wife I adore, I adore.'

Léontine (*aside*)   He's overdoing this.

Duchotel   What fishing! Oh, what fishing! The weather, you've no idea.

Léontine   That's why you changed your trousers?

Duchotel   Eh? Oh. Yes. You noticed that? Amazing, wives always notice.

Léontine   They don't quite fit.

Duchotel   They don't quite fit. Cassagne, that dear kind man, Cassagne, he said, 'You're soaked. You can't wear those trousers. I'll lend you a pair of mine.'

Léontine   That explains it.

Duchotel   It does, doesn't it? Better than catching a chill ... Babet, please fetch a pair of mine.

Babet   Yes, Monsieur.

Exit.

Duchotel   What a time I've been having! You've no idea.

Léontine   I haven't.

She sits, leans her elbows on the table, props her chin on her hands and gazes raptly at him.

Duchotel   And what a success! A salmon, a bloater, some pilchards ... And you should have seen the one that got away.

Léontine   Oh I wish I could.

Duchotel   They're all in here. Look: in this hamper.

Léontine   I'll get some scissors and cut the string.

Duchotel   You'll be amazed.

Léontine   I can hardly wait.

Exit.

Duchotel   So far so good. Thank God. Salmon, herring, pilchards . . . if you're telling whoppers, make them *good* ones. Nice hamper, too. So it ought to be.

He lifts it on to the table.

Forty francs. That fishmonger. All I said was, 'Pack me up some salmon, a bloater, some pilchards' – and this is the result. Forty francs. That reminds me, the bill . . .

He fishes in his pockets, finds a note.

My wife's writing. That's not it.

He puts it in his waistcoat pocket, and fishes out another note.

Here we are. Get rid of it – it could cause trouble later.

He tears it up and throws it in the fire. Enter **Léontine**, *with scissors.*

Léontine   Here we are. I'm so excited.

Duchotel   On the table, darling: my entire catch, just for you.

Léontine   You really caught all this?

Duchotel   With my own two hands.

Léontine   It's just that . . . you always look like someone who's never been fishing in his life.

Duchotel   Never been fishing? I bring a basketful home, each time.

Léontine   Trout and lobster.

Duchotel   Not this time!

He sits expectantly.

Go on, see for yourself. Open it.

Léontine   I am.

She cuts the string, opens the hamper and gazes inside.

My! You caught all these?

Duchotel   Every one of them.

Léontine *begins taking packets out of the hamper.*

Léontine   Smoked salmon?

Duchotel   What?

Léontine   Bloater paste? Tinned pilchards?

Duchotel   I had to think quickly, darling. You know, fish, when it's raining, they won't be caught.

Léontine   Oh, tell the truth.

Duchotel   Darling, please –

Léontine   Never mind 'Darling, please'.

Duchotel *(aside)*   I'll kill that fishmonger. *(Aloud.)* Darling.

Léontine   No.

Duchotel   You don't believe me?

Léontine   No.

Duchotel   You don't?

Léontine   I don't. I know you never went fishing. I know you were never in the country.

Duchotel   But Cassagne –

Léontine   Cassagne not only wasn't fishing, he's never been fishing in his life.

Duchotel   Who told you that?

Léontine   He did.

Duchotel   He's been here?

Léontine   Yesterday. Just after you went off to go fishing with him.

Duchotel (*aside*)   Whoops.

Léontine   You weren't expecting this.

Duchotel (*inventing feverishly*)   Cassagne said ... and you thought ... But surely you know about Cassagne? Sunstroke. In the Sahara. Entire memory gone, poor chap. You ask him, 'Do you ever go fishing?' He says, 'No.' Of course he says, 'No.' His memory's gone. He means every word of it. 'No.' Cassagne! The finest fisherman in France. I wish he was here, here now, Cassagne, we could ask him, if only he was here –

Babet (*at the door*)   Monsieur Cassagne.

Duchotel   Oh God.

Léontine   How convenient.

Duchotel (*aside*)   What a time to choose!

Enter **Cassagne**. *Exit* **Babet**.

Cassagne   Madame ... Justinien ...

Duchotel (*trying to get between him and* **Léontine**)   Fancy seeing you. (*Aside to him.*) Don't say a word.

Cassagne (*aloud*)   You what?

Duchotel (*vigorously shaking his hands*)   That's right, that's right. (*Aside to him.*) We've just been fishing. Together.

Cassagne (*aloud*)   No we haven't.

Duchotel (*aside*)   Yes we have, yes. (*Aloud, casually.*) How are things, since this morning?

Cassagne (*jovially*)   Same as yesterday, same as the day before, and the day before that. Nay, lad ...

Duchotel (*aside*)   Argh! (*Forcing the joviality.*) Silly fellow!

Léontine (*pushing him out of the way to get to*
Cassagne)   You don't understand. Justinien means since
this morning, this morning especially. When you both
went fishing.

Cassagne (*completely baffled; breaking into dialect*)   How
much?

Duchotel (*gesturing to him out of sight of* **Léontine**)
Fishing. You know, fishing.

Cassagne (*still not getting it*)   How d'you mean, fishing?

Duchotel   Fishing!

He makes even more urgent gestures, till he realises that **Léontine**
is watching.

Duchotel   My salmon, my bloater . . . the one that got
away.

Cassagne   Bloomin hummer.

Duchotel (*to* **Léontine**)   You see? It's coming back to
him.

Léontine (*to* **Cassagne**)   That's right, fishing. We've got
the evidence.

She goes to the table. **Duchotel** *starts coughing and spluttering in
a meaningful way, to attract* **Cassagne***'s attention to the hamper.*

Léontine   You *did* catch cold.

Duchotel (*choking back his coughs*)   No, no. Hargh.

Cassagne   Smoked salmon? Tins?

Léontine   He caught them.

Cassagne   You *caught* these?

Duchotel   Of course I didn't catch them. (*Aside to him.*)
Will you stop playing the idiot?

Cassagne   You what?

Léontine   You were there when he did it.

Cassagne   I were?

Duchotel   Yes. Yes.

Cassagne   Nay, lass, I weren't.

Léontine   You weren't?

Duchotel   Of course he was. (*To her.*) Sunstroke. In the Sahara.

Cassagne   Sunstroke?

Duchotel   Exactly. When you lost your memory. (*To* **Léontine**.) So sad, so sad. What are you looking at me like that for?

Léontine   What a performance!

Duchotel   Pardon?

Léontine   Telling me tales like that, expecting me to believe them. You must think I'm a total fool.

During what follows, **Cassagne** *tries to feign indifference, going round the room admiring pictures, plumping cushions, like a complete stranger in a gallery.*

Duchotel   Darling, I'm telling you –

Léontine   D'you think I don't know? Everything? You never go fishing: you pretend to go fishing, to play your little games. Why can't you admit it? Then at least I could say, 'He's a pig, but at least he *is* a man.'

She rings the bell.

Duchotel   But Léontine –

Léontine   Not another word!

Enter **Babet**.

Babet   Madame?

Léontine (*indicating the hamper*)   Get rid of this.

Babet   Yes, Madame. Your trousers, Monsieur. I had to brush them.

She goes for the hamper.

What are these?

Léontine   Monsieur caught them. Take them.

Babet (*not understanding at all*)   Yes, Madame.

Exit with the hamper.

Duchotel   Please, Léontine . . .

Léontine   No.

Exit, slamming the door.

Cassagne   Argy-bargy, eh?

Duchotel   This is all your fault.

Cassagne   You what?

Duchotel   You still don't get it, do you? I used you as a blind. I said I was fishing with you, so she wouldn't suspect, my wife.

Cassagne   Suspect what?

Duchotel   Suspect what! What d'you think? Er, never mind.

Cassagne   Sorry, I'm sure.

Duchotel *sits, back to the audience, changing his trousers.*

Duchotel (*furiously*)   Don't try to wriggle out of it. You don't set foot in this house for years – years! I use you as an alibi, and then you come barging in on the very day I'm supposed to be spending the day with you. Ruining everything, barging in.

Cassagne   How was I to know?

Duchotel   You never know anything. If someone never sets foot in someone else's house, you'd think the first thing he'd do before setting foot in it would be say to himself, 'Just a minute Suppose he's using me as an alibi?' Stands out a mile.

Cassagne   I'm not a mind-reader.

Duchotel   Some people just don't know when they're not wanted.

Cassagne (*aside*)   He does get grumpy, changing trousers.

Duchotel (*folding the trousers he's taken off*)   What are you here for, anyway? What is it you want?

Cassagne   Ah. You see, lad, it's a bit ... I may have been a bit ...

Duchotel *puts the trousers on the table.*

Duchotel   Oh, you might, you might.

Cassagne   What I mean is, I asked him to meet me here. The inspector.

Duchotel   What?

Cassagne   It seemed a good idea.

Duchotel   You've called the police? To my house? You've called the police?

Cassagne   That's right. To keep you in the picture. You see, lad, I've found it. Evidence. My wife: she provided evidence last night.

Duchotel   What? How?

Cassagne   I arranged it.

Duchotel (*aside*)   Of course he did! (*Aloud.*) 'You arranged it'? 'She provided evidence'? You can't have. She can't have. Unless they got the lover.

Cassagne   They did.

Duchotel   Beg pardon?

Cassagne   Red-handed.

Duchotel (*aside*)   I'm not hearing this.

Cassagne   Some fellow called Moricet.

Duchotel   What?

Cassagne   Moricet. Some kind of doctor. Medical.

Duchotel   He's ... confessed?

Cassagne   Of course he hasn't confessed. Says he was nowhere near. But they've proof. His trousers. He ran for it, and left his trousers.

Duchotel (*aside*)   My trousers! Good grief.

Cassagne   You don't by any chance know this Moricet?

Duchotel   Moricet ...? Moricet ...? Never heard of him.

Babet (*at the door*)   Monsieur Moricet.

Exit.

Duchotel (*aside*)   It's the end. No ... got it!

Cassagne   Did she say Moricet?

Duchotel   That's right.

Cassagne   You said you didn't know any Moricet.

Duchotel   Who said?

Cassagne   You said.

Duchotel   No I didn't.

Cassagne   I said to you, 'You don't by any chance know this Moricet?' –

Duchotel   'Moricet'? 'This Morris Hay,' you said.

Cassagne I never . . .

Duchotel You did. 'This Morris Hay.' It must be the way you say it. 'Morris Hay.' Of course I don't know 'Morris Hay'.

Cassagne All right then: Moricet.

Duchotel Oh, you mean Moricet. My tailor.

Cassagne Tailor?

Duchotel Makes all my shirts.

Cassagne Good, is he?

Duchotel The best.

Enter **Moricet**. **Duchotel** *runs to put himself between the other two.* **Moricet** *doesn't at first see* **Cassagne**.

Moricet (*cheerfully*) Got you! At last! You sly dog! You're for it this time.

Duchotel (*aside to him*) The husband. Shh.

Moricet (*aloud*) Pardon? Didn't quite catch . . .

Duchotel (*aside to him*) Cassagne. The husband.

Moricet (*aloud*) I know his name's Cassagne.

Duchotel (*aside to him*) You don't understand. Shut *up*! (*Aloud*.) Great to see you.

Moricet I didn't come here for chit-chat. I came for –

Duchotel Of course you did.

Cassagne (*drawing him aside*) Bit familiar for a tailor.

Duchotel (*to him*) We were at school together. (*Aloud*.) My dear Moricet, may I introduce my dear friend Cassagne.

Cassagne (*jovially*) Ow do.

Moricet (*briskly*) Morning. (*To* **Duchotel**.) This is urgent. Tell me –

Duchotel In a minute. You're so impatient. (*To* **Cassagne**.) He's so impatient.

Cassagne (*not interested*) Oh, aye? (*Urgent aside to him.*) Hang on a minute.

Duchotel What?

Cassagne I've had a thought. (*Aloud to* **Moricet**.) Nick of time, lad. I'll have two dozen.

Moricet Pardon?

Duchotel Oh God.

Cassagne No rubbish, mind. Fourteen francs, not a penny less.

Moricet (*after a blank moment or two*) I'm sorry. None of my business.

Cassagne You what?

Duchotel (*getting between them*) He means, what business are shirts of his?

Cassagne For heaven's sake, he makes them.

Moricet Never mind shirts. What about trousers? And by the way, my friend, I want a word with you.

Cassagne As many as you like.

Duchotel (*between them*) No. You don't. You don't.

Cassagne *and* **Moricet** I do.

Duchotel (*holding them apart*) Later! Later!

Cassagne 'I want a word,' he said.

Duchotel (*pulling him aside*) You don't want to listen. Shirt-making. That's all he ever talks about. Boring. Very, very boring. Go in there.

Cassagne Why?

Duchotel   Because! He's going to measure me. Stark naked. (*Displaying himself.*) Not a pretty sight. So wait in there.

Cassagne   But what if the inspector calls?

Duchotel   I'll call you. Go in, go in.

Cassagne   Whatever you say.

Exit. **Duchotel** *shuts the door and leans against it.*

Duchotel   Foo! What a morning.

He makes a supreme effort to be interested in **Moricet**.

Duchotel   What was it you wanted?

Moricet   Trousers. My trousers. I want my trousers.

Duchotel   Is that all? Why didn't you say so? You are a fusspot.

He hands him the trousers from the table.

Moricet (*clutching them to him*)   Ahhhh!

Duchotel   All that carry-on for trousers.

Moricet   And the things in the pockets?

Duchotel   They're there. Do you think I go through other people's pockets?

Moricet (*aside*)   Saved! (*Aloud.*) I suppose you're satisfied?

Duchotel   What?

Moricet   Last night. I suppose you're satisfied?

Duchotel (*sympathetically*)   Oh, that. Yes. They said you'd been arrested.

Moricet   In your trousers.

Duchotel   What can I say? These things happen. It could have been worse. It could have been me.

Moricet   Just a minute. 'It could have been me.' You're getting me out of this.

Duchotel   Oh, no I'm not.

Moricet   What?

Duchotel (*hotly*)   Well, for heaven's sake! You got arrested – is that my fault?

Moricet   *What?*

Duchotel   To save the honour of the woman I love, I jump out of windows, sprint along balconies, risk my very neck – and then some idiot gets arrested in his underwear . . .

Moricet   You had my trousers!

Duchotel   You should have been wearing them! Underwear! In a public hotel! If the Department of Medicine ever hears of this –

Moricet   I'm not having this. I tell you, I'm not having this.

Duchotel   All I know is, you were arrested and I wasn't.

Moricet   You –

Duchotel   Sh! Léontine.

Enter **Léontine**. *She is carrying a bundle of letters and newspapers. She pretends not to see the men, goes to the table and slams down the newspapers, then goes to bang the letters on the writing-desk.*

Duchotel (*aside*)   Still cross, then . . .

Moricet (*to* **Léontine**)   Madame, good morning.

Léontine (*not over-warmly*)   Oh, Moricet. Good morning.

Duchotel (*like a winsome little boy*)   Léontine . . .

Léontine (*icily*)   Yes?

Duchotel   Still cross with me?

Léontine   Ha, ha, ha! I've far more important things to do. (*To* **Moricet**.) What's that pair of trousers on your shoulder?

Moricet   Just a pair your husband gave me.

Duchotel (*aside*)   That's torn it.

Léontine   Cassagne's trousers? You've given them to Moricet?

Duchotel   Of course not. He was going, Cassagne, I had to put them somewhere. I put them on Moricet.

He takes one leg of the pair of trousers. **Moricet** *hangs on to the other leg.*

Moricet   Oh, no you don't.

Duchotel (*tugging*)   Oh, yes I do.

Moricet (*tugging*)   You don't.

Duchotel (*tugging*)   I do.

Léontine   Oh, let him have them. They *are* Cassagne's.

Moricet (*suddenly snatching them*)   They're not. They're mine.

Duchotel (*aside to him*)   Thanks for nothing.

Moricet   Thank *you*.

Duchotel   I've had enough of this.

He goes upstage to sulk. Meanwhile:

Moricet (*urgently to* **Léontine**)   Your note's in the pocket.

Léontine (*superbly calm*)   I knew it would be.

Moricet (*aside*)   What's she playing at now?

Duchotel (*coming downstage*)   Léontine, I can't take any more. It's time to tell the truth. Those are Moricet's trousers.

Léontine   There you are. And the fishing? The fishing?

Duchotel   Yes, what can I say? There's only one thing for it –

Léontine   I'm waiting.

Duchotel   I've never been fishing, with Cassagne or anyone else.

Léontine   I knew it!

Enter **Cassagne**.

Cassagne   I am still here, you know.

Duchotel   What? Of course you're still here.

Cassagne   Ah, Madame. I've something to tell you. I didn't quite understand what you were asking, a moment ago. About fishing. But now I remember. Of course we went fishing, your husband and me.

Duchotel   What?

Léontine *and* **Moricet** *burst out laughing.*

Léontine   You did?

Moricet   He does pick his moment.

Duchotel (*to* **Cassagne**)   No. For heaven's sake! What's all this rubbish about fishing?

Cassagne   You said –

Duchotel   No I didn't. My *wife* said – you heard her – we've never, ever been fishing. Why d'you have to tell such whoppers?

Cassagne   Hang on, it was you who –

Duchotel   Listen to him. You-who! Me-who! (*To* **Cassagne**.) Naughty. Time to go back in there.

He steers him towards the door.

Cassagne   I don't know whether I'm coming or going

with you.

Duchotel So long as you're not going fishing. Naughty, naughty.

Cassagne I'll go to the foot of our stairs.

Duchotel No, go in there.

Cassagne (*as he goes*) You'll call me when the inspector comes?

Duchotel Of course I will.

Cassagne (*muttering as he goes into the side room*) By, this is a cartload of monkeys, and no mistake.

Duchotel (*shutting the door after him*) Sunstroke. Worst case I've ever seen.

Léontine Why is the inspector coming to talk to Cassagne?

Duchotel What? Oh, nothing. He's got his evidence, that's all. His wife was caught red-handed, with another man.

Léontine That's right, with you.

Duchotel (*eagerly*) That's right. (*Realising what he's said.*) No it isn't! Why me? If it was me, why would he turn up here?

Léontine If it wasn't her you were with, who was it?

Duchotel I wasn't with anyone.

Léontine You're starting again, aren't you?

Duchotel Me, with a woman? Moricet, I mean . . . me, with a woman.

Moricet Leave me out of it.

Duchotel (*through his teeth*) Thanks.

Léontine So why did you keep pretending to go fishing?

Duchotel   Er . . . a surprise! I wanted to surprise you.

Léontine   Pardon?

Duchotel   A cottage, a cottage by the sea . . . For you, for me, for us.

Léontine   All this secrecy? For a cottage, no. For a mistress, yes.

Duchotel   A cottage, a cottage. Not a mistress by the sea, a cottage by the sea.

Léontine   And all this time, there was I, sat at home . . . innocent, trusting, accepting . . .

Duchotel   Léontine . . .

Léontine   The very picture of a model wife. A faithful, loyal wife. Wasn't I, Moricet?

Moricet   Yes, yes.

Duchotel   I was, too. A wife, er, husband. Faithful. Wasn't I, Moricet?

Moricet (*as if saying 'Who cares?'*)   Yes, yes.

Léontine   I'd never have dreamed of deceiving my husband. Would I, Moricet?

Moricet   Oh, no.

Duchotel   Well, I'd never have dreamed of deceiving my wife. Would I, Moricet?

Moricet   Oh, for heaven's sake, you're paragons. Paragons, the pair of you.

Babet (*at the door*)   Monsieur Gontran.

She goes, leaving a stunned silence: no one knows what to say or do.

Gontran (*entering*)   I say, do tell a chap: what were *you* doing at 40 rue d'Athènes last night?

Consternation. All hum and sing to drown out his voice.

All   Hum, hum, hum . . .

Duchotel (*effusively*)   My dear, dear nephew . . .

Léontine   Ah, Gontran, there you are . . .

They hurry at him from both sides, to get him in private. They tug. Stop pulling him.

Duchotel   You stop.

Moricet (*helping* **Léontine**)   Let him go.

Duchotel   You let go.

Gontran   What have I done?

Duchotel *wins with a particularly violent tug, and takes him aside.*

Duchotel (*low whisper*)   Five hundred francs if you shut up about last night.

He pushes him gently away. **Léontine** *grabs him and takes him aside.*

Léontine   Not a word about last night. It's worth five hundred francs.

All now pretend to be totally uninterested in **Gontran**. *He counts his imaginary takings.*

Gontran (*highly delighted*)   I say!

Long pause.

Duchotel (*breaking it at last*)   There, you see.

Léontine *and* **Moricet** *stare at him.*

Duchotel   You said stop tugging him. I stopped.

Léontine   Well, so did I.

Duchotel   Oh, so you did.

Moricet   As soon as you stopped, we stopped.

Duchotel   You did, you did.

Pause.

Pardon?

Léontine   I didn't say anything.

Duchotel   Ah.

Moricet   Nor me.

Duchotel   Exactly. (*He throws his eyes up to heaven.*) Phew, eh?

Léontine (*same business*)   Phew.

Moricet (*same business*)   Phew.

They stand there.

Gontran   What's wrong with them all?

Pause.

Duchotel (*brusquely to him*)   Well, well, well, well. Time you were going.

Léontine *and* **Moricet**   Time you were going.

Gontran   I've only just arrived.

Duchotel   Come back later. We'll talk to you then. (*Ushering him towards the door.*) Wait next door. I'll bring you five hundred francs.

Gontran   Ah. Bye, Auntie.

Léontine   Bye, Gontran. (*Going to him, as* **Duchotel** *comes downstage.*) Wait next door: five hundred francs.

Gontran (*aside*)   I say, what larks.

Exit.

Duchotel (*aside to the audience*)   Phew, eh?

Léontine *and* **Moricet** (*aside to each other*)   Phew, eh?

Pause. Moment of calm. Then a demonic ring at the bell, off. All jump; all panic.

Duchotel (*feigning indifference*)   Someone rang. Ha, ha, ha.

Léontine (*same business*)   Ha, ha, ha.

Moricet (*idiotically*)   On the bell.

They stare at him. Pause.

Duchotel   I wonder who it was.

Léontine   It could be anyone.

Moricet   I don't either.

Same business. Enter **Babet**.

Babet   Monsieur Bridois.

Duchotel (*to the others*)   Ha, ha, ha. Monsieur Bridois.

Léontine   Monsieur Bridois.

Moricet   Monsieur Bridois. Ha, ha, ha.

Duchotel (*to* **Léontine**)   You know him?

Léontine   Never heard of him. (*To* **Moricet**.) What about you?

Moricet   Complete stranger.

Duchotel   I don't either. (*To* **Babet**.) You'd better show him in.

Babet (*to* **Bridois**, *off*)   This way, Monsieur.

Enter **Bridois**. *He's carrying a package. They have their backs to him.*

Bridois   Gentlemen, Madame . . .

The others (*jumping out of their skins*)   The inspector!

Léontine (*aside to* **Moricet**)   Now what do we do?

Duchotel (*aside to the audience*)   Now what? (*Hastily, to* **Léontine**.) Cassagne, darling. It's that Cassagne business. I told you.

Léontine   Of course it is.

Bridois   Monsieur Duchotel . . . ?

Duchotel   It was him. I mean, that's me. (*Feigning extreme good fellowship and innocence.*) It's the Cassagne business, isn't it? He's just in there. I'll fetch him. You've met Doctor Moricet . . . ?

Bridois   Oh yes. And Madame Moricet.

Léontine *and* **Moricet** (*to him*)   No, no!

Duchotel   Madame Moricet? No, no, no. This is Madame Duchotel, my wife.

Bridois   Your wife?

Duchotel   My wife.

Bridois (*to* **Léontine**)   His wife?

Léontine   His wife.

Moricet   I'm afraid she is.

Duchotel   I'm glad that's cleared up.

Bridois   But I don't underst – (*Man-of-the-world.*) ah! I understand.

He nods, sagely.

Duchotel   Excuse me. Cassagne . . . I'll just . . .

Exit.

Léontine   Inspector, I can explain everything.

Moricet   It's very simple.

Bridois   No need. No need. The gentleman understands perfectly, and the public servant has no need at all to know.

Léontine *and* **Moricet** (*down*)   Ah.

Bridois   We're like priests: the confessional.

Léontine *and* **Moricet** (*up*)   Ah!

Enter **Duchotel** *and* **Cassagne**.

Duchotel   Here he is. Cassagne.

Cassagne   Inspector. Thank you for coming. I wanted everything settled here, where my dear friend Duchotel could hear.

Duchotel (*to* **Léontine**)   I told you.

Bridois   And I came at the express request of the guilty party, who said that here was the only place he could clear his name.

Moricet   Precisely.

Cassagne   What's he mean, precisely? He's a tailor, what's it to do with him?

Duchotel (*to* **Léontine**)   You see, darling. A private matter. Monsieur Cassagne's private matter . . . No need for you to stay.

Cassagne   Nay, nay. It doesn't mither me. Let her stay. Please stay, Madame.

Duchotel (*aside*)   He just *never* gets it right.

All sit. Awkward pause.

Bridois   Well then, if I could start by reminding you of all the facts. Last night, alerted by Monsieur Cassagne himself, I discovered Madame Cassagne red-handed with her lover.

Cassagne (*getting up, momentarily furious*)   And I say –

Bridois   Yes, Monsieur?

Cassagne (*calming himself*)   'Thanks very much.' That's what I say, thanks. Well, I mean, she is my wife.

Bridois That's right: she is.

Both sit.

To continue. What did we know about the lover? Two things only: he'd made his escape along the balcony, and he was in his underwear. We had his trousers in police custody. My lads went after him, and five minutes later we arrested a gentleman who answered the description exactly: Doctor Moricet.

Moricet (*jumping up*) Pure coincidence. Miscarriage of justice.

Cassagne (*jumping up*) Well, I'll be . . . !

All What is it?

Cassagne It's him! (*To* **Moricet**.) It's you.

Moricet What d'you mean, me?

Cassagne I've got it at last. (*Aside to* **Duchotel**.) You told me he was a tailor.

Duchotel (*jumping up*) Of course I did. You get so excited.

All sit again.

Bridois As you've all heard, Doctor Moricet strenuously denies all accusations. The evidence is circumstantial . . . and in fact one piece of evidence is strongly in his favour. We tried the trousers on him, and they're far too big.

Moricet Proof positive.

Bridois (*getting up and putting his package on the table*) I took the precaution of bringing them with me.

Duchotel (*jumping up hastily*) No, no, no, no, no. No need for that. You don't need the lover. You found Madame Cassagne, you found a pair of trousers, that's surely all you need.

Cassagne (*jumping up hotly*) It's all *I* need.

Duchotel Me too.

They sit.

Bridois Unfortunately, it's not all *I* need. Or rather, the Law. A woman and a pair of trousers – that won't stand up in court. If I could just produce exhibit A: the trousers.

He opens the packet and holds up the trousers. The others leap to their feet. **Duchotel** *makes a face at the audience: 'It's all up now.'* **Léontine** *stands with her arms folded, looking at him: 'Get out of this.'*

Bridois All we have to do is find the owner.

Léontine *mimes to* **Duchotel**: '*You.*' *He mimes back*: '*No, no, no.*' *She mimes*: '*I don't believe you.*' *He mimes*: '*I mean it.*' **Bridois** *is fascinated.*

Bridois Excuse me . . . ?

Duchotel *and* **Léontine** Sorry. Sorry.

Bridois (*continuing his line of thought*) The only problem is, how to find him?

Cassagne I wondered that.

Duchotel You'll never find him. It's impossible. Out of the question. You can't just stand in the street and force every passer-by to try them on. Case closed, inspector.

Bridois I'm sorry, that's not how we close our cases.

Duchotel (*aside*) I didn't think it would be.

Enter **Gontran**.

Gontran I say, a chap's being very patient, but – Good grief, my bags.

Amazement all round. **Duchotel** *drags* **Cassagne** *downstage.*

Duchotel You heard him? 'My bags,' he said. 'Good grief, my bags.' They're his.

Gontran Well, of course they're mine. Why shouldn't they be?

Duchotel No reason, no reason. (*Taking him aside.*) Five hundred francs if you insist they're yours.

Gontran What?

Bridois You admit these bags, ah, trousers are yours?

Gontran Oh, I'll say.

Bridois You further admit you were at 40 rue d'Athènes last night?

Gontran Golly, how did you know that?

Duchotel He admits it. You heard him. He admits it.

Gontran (*man-of-the-world*) After all, why shouldn't I?

Duchotel You see! (*Banging him on the shoulders.*) Well done, well done.

Bridois (*taking out notebook and pencil*) Your name?

Gontran Pardon?

Bridois I said, your name?

Gontran (*aside*) Who is he? (*Aloud.*) Gontran Morillon. Why?

Cassagne And why did you go to 40 rue d'Athènes last night?

Gontran To see my bit on the side, of course.

All Oh!

Cassagne Bit on the side, eh? Would it surprise you to hear that she belongs to me?

Gontran Yours? (*Thunderstruck.*) The old baboon!

All (*including* **Cassagne**) The baboon?

Gontran The baboon I hid from in the closet.

Cassagne (*furious*) Baboon. That does it. Do your duty, inspector. That's your man.

Gontran Inspector?

Cassagne The last piece of evidence. Divorce, at last.

Gontran Divorce? Who are you? *Not* the old baboon?

Cassagne No, the husband.

Gontran Monsieur Fifi! Oh, Monsieur, I'd no idea. She never said she was married. She never told me.

Cassagne (*triumphantly*) Thank you, Monsieur. That's all I need. Madame, Messieurs, excuse me.

Exit.

Gontran (*running upstage after him*) Wait, Monsieur. Wait.

Duchotel No, let him go.

Gontran (*to him*) I can't. (*Running after* **Cassagne**.) Please wait . . .

Exit.

Moricet I wish I knew what was going on.

Duchotel (*aside*) Going better, suddenly.

Bridois Well, I'll be off. Doctor Moricet, I do apologise.

Moricet That's all right.

Bridois Madame . . . Monsieur Duchotel . . .

Duchotel It's all right. I'll show you to the door.

Bridois How kind.

Duchotel Not at all, not at all. (*Aside as he goes.*) Very nearly very nasty . . .

He shows **Bridois** *out.*

Moricet All right for some . . .

Léontine I'm not going to change. He may have fooled the inspector, but he can't fool me. (*Change of tone.*) All right, no one else is here: give me back my letter.

Moricet Good idea. Where are *my* trousers? It's a trousery day, and no mistake.

Léontine Never mind being clever. Give me the letter.

Moricet All right, all right.

They take a leg each, and he searches the pockets.

Purse, handkerchief . . . not this side. Corkscrew. Look, it's the corkscrew from yesterday, the one you –

Léontine Get on with it.

Moricet I can't find it. It isn't here.

Léontine Of course it's here. Look properly.

Moricet Where? One leg, two legs . . . that's all there are.

They search again. Enter **Duchotel**. *He rushes to them.*

Duchotel Now what are you doing?

Moricet Eh? Showing your wife my trousers.

Duchotel What else? (*To* **Léontine**, *jovially.*) Who'd have thought it, eh? Gontran, eh? Madame Cassagne, eh? Madame Cassagne and Gontran, eh?

Léontine Yes.

Duchotel To think you suspected *me* – and it was Gontran, Gontran!

Léontine Of course it was Gontran. I knew all along it was Gontran. He told me so himself.

Duchotel What?

Léontine (*enjoying herself*) You mean *you* didn't know? That he . . . and Madame Cassagne . . . ?

Duchotel No, I didn't. (*Aside.*) I don't believe it.

Léontine Why else d'you think he borrowed all that money?

Duchotel You mean ... ? He borrowed ... I paid ... I paid *twice*?

Léontine The only cloud in his sky, poor boy, was that he had to share her. With some daft old fool.

Duchotel Who said he was old?

Léontine She did. To Gontran.

Duchotel Old! What a thing to say. She can't have meant it. Old!

Léontine You seem very concerned.

Duchotel I ... am ... not ... old!

Léontine Of course you aren't.

Duchotel (*realising that she's got him*) Ah. No. I meant –

Moricet Watch every word.

Duchotel (*crossly*) Are you still here?

Léontine I think we've got you.

Duchotel If you'd let me *explain* ...

Léontine Not explain, admit. I know everything. The man with Madame Cassagne last night – was you.

Duchotel Oh ... all right. It was. I admit it. I'm sick of all this. Yes, it was me, me, me.

Léontine You're sure?

Duchotel Of course I'm sure.

Léontine (*to* **Moricet**) He never could tell lies.

Moricet That's true. (*Edging away.*) Look, if I just –

Léontine No, no. Do stay. (*To* **Duchotel**.) Monsieur

Duchotel, goodbye.

Duchotel (*putting on his little-boy act*) Léontine, I'm sorry.

Léontine Too late.

Duchotel No, no. I *am*. (*To* **Moricet**.) Say something. Don't just stand there.

Moricet Oh, sorry. (*To* **Léontine**, *in a tone of utter indifference*.) Please, Léontine.

Duchotel There, you see? I'll never do it again. Not with Madame Cassagne, not with anybody.

Léontine Of course you won't.

Moricet (*as before*) Of course you won't.

Duchotel Shut up, you. (*To* **Léontine**.) No more lovers, no more fishing, no more hampers. (*Making a clean breast of it.*) Oh, that reminds me, the hamper. I forgot to tell you. I didn't catch it, I bought it. No, no, I swear. You don't believe me. I'll prove it. I've got the bill.

He burrows in his pockets.

No, that's right, I burned it.

He finds her letter to **Moricet**.

Just a minute, what's this?

Léontine (*aside*) Oh no!

Moricet No!

Duchotel (*opening it*) This is your writing.

Léontine Oh, so it is.

She tries to snatch the letter. He fends her off.

Duchotel No, it's interesting . . . Listen.

Moricet *and* **Léontine**. Oh no!

Duchotel (*reading*) 'Dear friend, what can I say? Nothing stands between us.' (*Repeating it.*) 'Nothing stands between us.' Why should you tell me that?

Léontine   I . . . I can't remember.

Moricet   I can. It was one evening –

Duchotel   How do *you* know? You don't know. Keep out of this. (*Reading.*) 'If it was up to me, you'd have my heart.' A-HAH!

Moricet *and* **Léontine**   What?

Duchotel   I remember.

Léontine *and* **Moricet**   He remembers.

Duchotel   The day before we got engaged. (*Reading.*) 'If it was up to me, you'd have my heart. But it belongs to another.' That's it. Your father.

Moricet   Her father?

Duchotel   Her father.

Moricet   Phew.

Duchotel (*to* **Léontine**)   D'you know, I'd forgotten all about this letter.

Léontine   How *could* you?

Duchotel   But I remember it now, of course. Perfectly. Oh, Léontine, darling, think back to those happy days, those happy, happy days. Forgive me –

Léontine   Certainly not.

Enter **Gontran**.

Gontran   He wouldn't listen, Monsieur Zizi . . .

Duchotel   Gontran, help me persuade your auntie.

Gontran   Rather. Pardon?

Duchotel   Léontine, I promise, I swear, I'll never stray again.

Moricet   Please say you forgive him.

Duchotel   That's right. I couldn't have put it better.

Moricet (*histrionically*)   He's guilty, guilty . . .

Duchotel   All right, that'll do.

Léontine   Never! Never!

Duchotel (*furious*)   What?

Gontran (*aside to her*)   Auntie, you must.

Léontine   I won't.

Gontran   For the sake of the lady I saw at 40 rue d'Athènes last night.

Léontine   What? Ah. (*To* **Duchotel**.) All right, I forgive you.

All   Ahhh!

Léontine   But no more fishing.

Duchotel   The one that got away . . .

Moricet (*hastily bundling up his trousers*)   You can say that again. Phee-oo!

Final curtain.

Now You See It

Le Système Ribadier

Characters

Summersby, *a man of affairs*
Marie-Louise, *his wife*
Shaftesbury-Phipps
Vole, *a wine-merchant*
Oriole, *Summersby's gentleman's-gentleman*

Scene: the elegantly furnished sitting-room of Summersby's house. There is a large bay window in an alcove. Time: Edwardian. There are two acts.

Act One

Afternoon. The window is half open. Outside, it's a beautiful summer's day. We hear distant children, birds singing, bees buzzing. A dog suddenly begins barking and growling. **Oriole** *climbs in through the window, with difficulty because he's drunk. He's trying to shush the unseen dog, outside.*

Oriole Go away. No, I won't. I said I would, but I won't. Stop making such a noise. Oh, for heaven's sake! (*He sings to it, sotto-voce:*)

'Oh Danny-boy, the pipes, the pipes are ca-alling . . .'

(*He speaks, as if soothing a baby.*) There, now. There, now. There.

He turns into the room, and starts straightening his clothes. The dog barks again.

Oh, for heaven's sake!

Not without difficulty, he takes off one shoe and throws it out of the window. The barking turns into whines and stops. He goes on straightening his coat. In his top pocket is a floppy silk handkerchief. He pulls it out to straighten it, and a stream of coloured handkerchiefs follows: this is a conjurer's coat. He tries to stuff them back in, finally mops his brow with them and puts them under a cushion on the sofa. He sits on the sofa, and takes out a cigarette. His coat starts bobbing and jerking, and he staggers to his feet. With great difficulty, he takes a folded top hat from one pocket. He opens it out, then reaches inside and takes out a large rabbit. He puts the hat rakishly on his head, tiptoes to the window and lowers the rabbit to the ground outside. He pats his other pockets. He finds a box of matches at last, and tries to take one out to light his cigarette. They spill. He scrabbles for them on the floor, but nearly loses his hat and his dignity. He straightens up and makes for the sideboard, where there's a lighter. But he sees a decanter and some glasses. He pours a large brandy, and is about to drink when he freezes. He tiptoes to the window.

Shh! Birdsh, beesh, all of you.

He is about to drink when we hear **Summersby** *and* **Marie-Louise**, *off.* **Oriole** *twines the curtain round himself and stands there stiff as a statue. Enter* **Summersby** *and* **Marie-Louise**. **Marie-Louise** *is carrying a tray of coffee things. She bangs it down on the sideboard. During what follows she pours, milks, sugars a cup, calmly, for all the fury she is in.*

Marie-Louise   Leave it. I said leave it. I've had enough. (*Calmly.*) Here.

She hands the coffee.

Summersby (*taking it calmly*)   Thanks. (*Furiously.*) What d'you mean, *you've* had enough? It's not your place to have enough. I'm the husband, you're the wife. I'm the one to have enough. I've far more right to have enough than you do.

Marie-Louise (*at the coffee-table*)   There's no milk, now. You've taken the last of the milk.

Summersby   You gave it to me.

Marie-Louise   Oriole!

Summersby   It's no good shouting for Oriole. He isn't here. He hasn't been here since breakfast.

Marie-Louise   That's another thing. Oriole! Do we have to put up with Oriole? He's drunk, he's never here, keeps doing those silly tricks. Why don't you get rid of him?

Summersby   I can't.

Marie-Louise   What d'you mean, you can't?

Summersby   I just can't.

Marie-Louise   Why not?

Summersby   He taught me all I know.

Marie-Louise   Oh, that's right. Blame him.

Summersby What are you talking about? And what about you? That business this morning, at the Suffrage Committee Meeting?

Marie-Louise How else could I be sure you were at a Suffrage Committee Meeting?

Summersby How could you be sure? I told you, with my own lips. 'I'll be at a Suffrage Committee Meeting.' Short words, plain English, I thought it was clear enough. But of course I should have known. For a man, it would have been enough. But not for a woman. Not for my own dear wife. She has to turn up to check, in person.

Marie-Louise (*calmly*) I'll drink this black.

Summersby Will you be quiet about that coffee? There we were . . . we'd approved the minutes, dealt with matters arising, were moving on to tactics when the door opens and a hurricane bursts in. My wife. Mrs Victor Summersby. 'Ha-HA!' she shouts. 'Caught you! Suffrage Committee Meeting! Caught you!' What do you think they *thought*?

Marie-Louise (*scornfully*) Thought? They're MPs.

Summersby Thank you. Thank you very much.

He sits angrily on the sofa. Fishes under him, pulls out the handkerchiefs hidden by **Oriole***, dumps them angrily on the floor and continues.*

Summersby Don't do it again, that's all. I didn't know where to put myself. The Chairman . . . Ponsonby-Charlesworth, you must have noticed the faces he was pulling. As soon as you were gone, he let me have it. Both barrels, right between the eyes. 'My dear fellow, do try to make Mrs Summersby understand in future, that meetings of the Suffrage Committee are for members only. Gentlemen. No ladies by request.' I was red with embarrassment. I didn't know what to say.

Marie-Louise You didn't stand up for me?

Summersby Of course I stood up for you. I said that, like all little ladies, from time to time . . . you do things that aren't quite . . . rational.

Marie-Louise You called me irrational?

Summersby They accepted that. You're my wife, for heaven's sake. It's not as if you were my brother.

Marie-Louise Thank you.

Summersby Well, what would you have said?

Marie-Louise I'd have said 'She came to do research. Research to see if any man, any man on earth, can be trusted for five minutes.'

Summersby Don't start again.

Marie-Louise I don't believe in your Suffrage Committee. I never have, and I never will.

Summersby Well, there you are, you see.

Marie-Louise What d'you mean, there I am?

Summersby Don't worry about it, darling. Don't worry your dear little head. I told you: it's to do with powers of reasoning. Men and women – we're completely different. It's perfectly natural. You don't need to be embarrassed.

Marie-Louise Powers of reasoning. What powers of reasoning?

Summersby You saw us with your own eyes.

Marie-Louise Oh I saw you. All of you, sitting there. What of it? Those committee rooms, that staff of yours, they know how to look after their members . . . avoid unpleasantness.

Summersby What unpleasantness?

Marie-Louise Don't tell me you hadn't time to hide them.

Summersby   Hide who?

Marie-Louise   The loose women.

Summersby   Loose women? My dear sweet darling, the gentlemen of the Suffrage Committee are, well, gentlemen. We've far more important things to think about than women. Loose women, I mean.

Marie-Louise   What sort of things?

Summersby   If I told you, you wouldn't understand.

Marie-Louise   You meet to talk about votes. A likely story.

Summersby   We do.

Marie-Louise   Never mind. It's done, let's forget it. Votes!

She goes to the sideboard to pour more coffee. **Summersby** *is speechless. In the pause, a snore from* **Oriole**. **Marie-Louise** *shrieks.* **Summersby** *goes to the window, unwinds the curtain, and reveals* **Oriole**.

Summersby   So that's where you were. Give me that brandy. No, I won't pick a card. Not now. Go and do the washing-up.

He bundles **Oriole** *out of the room, and goes to sit on the sofa.*

Summersby   You see, there's a rational explanation for everything. I've never given you the slightest reason to suspect me.

Marie-Louise   Of course you haven't. But *he* did. (*She is holding a framed photograph.*)

Summersby   Who did? Oh, Selby. Charlie Selby. It's not my fault if your first husband was a bounder. I can't help it if he chased every woman in London.

Marie-Louise   And the Home Counties.

Summersby   And the Home Counties. You can't blame me.

Marie-Louise I blame myself for loving him. If I'd suspected for just one moment . . . But it won't happen twice. A bounder, from his first long trousers till he had that argument with a number thirty-seven bus. Look at him! (*Affectionately, to the photo.*) Oh Charlie, Charlie, what a man you were.

Summersby He certainly was.

Marie-Louise (*to the photo*) I trusted you. I was your own adoring wife. I believed every word you said. Well, never again. Never, ever.

Summersby Ahem –

Marie-Louise You've opened my eyes. Thanks to you, I know all about men, about husbands . . . all there is to know.

Summersby Darling –

Marie-Louise No man, no husband, will ever make a fool of me again.

Summersby Marie-Louise! Lulu! Pull yourself together. Remember who else is here. I'm here.

Marie-Louise I'm sorry. I was talking to Charlie.

Summersby Well, don't. He's dead and gone. You're my wife now. My own little adoring little darling. You don't have to trust him now. I'm the one you trust.

Marie-Louise I get so cross every time I see this photo.

Summersby Then put it in the attic.

Marie-Louise I can't do that. It's a Pingly. Pingly of Balmoral, photographer royal.

Summersby What of it?

Marie-Louise You don't put Pinglies in the attic.

Summersby Women's logic! You don't put Pinglies in the attic, you keep them on the sideboard to annoy your husband.

Marie-Louise I keep Charlie on the sideboard to remind me not to trust you.

Summersby What?

Marie-Louise It's not your fault. He doesn't blame you personally. He tells me, 'All husbands are cads and bounders. It's in their blood.'

Summersby Charlie's photograph says that, and you believe it?

Marie-Louise That's not all he says. 'Look how I treated you,' he says. 'Look, and remember: all husbands are the same.'

Summersby We are not.

Marie-Louise 'Don't trust appearances. When things look safest, they're riskiest. Keep alert ... eyes, ears ... and if you find nothing, tell yourself: look harder.'

Summersby You're overwrought.

Marie-Louise I'm not.

Summersby This house is too much for you. Poor, helpless little darling. We'll get a maid.

Marie-Louise I don't want a maid. I'm not overwrought. I'm just doing what the photo says.

Summersby I'll throw it on the fire.

Marie-Louise You don't understand.

Summersby Of course I understand. I'm your husband. Poor, dear little darling. Don't you worry about anything. Leave everything to me. Trust everything to me.

Marie-Louise I trusted Charlie. I loved him and trusted him. And look where it got me. When I married

you, I said to myself, 'Remember Charlie. Darling
Charlie. Now you're married to Victor, remember how
Charlie fooled you, don't give an inch.'

Summersby   You mean you don't trust me?

Marie-Louise   I don't need to trust you. I'm watching
you. And now I know.

Summersby   Know what?

Marie-Louise   All the tricks. The husband's tricks.

Summersby   What tricks? How do you know?

Marie-Louise   Charlie told me. Look.

She takes out a leather-bound notebook.

Summersby   What's that?

Marie-Louise   Charlie's diary. On the day he argued
with that bus, I found it. In his hatbox.

Summersby   Hatbox?

Marie-Louise   He always did say, 'Keep it under your
hat.' He put everything in here. His diary. And after he
died, I found it.

Summersby   What a fool he was. You don't write
down things like that.

Marie-Louise   Oh I see: you don't.

Summersby   Well ... I mean ... I don't. Of course I
don't.

Marie-Louise   Well, Charlie did. Day after day after
day.

Summersby   He was a bounder.

Marie-Louise   Just an accountant. He gave an account
of everything. Every affair, every lie, every trick. Look,

here: country buses.

Summersby   What d'you mean, country buses?

Marie-Louise   'Thursday 18th. Spent evening with
Victoria. Told M-L bus was three hours late.'

Summersby   Well, personally, as you know, I take the
train.

Marie-Louise   Oh, Charlie took trains. (*Riffling through.*)
'Friday 27th. Train to Reading. First-class compartment.
Alexandra, self. Drew blinds, locked door. First-class
service. Memo: bill Gasworks.'

Summersby   Why 'bill Gasworks'?

Marie-Louise   Two fares: self and personal assistant.
He was auditing their accounts. Here's another one.
'Wednesday 7th. Executive Committee Meeting.'

Summersby (*startled*)   Let me see that.

Marie-Louise   There. Look. 'Executive Committee
Meeting. Club. Each member, private room. Ernestine
Ebbsmith: any other business. Three stars.'

Summersby   Three stars?

Marie-Louise   Big red stars. Look.

Summersby   And that's why you came to the
committee this morning . . . ? I don't believe this.

Marie-Louise   'All husbands are the same. It's in the
blood.'

Summersby   My dear feather-headed darling, you're
completely mistaken. You read a diary, you listen to a
photograph, you suspect the worst.

Marie-Louise   He was an accountant.

Summersby   He was a fool and a bounder. Writing
everything down like that. A fool.

Marie-Louise   I see. You can do what you like, so long as you don't write it down?

Summersby   That wasn't what I said.

Marie-Louise   It's what you meant.

Summersby   Darling, do try to be reasonable. Men aren't like women. They have responsibilities, they're in control, they're used to making decisions. When a new situation comes along, a man has precedents to go by. A woman makes her mind up afresh each time.

Marie-Louise   You know so much about women.

Summersby   Of course I do. It's part of the job. If this committee is to do anything to improve the position of women in the country, we have to begin by finding out everything about them. Their backgrounds, their daily lives, their little preoccupations, the way their minds work. Research. It's how we do our work.

Marie-Louise   That's what Charlie called what he did. Research.

Summersby   And you trusted him. You see! There's so much we still don't know about women. The way they look at things, try to make sense of things.

Marie-Louise   If I find out you're doing research in first-class compartments, on country buses, in private committee rooms, in Reading, I'll show you how I make sense of things.

Summersby   My dear sweet –

Marie-Louise   Just remember, Victor. I've read Charlie's diary. I've learned every little trick. And I'm watching you like a hawk.

She sits angrily on the sofa. **Summersby** *picks up the photo and talks to it.*

Summersby   Well, thank you very much. You ruin

your own marriage, and now you ruin mine. You and your diary. You bounder. You cad. You fool.

He looks to see what effect this is having on **Marie-Louise**. *None, apparently. He sits huffily on the other end of the sofa. Long pause. He sighs, histrionically. Pause. He feigns nonchalance. This is a long practised technique in their marriage: to wear her down by silence. At last, this time too, she seems to weaken.*

Marie-Louise   Victor . . .

Summersby   Yes?

Marie-Louise   I went too far. I'm sorry.

Summersby   You see what I mean, my poor, sweet darling? It's quite all right. I understand. We've been through it all before. If you had the slightest ability to stand outside yourself, to watch your own behaviour, you'd see it at once. I'm always right, and you always admit it in the end. You're always sorry – and you always start again five minutes later. You're like a little child.

Marie-Louise   I really meant it.

Summersby   You always do.

Marie-Louise   Please?

Summersby   Oh, all right. This time.

He kisses her.

Poor darling, it's all right. I'm not angry. I forgive you. I understand. But in future, do try to remember. I'm a busy man: my work for women takes up all my time. I can't allow myself to be distracted by scenes like these. It's for your own sex, darling, for the good of your own unpredictable, adorable, exasperating sex.

Marie-Louise   I'll remember, Victor. I was wrong to suspect you, and I'm sorry I distracted you.

Summersby   We'll say no more about it.

Marie-Louise   Look, two letters. They came last Tuesday.

Summersby   'Victor Summersby, MP.' 'Victor Summersby, Esquire.' These are addressed to me.

Marie-Louise   Yes, Victor.

Summersby   I don't understand. You kept them back?

Marie-Louise   I didn't open them.

Summersby   I don't know what to say.

Marie-Louise   It's not that I don't trust you. It's just that ... Charlie was always getting letters.

Summersby (*wearily*)   Yes, yes.

Marie-Louise (*after a pause*)   Aren't you going to read them?

Summersby   Later.

Marie-Louise   I don't mind. You can read them, now.

Summersby   This is ridiculous. First you say you trust me, then you want me to open my letters and read them in front of you. Here, you read them, if you're so interested, you read them.

He hands her the letters and sulks again.

Marie-Louise   'Dear friend, please don't think I've forgotten the thirty pounds, two and fivepence you so kindly lent me last Derby day. It'll be Ascot in three weeks' time. If you could see your way to lending me another nineteen pounds, seventeen and sevenpence, that would make it a nice round figure I owe you.'

Summersby   Thirty pounds, two and fivepence ... nineteen pounds, seventeen and sevenpence ... Fifty pounds. He's right.

Marie-Louise   He's the Chancellor of the Exchequer.

Summersby There you are, then.

Marie-Louise Sponging off a friend!

Summersby Sponging! I was his fag at school.

Marie-Louise I'd no idea.

Summersby You really should think before you speak.

Marie-Louise What about this one? What disgusting perfume. And what fancy writing. 'An Evening of Delight and Froodeefroo'. Look, here on the envelope: 'An Evening of Delight and Froodeefroo'.

Summersby (*grabbing the letter*) Give me that.

Marie-Louise You've never met this woman?

Summersby 'Dear Sir, Thanks to the unprecedented success of our latest invention, the Combined Gazogene and Perfume Atomiser (Patent Applied For), we are in the happy position of being able to offer, for a limited period only, with every purchase of the Combined Gazogene and Perfume Atomiser (Patent Applied For) (Larger Size), one six-dram, cut-glass phial of the new fragrance from Messrs Craikhollow and Wellbeloved, Perfume-makers to Her Majesty the Queen. The fragrance in question consists of a fine blend of Craikhollow's long-established "An Evening of Delight", and Wellbeloved's latest, up-to-the-minute creation for the Lady of Refinement, "Froodeefroo". Stocks Limited. Apply at your Earliest Convenience. Yours, etc.' Her Majesty the Queen. No, I've never met this woman.

Marie-Louise 'An Evening of Delight and Froodeefroo'. What else was I supposed to think?

Summersby You were supposed to trust. I've had enough of this. You suspect me, you read my letters, you spy on me, find secrets in everything I do. If I ask the woman in the cakeshop for a lemon slice, you pretend it's the Fall of Ancient Rome. I won't have any more of it.

He sulks again.

Marie-Louise   You look like a furious ferret.

Summersby   This is my house. You're my wife. Those are my letters. I'll look like a ferret if I feel like a ferret.

Marie-Louise   Victor, I'm sorry.

Summersby   Oh, again.

Marie-Louise   I should have trusted you.

Summersby   Yes, you should.

Marie-Louise   It's all Charlie's fault.

Summersby   How, Charlie's fault?

Marie-Louise   His tricks. His diary.

Summersby   His tricks? You still don't understand. Even if I was . . . carrying on, d'you think I'd use one of his tricks? One of Charlie's tricks? I'm an educated man, I went to Cambridge University, I've tricks of my own, far more interesting than Charlie's tricks. (*Realising what he's said, tailing off.*) I mean, if I had, I would have . . .

Marie-Louise   Oh, don't have.

Summersby   Of course I won't have. Haven't! I'm a man of affairs, a public figure, a Member of Parliament. Who d'you take me for? Casanova?

Marie-Louise   It's not as if you played the violin.

Summersby   Exactly. But if you go on checking up on me, distracting me, I may just learn.

Marie-Louise   Oh, don't.

Summersby   I might.

Marie-Louise   The point is, darling, I depend on you.

Summersby   Of course you do. Every woman does. Her husband, her shining star, the still point and centre of her universe. Who else should you depend on?

Marie-Louise Please don't be cross.

Summersby   How can I help being cross? If you want to stop me being cross, you'll have to change your ways entirely.

Marie-Louise I will.

Summersby No more suspecting. No more checking. No more keeping back my letters.

Marie-Louise No.

Summersby (*after a pause*) Well, then.

Marie-Louise Please kiss me, Victor. To show me you've forgiven me.

Summersby Oh. There. There's a good little girl.

Marie-Louise (*like a child*) Oh thank you. Good little girl. Daddy's good little girl!

She dances. **Summersby**, *who has missed the irony entirely, gives the audience a 'here-we-go-again' look. Enter* **Oriole**. *He sees* **Marie-Louise** *dancing, joins hands with her, and gravely dances, until he catches* **Summersby**'s *look.*

Summersby What do you want?

Oriole Nothing, sir.

Summersby As usual.

Marie-Louise Come on, Oriole, you came in. You must want something.

Oriole We all want something, madam. It's the human condition. We all have our little needs.

Pause.

Summersby My wife doesn't mean you must want something – she means, you must *want* something.

Oriole   I don't think so.

Summersby   Oh, for heaven's sake.

Oriole   Unless . . . It is Tuesday.

Summersby   You'd rather have Wednesday? Is that what you want?

Oriole (*with dignity*)   I'm sorry, sir. You don't understand. Pelmanism. It's a memory technique. You remember things by association. You think of one thing, and it reminds you of the thing you want to remember.

Pause.

Summersby   Well?

Oriole   Tuesday.

Pause.

No. It's gone. Well, never mind. Madam, this is for you.

Marie-Louise   A telegram.

Oriole   It came . . . I can't remember when. A telegram for sir.

Marie-Louise   Well, give it to him.

Oriole   But you told me always to give them to –

Marie-Louise (*quickly*)   Oh my goodness. It's Tuesday. You did say it was Tuesday. I must water the tomatoes. Tuesday!

Exit hurriedly.

Summersby   What's got into her today? We don't have any tomatoes. Now, you . . .

Oriole   Yes, sir?

Summersby   My telegram.

Oriole   Ah.

He hands it over.

Summersby 'HAPPY CHRISTMAS, PEREGRINE.' How long have you had this?

Oriole Since Christmas, sir.

Summersby Who's Peregrine?

Oriole I'm sure I can't remember, sir.

Summersby Never mind. This was my telegram. My telegram. Why were you going to give my wife my telegram?

Oriole Madam told me to.

Summersby Oh, she did? And why?

Oriole Sir, we all have our little wants.

Summersby H'm. And what's your little want? I seem to have had this conversation before.

Oriole In *The Stage*, sir. The small advertisements. Equipment.

Summersby What sort of equipment?

Oriole It would realise a dream.

Summersby Well, I won't pry. Look, get the equipment, charge it to me, and in future, deliver all my telegrams to me.

Oriole Very good, sir.

Summersby It might be better . . . if you delivered them when my wife was somewhere else.

Oriole Yes, sir. Anywhere in particular?

Summersby Just don't forget.

Oriole I am a student of Pelmanism, sir.

Summersby Where did you learn it?

Oriole   I can't remember.

Summersby   Oh God.

Oriole   Sir, if I was to buy all the equipment...

Summersby   I'm listening.

Oriole   I might be able to deliver madam's telegrams to you.

Summersby   My wife gets telegrams?

Oriole   Oh, no sir.

Summersby   Go away.

Oriole   Yes, sir.

He stays.

Summersby (*looking at his telegram*)   Peregrine.

He picks up the photo of Selby, and speaks to it.

You must have known a Peregrine...

He puts the photo down, sees **Oriole**.

Summersby   What now?

Oriole   I've remembered.

Summersby   Remembered what?

Oriole   Tuesday. Mr Shaftesbury-Phipps is here.

Summersby   What's that got to do with Tuesday? Never mind. And who on earth is Mr Shaftesbury-Phipps?

Oriole   You remember, sir. You can't have forgotten him.

Summersby   I have.

Oriole   I'm sure it was Tuesday.

Summersby   Oh, show him in. Tell him I won't be a

moment. This telegram was prepaid. From Peregrine. I'll just go and answer it.

Exit.

Oriole Yes, sir.

He steers himself to the sideboard, pours a drink, notices the photo of Selby looking at him, turns it face downwards, drinks. Pause. He's trying to remember something. At last:

Oriole Tuesday!

He goes to the door, and shows in **Shaftesbury-Phipps**.

Oriole This way, sir. There's no one here.

Shaftesbury-Phipps I say. You do keep a chap waiting, what?

Oriole What?

Shaftesbury-Phipps What? Oh, what? I mean, I counted the roses on that hall-wallpaper sixteen times. Thirty-seven. Odd, that, thirty-seven. You'd think they'd have made it thirty-six. Or thirty-eight.

Oriole Ahem.

Shaftesbury-Phipps I say, you said there was no one here.

Oriole I don't remember.

Shaftesbury-Phipps Well, tell your mistress I've arrived, there's a good fellow.

Oriole Yes, sir. (*Pause.*) I'm afraid I've forgotten your name.

Shaftesbury-Phipps Shaftesbury-Phipps. For heaven's sake. Despard Shaftesbury-Phipps. From India.

Oriole Sir is Indian?

Shaftesbury-Phipps Haw-haw. Came as soon as I heard the news.

Oriole   News, sir?

Shaftesbury-Phipps   Mr Selby.

Oriole   Mr Selby?

Shaftesbury-Phipps   Madam's husband. Sir.

Oriole   Ah.

He backs towards the sideboard, and stealthily puts the photo right way up.

That was two years ago, sir.

Shaftesbury-Phipps   Two years. I know. Two years, and still one sheds a silent tear.

Oriole   Sorrow lasts and lasts.

Shaftesbury-Phipps   Well, not exactly. I only heard fifteen minutes ago. At the club. 'He's gorn, old Selby. Gorn.' Went round to his place right away. Moved, of course. Quite a long way, in fact. So naturally, hurried here. I mean, they gave me the address. Otherwise, wouldn't have known –

*He tails off, aware that **Oriole** is looking at him.*

Shaftesbury-Phipps   What is it?

Oriole   Nothing, sir. I was thinking of *The Stage.*

Shaftesbury-Phipps   Oh. Well, well, well, well, well. Look: photo. What a likeness. Him, all right. Looked better then. Alive, for a start. But definitely him.

Oriole   I'll fetch madam.

Shaftesbury-Phipps   Right.

Oriole *makes a false exit into the cupboard, then crosses the room and passes him again.*

Shaftesbury-Phipps   Right.

*Exit **Oriole**. **Shaftesbury-Phipps** talks to the photo.*

Shaftesbury-Phipps   My dear fellow. Dreadfully sorry.
I'll be marrying your wife. Couldn't before . . . not cricket.
One's dearest friend. Loved like a brother. Well,
practically. Not the done thing at all. Especially after . . .
Stella. Remember Stella? Chorus, second row. Mad for
her. On way to propose. After second house, Friday night.
And what did you say? 'Don't do it, old man. Swelling
reasons. You'll see soon enough.' So off I held, and sure
enough, six months later, twins. Did me a good turn
there, all right. What friends we were! Loved you like a
brother. My house your house, your house my house, my
caddy your caddy, your wife my – No. That was whole
point, d'you see? Why else should I go to India? Hot day
. . . you at office . . . tea in garden, Marie-Louise, self.
Stormy with sunny spells. Eighty in shade. Buddleia. Bees,
butterflies, all that. Ah, Marie-Louise! Screamed, suddenly.
'Ahah!' Well, more like, 'Ahaah!' Caterpillar. Huge great
thing. On neck. Well, naturally, picked it off. Then . . .
then . . . puckered lips, bent, lower, lower . . . No, no, no.
Boat train. First thing. Bombay. Never even made it.
Candibar, some such place. Vice-consul. Never did get the
hang of that. Punkah-wallahs. What are punkah-wallahs?
Still, over now. You too, over. Poor old man. Field clear,
no heeltaps, straight down fairway . . . Down on one knee.
Bouquet of flowers. 'I say, old girl, what about it, what?'

He kneels. Enter **Marie-Louise**. *She can't see him.*

Marie-Louise   Hello-oh. Oh no, he's from India. Sala-
am!

Shaftesbury-Phipps (*jumping up*)   Lulu!

Marie-Louise   You-you!

Shaftesbury-Phipps   Who-who? Oh, me. I think so.
Yes. Me. Back.

Marie-Louise   But whyever did you go? You didn't
even drink your tea.

Shaftesbury-Phipps   It was all because of you. I

adored you, dash it.

Marie-Louise Don't be silly.

Shaftesbury-Phipps Silent adoration. Worship from afar. That kind of thing. You know what the poet says, er . . . that kind of thing.

Marie-Louise You must never say that again.

Shaftesbury-Phipps Pardon?

Marie-Louise In front of my husband.

Shaftesbury-Phipps That's not your husband. It's a photo.

Marie-Louise No, no, no, no.

Shaftesbury-Phipps See what you mean. A shrine. Shrine to his memory. Quite right, too. A saint, a saint.

Marie-Louise He wasn't.

Shaftesbury-Phipps Beg pardon?

Marie-Louise I see you were like me. He pulled the wool over both our eyes.

Shaftesbury-Phipps I don't follow.

Marie-Louise He had a lady-friend in every house in town.

Shaftesbury-Phipps I say.

Marie-Louise I've upset you.

Shaftesbury-Phipps Not in the least. In fact, what you've told me . . . I'm overwhelmed.

Marie-Louise Why?

Shaftesbury-Phipps Because it puts my mind at rest. Don't you understand? Chap's alive . . . casts giant shadow . . . one feels, well, shadowed. Now he's dead . . . truth comes out . . . one's bound to be seen in a better light.

Marie-Louise What better light?

Shaftesbury-Phipps In the race of life. Stumbling-block ... dash off to India ... come back ... stumbling-block gone.

Marie-Louise I still don't –

Shaftesbury-Phipps (*on his knees*) I say, old girl, what about it, what?

Marie-Louise What are you doing? Get up. You're joking.

Shaftesbury-Phipps What's the matter?

Marie-Louise We can't.

Shaftesbury-Phipps Why not?

Marie-Louise There's a stumbling-block.

Shaftesbury-Phipps Another one? I'll kick it aside. What is it?

Marie-Louise My husband.

Shaftesbury-Phipps Don't be silly. Keep telling you: it's a photograph.

Marie-Louise Not Charlie. The other one.

Shaftesbury-Phipps What other one?

Marie-Louise The one I married later.

Shaftesbury-Phipps I say, not cricket. To pull a chap's leg like that. Some kind of test?

Marie-Louise No test.

Shaftesbury-Phipps You can't have.

Marie-Louise I did.

Shaftesbury-Phipps I don't believe it.

Marie-Louise Ask him yourself. He's here.

Enter **Summersby**.

Shaftesbury-Phipps   Good God, it's you.

Summersby   Good God, it's you.

Shaftesbury-Phipps (*to* **Marie-Louise**)   It's him.

Summersby   You never said you were back in town.

Shaftesbury-Phipps   I've only just arrived.

Summersby   What's wrong with you?

Shaftesbury-Phipps   Nothing. I. Gosh. I say.

Summersby   You've met my wife? Yes, I see you have. Let me introduce you . . .

Shaftesbury-Phipps   No, no. We knew each other . . . before.

Summersby   Before what?

Shaftesbury-Phipps   In poor dear Selby's time. When he was . . . I mean . . . what a sterling chap. Loved him like a brother. Sterling.

Summersby   Yes.

Shaftesbury-Phipps   How you must miss him. Well, not you, of course.

Summersby   I know what you mean.

Shaftesbury-Phipps   Popping off like that. A chap so full of . . . full of . . .

Marie-Louise   Will you be long in town?

Shaftesbury-Phipps   Oh, this I'm time back for good. No more India. I say, hang on, though . . .

Summersby   Got it in the blood, eh? Elephants, mulligatawny, maharajahs, you can't get enough.

Shaftesbury-Phipps   No, no. Thing is, one came back expecting . . . then it didn't quite . . . perhaps one'd better . . .

Summersby   Ah. (*To* **Marie-Louise**.) He means a woman.

Shaftesbury-Phipps (*nervously*)   Haha.

Summersby   Don't be bashful. We know what it's like. (*Gently mocking him.*) Two hearts beating as one . . . loving glances . . . call of duty . . . serve one's country . . . sundered . . . East is East, all that . . .

Shaftesbury-Phipps   Nothing of the sort at all.

Summersby   Found someone else, did she?

Shaftesbury-Phipps   In a manner of speaking . . .

Summersby   Well, there you are. Your turn will come.

Shaftesbury-Phipps   Mm.

Summersby   Excuse me just a moment. Lulu, darling, was there someone else here just now?

Marie-Louise   I don't think so. Why?

Summersby   Oriole came out with the most amazing name. Salisbury Tips. Canterbury Slips. Westminster Flips.

Shaftesbury-Phipps   Shaftesbury-Phipps.

Summersby   Pardon?

Shaftesbury-Phipps   Shaftesbury-Phipps.

Summersby   You spoke to him.

Shaftesbury-Phipps   No, no. That's me.

Summersby   No, it isn't.

Shaftesbury-Phipps   It is. It is.

Summersby   Your name's Cheese. Arthur Henry Cheese. Or at least it was at school. (*To* **Marie-Louise**.) We called him Mousetrap. Didn't we, Mousetrap?

Shaftesbury-Phipps   I changed it. Went to India, changed it.

Marie-Louise   Whatever for?

Shaftesbury-Phipps   You can't run an Empire under the name of Cheese. Arthur Cheese. It's just not done.

Summersby   So you changed it to something more sensible.

Shaftesbury-Phipps   One did one's best.

Summersby   Well, never mind. We were talking about women. My dear old Mousetrap ... er ... whatever it is ... your turn will come.

Shaftesbury-Phipps   Beg pardon?

Summersby   I guarantee it. And till it does, where are your things?

Shaftesbury-Phipps   Things?

Summersby   From India. Pith helmet, polo sticks ... things.

Shaftesbury-Phipps   At the station. Left-luggage.

Summersby   I'll send Oriole.

Shaftesbury-Phipps   What for?

Summersby   My dear chap, until you find the woman you love, your place is here. With us.

Marie-Louise *and* **Shaftesbury-Phipps** *are gaping.*

Summersby   In the summer house. For as long as you like. It's yours.

Shaftesbury-Phipps   But I can't.

Summersby   Of course you can.

Marie-Louise   It hasn't been decorated.

Summersby   He's been in India. Rude huts. It'll make

him feel at home. (*To* **Shaftesbury-Phipps**.) You don't mind a few cockroaches?

Shaftesbury-Phipps (*feebly*) Cockroaches?

Summersby They're why we've never rented it. You can't ask strangers to ... But for friends ... after India, big-game hunting, what could be better?

Shaftesbury-Phipps No cockroaches in India. Scorpions.

Summersby Scorpions?

Shaftesbury-Phipps Size of dinner-plates.

Summersby I know. The Zoo. I'll send Oriole. You know, it's a damn good thing you came. I thought we'd never rent out that summer house.

Exit.

Shaftesbury-Phipps I can't stay here.

Marie-Louise Of course you can't. You mustn't.

Shaftesbury-Phipps Why not?

Marie-Louise For my sake.

Shaftesbury-Phipps Pardon?

Marie-Louise After what you told me before Victor came in, after all those glances you sent me after Victor did come in, after all we've been through together.

Shaftesbury-Phipps We haven't been through anything.

Marie-Louise Of course we have. That hot summer, that stormy, sunny day, that caterpillar ... No, it's no use. What's done is done. We can't put it behind us. Not a day like that, a day of destiny.

Shaftesbury-Phipps I puckered my lips, I bent ...

Marie-Louise My heart was pounding, pounding. But

it was hopeless. It was not to be. I did love Charlie, after all.

Shaftesbury-Phipps   So did I. Like a brother.

Marie-Louise   You rushed off to India just in time. Oh, why were you so bashful . . . ?

Shaftesbury-Phipps   Damn fool thing to be.

Marie-Louise   No, no, we mustn't. It must never be. We can't . . . live in the same . . . house, see each other, day after day. Gaze at each other. Say 'Good morning. Lovely day.'

Shaftesbury-Phipps   'Good morning. Lovely day.'

Marie-Louise   What?

Shaftesbury-Phipps   You said, 'Say "Good morning. Lovely day."'

Marie-Louise   You see? We could never keep it up.

Shaftesbury-Phipps   We couldn't.

Marie-Louise   There'd always be a stumbling-block. My husband.

Shaftesbury-Phipps   Life's so unfair. There we were: garden. Lapsang Souchong. Cucumber sandwiches. Buddleia. Butterflies, heedlessly flitting, flitting. Storm. Caterpillar. Pluck it off. Lips puckered. Bend. Boat train, dash it. Bombay . . . well, Candibar. Husband in way. Husband dies. Will she wait for beloved till end of time? No, she marries another husband. Another one! Life's so unfair.

Marie-Louise   We're victims, my darling, victims of the gods.

Shaftesbury-Phipps   One does see that. But what I don't see . . . why should I have to stop seeing you, just because you married a second husband?

Marie-Louise It's for your own good.

Shaftesbury-Phipps His good, you mean. Want me to
tear myself, wrench myself, away ... for Summersby. You
must have loved him very dearly.

Marie-Louise Not exactly.

Shaftesbury-Phipps I say.

Marie-Louise Put yourself in my place.

Shaftesbury-Phipps Steady on.

Marie-Louise He was such a ... powerful man. A
man of power. Authority. And then there was his name.

Shaftesbury-Phipps What d'you mean, his name?

Marie-Louise Summersby.

Shaftesbury-Phipps You married him because of his
name?

Marie-Louise Well, of course I did.

Shaftesbury-Phipps But why?

Marie-Louise It's obvious. Selby, Summersby.
Summersby, Selby. We had monogrammed table napkins.
It was meant to be.

Shaftesbury-Phipps It's baffling. Head-whirling. Why
do people marry? For love? For companionship? For
table napkins? If that's all it was, you could have married
me.

Marie-Louise I don't follow.

Shaftesbury-Phipps Shaftesbury-Phipps! Shaftesbury-
Phipps!

Marie-Louise I still don't follow.

Shaftesbury-Phipps The table napkins would still have
done.

Marie-Louise   Ah yes, but I thought your name was Cheese. In any case, he's my husband. It's my duty to love him.

Shaftesbury-Phipps   You say that to me? You stand there, say it to my face? You love your husband?

Marie-Louise   Love, honour and obey.

Shaftesbury-Phipps   Twist the dagger, twist the dagger.

Marie-Louise   That's why we have to part.

Shaftesbury-Phipps   Quite understand. (*Bitterly.*) Come all the way from India, turn round, go back again.

Marie-Louise   When?

Shaftesbury-Phipps   Tomorrow. I only arrived this lunchtime. What to do this afternoon? Perhaps, the Zoo.

Marie-Louise   What a good idea. Go to the Zoo, then go to India. And on the way, explain everything to Summersby.

Shaftesbury-Phipps   Summersby!

Marie-Louise   My husband. And now, goodbye, my darling, goodbye for ever.

Shaftesbury-Phipps   Er . . . darling . . .

Marie-Louise   Yes, darling?

Shaftesbury-Phipps   One thing, darling. Promise –

Marie-Louise   Anything, darling.

Shaftesbury-Phipps   We're all mortal . . . we mortals. If Summersby should happen to . . . I mean if he . . .

Marie-Louise   You mean if he . . .

Shaftesbury-Phipps   Oh, yes. Write, darling. Send a telegram, even. 'COME HOTFOOT. I'M FREE.'

Marie-Louise   Hotfoot? In a telegram? What do you take me for? (*Lip quivering.*) You're so ... so ... impulsive!

Exit.

Shaftesbury-Phipps (*on his knees*)   I am! My love, my own – Oh, she's gone. (*Getting up.*) Didn't even say goodbye. She's right. It's hopeless. She loves her husband. Heart broken. Better off in India.

He slumps on the sofa. Enter **Oriole**.

Oriole   Your scorpions, sir.

Shaftesbury-Phipps   Erg?

Oriole   They're for the summer house.

Shaftesbury-Phipps   Summer house. Summersby summer house. Oh God.

He slumps again, clutching the box of scorpions. **Oriole** *meanwhile has begun fetching in and assembling two trestles, a bottom-board and the side-panels of a hinged, hollow-ended coffin – the sort magicians put people in to saw them in half. He has extreme difficulty putting it together. At last he succeeds.*

Oriole   Sir ...

Shaftesbury-Phipps (*dully*)   Yes?

Oriole   I wonder if you'd be kind enough to lie down in here for me.

Shaftesbury-Phipps   Pardon?

Oriole   I wonder if you'd be kind enough to lie down in here for me.

Shaftesbury-Phipps   Why?

Oriole   It was in *The Stage*, sir. This morning. It's an illusion I've always admired. But until this morning, I've never had the chance.

He fetches a large saw.

In the box, sir, if you'd be so kind.

Shaftesbury-Phipps   Oh dash it, anything's better than India.

He clambers into the coffin. It collapses in a heap round him. Enter **Summersby**.

Summersby   Ah, there you are. Have you seen Marie-Louise?

Shaftesbury-Phipps   No! Not here. Was never here. Left.

Summersby   She'll be fetching pillows for the summer house.

Shaftesbury-Phipps   You don't understand. I can't. I can't.

Summersby   Is it the cockroaches?

Shaftesbury-Phipps   No, no, Pit of Despond.

Summersby   It's only a summer house.

Shaftesbury-Phipps   I'll never be happy again.

Summersby   You do need cheering up. Aren't you pleased to see me again?

Shaftesbury-Phipps   Oh. Yes.

Summersby   And you like Marie-Louise.

Shaftesbury-Phipps   What? Yes.

Summersby   So why are you so gloomy?

Shaftesbury-Phipps   Not gloomy. In hurry. Can't stay here. Going back to India.

Summersby   I know what it is.

Shaftesbury-Phipps   You do?

Summersby It's love. Unrequited love.

Shaftesbury-Phipps I say. You know. How do you know?

Summersby You told me. It's why you went to India in the first place. Well, one thing's for sure. She won't come looking for you there.

Shaftesbury-Phipps Won't come looking anywhere.

Summersby Don't run yourself down like that. Your problem is, you don't understand women. You've no experience. You need expert tuition. Put yourself in my hands.

Shaftesbury-Phipps What d'you mean?

Summersby Expert tuition. I'll show you how it's done. By a real expert. The spoor ... the stalk ... the pounce.

Shaftesbury-Phipps What d'you mean, spoor, stalk, pounce?

Summersby You're like a little child. So innocent. I'll show you. It's a matter of tactics. Siege tactics. You reconnoitre. Spy out the citadel. Survey the defences, the battlements, find a weak link, then in you go, tally-ho, all guns blazing.

Shaftesbury-Phipps No, no, no, no, no.

Summersby Ah! Got it. You're scared. You're scared of me.

Shaftesbury-Phipps Pardon?

Summersby Man of the world ... your little lady ... you're afraid I'll steal her heart.

Shaftesbury-Phipps Really, no.

Summersby No need to worry. That's not my way at all. No, no, put yourself in my hands. Leave everything to me.

Shaftesbury-Phipps You're crazy. You're married.

Summersby What's that to do with it?

Shaftesbury-Phipps Sacred bond. Two hearts beat as one. Love, honour, obey . . . Cherish . . . that kind of thing. Not . . . the other kind of thing.

Summersby Don't be ridiculous. I'm a Member of Parliament. In any case: Baden-Powell.

Shaftesbury-Phipps What about Baden-Powell?

Summersby Dictates to two secretaries at the same time. Famous for it.

Shaftesbury-Phipps Who's talking about secretaries?

Summersby I'm not.

Shaftesbury-Phipps You brought it up.

Summersby It was an example. He's a happily married man.

Shaftesbury-Phipps Who is?

Summersby Baden-Powell is.

Shaftesbury-Phipps And so are you. Whole point of the thing. Happily married man. And so are you.

Summersby You think so?

Shaftesbury-Phipps I say!

Summersby She was so trusting, so innocent. I saw straight away that she was the wife for me. One in a million. So trusting, so innocent. As you must have known.

Shaftesbury-Phipps Eh?

Summersby Selby must have told you.

Shaftesbury-Phipps Oh, Selby. Yes. Often!

Summersby That man was a fool.

Shaftesbury-Phipps Steady on. Loved him like a brother.

Summersby D'you know what he did? Kept a diary, that's all.

Shaftesbury-Phipps Nothing wrong in that. Keep one self.

Summersby Of course there's nothing wrong in that. But he put everything in – and then Marie-Louise found it. Read it. The scales fell from her eyes. 'So that's what husbands get up to,' she said to herself. Not just Selby, all husbands, any husband. You can imagine the position it puts me in, for a start.

Shaftesbury-Phipps No.

Summersby I told you. So trusting. So innocent. That's why I married her.

Shaftesbury-Phipps *looks at him blankly*.

Sommersby Listen. Right now, right at this moment, I've . . . an interest.

Shaftesbury-Phipps Interest? Oh, interest. Ohh!

Summersby Her husband's a wine-merchant. She's . . . how can I put it . . . robust, full-bodied, merest hint of fizz . . .

Shaftesbury-Phipps Didn't know you were a wine-man.

Summersby I'm a connoisseur, a connoisseur.

Shaftesbury-Phipps But the diary. Marie-Louise. The diary.

Summersby No problem.

Shaftesbury-Phipps She'll know every trick.

Summersby   She'll know all Charlie's tricks. Not mine.
I know you loved him like a brother, but he was a fool,
an amateur. What's needed here is science.

Shaftesbury-Phipps   You've lost me again.

Summersby   It's very simple. I'll give you a
demonstration. But only if you stay here.

Shaftesbury-Phipps   Eh?

Summersby   No running off to India.

Shaftesbury-Phipps   Oh. No. (*Reflectively.*) Don't think
I'll be running to India, after all.

Summersby   Good man.

Shaftesbury-Phipps   Thank you.

Summersby   Shake on it, then. Shake on it.

Shaftesbury-Phipps   Whatever you say.

Summersby   I think it calls for a drink. Oriole!

Oriole   Yes sir?

Shaftesbury-Phipps   Good God, he's here.

Summersby   Of course he's here.

Shaftesbury-Phipps   But suppose he . . . what if
he . . . ?

Summersby   It's all right. He knows everything.

Shaftesbury-Phipps   Hargh?

Summersby   He taught me all I know.

Oriole *serves drinks. They all three drink.*

Summersby   Wives, God bless 'em.

Shaftesbury-Phipps   You don't know what you're
saying. Oh, wives.

Oriole   Wives. Of course I never married. I married the business. I was fourteen years old, and there it was. On the village green, a circus. Horses, clowns, tightrope walkers. Tigers, elephants, a human cannonball. I started at the bottom. Juggling, stilt-walking. Base of the human pyramid. I loved them, I loved them all. Roger the Rubber Man, Beatrice the Bearded Lady – she was like a father to me – the Soaring Sidneys, the Horace Hoxton Accordion Ensemble, Marvello the Magician. Oh, Marvello! I loved him like a brother. Mice. Rabbits. Doves. Card-tricks, mind-reading, escapology. He gave me this coat. He taught me all I know. (*He drinks.*) Marvello!

Summersby Did you get those scorpions?

Shaftesbury-Phipps He gave them to me.

Summersby Where are they?

Shaftesbury-Phipps Here. Here. I've got them here.

Summersby You certainly know how to handle game.

Oriole This came for you.

Summersby A note.

Oriole Yes. From the Zoo.

Summersby I don't know anyone at the Zoo.

Oriole I'd been to the Insect House. I was passing the reptiles. I always pass the reptiles. I find they soothe the nerves. Chameleons, especially. I was looking at the chameleons. They never blink, you know. They swivel their eyes, but they never blink. All at once, someone plucked my sleeve. A woman, muffled. A woman of mystery. She pressed this note into my hands, and then she was gone.

Summersby All right, all right. The note.

Oriole Pardon? Oh.

He hands over the note. **Summersby** *reads.*

Summersby   Aha!

Shaftesbury-Phipps   Aah!

Summersby   My dear Watson, the game's afoot.

Shaftesbury-Phipps   What d'you mean?

Summersby   This is from her. My . . . little glass of bubbly. 'Come tonight. Clarence away on claret business. Hurry. Pusskin.'

Shaftesbury-Phipps   Pusskin?

Summersby   Nothing. A kind of code. Well, now you can see for yourself.

Shaftesbury-Phipps   See what?

Summersby   I said I'd show you. How a scientist, a wine-lover, goes about these things. Oriole, take Mr . . . Whateverhisnameis . . . to the summer house. And you, my dear fellow, get those scorpions settled in and come straight back here.

Shaftesbury-Phipps   Oh.

Oriole   This way, sir.

Exeunt **Oriole** *and* **Shaftesbury-Phipps**.

Summersby   'Come tonight. Clarence away on claret business. Hurry.' Oh!

He hurries, and falls over the bits of coffin.

For heaven's sake!

He starts hurling them out of the window.

Oriole!

Enter **Marie-Louise**.

Marie-Louise   He's gone, your friend?

Summersby   Yes, to the summer house.

Marie-Louise   I thought he was going to India.

Summersby   He changed his mind.

Marie-Louise   Oh!

Summersby   It's all right, darling. What's the matter? Don't worry. I'll take charge. I'll entertain him. I've got it all in hand. You just sit there, smile, ornament the room.

He goes to her.

Poor darling. You are upset. Who's been upsetting you? Let me see to it, sort it out. I'm your husband, your Lancelot, your knight in shining armour, and you're my own sweet gentle darling. There, darling. There there. Sit on the sofa, beside me, here. Take my hands. That's right. Dear little darling. Look at me, darling. How strong I am, how wrong you were to doubt me. Look at me, darling. Look into my eyes and say you trust me.

Marie-Louise   I . . . trust you.

Summersby   And I love you. How could you ever doubt me? I love you, darling, I love you. Love you, love you, love you . . .

Marie-Louise (*in a trance*)   Love me, love me . . .

She's hypnotised.

Summersby   There, Charlie Selby. How's *that* for tricks?

Enter **Shaftesbury-Phipps**.

Shaftesbury-Phipps   I think they'll settle.

Summersby   Fine. I have to go out. Are you going into town?

Shaftesbury-Phipps   I – eugh! Marie-Louise! What's she doing?

Summersby   It's quite all right.

Shaftesbury-Phipps   But she's . . . she's . . . look at her! What's wrong with her?

Summersby   I told you. Science. Hypnotism. I learned it from Oriole. He taught me all I know.

Shaftesbury-Phipps   Is she all right?

Summersby   She'll be fine till I get back. Then I take her hands in mine, blow into the palms – *ffufufu, ffufufu* – and hey presto! None the worse. Sometimes she doesn't even know she's been asleep.

Shaftesbury-Phipps   Sometimes? You mean . . . other times?

Summersby   I'm a connoisseur. I told you.

Shaftesbury-Phipps   I say.

Summersby   Watch me, my boy, watch me and learn. Come on.

Shaftesbury-Phipps   Where are we going?

Summersby   My . . . wine-merchant. My . . . pert little vintage. Pusskin.

Shaftesbury-Phipps   I can't go there. Don't even know the woman.

Summersby   You want some pointers, don't you? How these things are done? A lesson or two in science? I'll tell you on the way.

Shaftesbury-Phipps   But when we get there?

Summersby   You can wait in the garden. Twenty minutes. These things never take longer than twenty minutes. On we go!

Exeunt. Curtain.

Act Two

The same. Evening. **Marie-Louise** *is still asleep where she was. There is a discreet tap at the door, and* **Shaftesbury-Phipps** *creeps in, clutching a bunch of flowers.*

Shaftesbury-Phipps I say, are you ... ? Gosh. Yes. (*To the audience.*) Nine o'clock. Dashed late to be out. Adventuring. In India, port and nuts by now. Funny place, India. So ... Indian. Anyway, no time for port now. Or nuts. Just managed to sneak away. Took me with him. Summersby. Dashed embarrassing. Cab to High Street. Seventy-seven bus. Get on, sixpennny ride, get off. Flowerstall. Flowers. Down street past post office. Mews. Back door. Embarrassing. Summersby: key. Door open. In. Wine-shop. Back regions. Bottles, corkscrews. 'I can't come upstairs,' I said. 'Pardon?' he said. 'I can't come upstairs,' I said. 'Don't be ridiculous,' he said. 'What d'you mean?' I said. 'You're supposed to stay here,' he said. 'Qui vive.' I mean, what did he mean, qui vive? Would have asked, but he'd gone. Forced to stay where was. Three hours. Fiddled with corkscrews. Read wine labels. Read labels again. Foreign languages. Why? Foot went to sleep. Watched spider in corner. Unravelling web. Packing up for night. Thought, 'Well, if he can, I can.' Not spider, Summersby. If he can, other man's wife, I can, his wife. Put down bottle I was reading – in Portuguese, I think it was – tiptoed out. Foot still asleep. Barked shin. Up mews. Past flowerstall. Bus. Taxi. Gate. Door. Oriole in cubbyhole. Muttering. Clinking glass. Practising some kind of trick. Climbed stairs. Tapped on door. Opened door. Walked into room. Saw you. Good of you to come. Started talking to you. Foot still asleep. What do next? Dash it, not used to this. Another chap's wife. Not first-team stuff at all. Hardly reserves, even. Still, his fault. All his fault. Wine-shop!

He dithers, plucking up his courage.

Seems so dashed rude. One's host, after all. Summer
house. Summersby summer house. Summersby Lulu.
Mind you, chap's a bounder. Absolute bounder. Not as if
dearest friend. Not like brother. Do it. Do it. (*He tries
again.*) Now other foot gone to sleep. Dark, too. Lamp.
Call for lamp-wallah. No, no, put on lamp oneself. How
do that? Where do that? Ah.

He switches on a standard lamp, gazes at **Marie-Louise**,
transfixed.

I say! Just like that picture. You know the one ... No,
not that one, the other one. Kneel at her feet. Her feet.
Offer flowers. Heart pounding, tick tock, tick tock, rather
like ... clock. Get to it, man. Eye on ball, straight down
fairway, fore!

He kneels.

It's me. Me. My darling. My angel. Hang on. Asleep.
Can't hear a word I'm saying. Bit louder. Ahem. A-hem!
Nothing. What next? Shake shoulders? No, no: gentleman.
Fire off revolver? No, dangerous. Only got penknife,
anyway. Mrs Summersby ... Marie-Louise ... Lulu ...
Dashed hard on knees, all this. Not man of world, not
man of world at all. Summersby. What would he do,
Summersby? Man of world all right. And man of science.
Said so himself. Of course! Science. Take hold of hands,
blow on palms, he said. Take hold of hands ... blow on
palms ...

Marie-Louise   Where am I? What a lovely sleep.

Shaftesbury-Phipps (*still on his knees*)   Lulu. I say.

Marie-Louise   You!

Shaftesbury-Phipps   Yes, me. Don't heed them,
Marie-Louise, my darling, the raised eyebrows of society.
Heed only the pounding of my heart.

Marie-Louise   What?

Shaftesbury-Phipps   Tick, tock, tick, tock. I was telling them. Of course, you were asleep.

Marie-Louise   What are you talking about?

Shaftesbury-Phipps   I love you.

Marie-Louise   We talked about this before. My husband!

She moves away. He follows, on his knees.

Shaftesbury-Phipps   It's all right. He'll never know. My knees! He's out.

Marie-Louise   Out? Where?

Shaftesbury-Phipps   Cigarettes. Ran out of cigarettes.

Marie-Louise   Get up, you fool. The tobacco shop's next door.

Shaftesbury-Phipps   Closed. They were closed. He took a taxi. Oh Lulu, Lulu, I love you, Lulu.

Marie-Louise   I refuse to listen.

Shaftesbury-Phipps   No, no, listen. It's just like that film. You remember . . .

He mimes a passionate declaration from a 1920s silent film.

Marie-Louise   Pardon?

He does it again.

Marie-Louise   I'm sorry, I didn't quite catch –

Shaftesbury-Phipps   It's not the same without the orchestra. I love you, dash it, love you.

Marie-Louise   But I can't love you. I told you.

Shaftesbury-Phipps   Of course you can. You did. Do try to remember. Hot afternoon, garden, caterpillar . . .

Marie-Louise   We must crush that memory. A moment's weakness.

Shaftesbury-Phipps   Another. That's all I ask.
Another!

He staggers to his feet, cramped.

Oh Lulu, Lulu.

Marie-Louise   We can't! He's a good, kind man. I'm
his wife. And you're his friend. His schoolfriend.
Mousetrap! You're a guest in his summer house. It's
unthinkable.

Shaftesbury-Phipps   Unthinkable but human. My
darling . . .

Marie-Louise   We mustn't give way. After all he's done
for women.

Shaftesbury-Phipps (*darkly*)   I know what you mean.

Marie-Louise   It would be infamous. Infamous. Can't
you understand?

Shaftesbury-Phipps   Did cross one's mind. In the
wine-shop. 'Infamous' – like that. Then again –
'Infamous'. Then again. A dozen times. Twenty times.

Marie-Louise   Well then?

Shaftesbury-Phipps   By the twenty-first time, I'd got
used to it.

Marie-Louise   What wine-shop?

Shaftesbury-Phipps   Ah that, my darling, you must
never, never know.

Marie-Louise   You said you were going back to India.

Shaftesbury-Phipps   India! Ha! I offer love, she insists
on India! Just like before.

Marie-Louise   Before what?

Shaftesbury-Phipps   Before I went to India, last time.
In the garden. After the caterpillar. 'I think I'll be off to

India,' I said. 'Oh,' you said.

Marie-Louise What's wrong with that?

Shaftesbury-Phipps 'Oh.' One knew what it meant.
'Oh.' It hurt, deep down. But one knew what it meant.
And one knew what one had to do. For his sake. For
Charlie. Loved him like a brother.

Marie-Louise Not again.

Shaftesbury-Phipps Exactly. Not again. For him, yes,
but not for everyone else you choose to marry.

Marie-Louise Arthur!

Shaftesbury-Phipps Despard. Wish I'd never gone.

Marie-Louise You enjoyed India.

Shaftesbury-Phipps (*bitterly*) Oh yes. Enjoyed.
Stamping passports. Tiger-licences. And all the time – he
dies, you marry someone else.

Marie-Louise It seemed such a good idea.

Shaftesbury-Phipps I love you. Don't you
understand? Every time I think of you, head fills with
poetry.

Marie-Louise Poetry?

Shaftesbury-Phipps Poetry. 'Love like red, red rose',
that kind of thing. Oh, tell me you love me too.

Marie-Louise On one condition.

Shaftesbury-Phipps (*as before*) I knew you'd never –
(*Realising.*) What?

Marie-Louise On one condition.

Shaftesbury-Phipps You mean, you . . . you . . . me
. . . you . . . Anything! Gun, deadly snake, penknife, die
for love, all that.

Marie-Louise For my sake, if you love me, Despard,
darling –

Shaftesbury-Phipps   Yes?

Marie-Louise   Go back to India tonight.

Shaftesbury-Phipps   What?

Marie-Louise   It isn't much to ask.

Shaftesbury-Phipps   Not much? Cross continents, seas, catch boat-trains ... not much to ask?

Marie-Louise   It's a measure of what you feel for me.

Shaftesbury-Phipps   Can't measure feelings by seas and continents.

Marie-Louise   You don't really love me.

Shaftesbury-Phipps   Of course I love you. That's why I want to stay. You don't know what you're asking. Heat, endless dinner parties, gin ... All the time waiting. Waiting – for what? Someone else to die. Not like a brother, but even so. Good God. What thinking of? Step into dead man's shoes? No, no. Make love to wife now. No need for poor chap to die.

Marie-Louise   What are you suggesting?

Shaftesbury-Phipps   Nothing complicated. Simple. Man, wife, lover. House, garden, summer house. No need for anyone to die.

Marie-Louise   You're out of your mind.

Shaftesbury-Phipps   No problem. Be nice to him. We'll both be nice to him.

Marie-Louise   It's unheard-of.

Shaftesbury-Phipps   Of course it's not unheard-of. History's crammed with cases. Boadicea ... no, not Boadicea. Cleopatra. Cleopatra, yes.

Marie-Louise   You want me to be Cleopatra?

Shaftesbury-Phipps   And I'll be Lancelot. My darling. My own, my own!

Marie-Louise   We mustn't. Go to India. I'll scream.

Shaftesbury-Phipps   Don't care. On fire, rain kisses, love –

Marie-Louise   I'll shout for my husband.

Shaftesbury-Phipps   Won't hear you.

Marie-Louise   He's only gone for cigarettes.

Shaftesbury-Phipps   Turkish. May be away some time.

Marie-Louise   What was that? Listen!

Shaftesbury-Phipps   Nothing.

Marie-Louise   The front gate. He's coming.

Shaftesbury-Phipps   What?

He runs to the window.

Good grief, it's him. Now what? Red-handed. Hide. Where hide?

He tries to hide.

Too obvious. Wife standing there, guilty look, lover in cupboard. Standing there! Oh my God. Asleep! Should be still asleep. Man of science. Now what?

He runs to her and tries to hypnotise her.

Look at me. You're feeling sleepy.

Marie-Louise   No I'm not.

Shaftesbury-Phipps   Dash it, you are. Drowsy. Eyelids heavy. Arms floppy. Sleepy . . . sleepy . . .

He snores.

Marie-Louise   What are you doing? Wake up! Wake up!

She kicks him on the shin.

Shaftesbury-Phipps　Ow! Where am I? Lovely snooze. Oh God. Look, here. In eyes. Closer. Don't you sense anything?

Marie-Louise　Hair-cream. Revolting.

Shaftesbury-Phipps　Indian muck. Never mind. Feel eyes drooping? Sleepy?

Marie-Louise　Don't keep saying that.

Shaftesbury-Phipps　Do try. Do try.

He makes hypnotist's passes at her.

No use. No science. Look. Lie here, on sofa. Pretend sleep. When Summersby comes. Especially when Summersby comes. Don't open eyes, don't speak, play sleep.

Marie-Louise　But why?

Shaftesbury-Phipps　No time explain. Lie, lie.

He gets her to lie on the sofa.

Lamp.

He switches off the lamp.

Marie-Louise　What are you doing?

Shaftesbury-Phipps　Don't ask. Just sleep. Goodbye!

He jumps out of the window. **Marie-Louise** *falls back on the sofa as if asleep, with a fixed grin on her face. Enter* **Summersby** *and* **Vole**. *Each is carrying a hat, and each is furious.* **Summersby** *tries to shut the door on* **Vole**.

Summersby　Go away.

Vole　I said I was coming in, and coming in I am.

Summersby　You aren't.

Vole　I am.

Summersby You aren't.

Vole I am.

He gives a convulsive heave on the door, and bursts into the room.

Summersby But what is it you want?

Vole I want you. And I've got you. Now.

Summersby At least let me put a light on.

Vole Put! Put! Put!

Summersby *goes to switch on the lamp. On the way he passes* **Marie-Louise***, and waves a hand in front of her face to make sure that she's still asleep. Reassured, he switches on the light.*

Summersby Now then, you. Good God, is that what you look like? What is it you want?

Vole Stop shouting. I'll tell you. First get rid of your daughter.

Summersby That's not my daughter, that's my wife.

Vole Amazing. Get rid of her.

Summersby I will not.

Vole You will.

Summersby I won't.

Vole It's none of her business.

Summersby I'll decide that. She's my wife. I'll decide.

Vole She won't like it.

Summersby She's asleep, dammit. Can't you see? Asleep!

Vole Very well. You give me no choice. This won't take long. Two words.

Summersby I refuse to play charades.

Vole Not two words, two words. I'm *Vole.*

Summersby   Vole?

Marie-Louise (*silent aside*)   Vole?

Vole   Vole!

Summersby   I'm not with you.

Vole   No. That's the whole point. You're with my wife.

Summersby   I beg your pardon?

Vole   My wife. You. She. You're lovers!

Marie-Louise *starts up, glares at* **Summersby**, *then falls back before anyone sees her.*

Summersby   You? Me? She? Lovers? I've never even heard of her.

Vole   You've only just left her, dammit. I come in the door, you jump out of the window.

Summersby   You're joking. Me, jump out of windows, a man in my position?

Vole   They always jump out of windows. Lovers. That's your position.

Summersby   I assure you I've never met your wife.

Vole   Oh yes you have. I put my key in the door, you grabbed a hat, you jumped.

Summersby   Hat? Hat?

Vole   Yes, hat.

Summersby   You're being ridiculous.

Vole   Try it on, then. Go on, try it on.

Summersby   Certainly.

He tries on the hat. It's too small.

Vole   See? See? And this one's yours.

He puts on the other hat. It's too big.

Summersby That proves nothing. Just because you've got a small head.

Vole I've got a small label. Inside my hat. Look and see.

Summersby (*examining the hat*) My God, you're Vole.

Vole I keep telling you I'm Vole.

Summersby The wine-merchant.

Vole Vole's Vintages. Exactly.

Summersby Ah. Well, in that case, why should I hide it? I love your wife.

Marie-Louise *bounds to her feet, glaring, hands out as if to strangle him. He and* **Vole** *are too furious to notice. As they whirl and turn, she falls back on the sofa just in time.*

Vole I keep telling you that.

Summersby So what about it?

Vole What about it? You're making me look a fool.

Summersby You don't need me for that.

Vole What?

Summersby All husbands look fools when their wives take lovers. If you don't believe me, ask your wife.

Vole I'm not a violent man. I'm a wine-merchant. You have to keep calm. But I'm warning you, if anyone finds out my wife has a lover, and the lover is you, I'll fillet you.

Summersby Fillet me?

Vole Bare-handed.

Summersby Charming.

Vole It's not that I've anything against you personally. I hardly know you. It's the look of the thing.

Summersby   You've lost me again.

Vole   Wine-merchants. Leaders of society. We can't have wives who have lovers. The nudges, the gossip, the giggles. Highly bad for trade.

Summersby   Highly bad?

Vole   Eight days, I'd be out of business.

Summersby   I see what you mean.

Vole   So, sir, I insist on silence.

Summersby   My lips are sealed.

Vole   Or else you get filleted.

He is now at the sideboard. Absent-mindedly, he begins to pour two glasses of brandy.

Summersby   You've got it all worked out. Except for one thing. Suppose it's me that does the filleting?

Vole   You're not a filleter.

Summersby   What makes you so sure?

Vole   Lovers don't fillet. Only husbands fillet.

Summersby   Not necessarily.

Vole   Oh yes.

He hands him one of the glasses.

Lover loves wife, husband finds out, husband fillets. That's how it goes. Cheers.

Summersby   Cheers.

Vole   Not bad.

Summersby   Oh, thank you. '87.

Vole   What did you pay for it? If you don't mind my asking?

Summersby   Sixteen and ten.

Vole   They're robbing you. (*To* **Marie-Louise**.) They're robbing him. (*To* **Summersby**.) Look, I don't do this for everyone, but I can let you have a case for fifteen-and-six the bottle.

Summersby   You're joking.

Vole   No, no. Business is business. But you'll have to be quick. I've only four left.

Summersby   I'll take them.

Vole   You won't regret it. Just let me make a note.

He takes out a notepad and pencil.

Mr . . . ? I don't even know your name.

Summersby   It's –

Vole   No, no. How silly of me. My wife'll know. 'Four cases, '85 cognac.' Is that account or cash? For cash, we allow five per cent per case.

Summersby   Well, cash, then, naturally.

Vole   Thank you very much.

Summersby   Thank you.

Vole   You'll really enjoy it.

Summersby   I look forward to it.

Marie-Louise *is seething behind her grin.*

Vole   Well, I'll say good evening.

Summersby   Good evening.

Vole   And don't forget, that other thing. Mum's the word.

Summersby   Oh, naturally.

Vole   Or else I fillet you.

He puts on the hat. It's the wrong one.

No, no, silly me.

They exchange hats. Business. At last it's sorted.

Are you sure that's your wife? Not a dressmaker's dummy?

He touches her, then leaps back.

Good God, she's alive.

Summersby   Of course she's alive.

Vole (*looking at Selby's photo*)   Nice photo. Anyone I know?

Summersby   Her husband.

Vole   You share?

Summersby   Only with a photo.

Vole   She's a very heavy sleeper. A sleeping wife, a photo. I'll make it seven per cent.

Summersby   That's very understanding.

Vole   The least I can do . . .

Exeunt, very chummily. **Marie-Louise** *bounds to her feet.*

Marie-Louise   Aaaaaaaaargh! Swine, swine, swine. I'll give you 'share'. I'll 'allow you seven per cent'. Turkish cigarettes. You swine, you swine.

She paces. **Summersby** *comes back. He doesn't see her.*

Summersby (*calling off*)   I'll expect delivery tomorrow. Good night, good night. What a charming man.

He suddenly comes face to face with **Marie-Louise**.

Summersby   Euuuugh! You're awake.

Marie-Louise   Of course I'm awake.

Summersby   How on earth did that happen?

Marie-Louise   Never mind. Explain!

Summersby   What is there to explain?

Marie-Louise   You can start with Mrs Vole.

Summersby   Who's Mrs Vole?

Marie-Louise   Vole's wife. The wife of Vole.

Summersby   Vole ... Vole ...

Marie-Louise   He was here just now.

Summersby   He was?

Marie-Louise   He's just this minute gone.

Summersby   Oh, him! What a fool.

Marie-Louise   It's not him we're talking about. It's her.

Summersby   Who's her?

Marie-Louise   His wife. Your lover.

Summersby   You think I love his wife? (*He laughs, heartily.*)

Marie-Louise   Stop doing that. You sound like a carpet-sweeper.

Summersby   You ... think ... I ... love ... his ... wife?

Marie-Louise   I heard you.

Summersby   Heard me? Oh, the play.

Marie-Louise   What play?

Summersby   We were rehearsing. The Suffrage Society play. The annual play. That man who was here –

Marie-Louise   Vole.

Summersby   Vole? Vole? Not Vole. His name's ... er, Duxbury.

Marie-Louise   Duxbury. From the Suffrage Society.

Summersby   He always plays the wronged husband. Every year. And this year, I play the lover. I didn't want to. No experience. The President insisted. 'You've got the shoulders for it,' that kind of thing.

Marie-Louise   The shoulders.

Summersby   That's what he said.

Marie-Louise   So it's just a play. What play?

Summersby   Well, you know. *Othello*.

Marie-Louise   Shakespeare's *Othello*?

Summersby   That's the one we chose.

Marie-Louise   The one where Othello argues with Vole the wine-merchant.

Summersby   That's the one.

Marie-Louise   The one written in poetry.

Summersby   What? Oh.

Marie-Louise   Tell me some. You seem to know all the part.

Summersby   I . . . euh . . .

Marie-Louise   Yes?

Summersby   I can't just do it. I have to get into the mood. Euh . . . I know. (*As if quoting.*) 'Enter Vole, with two glasses.

Here's Othello now. That's handy.
I'll give the dear old chap a glass of brandy.'

Marie-Louise   Shakespeare.

Summersby   Good, isn't it?

Marie-Louise   Go on.

Summersby   What?

Marie-Louise The next bit. The bit you were rehearsing just now, with . . . er, Duxbury.

Summersby Who's Duxbury?

Marie-Louise You're not very good at this. Stay exactly where you are.

Summersby Where are you going?

Marie-Louise You'll find out. Stay exactly where you are.

Exit.

Summersby She's awake. How did that happen? You can't wake yourself up. Someone else must have . . . The swine. The swine.

Shaftesbury-Phipps *looks gingerly in.*

Shaftesbury-Phipps Ah. Um. I say.

Summersby My dear fellow, come in, come in.

Shaftesbury-Phipps Dear fellow? Ah. (*Inching in.*) I say, is . . . ?

Summersby You've no idea what's happened. My wife. Marie-Louise. Lulu.

Shaftesbury-Phipps (*carefully*) Yes?

Summersby She's awake.

Shaftesbury-Phipps No!

Summersby Yes.

Shaftesbury-Phipps I don't believe it.

Summersby But what I want to know is, who was that swine?

Shaftesbury-Phipps What swine?

Summersby The one who woke her up. Just let me get my hands on him. I'll wake him up. I'll . . . I'll . . .

He grabs **Shaftesbury-Phipps** *and throttles him.*

Shaftesbury-Phipps   Haargh.

Summersby   Pardon? Oh, sorry. Carried away.

Shaftesbury-Phipps (*in a half-choked voice*)   It's quite all right.

Summersby   It's all his fault. Whoever he is. He woke her up. She was awake. She heard . . . everything.

Shaftesbury-Phipps (*blankly*)   Ah.

Summersby   All that rubbish about Othello.

Shaftesbury-Phipps   Yes.

Summersby   I mean, I'm not a poet. Never claimed to be.

Shaftesbury-Phipps   No, no.

Summersby   When I catch him, I'll fillet him.

Shaftesbury-Phipps (*feebly*)   Yes?

Summersby   Yes!

Shaftesbury-Phipps   Yes . . .

Enter **Vole**. *He is in another towering rage.*

Vole   Right, you.

Summersby   Not you again.

Vole   Yes, me again. I want a word with you. Get rid of your son.

Summersby   He's not my son.

Vole   You're not going to tell me he's your husband.

Summersby   He's my . . . he's my . . . (*To* **Shaftesbury-Phipps**.) What are you?

Shaftesbury-Phipps   I'm his . . . scorpion expert. How do you do?

Vole   Get rid of him.

Summersby   Oh all right. (*To* **Shaftesbury-Phipps**.) Look, wait somewhere, would you?

Shaftesbury-Phipps   Where?

Summersby   Anywhere! Anywhere you like!

Wildly, **Shaftesbury-Phipps** *rushes to the nearest door.*

Shaftesbury-Phipps   In here?

Summersby   Yes!

Shaftesbury-Phipps (*opening the door*)   It's a cupboard.

Summersby   Never mind!

Shaftesbury-Phipps   I say.

He goes into the cupboard and shuts the door.

Summersby   All right, get on with it. What is it?

Vole   You come with me.

Summersby   Come where?

Vole   To see my wife.

Summersby   No, really. It's quite all right. Not again, so soon.

Vole   What is it you do to women?

Summersby   How d'you mean?

Vole   I mean she's asleep. My wife, asleep. I come in here, your wife's asleep, I go back home, my wife's asleep. What is it you do to them?

Summersby   I'm so sorry. I'd no idea. It's something I say to them. It's ... Tell me, what did you do when you found her?

Vole   What did I do? I clapped my hand to my head, I shouted 'My God, my wife!' What did you expect me to do?

Summersby I mean, didn't you try to wake her up?

Vole Of course I didn't try to wake her up. What d'you take me for, an idiot? I said, 'He did this. Mr Seven-per-cent. He did it, he can sort it out.' So I came straight round.

Summersby How kind of you.

Vole So put your hat on and come along.

He starts pulling him towards the door.

Summersby This is ridiculous. I'm staying here. Wake her up yourself.

Vole How, exactly?

Summersby Will you stop shouting?

Vole Why should I?

Summersby You'll disturb my wife.

Vole (*loud*) Oh, sorry. (*Low.*) How, exactly?

Summersby Breathe on her palms.

Vole Pardon?

Summersby Breathe on her palms.

Vole I thought you said, 'Breathe on her palms.'

Summersby (*at the top of his voice*) I did. Breathe on her palms.

Vole (*loud*) There's no need to shout. I heard you the first time. Breathe on her palms.

Summersby So go.

Vole Pardon?

Summersby Go! Go! Go!

Vole I'll go.

False exit. Then he comes back and whispers:

One breath or two?

Summersby What?

Vole (*loud*) On each of her palms. One breath or two?

Summersby Right. That does it.

He advances on him.

Marie-Louise (*offstage*) Victor! Victor!

Summersby My God, now she's here. Quick, you.
Here.

He bundles **Vole** *out of the window, and sits nonchalantly on the
sofa. Enter* **Marie-Louise**. *She is wearing hat and coat.*

Marie-Louise What's all the shouting? More rehearsal?

Summersby Yes, yes, yes.

Marie-Louise A solo scene?

Summersby Pardon?

Marie-Louise You were shouting at yourself.

Summersby Ah. I was ... I was gargling.

Marie-Louise Well, I was shouting. In the hall. Have
you seen my umbrella?

Summersby No. (*Carefully.*) What d'you want your
umbrella for?

Marie-Louise In case it rains.

Summersby Ah, in case it ...! You're not going out?

Marie-Louise I'm going out.

Summersby At this time of night?

Marie-Louise Why not?

Summersby Where are you going?

Marie-Louise   To the President of the Suffrage Society.
To ask for a ticket for *Othello*.

Summersby   You can't do that.

Marie-Louise   Why not?

Summersby   It's private. Members only. They've no
tickets left.

Marie-Louise   In that case, I'm going home to Mother.

Summersby   Look, Lulu –

Marie-Louise   And tomorrow morning, I'm putting an
announcement in the paper. 'Victor Summersby, MP,
loves Mrs Vole.'

Summersby   You can't do that.

Marie-Louise   I think I can.

Summersby   He'll fillet me.

Marie-Louise   Exactly. Vole will fillet you. Then he'll
divorce his wife. But never mind. She'll soon find
someone else.

Summersby   Marie-Louise, I forbid it.

Marie-Louise   Stand out of my way.

Summersby   Now where are you – ?

Marie-Louise   My umbrella. The cupboard.

Summersby   Euuuuugh.

Marie-Louise   Stand still. You're like a whirling
dervish.

Summersby   Let me get it for you. The umbrella. Get
it for you . . .

He dances in front of her, to the cupboard. **Shaftesbury-
Phipps**'s *hand passes out an umbrella to him. He gives it to*
Marie-Louise.

Marie-Louise Who've you got in there?

Summersby No one, darling. Nothing.

Marie-Louise Get out of the way.

Summersby It's all right. Calm down. You're so excitable. Don't you trust me? Look at me. You can trust me, darling. Trust me. I love you. Love you, love you, love you.

Marie-Louise Love you, love you . . .

She falls under the influence, and he guides her to the sofa, where she falls asleep as before. He flops beside her, and mops his brow.

Summersby Thank God. Now just stay there. Don't move. Don't speak. Just sleep. Till this all blows over. However long it takes. Ten days, ten months, ten years. Pretend you're an ornament. (*To himself.*) Oh my God, the umbrella, the hat, the coat . . .

Shaftesbury-Phipps *pokes his head out of the cupboard.*

Shaftesbury-Phipps I say –

Summersby Oh come out, come out.

Shaftesbury-Phipps (*coming out*) Dark in there, what? Poky. Brooms, moths, spiders. Argument, feather duster. (*Sneezing vigorously.*) Foo-aaargh!

He sees **Marie-Louise**.

Shaftesbury-Phipps It's her.

Summersby Never mind that. Sit down. At the table. There.

Shaftesbury-Phipps What for?

Summersby What d'you mean, what for? A game of snap.

Shaftesbury-Phipps At this time of night?

Summersby (*through his teeth*)   If I say so, yes.

Shaftesbury-Phipps   I don't know how to play.

Summersby   What does that matter? I'd win anyway. Deal the cards.

Shaftesbury-Phipps   I don't know how to. Why can't you?

Summersby   I'm busy. I'm undressing my wife.

Shaftesbury-Phipps   Ah. I think I'd better –

Summersby   Deal the cards! Sit down!

Meanwhile he's taken off **Marie-Louise**'s *coat and hat, and stuffed them and the umbrella in the cupboard. He looks at the effect.*

Summersby   Not natural enough. I know. A book, a book . . .

He fetches a book, opens it and props it in her hands.

That's better. Isn't that better?

Shaftesbury-Phipps (*sulkily*)   Hanged if I know.

Summersby   It's got to look natural.

Shaftesbury-Phipps   Oh well, naturally . . . natural.

Summersby   She knows everything.

Shaftesbury-Phipps   Wish I did.

Summersby   That's why we're playing snap.

Shaftesbury-Phipps   Of course! Why?

Summersby   For her!

Shaftesbury-Phipps   I say. Wouldn't a duel be better?

Summersby   What are you talking about?

Shaftesbury-Phipps   I mean, chaps don't play chaps for women, at snap.

Summersby   We're not playing for her, we're playing for her. In case she wakes up.

Shaftesbury-Phipps (*with blank enthusiasm*)   Of course!

Summersby   It's perfectly simple. Just copy me.

Shaftesbury-Phipps   Whatever you say.

Summersby   I pick up my cards.

Shaftesbury-Phipps (*identical inflexion*)   I pick up my cards.

Summersby   I don't look at them.

Shaftesbury-Phipps   I don't look at them.

Summersby   I play the top card.

Shaftesbury-Phipps   I play the top card.

Summersby   Mine.

Shaftesbury-Phipps   Mine.

Summersby   Excuse me, mine.

Shaftesbury-Phipps   Excuse me, mine.

Summersby   Will you stop that?

Shaftesbury-Phipps   Will you stop that?

Summersby   Stop saying everything I say!

Shaftesbury-Phipps   You told me to.

Summersby   I didn't mean that. I didn't mean now. When she wakes up, do exactly what I do. Follow suit.

Shaftesbury-Phipps   I keep telling you: I don't know how to play.

Summersby   Just hold the cards. And smile.

*He goes and blows gently on **Marie-Louise**'s palms, then scuttles back to the table.*

Summersby　King.

Shaftesbury-Phipps　King.

Summersby　Snap.

Shaftesbury-Phipps　I say.

Marie-Louise (*waking up*)　What a lovely sleep.

Summersby (*very loud*)　Two of hearts.

Marie-Louise　What are you doing, darling?

Summersby　Playing cards with Shaftesbury-Phipps. Winning.

Shaftesbury-Phipps　Cheating. (*As he's kicked under the table.*) Ow!

Summersby　Snap. My round.

Marie-Louise　Darling . . .

Summersby　Did you sleep well, darling?

Marie-Louise　I think so. I was . . .

Summersby　You've been out like a light, darling. For at least an hour. (*To* **Shaftesbury-Phipps**.) Eh? Eh?

Shaftesbury-Phipps　Ow! Yes, darling. I mean, yes.

Marie-Louise　I've had the oddest dream.

Summersby　Dream, darling?

Shaftesbury-Phipps　Dream, dar – ?

Marie-Louise　I was wearing my hat and coat . . .

Summersby　To read a book?

Marie-Louise　I was holding my umbrella . . .

Summersby　You're still half asleep.

Marie-Louise　You've been here all evening?

Summersby　With Shaftesbury-Phipps? Of course.

Shaftesbury-Phipps Of course.

Marie-Louise You didn't go out?

Summersby Go out, me? Hahahaha. Shaftesbury-Phipps, she thinks we went out. Hahahahaha.

Shaftesbury-Phipps Heeheeheeheehee.

Marie-Louise A man didn't come?

Summersby What man?

Marie-Louise A man called Vole.

Summersby Vole, Vole . . . (*To* **Shaftesbury-Phipps**.) Do you know a man called Vole?

Shaftesbury-Phipps I knew a Vole once. General-Assistant-Adjutant to the Assistant-Adjutant-General, ninety-seven.

Marie-Louise Not him. The Vole whose wife is my husband's mistress.

Shaftesbury-Phipps Oh, that Vole. Ow! No, no, never heard of him.

Summersby Mistress. She dreamed I've a mistress. Hohohohoho. (*Pointedly to him.*) Hohoho.

Shaftesbury-Phipps Oh. Hohohohoho.

Marie-Louise You mean, you haven't?

Summersby Hahahaha.

Marie-Louise Hahahaha.

Summersby *and* **Shaftesbury-Phipps** (*pretending to burst their sides*) Hahahahahahahaha.

Marie-Louise It was all a dream.

Summersby (*as if he can't control himself*) All . . . a . . . dream . . . Hohohohohohohoho.

Marie-Louise (*weak with laughing*) His name was . . .
Vole . . .

Shaftesbury-Phipps Vole! Heeheeheehee. Vole! Voley,
Voley, Vole.

Summersby (*aside to him*) Don't overdo it.

Marie-Louise He came here. He sold you brandy. You
acted a play.

Summersby *and* **Shaftesbury-Phipps** Hahahahaha.

Marie-Louise He . . . he . . . hahahaha . . . he said
he'd fillet you.

Shaftesbury-Phipps (*practically rolling on the floor*)
HAHAHAHAHAHA.

Summersby (*coldly*) That's not funny.

Marie-Louise It is, it is.

Shaftesbury-Phipps It is.

Marie-Louise If it was a dream.

Summersby What? Of course it was a dream. Vole . . .

Shaftesbury-Phipps Wine-shop . . .

Marie-Louise Fillet you . . .

*They all burst into uncontrollable guffaws. They dance round the
room. The dancing gets wilder and wilder. It takes in another figure,*
Vole, *who has arrived and is swept up in it. No one seems to
notice. But they do notice the arrival of* **Oriole**, *because he is dead
drunk, riding a unicyle and brandishing a gun. (Or: carrying a
unicycle and a chair in one hand, and a gun in the other.) He
waves the gun about, and they scatter.* **Vole**, *in the confusion, is
spun into a corner of the room, where he crouches as inconspicuously
as he can.* **Summersby** *must not, at this stage, see him at all.*

Oriole There's far too much noise in here. A man can't
concentrate.

Summersby Oriole. Put down the gun, there's a good chap.

Oriole No, no, no. I'm perfectly in control. Perfectly. Steady hand, nerves of steel. I never thought I'd find one of these again. In *The Stage*, this morning. I haven't ridden one in forty-seven years. In all that time, never had an accident. Well, only the one. Once you've learned the knack, you never lose it. It's like riding a bicycle. It is riding a bicycle. Look. (*Lurch.*) I learned to do it in Basingstoke. The back garden of England. That's what we called it in the business. Tenth week of the summer tour. Did I ever tell you I was with a Wild West show? Big Bill Henderson and his Rogue Riders. I was a Rogue ... rode my unicycle, aimed my gun, shot cigarettes from people's mouths. (*Wistfully.*) No one smoking here? What a shame, tsk tsk tsk. It was the peak of my career, the pinnacle. I did it for the moving pictures once. On a tightrope, across the Avon Gorge. My lovely assistant went ahead ... Daredevil Dolly, a Tutu and a Tightrope ... I went next, *on* the unicycle, *with* the gun ... then came the cameraman and the director. We had terrible trouble getting a director. In the end Wizzo the Human Cannonball agreed to do it ... He was fired soon afterwards. Funny thing, I swear I saw him just last week. At the Empire. Pantomime cow. Back end. But you could see it was him, so light on his feet ... Tell me if you find this boring. The way it's done, you sit on the bike ... you get your balance ... you look straight ahead, not down ... you lift the gun ... you release the safety catch ... safety catch ... you start the song ... with me, it was always 'Your Tiny Hand is Frozen', mine was a high-class act ... you give the left-hand pedal a half-turn, and ...

He sets off, lurches and collapses in a heap.

Summersby Quick! Mousetrap! The gun! The gun!

He sits on **Oriole**. **Shaftesbury-Phipps** *takes the gun. He turns it over and over, sights down the barrel, aims it, preens.*

Shaftesbury-Phipps   Never held a gun before. Funny feeling. Aim like this? Tight trigger. Whoops!

The gun goes off. A flag saying 'Bang' comes out of it.

I say.

Summersby   Will you put that down! Give me a hand with this.

Shaftesbury-Phipps   Out, I'd say.

Summersby   Yes.

Shaftesbury-Phipps   Snoring. Knew a fellow once, in Dinnagong . . .

Summersby   Will you stop wittering about India and help me?

Shaftesbury-Phipps   Sorry. How?

Summersby   We'll dump him in the kitchen till tomorrow. Take an end.

Shaftesbury-Phipps   Which end?

Summersby   What does it matter? The nearest end!

Shaftesbury-Phipps   No need to get huffy.

They pick **Oriole** *up. Then:*

Shaftesbury-Phipps   I say –

He drops his end.

Summersby   What now?

Shaftesbury-Phipps   That fellow. Telling you about. In Dinnagong. Not kitchen. Wine-cellar.

Summersby   Pardon?

Shaftesbury-Phipps   Put him in wine-cellar. Hair of dog, all that. (*He taps his nose.*) Trust me. Know all about these things.

Summersby We'll put him in the wine-cellar, then.

Shaftesbury-Phipps I say, have you got one?

Summersby No, but we've got a rack.

Shaftesbury-Phipps Bit drastic.

Summersby Wine-rack, you fool. Come ON!

They pick **Oriole** *up again.*

Shaftesbury-Phipps Got him. Hup! Bring bike as well?

Summersby Just leave the bike. Come ON! Lulu, please hold the door.

Exeunt, carrying **Oriole**. **Marie-Louise** *closes the door behind them, turns round and is confronted by* **Vole**.

Marie-Louise Ah! You!

Vole I had to come.

Marie-Louise You do exist.

Vole I blew once, I blew twice. Nothing. I had to come.

Marie-Louise Is your name Vole?

Vole Vole's Vintages. The same.

Marie-Louise You're real.

Vole I can't wake her at all.

Marie-Louise You're not a dream.

Vole I can see you're surprised to see me. That's not surprising. I wouldn't have come. I'd have sent my seconds. But this is an emergency.

Marie-Louise I don't follow.

Vole My dear madam, your husband was with my wife.

Marie-Louise I follow.

Vole   You're very kind. But I played fair. I said to him, don't tell a soul.

Marie-Louise   Very generous.

Vole   Well, under the circumstances . . . Unfortunately, he did. So we have to.

Marie-Louise   Have to what?

Vole   Fight a duel. But not because of her. We'll say we were at a dinner party. I was the host. Lavish, generous affair. Fine wine. 'Bordeaux,' he said. 'No, Burgundy,' I said. 'Bordeaux . . .' 'Burgundy . . .' A duel's the only way to settle it. Duel to the death.

Marie-Louise   No one'll believe you.

Vole   My customers will understand.

Marie-Louise   You'll have to talk to my husband. It's nothing to do with me. After what you've told me, he's nothing to do with me.

Vole   I know what the matter is. You're furious.

Marie-Louise   Of course I'm furious.

Vole   You'd like to scream, kick the furniture, wring his wretched neck.

Marie-Louise   Well, I –

Vole   I know what it's like. I've walked those paths.

Marie-Louise   You have?

Vole   Tonight. Half an hour ago. I'll explain.

Marie-Louise   It's all right . . .

Vole   I'd been away on business. The Great Western Railways Claret Concession. Did you know, on the Temple Meads–Paddington run alone, they use forty-seven cases a week? Not to mention spirits.

Marie-Louise   I'd no idea.

Vole It's big business: bulk shipping, warehousing, glass-packers –

Marie-Louise Glass-packers?

Vole To pack the glasses.

Marie-Louise Of course.

Vole You can imagine the state I was in. I hurried home, took a cab. I usually go by bus. And when I get there, my wife's asleep on the sofa, and on the floor beside her, an enormous hat.

Marie-Louise That doesn't prove my husband –

Vole Of course it doesn't. This does.

He brandishes a letter.

Marie-Louise He wrote you a letter?

Vole Not me. My wife. I found it in her handbag.

Marie-Louise How?

Vole By looking. Listen. 'Pusskin . . .'

Marie-Louise What?

Vole That's how it starts. 'Pusskin.' That proves it's her.

Marie-Louise How?

Vole Because I always call her 'Kittikins'.

Marie-Louise Do go on.

Vole 'Pusskin, What I saw today convinced me. That photo of your husband. No wonder you're not in love with him. He's nothing but a . . .' You read the next bit. I can't go on.

Marie-Louise 'He's nothing but a . . .' I see what you mean. 'You're the darlingest little darling in all the world. The wonderfullest, preciousest little Pusskin. Especially when I compare you to my wife, that . . .' You read the next bit. I can't go on.

Vole   '... compare you to my wife, that ... h'm ...'
(*He looks at her.*) 'That ... h'm ...' (*He looks again.*)

Marie-Louise   Oh, give it to me. 'Thank goodness we
have my little secret. She doesn't suspect, and she'll never
know.' What?

Vole   Let me.

He takes the letter.

'Each time your fool of a husband goes away on
business ...'

Marie-Louise   I think you're reading my bit.

Vole   'I look into her eyes, deep into her eyes, she falls
into a deep sleep, and we have all the time in the world
to ... to ...' The swine!

Marie-Louise (*taking the letter*)   'All the time in the world
to ...' You're right. The swine! I thought I'd been feeling
very sleepy lately. And all the time it was him. He was
... The swine!

Vole   'If you only knew how much I ache for you ...'

Marie-Louise   Ache for you! Aaaah!

She leaps for his throat.

Sorry. Carried away. Give me the letter.

Vole   No.

Marie-Louise   My husband wrote it. It belongs to me.

Vole   He wrote it to my wife. It belongs to me.

Marie-Louise   Give it to me.

In the struggle, the letter is torn in half.

Half each. That's fair.

Vole   I've got the blank half.

Marie-Louise Never mind. This is the proof I need. He put me to sleep. Whenever he wanted to ... to ... The swine!

Vole Not to mention Kittikins.

Marie-Louise I know exactly what to do.

Vole So do I.

Marie-Louise Divorce.

Vole Exactly.

Marie-Louise He can pay back the dowry.

Vole So can – What did you say?

Marie-Louise I said, he can pay back the dowry.

Vole So you did. Damn, damn, damn.

Marie-Louise What d'you mean, Damn, damn, damn?

Vole I don't mean Damn, damn, damn for him. I mean Damn, damn, damn for me.

Marie-Louise But why?

Vole I hadn't thought of dowries. When we got married, Kittikins and I, her father set me up in business. Vole's Vintages.

Marie-Louise What were you before?

Vole Waiter. Railway Hotel. First-class dining room. But it's not the same.

Marie-Louise Pardon?

Vole I could never go back to that.

Marie-Louise I don't see the problem.

Vole Were you ever a waiter? No, no. You can't have been. You'd know. Wine-selling's in the blood. Once you start, you can't possibly ... No, no, no. Kittikins I can do without. But not Vole's Vintages. You do see that?

Marie-Louise It's nothing to do with me.

Vole Ah well. Life's a corkscrew, and no mistake. As we say in the wine business. If you'll excuse me . . .

Marie-Louise You're not going back to her?

Vole We'll work something out. Forty-seven cases a week! Plus spirits. We'll have a little talk. If I can only wake her up . . .

Exit. **Marie-Louise** *is absolutely furious. She paces round the room, sits on the sofa, opens the window, shuts the window, sits again, opens the cupboard to put on her hat and coat, takes them off again, picks up the photo of Charlie Selby and sits on the sofa to stare at it, then dumps it in the wastepaper basket and sits down again, still so cross that she doesn't know what to do with herself.*

Marie-Louise Men!

Enter **Summersby**.

Summersby We've dealt with him.

Marie-Louise (*through her teeth*) Grr.

Summersby We put him on the floor next to the wine-rack. He's cradling that magnum the Temperance Subcommittee sent last Christmas. He's sleeping like a baby.

Marie-Louise *doesn't answer. She is staring out front, rigid with fury.*

Summersby Marie-Louise? Lulu? Oh God, she's not . . . ? Darling? I thought I heard voices in here just now. Someone for me?

Marie-Louise Just Mr Vole. He talked to me. He won't be filleting you after all.

Summersby Well, isn't that a comfort?

Marie-Louise I will.

Summersby Pardon?

Marie-Louise (*sweetly*) He showed me a letter. I read it. I know everything. In a minute I'm going to take you to the summer house. I'm going to cut you into little pieces and feed you to the scorpions.

Summersby Lulu, darling, are you sure you've got this right? Are you sure you're not overwrought? I mean, just this afternoon you could talk of nothing but wifely duty.

Marie-Louise Wifely duty. Let's talk about husbandly duty. For example, hypnotising your beloved wife, leaving her stranded here on the sofa like a . . . like a –

Summersby Like a puppet.

Marie-Louise Thank you. Like a puppet, while you go out to play with Pusskin.

Summersby Well, that's exactly what I mean. Are you sure you've got it right? Just let me explain.

Marie-Louise I don't think you should. I really don't think you should.

Summersby It's all a mistake. It's that silly business of the Suffrage Society, all over again.

Marie-Louise What did you say?

Summersby You get things wrong. It's understandable. You're a woman, darling. A dear, sweet, adorable darling, but a woman. You misunderstand these things.

Marie-Louise It's all my fault?

Summersby I didn't say that. I don't mean that. It's just that . . . well, men take a longer view. You were perfectly happy with Charlie.

Marie-Louise Until I knew.

Summersby Until you knew, yes. But this is different.

Marie-Louise You don't keep a diary?

Summersby You don't know all the circumstances.

Marie-Louise   I know more than you think.

Summersby   This is men's work, not women's. I warn you, Lulu, if you persist in behaving in this outrageous fashion, I'll divorce you. It's three years till the General Election. I'll divorce you.

Marie-Louise   I don't think you will. If there's divorcing to be done, I'll do it.

Summersby   My darling little Lulu, you're playing with fire.

Marie-Louise   But I won't divorce you yet. Not yet.

Summersby   My darling, it's hardly for you to say.

Marie-Louise   I think it is. When I'm good and ready, I'll divorce you. But first, I want revenge.

Summersby (*tickled*)   Revenge?

Marie-Louise   Yes.

Summersby   For what?

Marie-Louise   For you being the man you are.

Summersby   All I did was practise a little domestic hypnotism.

Marie-Louise   That's how you think of it? That's all it was? You hypnotised your wife, left her lying on the sofa and went out for a little domestic adultery. But suppose, while you were out on the tiles, something else was happening back here?

Summersby   Pardon?

Marie-Louise   Imagine it, darling. The husband's away. The wife's deliciously asleep on the sofa. The window opens . . . and he comes in.

Summersby   Who comes in?

Marie-Louise   He does.

Summersby You mean this afternoon, when I . . . when you . . . he . . . you . . . ? I'll murder the swine. What's his name?

Marie-Louise I was asleep, remember?

Summersby And that swine climbed in and took advantage?

Marie-Louise I encouraged him.

Summersby I thought you said you were asleep.

Marie-Louise It was all like a lovely dream.

Summersby I'll dream him when I catch him. I'll round up everyone who was here this afternoon, and kill them all.

Marie-Louise Oh, it wasn't just this afternoon.

Summersby What did you say?

Marie-Louise How often have you slipped out to visit Pusskin?

Summersby You mean, every time – ?

Marie-Louise Don't blame yourself, my darling. A little domestic hypnotism. You weren't to know.

Summersby Why didn't you scream?

Marie-Louise No one screams. Except in nightmares. And these were dreams, not nightmares.

Summersby How can you say that?

Marie-Louise Perhaps I was dreaming it was you.

Summersby You were? You were?

Marie-Louise Of course I wasn't.

Summersby Now where are you going?

Marie-Louise The kitchen.

Summersby You're not starting to cook at this time of night.

Marie-Louise Black coffee. I've things to say to Oriole.

Summersby What's this to do with Oriole?

Marie-Louise Excuse me.

Exit. **Summersby** *goes to the window, flings it up and shouts furiously.*

Summersby Mousetrap! Cheese! Put down those scorpions and get in here!

He pours himself a drink, glowering. After a moment,
Shaftesbury-Phipps *laboriously climbs in at the window.*

Summersby What the hell d'you think you're doing?

Shaftesbury-Phipps You told me. Put down scorpions. Get in here now.

Summersby (*furiously*) Why are you like this?

Shaftesbury-Phipps Pardon? (*Looking at himself, shrugging.*) Just how I am.

Summersby Is there more? Is there any more?

Shaftesbury-Phipps You've lost me, old boy.

Summersby I'm at a crisis in my life. My own wife, the wife I loved and trusted, the wife I caringly – caringly – left asleep, in all her innocence, each time I – in all her innocence – and all you can do is play with your scorpions, climb in and out of windows, and shrug at me?

Shaftesbury-Phipps (*shrugging, then realising*) Sorry.

Summersby DON'T KEEP ON SAYING SORRY!

Shaftesbury-Phipps Sor – Oh. Rather.

Summersby Here. Drink this.

Shaftesbury-Phipps Something's upsetting you.

Summersby Oh, you've noticed?

Shaftesbury-Phipps You gave me an empty glass.

Summersby I'll give you more than an empty glass. After everything that's happened. Stand still and listen. Every time I leave her sleeping on the sofa, and slip out to see Zelda –

Shaftesbury-Phipps Hang on. Zelda?

Summersby Zelda Vole.

Shaftesbury-Phipps Oh, Pusskin. Go on.

Summersby Every time, every single time, some swine climbs in that window and –

Shaftesbury-Phipps (*after a blank pause, encouragingly*) Yes . . . ?

Summersby (*beside himself*) What d'you mean, 'Yes'? He climbs in at the window and –

Shaftesbury-Phipps Ah. Climbs in and –

Summersby Exactly.

Shaftesbury-Phipps I say, I hope you don't think . . .

Summersby Think? What?

Shaftesbury-Phipps I mean, when I climbed in just now . . .

Summersby You? Don't be ridiculous.

Shaftesbury-Phipps Beg pardon?

Summersby You don't love my wife.

Shaftesbury-Phipps (*relieved*) Oh. See what you mean. Yes. Rather. Not.

Summersby I'm going to catch the swine. I'm going to tear him limb from limb. I'm going to –

Shaftesbury-Phipps Fillet him?

Summersby   Watch me!

Shaftesbury-Phipps   Small chap, is he?

Summersby   What d'you mean, small chap?

Shaftesbury-Phipps   Smaller than you, I mean.

Summersby   What's that got to do with it?

Shaftesbury-Phipps   Bit of advice, old man. Old India hand. When it comes to filleting chaps, always check they're smaller first. First check, then fillet.

Summersby   I don't know who it is!

Shaftesbury-Phipps   Ah. May be able to help you there.

Summersby   Help? Help? How help?

Shaftesbury-Phipps   Window. Was climbing in just now. Foot caught on something. Something in flowerbed. This.

He holds out a man's shoe.

Summersby   What is it?

Shaftesbury-Phipps   Shoe. Patent-leather. Not yours. Funny thing. Not mine. Who else in this house – ?

Summersby *goes and yells through the kitchen door.*

Summersby   Oriole!

Shaftesbury-Phipps   I say. You don't think –

Summersby   This is one circus trick too many. Oriole! Are you coming in here, or do I fillet you out there?

Enter **Marie-Louise**.

Marie-Louise   Do stop shouting, Victor. And don't stand on one leg like that. You look like an outraged ostrich.

Summersby   I do, do I? And what are you doing in

here? I shouted for Oriole. I didn't shout for you.

Marie-Louise   This is my house. I can go where I like. I don't have to be shouted for.

Summersby   Your house! This is my house! I'm the master of this house.

Marie-Louise   This is our house. A marriage, a partnership of equals. Remember who said that?

Summersby   Of course I don't remember.

Marie-Louise   You did. In the *Morning Post* last Thursday. 'Wives of Britain, Stand Up for Your Rights. A clarion call by Victor Summersby.'

Summersby   That was business. This is private.

Marie-Louise   You've been on your soapbox about equality for seven years.

Summersby   On my soapbox?

Marie-Louise   Lectures, articles, evidence to committees. You're a busy and important man.

Summersby   I don't –

Marie-Louise   You told me so yourself. 'Watch me and learn,' you said. 'Women are weak; men are strong. I'll put my weight behind this campaign, like Joshua at the walls of Jericho.'

Shaftesbury-Phipps   Gosh. Joshua!

Marie-Louise   That was just before you said, 'Please don't interrupt. Dear sweet little darling, I'm your husband, your strong right arm, and husbands need peace and quiet to think. Can't you read, or sew, or something? Would you like a pet?'

Summersby   You refused to have a pet.

Marie-Louise   Then you took me in your arms, and looked into my eyes, and told me you loved me, and next minute I was deliciously asleep.

Summersby You'd had an exhausting day.

Marie-Louise And you were planning an exhausting night. With Pusskin. Well, unfortunately for you, all that's over. Vole was here. He's got your letter. He knows everything. He showed it to me, so I know everything. And tomorrow he's planning to show it to the *Morning Post*. So they'll know everything.

Summersby It's a forgery. Who'll believe it?

Marie-Louise Everyone, when they see the photographs.

Summersby There aren't any photographs.

Marie-Louise You can come in now, Oriole.

Enter **Oriole**, *with an old-fashioned plate camera.*

Summersby He's not a photographer.

Marie-Louise Of course he's a photographer. Six years on Brighton Pier. Snappy Sidney, the Prince of Portraiteers. He told me so himself.

Summersby Just a minute. Come here, you. What exactly were you doing to my wife this afternoon?

Marie-Louise Don't shout at him. I gave him three potfuls of coffee, but his head's still sore.

Summersby He'll have more than a sore head in a minute. (*To* **Oriole**.) How d'you explain this, eh? This? (*To* **Shaftesbury-Phipps**.) The shoe, the shoe!

Shaftesbury-Phipps Oh, sorry. Here.

Marie-Louise (*to* **Oriole**) There you are, Hesketh. I told you it couldn't be far away.

Summersby Hesketh! He lets you call him Hesketh?

Marie-Louise It is his name.

Summersby But you're a wife. Not his wife. My wife. Mine. You belong to me.

Marie-Louise Are you going to put that in the paper too?

Summersby How dare you? After you ... you ... you ... with him ... ?

Marie-Louise I don't know what you mean.

Summersby Every afternoon. You're asleep. On the sofa. And he climbs in, and ... and ...

Marie-Louise Who does?

Summersby Hesketh. Oriole.

Marie-Louise Oriole does what, my darling?

Summersby Well, he ... You told me so yourself.

Marie-Louise I never mentioned Oriole.

Summersby You mean there were others?

Marie-Louise I never saw their faces.

Summersby You dare say that to me? Your husband. My wife. You dare say that to me?

Marie-Louise I told you: it was a dream. I dreamed of a lover. A lovely garden, a lovely day, a lovely, lovely caterpillar, a lovely dream.

Summersby Mousetrap, Shaftesbury-Phipps, whatever your damn name is. Did you hear that?

Shaftesbury-Phipps (*ecstatic*) Ra-THER.

Summersby Women! Why do we bother? I'll never understand.

Marie-Louise It's all right. After tomorrow afternoon's paper, you may not have to.

Summersby I don't know what you mean.

Marie-Louise The photographs, darling.

Summersby There aren't any photographs.

Marie-Louise But Oriole's got his camera. And he's got his friend. Flirtatious Flossie, the Siren with the Serpent.

Summersby What?

Marie-Louise She's coming round in half an hour. With serpent.

Summersby I won't take this lying down.

Marie-Louise (*change of tone*) Of course you won't. Poor darling. Did you really believe all that? Did oo weally believe all little wifie said? Is oo head all hot? Come to wifiekins. Sit here. Sit comfy. There. There, there. Look into wifie's eyes. Poor darling, does little wifie love you, love you, love you?

Summersby Love you, love you . . .

He falls back on the sofa, hypnotised. **Shaftesbury-Phipps** *is goggling.*

Shaftesbury-Phipps I say, did you do that?

Marie-Louise Some have the knack, some haven't.

Shaftesbury-Phipps What happens now?

Marie-Louise Oriole sets up his camera. Flirtatious Flossie knocks on the door. She has her serpent. Oriole takes his photos. The *Morning Post* reporter comes. He knocks on the door – and before they open it, they wake poor dear Victor up to face the music.

Shaftesbury-Phipps And what about us?

Marie-Louise You and I, my darling, will be on the milk train to Southampton. Tomorrow morning, we set sail for India, our new life begins, and my revenge is complete.

Shaftesbury-Phipps You are wonderful. But you're a woman. I mean, not a man. However did you think of a plan like this?

Marie-Louise Oh, I'd never have managed it all on my own. It was Victor, darling. Victor. He taught me all I know.

Final curtain.

Pig in a Poke

Chat en poche

Characters

Wembley, *a London merchant*
Martha, *his wife*
Julie, *their daughter*
Oakleigh, *a society doctor, Wembley's friend*
Ernestine, *his wife*
George, *a servant*
Pennyfeather
Winstanley

The action takes place in the conservatory of Wembley's house in London, during the Edwardian age. The play is in three acts.

This version of *Pig in a Poke* was first performed, at the Oxford Playhouse and on tour, by the Oxford Stage Company in October–December 1992, with the following cast:

Wembley	Paul Greenwood
Martha	Tessa Wyatt
Julie	Tamsin Olivier
Oakleigh	Ian Burford
Ernestine	Linda Spurrier
George	Hugh Sachs
Pennyfeather	Robin Kermode
Winstanley	Grant Parsons

Directed by Mark Dornford May
Designed by Claudia Mayer
Music by Matthew Scott

In this production, the interval was placed after Act Two. There was an entracte between the first and second Acts, and Act Three was preceded by a brief dumb-show. These are printed at the end of the play and are of course optional.

Act One

The conservatory, opening on to the garden. Cane chairs, occasional tables, plants in pots, etc. A piano, littered with sheet music and music paper. It is a warm evening in summer. A meal has ended (i.e. offstage), and **Wembley**, **Martha**, **Ernestine** *and* **Oakleigh** *are drinking coffee, very relaxed and cheerful.* **Julie** *is toying dreamily with the piano.* **George** *is hovering, trying to combine his duties as coffee-server with his wish to watch what* **Julie** *is doing, and learn from it.*

Wembley   Martha my dear, that duck was delicious.

Oakleigh (*with a flourish*)   A duck of the gods.

Wembley   What?

Oakleigh   A duck of the gods.

Wembley (*unconvinced, to* **Martha**)   A duck of the gods.

Martha   Thank you. And thank *you*, Ernestine.

Wembley   What did she do?

Martha   She gave me the recipe.

Ernestine   It was nothing, nothing really. It was Albert's table.

Wembley   And George's cooking.

Martha   And Doctor Oakleigh's duck.

Oakleigh   Bagged it myself, don't you know. Dickie Daventry's shoot. Last week.

Wembley   You told us bef –

Oakleigh   Dear old Dickie. Treated her ladyship all last winter.

Wembley   You told us –

Oakleigh   Liver-spots, know what I mean? Martyr to

liver-spots. Had to spend the entire winter in Biarritz.

Wembley Biarritz, I –

Oakleigh But what can you do, eh? *Have* to make sacrifices.

Wembley Of course I –

Oakleigh As for the duck, old Indian Army recipe. Gave it to Ernestine myself. Didn't I, Teenie?

Ernestine Yes. (*To the others.*) You see, you –

Oakleigh 'Take one duck' – actually, in India it's usually 'Take one ostrich' –

Wembley Do they have ostriches in – ?

Oakleigh 'Take one duck, place hands round neck and – ' Teenie could never get the hang of this bit. Could you, old girl? 'Squeeze, old girl,' I used to say to her. Didn't I, Teenie. 'Squeeze away like a good 'un!' She had to get the ostrich-wallah in, every single time. Just couldn't seem to –

Ernestine Osbert!

Oakleigh Anyway, you take a duck, squeeze, and Bob's your uncle.

Wembley Well, whatever you did to it, it was delicious.

Oakleigh A duck of the gods. And that asparagus! Ambrosia.

Wembley No, Harrods. Martha chose it herself. My dear wife . . . the vegetable hall . . . her own fair hands.

Martha I just happened to see it. And do you know, I was so delighted with the asparagus, I left my purse on the counter. I was on the tram when I found out. If it hadn't been for a kind young man who lent me sixpence, I don't know *where* I'd be by now.

Ernestine For some people, there's always a young

man around at the right moment.

Martha   Oh, Teenie!

Wembley   Well, talking of right moments ... George, stop mooning round that piano, and bring the champagne.

George *starts to uncork and serve champagne.*

Ernestine   Champagne! How I adore champagne.

Wembley   Hold out your glasses. This is the genuine article ... all the way from Argentina.

Oakleigh   Aha! Argentina, where that dance comes from.

Wembley   What dance?

Oakleigh   The tango. (*Half-singing.*) DUM-dum-dum, da-DUM-dum-dum ...

Ernestine   Not *now*, Osbert!

Julie   Daddy, really, how can it be genuine champagne if it comes from Argentina?

Wembley   No problem at all. It says so on the bottle. 'Genuine Argentinian champagne.'

He gets to his feet.

Now then ... ladies and gentlemen ...

Ernestine (*eagerly*)   He's making a speech.

Oakleigh (*not so eagerly*)   He's always making speeches.

Martha   He's very good at them. Go on Albert, we're listening. Teenie, Julie, sit here next to me.

Clatter as they all settle their chairs to listen. **Wembley** *struggles above the noise.*

Wembley   Fellow shareholders ... er, my friends ... this has been a most profitable year to date. And so, in –

Martha Sewing! That reminds me, Teenie: I found that sewing-basket of yours this morning.

Ernestine Oh thank goodness. I thought I'd lost it.

Oakleigh Ladies . . .

Julie Shh!

Wembley Ahem!

Martha Sorry, Albert. (*To* **Ernestine**.) Remind me to give it back to you, afterwards.

Wembley (*quickly recapitulating his learned text*) Fellow share . . . my friends . . . most profitable year to date . . . and so, in celebration, I'd like to offer you a little surprise. You must all know by now that Julie . . . my daughter . . . has brought great honour to the family by composing an opera. She's written a second *Carmen*. It's full of tunes. Far better than all that Bizet business. Singing bull-fighters? No singing bull-fighters here. Anyway, I've decided to have your *Carmen* performed at Covent Garden. That's the surprise.

Applause and delighted cries from the others. He tries to make himself heard above the row.

After all, I've made a fortune out of manufacturing glucose sweets for diabetics . . . now I need something to bring lustre to the family name. And that, my dear Julie, is exactly what your *Carmen* will do. You're my child, the opera's your child . . . and since our children's children count as our own flesh and blood, I look on *Carmen* as my own creation. There. Finished.

Greatly moved, he sips champagne.

All Bravo! Bravo!

Oakleigh But how will you get it put on? I mean, dash it all, an *opera*. Covent Garden would never . . .

Wembley Ah! That's where business acumen comes in.

I heard the other day that Covent Garden are proposing to offer a contract to a great tenor ... a South American, been singing in Argentina. Amoroso.

Women   Amoroso! Oh, Amoroso! Oh!

Wembley   Yes, *that* Amoroso. You can guess what happened next. (*Pause.*) Oh, all right, I'll tell you. I sent a telegram to my old friend Pennyfeather in Buenos Aires. You don't know Pennyfeather. We were at school together. In Bolsover. That was before he went to Argentina, of course. The River Plate Fine Wines and Black Pudding Company. Anyway, I sent him a telegram. 'ENGAGE TENOR AMOROSO STOP PRICE NO OBJECT STOP SEND AT ONCE TO LONDON STOP' Now d'you see?

Another blank pause. He explains, patiently.

I get hold of this tenor ... I bind him to me with a contract ... a contract of steel ... Covent Garden comes knocking at my door, and I refuse to let them have my tenor unless they take my opera as well. That's how Wembley's *Carmen* goes down in history. Ladies and gentlemen, *Carmen*!

All   *Carmen*!

They drink. **Julie** *runs to embrace* **Wembley**.

Julie   Oh Daddy!

Wembley   Careful! I'm not an ostrich. Kiss your stepmother.

Martha   I wish you wouldn't keep calling me her stepmother. It makes me sound so old ... like some sort of preserved fruit.

Ernestine (*archly*)   Ah, Martha! Preserved fruits are often the sweetest.

Oakleigh   Take it from one who knows.

Somewhat awkward silence. Enter **George**.

George Sir, there's a gentleman from Argentina at the door. He says Mr Pennyfeather . . .

Wembley Pennyfeather! It's him . . . it's Amoroso! Quickly . . . Let's give him a really operatic welcome. You know what these tenors are like. Julie, to the piano! Your party-piece. Ernestine and Martha, tap your glasses with your spoons. Oakleigh, take the other end of this table-cloth. Bull-fighter, you fool. I'll be the bull. Ready? George, show Mr Pennyfeather in.

George *ushers in* **Pennyfeather**, *who is holding a parrot in a cage. He* (**Pennyfeather**) *is greeted by an astounding cacophony.* **George** *starts fetching in all* **Pennyfeather***'s luggage.*

Pennyfeather It's a madhouse. I've come to the wrong address. (*Shouting above the noise.*) Excuse me.

They all stop in mid-movement. Silence.

Wembley (*standing on one leg*) Well?

Pennyfeather Nothing, nothing. It's quite all right. I . . . I'll just put the parrot down. Don't mind me . . . Very nice . . . There, there . . .

Wembley (*to the others*) I told you they'd adore it. Once again, now.

The noise is renewed. **Pennyfeather** *tries again to slip out.*

Wembley Now where are you going? Artistic temperament!

Pennyfeather I wasn't going anywhere. (*Aside.*) I'm outnumbered.

The 'welcome' continues to its conclusion. Everyone flushed and panting. **Pennyfeather** *extremely apprehensive.*

Wembley Now we can talk. First of all, let me introduce everybody. (*Rapidly.*) My daughter . . . my dear wife . . . Doctor and Mrs Oakleigh, our dear friends, who're spending a few weeks as our guests . . .

Martha (*aside*)   The young man from the tram, who lent me sixpence.

Pennyfeather (*aside*)   The lady who lost her purse. In a madhouse. What a shame.

Wembley   There. Now you know everyone. I'm really glad to meet you at last. Tell me, how is Pennyfeather?

Pennyfeather   Who? Father?

Wembley   Father? You don't understand. I asked if Pennyfeather . . .

Pennyfeather   You did say Pennyfeather?

Wembley   Of course I said Pennyfeather. (*To the others.*) What's wrong with him?

Pennyfeather   You *are* Mr Wembley?

Wembley   Well, naturally. Who did you think I was?

Pennyfeather   I thought I was in a madhouse.

Wembley   A madhouse? This house? A madhouse?

Pennyfeather   You mean that banging, that singing . . . that's *normal* in England?

Ernestine   We were giving you an operatic welcome.

Pennyfeather   Ai marmelita.

Ernestine (*aside*)   'That's *normal* in England?' What dulcet tones!

Pennyfeather   Well, Mr Wembley, I'm really pleased to meet you. I've got a letter for you, at the bottom of one of these suitcases.

Wembley   A letter? From Pennyfeather? One of my oldest friends. How is he, Pennyfeather?

Pennyfeather   He's very well, Father, thank you.

He rummages in one of the suitcases. Meanwhile.

Wembley (*aside*)   Why does he keep saying Father? He must be a Roman Catholic. I suppose, in Argentina, they all are. (*To the others.*) Well, how d'you like my tenor?

Martha   Magnificent!

Ernestine   Superb!

Oakleigh   He looks fit as a fiddle. They care a lot about that, you know, their health. Knew a chappie once, in Poona . . .

Ernestine   Osbert, *what* was that dance again?

Oakleigh   The tango. Want me to show you how?

Ernestine   Not now. (*Smouldering at* **Pennyfeather**.) But yes.

Martha (*also smouldering*)   You can show me, too.

Pennyfeather (*as he rummages, aside*)   What funny people! Father said to me in Buenos Aires, six months ago yesterday, 'Look, son, you've got to go to England. Learn the black-pudding business from the bottom up. But I don't want you sowing wild oats in that country of wickedness and vice. Go to Wembley. Stay with my old friend Wembley. Be like a son to him; do anything he says. He knows what's what. He's made his way in business. He knows how things are done.' That's true. You can tell at a glance. He'll stop me sowing wild oats, I'm sure of that.

Wembley (*coming to join him*)   I really am delighted to meet you. Have you eaten yet?

Pennyfeather   Nothing since this morning but ensaimadas.

Wembley   I knew it: you've got that look about you. What would you like? An Eccles cake? Black pudding? A plate of tripe?

Pennyfeather   Is that what you eat in England?

Martha   No, no, no. Remember your *voice*.

Pennyfeather   Personally, I always try to forget it.

Ernestine (*archly*)   What a blessing we're not all like you!

Pennyfeather   I can see you're a singer.

Ernestine   A singer? Silly boy!

Wembley   George. George! Come away from that piano. Bring food. Food.

George *shoots him a look.*

Wembley   *I* don't know what. Whatever the ladies here decide.

Martha   Don't worry. We'll find *just* the thing.

The women and **George** *go into a huddle.*

Pennyfeather (*aside*)   Isn't she delightful? But whose wife is she? Wembley's or the other one's? They were all introduced in a bunch.

Exit **George**.

Wembley   Do sit down. We've finished supper. We were having coffee. And champagne. We often have champagne.

Pennyfeather   Champagne. Well, don't mind me. I'll join in, wherever you've got to. I won't disturb you.

Wembley   Oakleigh, pour him a glass, there's a good fellow.

Oakleigh   There's none left. The bottle's empty.

Wembley   Well give him yours, then.

Oakleigh   I say!

Pennyfeather   Gentlemen . . . and ladies . . . your health.

All but **Oakleigh** *drink the toast.*

Oakleigh (*muttering*)   Health, I'm sure.

Enter **George**.

George   I'm back, sir.

Wembley   Well?

George   Yes, sir.

Wembley   Did you bring it?

Blank look from **George**.

Wembley   The food!

George   No. But I did bring this. It was in the kitchen.

He holds up **Ernestine**'*s sewing-basket.*

Martha   Ah. The sewing-basket.

Ernestine   Oh, yes.

Martha (*brightly, to* **Pennyfeather**)   George had it all the time.

Pennyfeather   How nice.

Martha   It was lost, and now it's found. Teenie was *beside* herself. Weren't you, *beside* yourself?

Ernestine (*through her teeth*)   If you say so.

Wembley   Now then, young man. I won't hear of you lodging anywhere but here. Stoke Newington's nice and open – excellent for the voice. No, don't refuse. I'll put you in the room next to mine, overlooking the garden. Your own piano . . .

Pennyfeather   Piano? What will I want with a . . . ?

Wembley (*roguishly*)   *You'll* find a use for it.

Pennyfeather   I suppose I can hang my suits on it.

Julie   Would you like some coffee?

Wembley (*snatching the cup*)   No no, it's too stimulating!

Give him a cup of hot milk.

Pennyfeather But I hate . . .

Oakleigh Don't be silly. It soothes the throat.

Pennyfeather My throat doesn't need soothing.

Oakleigh Dear boy, don't argue. When I was in Ranjipoor . . .

Ernestine That'll do, Osbert.

Oakleigh I was just tellin' the fellow –

Ernestine That'll do. (*To* **Pennyfeather**.) You *must* have milk.

Julie George will fetch you a cup.

Wembley That's right, ladies. Look after our future star. (*To* **Pennyfeather**.) This is the young lady who wrote the opera.

Pennyfeather Saint Cecilia herself!

Wembley No, Julie.

Pennyfeather The goddess of music.

Julie (*simpering*) Oh . . .

Wembley I'm sure Pennyfeather told you all about it.

Pennyfeather Not exactly. I mean, he didn't go into details.

Wembley Well, she's the one that wrote it.

Pennyfeather (*somewhat blankly*) Splendid! Excellent!

Wembley (*aside to* **Julie**) Did you hear that? 'Excellent'!

Julie (*to him*) He's so . . . so *different* from my fiancé. I wonder if he knows how to dance the tango. Daddy, you must give him *anything* he asks.

Martha (*to* **Pennyfeather**) Can I tempt you?

Pennyfeather   Pardon? Oh, a drink. My dear lady, tempt me, yes of course. What kind is it? (*Reading label.*) Macclesfield cognac. (*Hastily.*) Another time, perhaps.

Martha (*grandly*)   Is, ah, tout le monde fini? In that case, shall we withdraw to the, ah, withdrawing room?

Ernestine   The withdrawing room?

Martha (*aside, through her teeth*)   Through here. (*Gaily.*) Follow me, everyone.

Wembley   Leave the young man in here with me, if you don't mind. He and I have matters to discuss.

Martha   Certainly, Albert. (*Roguishly to* **Pennyfeather**.) Don't be long!

All save **Wembley** *and* **Pennyfeather** *take coffee-cups and liqueur glasses and exeunt.*

Wembley   Right. Let's get down to business right away. No sense in beating about the bush.

Pennyfeather   No, no.

Wembley   All I want to know is, will you accept three hundred a month?

Pennyfeather   Three hundred?

Wembley   Three hundred pounds a month, plus free board, lodging, and laundry.

Pennyfeather   Laundry?

Wembley   Well, naturally laundry.

Pennyfeather   Oh, naturally, laundry. Naturally.

Wembley   Well?

Pennyfeather   You're joking.

Wembley   Of course I'm not joking. What did you get in Argentina, for heaven's sake?

Pennyfeather   Ten pounds.

Wembley   Well, that's three hundred, isn't it?

Pennyfeather   How d'you mean, ten pounds is three hundred?

Wembley   For goodness' sake! There are thirty days in a month. Thirty times ten, three hundred pounds.

Pennyfeather   But...

Wembley   All right, I won't haggle. Three hundred and fifty. Will three hundred and fifty pounds a month suit you?

Pennyfeather   Ai marmelita.

Wembley   Never mind 'I marmalade'. Do you accept?

Pennyfeather   Good heavens!

Wembley   We'll sign an official contract, so that each of us knows where he stands. We must know where we stand.

Pennyfeather   So long as it's watertight.

Wembley   Eh?

Pennyfeather   Not stand on the burning deck.

Wembley   Oh. Theatre slang.

He takes an impressive contract from the escritoire.

The most important thing is to have a heavy penalty clause. £4000 if you break contract, that sort of thing.

Pennyfeather   Don't worry, I won't break contract. But £350 a month. What on earth do *I* have to do for *you*?

Wembley   Sing. Whenever and wherever I decide.

Pennyfeather   You're joking. Sing?

Wembley   It's what you're being paid for, isn't it?

Pennyfeather You *are* joking.

Wembley At these prices, I never joke. You're not refusing, are you?

Pennyfeather At these prices, I never refuse. But I really ought to warn you, in Argentina whenever I tried to sing, they shouted 'Shut your mouth before a bird flies in.'

Wembley It's a ten-year contract. All you have to do is sign. Have a look. (*As* **Pennyfeather** *pores over the contract.*) Look, here. £350 on the one side, and £4000 on the other. That's the important part.

Pennyfeather 'In the presence of X and Y' . . . ?

Wembley We'll find X and Y later. 'This agreement was signed between Albert Sleightholme Wembley, glucose manufacturer of the first part, and Amoroso . . .'

Pennyfeather Who's Amoroso?

Wembley You are, you fool.

Pennyfeather Amoroso? Ah, a stage name.

Wembley Oh, is it really? What's your real name, then?

Pennyfeather Well, naturally, the same as my father's.

Wembley Well, naturally. But what is it?

Pennyfeather Pennyfeather, of course. Miguel Rodrigo Jesus-Maria de las Mantillas y Commancheros Pennyfeather.

Wembley Pennyfeather! No, no, not another word! You poor fellow, now I see. Pennyfeather's your *father*.

Pennyfeather I know he is. (*Aside.*) He's very strange.

Wembley (*aside, in anguish*) Pennyfeather's son! He's got a son! Who'd have thought it? A married man, with children – he's got a son.

Pennyfeather Father said to me, go and see
Wembley . . .

Wembley (*interrupting*) Father? He lets you call him
Father?

Pennyfeather Why should he not?

Wembley You're sure he *is* your father?

Pennyfeather What?

Wembley I mean, what does his wife say?

Pennyfeather What d'you expect her to say?

Wembley She does know you're his son?

Pennyfeather Who? Dona Barbara-Luisa de Santu
Espirito y Tapas? Mama?

Wembley Mama. Oh! She lets you call her mama?

Pennyfeather In Argentina, we do this thing.

Wembley But his son – what does his son think of it?
Seeing you in the family, in the place that should be his
alone?

Pennyfeather What son?

Wembley Your father's son, of course.

Pennyfeather (*amazed*) You mean . . . Father's got a
son?

Wembley I last met him thirteen years ago. He was a
lot younger than you are, then.

Pennyfeather A son! Whose son is this?

Wembley Well, whose d'you think? (*As* **Pennyfeather**
still looks blank.) Ah! I've got it. You've never met, the two
of you.

Pennyfeather Never. I don't believe it. I'm going to
write to Father.

Wembley No, no. That would never do. The bastard

son fighting the legitimate heir!

Pennyfeather   I'd have a perfect right.

Wembley   Calm down. Don't excite yourself. What's past is past. To know all is to forgive all. Least said, soonest mended. We'll say no more about it. Let's sign the contract.

Grumpily, **Pennyfeather** *signs.*

Wembley   Oh! You're putting 'Pennyfeather'. How embarrassing! Look, put after it, 'also known as Amoroso'. That'll make everything crystal clear.

Pennyfeather   There.

Wembley   Good. Here's a copy for you ... and one for me. Now you're my own private tenor.

Pennyfeather (*formally*)   I weesh you yoy.

Wembley   I've been a patron of the arts since I was *this* high. Now, come with me. I'll show you your room. Oh, one thing. You won't play the piano too early in the morning, will you, and wake everyone up?

Pennyfeather   Don't worry. No fear of that.

He picks up the parrot.

Wembley   The ladies here like to sleep in.

Pennyfeather   Ah, the ladies! (*Aside to parrot.*) Especially that adorable creature, Mrs ... what's her name? I've not been able to think of anything else, since the tram this morning.

Wembley (*at the door*)   This way ...

Exit. **Pennyfeather** *is about to follow, when he finds* **Ernestine***'s sewing-basket.*

Pennyfeather   The sewing-basket! It's hers! 'It was lost, and now it's found,' she said. I know. I'll write her a note.

He does.

'Ever since I bumped into you, I've loved you passionately.' There! Now, into the basket...

Wembley *returns.*

Wembley   Isn't that Mrs Oakleigh's sewing-basket?

Pennyfeather   Mrs Oakleigh ... Ah! Not your wife's.

Wembley   Wrong colour.

Pennyfeather   Ai Pepita! Marmelito mio!

Wembley   Marmalade again! Is something the matter?

Pennyfeather   No, no, no, no, no, no. Mr Wembley, can you keep a secret?

Wembley   Of course I can. If there's no alternative.

Pennyfeather   I find Mrs Oakleigh adorable. Qué confusión!

Wembley   You're joking. Are your eyes quite ...? She's got a face like a ... And her bosom ... it's never-ending ... it goes on and on...

Pennyfeather   I'm intoxicated by it. I can't help myself.

Wembley   Amazing. Artistic temperament.

Pennyfeather   Pardon?

Wembley   Incredible.

They look at each other. **George** *ushers in* **Winstanley**.

George   Mr Winstanley, sir.

Winstanley (*shaking hands*)   Good evening, father-in-law-to-be.

Wembley (*introducing them*)   Mr Winstanley, my future son-in-law ... Mr Pennyfeather, our own little Caruso.

Winstanley   Ah! You're a painter.

Wembley   No, no. He's at Covent Garden.

Winstanley   A vegetable-porter?

Wembley   No, no. (*Aside to* **Pennyfeather**.) Sherlock Holmes has nothing to fear from *this* one.

Pennyfeather   A detective, is he?

Winstanley   I'm studying to be a painter. Like my father.

Pennyfeather   I see. Your father's studying . . .

Winstanley   No, no. He's dead. He painted animals.

Wembley   He painted my son-in-law once. What a likeness!

Winstanley   So I thought I might do the same. One day. After all, one has to do something.

Pennyfeather   Well, my father deals in spirits.

Winstanley   He's a medium?

Pennyfeather   A wine-merchant. Well, black-puddings too. But chiefly wines and spirits. I deal in those too, whenever I get the chance.

Winstanley   I feel really at home with animals.

Pennyfeather   I feel really at home with alcohol.

They shake hands.

Pennyfeather   Delighted.

Winstanley   Enchanted.

Wembley   Well, now, Winstanley, we'll leave you. I'll send Julie in.

Winstanley   Yes please.

Wembley   This way, Pennyfeather.

He and **Pennyfeather** *go.* **Winstanley** *speaks to the mirror.*

Winstanley   Mama said to me, take your fiancée a
bouquet of flowers ... it's the done thing. So, I bought a
bouquet. Then, on the way, I called on Daisy, and she
thought it was for her. That's why I haven't ... Daisy,
yes. Oh, you know Daisy? Adorable creature ... and so
fit. All that cycling. (*Singing.*) 'Daisy, Daisy, give me your
answer, do ...' With her all I have to do is pedal. I don't
have to stammer all the time. Stammer, that's right.
Mama advised me to do that here every time I said
anything ... to give me time to think. Oh, you have that
problem too? How silly marriage is! Daisy agrees with me.
She even told me my fortune. We were on the tandem.
In Esher, I think it was.

'If Winstanley pedals alone, he'll find life uphill;
    If he shares it with Daisy, it'll be such a thrill.'

So there you are. I can't fight poetry.

He strikes poses, preening. Enter **Julie**.

Julie   (*muttering to herself*)   'Go and talk to your fiancé. Go
along.' Oh really, Father. Can't you see my fiancé bores
me? That silly stammer. (*Seeing* **Winstanley**.) Oh.

Winstanley   Miss Wembley. Ah! (*Holding out his hand.*) G-
g-good evening, J-J-Julie. H-h-how are you?

Instead of stammering, **Julie** *giggles in a silly but musical way
before she speaks.*

Julie   Hee-hee-hee. How's your mama? Well, I trust.

Winstanley   V-v-very well, in herself. But her s-s-sister's
s-s-sick, and her p-p-pet p-p-poodle p-p-passed away. She's
struck all of a he-he-heap.

Julie   Hee-hee-hee. How sad.

Winstanley   S-s-sad.

Pause. They stare pensively at the audience.

Julie   Hee-hee-hee. You seem pensive.

Winstanley Y-y-yes. I'm l-l-like that. I l-l-look before I l-l-leap.

Julie Hee-hee-hee. How sensible!

Another pause, then they blurt out together.

Both Miss Wembley/Mr Winstanley . . . after you . . . no, no, after you.

Julie Sssh! Mrs Oakleigh! Later!

*Enter **Ernestine**. She is dreamily imagining herself dancing the tango.*

Winstanley But I say, we –

Julie Later.

Winstanley Goo-good evening, dear lady.

Ernestine Don't let me disturb you. Don't mind me.

***Julie** and **Winstanley** sit down, formally apart. **Ernestine** is upstage. She finds the sewing-basket and talks to it.*

Ernestine Keep an eye on them. That's what Albert said. And don't make it obvious. Martha's taking second watch.

Winstanley Y-y-you'd hardly b-b-believe it, my d-d-dear, but in this heat I drink g-g-gallons of t-t-tea.

Julie Hee-hee-hee. How fascinating.

***Ernestine** has opened her sewing-basket.*

Ernestine Goodness!

Julie What's the matter?

Ernestine Nothing. Nothing at all. My sewing-basket.

*She surreptitiously opens **Pennyfeather***'s note.*

Ernestine 'Ever since I bumped into you, I've loved you passionately.' It's him. The tenor! I knew at once that he was interested. 'Ever since I bumped into you . . .'

Heavens, he must have been the one. In Trafalgar
Square, in the fog this morning. 'Good grief, how lumpy
Nelson's Column is!' It must have been him. What shall I
do? Shall I encourage him? Shall I take pity on the poor
young man . . . ?

She gets up, agitated. The young people rise politely.

Don't get up, children. Don't get up for Teenie.

Exit.

Winstanley Now, what did you want to say to me?

Julie I daren't tell you. You go first.

Winstanley I daren't either.

Julie I'd rather write a note.

Winstanley So would I.

Julie Here's some paper.

They write, then exchange notes and read together.

Both 'Love cannot be forced on anyone . . .' Oh.

Julie Have we got the wrong notes?

They change notes, and start again.

Both 'Love cannot be forced on anyone. We were not
made for each other . . .'

Julie Extraordinary.

Winstanley How wonderful.

Julie You mean . . .

Both . . . you aren't in love with me?

Julie Just a minute! It's gone . . . your stammer.

Winstanley That's not a stammer, it's a precaution.
Mama said . . .

Julie Just like my Hee-hee-hee . . .

Winstanley   And I thought 'She's a musician. She's practising her scales.'

Julie   How well we'll get on now we're not going to be married.

Winstanley   I do hope so.

Julie   Do you know the tango?

Winstanley   Rath-ER!

Julie   I've been learning too.

They tango a bit.

Winstanley   I say, do you ride a bicycle at all?

Julie   No, no, we mustn't. Daddy.

Winstanley   Ah yes. Mama.

Julie   For their sakes . . .

Winstanley   We must go on pretending . . .

Julie   That nothing's changed . . .

Winstanley   That everything's . . .

Both   Just as it was before.

Julie   Ssh! My stepmother!

Enter **Martha**.

Winstanley   D-d-dear lady . . .

Martha   Don't let me disturb you. Julie, you haven't seen the tenor, have you?

Julie   No.

Martha   I can't find him anywhere. I must pay him back the sixpence I borrowed. Isn't there some paper here I could wrap it in? It looks so *common*, giving people unclothed money.

Winstanley   Hee-hee-hee. If you'll excuse me, Miss

Wembley.

Julie C-c-certainly.

Martha Mr Winstanley, must you really go?

Winstanley For the moment, dear lady. (*To* **Julie**.)
Hee-hee-hee . . .

Julie I'll s-s-see you to the d-d-door.

Exeunt. **Martha** *has found some paper, an old letter, and reads it.*

Martha An old letter Ernestine wrote me when she was
in Bournemouth with her husband. 'You'll never imagine
the souvenirs I've bought . . . trunksful . . . I know I'm
acting foolishly, and shall again. My husband must never
know. Look after Tweetie-pie . . . and if you could be an
angel, and buy me a pair of garters . . . Hugs and kisses,
Ernestine Oakleigh.' I shan't need this again.

She wraps the sixpence up in the letter.

There, wrapped up like that . . . much less obvious.

Enter **Pennyfeather**, *muffled in scarves.*

Pennyfeather Phew! If I don't catch my death of heat,
I'll be lucky.

Martha The tenor! Good gracious, are you cold?

Pennyfeather No, Mr Wembley is. (*Aside.*) The basket's
been moved. She must have found . . .

Martha (*formally: she wants to return the sixpence*) Mr
Pennyfeather . . .

Pennyfeather Yes, dear lady?

Martha I've been trying to find you all evening,
because of what I had from you.

Pennyfeather (*aside*) My note! (*Aloud.*) You weren't
offended?

Martha One should never be offended by a chivalrous
action.

Pennyfeather   I reesk-éd everytheeng . . .

Martha   No, no, I was grateful.

Pennyfeather   Grateful?

Martha   Grateful.

Pennyfeather (*aside*)   Ai-me! (*To her.*) What more can I say?

Martha   Oh, there's no need for more. What there was was quite enough.

Pennyfeather   You say me: *enough*?

Martha   Do you do things differently in Argentina?

Pennyfeather (*over-cheerfully*)   Well now, fair lady, it depends how well you get on.

Martha (*blankly*)   Pardon? Oh, with the conductor, you mean.

Pennyfeather   With the conductor! You can tell this is a musical household. But never mind. The main thing is that you weren't offended.

Martha   Of course I wasn't. You were doing me a favour.

Pennyfeather   I see what you mean. If you put it like that . . .

Martha (*warmly*)   And I certainly don't intend to be outdone.

She hands him the wrapped money.

Here you are.

Pennyfeather (*taken aback*)   An answer . . . so soon? In London you waste no time. But what is this? A pebb-el.

He shakes the note and holds it to his ear.

Martha   You can open it later. If you'll excuse me, now . . .

Pennyfeather   I'll treasure thees . . . what you give me here . . . for the rest of my life. Treasure eet.

Martha   Well, if you want to. Thrift is a noble virtue, after all.

She smiles and exit.

Pennyfeather   Now, what did she write to me?

He opens the package.

Goodness, it was not a pebb-el, it was money. The sixpence. She needn't have paid that back. (*Reads.*) 'I know I'm acting foolishly, and shall again . . .' (*Aloud.*) Dios mio! (*Reads.*) 'My husband must never know.' I do agree. 'Look after Tweetie-pie . . .' Tweetie-pie? The husband. 'If you could be an angel, and buy me a pair of garters . . .' Garters! So soon! It's that London rush again. I'll buy her a boxful, right away. 'Hugs and kisses. Ernestine Oakleigh.' Ai Pepita! Qué confusión!

Enter **Ernestine** *upstage, unnoticed.*

Ernestine (*aside*)   The tenor!

Pennyfeather   Oh, Ernestine, Ernestine my darling . . .

Ernestine   Oh!

Pennyfeather   Garters, my sweet? You shall have them! A dozen, a bushel, a hundredweight. Promise to be true to me, Ernestine, just promise to be true.

Ernestine (*coming forward*)   Sir, I love another . . . my husband.

Pennyfeather   Eh? (*Coldly formal.*) Dear lady, I'm sure you do.

Ernestine (*hastily*)   I mean, I love my husband . . . but not to the exclusion of all *other* affections . . .

Pennyfeather (*even more frostily*)   Really?

Ernestine   Don't blush.

Pennyfeather   I'm not blushing.

Ernestine   When I think of Nelson's Column ... Don't blench.

Pennyfeather   I don't know how to blench.

Ernestine   People bump into each other all the time. It's the speed of modern life. This time was no different from any other. One coming down the steps, the other going up. I pressed myself against the Column, and ... *he* ... bumped into me. Don't turn green.

Pennyfeather   I'm not a chameleon.

Ernestine   This chance meeting kindled a spark. I couldn't see him, thanks to the fog, but I heard his enthralling voice.

Pennyfeather   What voice is thees?

Ernestine   Please, let me hear you say (*With passion.*) 'Good grief, how lumpy Nelson's Column is.'

Pennyfeather (*flatly*)   Good grief, how lumpy Nelson's Column is.

Ernestine   It's not the same voice at all. But of course! There isn't any fog.

Pennyfeather   In here? I'm not so sure.

Ernestine   How can I tell you how that meeting by Nelson's Column crushed me ... bruised me ... ?

Pennyfeather   It *is* made of solid stone.

Ernestine   I've been haunted ever since, by the very thought. The blood pounds in my veins ... my heart throbs wildly ... thud, thud, thud, all the time.

Pennyfeather   Dear lady!

He half moves to her; she half moves to him. They stand a moment, wondering what to do next. Enter **Wembley**, **Martha**, **Julie** *and* **Oakleigh**.

Wembley   My dears, I'm so excited. What a voice he has! Enthralling!

Oakleigh   I say! You've heard him sing?

Wembley   No, but I've heard him cough. What depth! What range!

Oakleigh   I say!

Wembley   I wrote off at once to Covent Garden for an audition.

Martha   Couldn't you persuade him to sing something for us now?

Wembley   With pleasure. My dear Pennyfeather ... (*Hastily, to the others.*) By the way, I forgot to mention, he's Pennyfeather's illegitimate son. But don't bring it up in conversation. You'll embarrass him.

Oakleigh   Poor fellow.

He shakes **Pennyfeather**'s *hand.*

Oakleigh   My dear old boy, one does understand.

Pennyfeather   How kind of you.

Oakleigh   The wounds of the heart: one understands *entirely*.

Wembley   Now, lad, I was wondering ... would you sing something for us?

Pennyfeather   You're joking.

Wembley   No, no. The contract ...

Martha   Please say you will ... for my sake.

Pennyfeather   Ah! But I haven't any voice.

Ernestine Aha, they all say that.

Pennyfeather Do they? (*Aside.*) Who do?

Julie I'll accompany you.

Pennyfeather Where, Miss Wembley?

Julie At the piano, of course.

Pennyfeather There's no need. I'll get there on my own . . .

Julie I mean, I'll play your accompaniment on the piano.

Pennyfeather Oh . . . you . . . my . . . What I meant was, pianos always seem to be out of tune, when I sing.

Martha Never mind. We'll make allowances.

Pennyfeather Well, if you insist, I'll do my best.

All (*delighted*) Aah.

Pennyfeather (*aside to* **Martha**) You've made me very happy.

Martha Pardon?

Pennyfeather I'll get you all the garters you'll ever need.

Martha Garters?

Julie What would you like to sing?

Pennyfeather Oh, songs are all the same to me. I know one piece quite well. 'Come into the garden, Ma-ood.'

Julie I know that too. I've made an arrangement.

Pennyfeather Who with?

Ernestine (*aside to* **Martha**) What did he say to you?

Martha He offered me garters.

Ernestine   Me too. He must be some kind of salesman.

Julie (*at the piano*)   Are you ready?

Pennyfeather (*striking a pose*)   Ready.

*He beams at the company, especially at **Martha**.*

Martha (*flustered*). Hahaha!

Julie *starts her introduction.* **Pennyfeather** *clears his throat.*

Pennyfeather   Haarrrgh! Ahaaaaaaaaargh!

Patter of delighted applause.

Wembley   What did I tell you?

Martha   A true artist.

Ernestine   And such a sweet boy.

Oakleigh   Ssh!

Pennyfeather (*to* **Julie**)   Begin again, my dear. I catch you up.

She plays. He sings, at last. Tonelessly.

'Come into the garden, Ma-ood,
For the bat-black night has fled.
Come into the garden, Ma-ood . . .'

– and so on, to the end of the stanza. Then he bows and smiles. Tableau: stunned silence. Quick curtain.

Act Two

As the curtain rises, **Oakleigh** *and* **Ernestine** *are discovered.* **Oakleigh** *is teaching her the tango. She is distracted, and rather cross with him.*

Oakleigh No, no, no, old girl. Slide, slide.

Ernestine I can't do this.

Oakleigh Of course you can. Look here, watch me.

Ernestine (*distractedly*) No, I mean, I can't do this now. Can't you see I'm busy?

Oakleigh You aren't.

Ernestine I am. Please go away. (*Crossly.*) Oh, later, Osbert, later.

Oakleigh Very well. I'll find Martha. She was asking for a lesson too.

He tangoes out. **Ernestine** *starts searching.*

Ernestine (*to herself*) Where on earth can I have left it? It was here earlier on. Surely he can't have ... Ah!

She finds her sewing-basket, and sits down with it.

I hope my needle-case is still ... Good heavens! Another note. It's from Pennyfeather. He's so headstrong, leaving them in here. Anyone could find them ...

She opens the note and reads, not noticing that **Winstanley** *has come quietly in and now stands irresolute, not seeing her.*

Ernestine 'I've got to talk to you ...'

Winstanley (*startled*) Harg.

Ernestine 'You chose to encourage me. I risk everything.'

Winstanley Pardon?

Ernestine (*to herself*) I don't understand him at all: so hot-blooded on paper, so frosty when he speaks.

Winstanley She must be as deaf as a post. Madam!

Ernestine (*jumping*) Aah! What is it?

Winstanley (*shouting*) It's all right.

Ernestine There's no need to shout.

Winstanley I'm sorry. I murmured . . . twice. I was just –

Ernestine (*distractedly*) In a moment, in a moment. (*Reading.*) 'I risk everything . . .'

Winstanley I've had a dismal night.

Ernestine 'Too many people can disturb us during the day. Meet me tonight . . .'

Winstanley The thing is: you don't happen to know: my fiancée . . . ?

Ernestine 'In the greenhouse.'

Winstanley Ah. Thank you. I'll go at once.

Exit.

Ernestine The greenhouse! He's sure of himself. (*Reading.*) 'I swear your honour will not be compromised.' (*Regretfully.*) Oh . . . ! 'If you agree to meet me, tell your husband to wave his handkerchief in the air the next time he sees me, turn around and sing either 'Goosy Goosy Gander' or 'The Grand Old Duke of York', whichever you prefer. Let me know the hour by drawing lines on his back in chalk. You don't know how happy you'll make me. By the way, I've found a garter-shop, but they want to know the size.' He thinks of nothing else!

Oakleigh *comes in, very roguish and ebullient.*

Oakleigh *She* got it in a moment.

Ernestine (*guilty start*) Ah!

Oakleigh It really is easy, once you know the steps.

He tangoes about, sees **Ernestine** *trying to hide the letter.*

Oakleigh What's that you're reading, Teenie? A love-letter?

Ernestine Nothing. A silly note. Nothing important.

Oakleigh (*exaggeratedly*) Nonsense, Ernestine. You're deceiving me. It's a love-letter. At your age! Let me see it at once!

Ernestine I will not.

Oakleigh You will!

Ernestine I won't!

Oakleigh Yes!

Ernestine No!

Oakleigh (*snatching at it*) Yes!

Ernestine Heavens, what an Othello you are.

She gives him the letter.

Oakleigh This is that tenor's writing. *Very* South American.

Ernestine Osbert, don't read it. It's not my letter.

Oakleigh Pardon?

Ernestine Can you keep a secret to the grave?

Oakleigh And beyond. If it's grave enough. Har, har.

Ernestine All right. That letter belongs to ... Martha Wembley.

Oakleigh Martha? I'm not a bit surprised. Chappie did tell her he loved her, right in front of me. So there's no reason for not putting it in a letter, later.

Ernestine   A letter?

Oakleigh   Later. Well, 'nuff said. 'Nuff said.

Ernestine   What d'you mean?

Oakleigh   Simple: I deliver it.

Ernestine   Oh, no.

Oakleigh   Whyever not?

Ernestine   You can't.

Oakleigh   I'll do my damnedest.

Ernestine   It's quite impossible.

Oakleigh   No, no, no. It's addressed to her ... I deliver it. It's simple.

Enter **Martha**.

Ernestine   Oh, no!

She rushes out.

Martha   Osbert. Here you are.

Oakleigh   Here I am, my dear.

Martha   Wasn't that Teenie, running away?

Oakleigh   'Spect so. Yes. Entirely.

Martha   Were you teaching her the tango again?

Oakleigh   Not that exactly.

Martha   We'll all be expert soon. I've been showing Albert.

Oakleigh   Yes. (*Suddenly serious.*) Haarumph. How is Albert?

Martha   He's really rather good at it. Except that he keeps thinking it's a waltz. He *twirls*.

Oakleigh   No, no, no. I mean, how *is* Albert. After that

Ma-ood business in here last night?

Martha   Oh, quite recovered. He got up, ate his breakfast, had his tango lesson, and now he's gone to Covent Garden. Mr Pennyfeather's being auditioned this morning, and Albert wanted to be there to see his triumph.

Oakleigh   Ah. Triumph. He has a magnificent voice, that young man. At least, so they say in Argentina.

Martha   And he's such a charming boy . . . !

Oakleigh   Haarumph. While we're on that subject . . . he gave me a little note to deliver to you.

Martha   Oh. Thank you.

Composedly she takes the note and reads.

'I've got to see you.' (*To* **Oakleigh**.) It's nothing. I know all about it. Just something I asked him yesterday.

Oakleigh   Pardon? You mean you *knew* about it?

Martha   Oh yes. It's quite all right.

Oakleigh (*aside*)   Well, at least it's not Teenie. It's not *all* bad news.

He totters out.

Martha   Fancy giving a letter like that to a third party to deliver. Thank heavens Oakleigh's not a man to suspect. Now then . . .

She buries herself in the letter, and reads. Enter **Winstanley**.

Winstanley   She wasn't in the greenhouse at all. Oh! You've changed into Mrs Wembley. How confusing everything is.

Martha *hasn't seen him at all.*

Martha (*reading*)   'I've got to talk to you . . .'

Winstanley   She's reading too. What a literary

household.

He sags and waits.

Martha 'I've got to talk to you. You chose to ... You chose to ...' What's that word? I can't make it out.

Winstanley (*as if reciting a lesson*) 'You chose to encourage me. I risk everything. Too many people can disturb us during the day.'

Martha Good heavens, how did *you* know?

Winstanley Dear lady, it's a circular!

Martha You've had one too?

Winstanley I know the opening lines. A begging letter, is it?

Martha Oh yes.

Winstanley (*politely*) Well, well, well, step-mother-in-law-to-be, and how are you this morning?

Martha (*abstractedly*) Fine, thank you.

Winstanley I've had a dismal night.

Martha I'm delighted to hear it.

Winstanley I'm trying to find my fiancée. But she wasn't in the greenhouse. Mrs Oakleigh said so.

Martha Said what?

Winstanley She was in the greenhouse.

Martha Mrs Oakleigh?

Winstanley No, no.

Martha Look, please do excuse me. (*Reads.*) 'Anyone can disturb us during the day ...'

Winstanley I suppose you don't know where I could find her?

Martha   Who?

Winstanley   My fiancée.

Martha (*crossly*)   In the potting shed.

Winstanley   The potting shed? How absolutely odd!
Excuse me, dear step-mother-in-law-to-be. The potting
shed . . . I say . . .

Exit.

Martha   At last. Now . . . (*Reading.*) 'Meet me tonight, in
the greenhouse.' What does he take me for? 'I swear your
honour will not be compromised.' What nonsense. He's
South American. 'If you agree to meet me, tell your
husband to wave his handkerchief in the air the next time
he sees me, turn round, and sing either 'Goosy Goosy
Gander' or 'The Grand Old Duke of York', whichever
you prefer. Let me know the hour by drawing lines on his
back in chalk.' That's going too far. Chalk my own
husband? Whatever next? 'By the way, I've found a
garter-shop, but they want to know the size.' He must
own shares in a factory.

Enter **Ernestine**.

Ernestine   Martha!

Martha   Teenie!

Mutual embarrassment.

Ernestine   Don't let me disturb you.

Martha   That's all right.

Ernestine   Have you seen my husband?

Martha   Your husband?

Ernestine   Doctor Oakleigh. Osbert.

Martha   Yes.

Ernestine   Yes?

Martha Yes.

Ernestine Did he . . . give you a note?

Martha You *know* about it?

Ernestine I had it in my hand a moment ago.

Martha You . . . had it in your hand?

Again, mutual embarrassment. Each suspects the other.

Ernestine I haven't read it, of course.

Martha Of course not.

Ernestine No more than you, I hope.

Martha I never read that kind of note.

Ernestine It's a matter of principle.

Martha I tore it up.

Ernestine *starts.*

Martha What else could I do?

Ernestine You could have given it to *me*.

Martha It was better to tear it up.

Ernestine I suppose it was . . . some timid lover's declaration of passion . . .

Martha Not in the least.

Ernestine You're sure you didn't read it?

Martha I'm sure I'm sure.

Ernestine Even if it had been . . . er . . . one isn't responsible for the feelings one inspires in others.

Martha (*offended*) Whatever do you mean?

Ernestine Pardon?

Martha He could have saved his ink. The object of his love simply isn't worth it.

Ernestine (*offended*) Really? The ... object ... isn't worth it? Of course the object's worth it.

Martha (*mistaking her*) You're very kind. But no. It's no use deluding ourselves. The object of his love is *quite* past the age for that kind of thing.

Ernestine (*through tight lips*) I assure you she's as capable of inspiring passion as the next woman.

Martha What next woman?

Ernestine Well ... as some people here in this room.

Martha (*modestly*) It would be self-deception to think so.

Ernestine (*nettled*) The world doesn't share your view. If Nelson's Column could only speak ...

Martha What's Nelson's Column to do with it?

Ernestine (*gnomically*) I like a solid base to my remarks. It's easy to talk; proof is what's needed. Not everyone has Nelson's Column to fall back on.

Martha I don't understand.

Ernestine To put it quite bluntly, Martha dear, this time you've gone too far. I don't mind saying it to your face.

Martha (*flattered*) What a friend you are. You even defend me against myself. All right, let's pretend I said nothing.

Ernestine We can't. You used the word ... object.

Martha Oh, I take it back. I didn't mean it anyway.

Ernestine Didn't mean it? I'm so glad. It hurt me.

Martha What a friend you are!

Ernestine And you won't say any more about 'past the age for that kind of thing'?

Martha Of course not. Some compliments are

absolutely meaningless . . .

Ernestine We know each other too well for *those*.

Martha If you prefer, I'll say we're dealing with . . . (*Archly.*) the most beautiful, most exquisite, most charming woman in the world.

Ernestine (*fluttering her eyelashes*) Now you're going to the other extreme. Passable's the word.

Martha (*crossly*) Passable?

Ernestine No longer alluring . . . no, definitely not. But even so, if the man wasn't too old . . . or too fussy . . .

Martha Really?

Ernestine It can happen. Now and then. Look at Nelson's Column.

Martha (*very cross*) Nelson's Column again! Why not Euston Station while you're about it?

Ernestine Whatever's the matter?

Martha I find your remarks in very bad taste.

Ernestine Pardon? No, no, you're far too generous . . . too kind . . .

Martha You can't *talk* like that to people.

Ernestine Oh, my dear, you're far too kind. But, if you insist, I'll take back every word. (*Archly.*) I suppose I *was* a little hard.

Martha You most certainly were.

Ernestine What a friend you are!

They embrace. Enter **George**.

George Madam, Mr Wembley's back . . . in a terrible state!

Ernestine Good gracious!

Martha   What's happened?

Enter **Oakleigh** *and* **Julie**, *supporting* **Wembley**, *who is in an apoplectic state. They sit him down and fan him with handkerchiefs.*

Wembley   Brandy! Brandy, for heaven's sake! What an experience!

They give him brandy. He drinks, coughs, gasps.

His audition . . . he's had it. A disaster! A catastrophe!

All   Oh!

Wembley (*sipping feebly*)   If I'd ever imagined . . . Even yesterday, when we asked him to sing, all that Ma-ood business, I thought . . . and so did you, Oakleigh . . . But then I said to myself 'No, we're not musicians. He's famous; it stands to reason he must have a good voice.' Well, I'm telling you his reputation is exaggerated. If that's all you need to make your name in Argentina . . .

Oakleigh   But what happened?

Wembley   I'll tell you. We arrived at Covent Garden, as arranged. The directors were there to meet us. We were shown on to the stage. There was no one else: just the two of us and the jury. The jury consisted of the directors, the conductor, and a commissionaire who kept walking up and down. He seemed to be there as an adviser. But no one asked his advice, so he didn't give it. The conductor was to accompany. He asked Pennyfeather what arias he knew, and he made some joke about 'the more the maria'. Then he said he'd sing 'Three little maids from school'. They told him it needed three sopranos, and he said 'Don't we all?' Then he offered them that infernal 'Come into the garden, Ma-ood', and I thought 'Ah well, only God can help us now.' He started singing – Pennyfeather, I mean – if you can call it singing. It was out of tune, in the wrong time. He kept saying the piano was flat, and the accompanist was going too fast. But you could see they didn't believe him. The directors were looking at each other in amazement. The commissionaire didn't say a word ... but he didn't look at all happy. The accompanist was sweating like a pig. He kept saying 'Faster, faster', and Pennyfeather kept saying 'It's not a race, you know'. I could feel them all looking at me. I was red with embarrassment. As we left, they told me the theatre was no place for practical jokers, and they suggested we try the post office. Oh, the fraud!

Julie   Calm down, Father.

Wembley   Calm down! It's easy to say 'Calm down' – I'm paying the man £350 a month! £350 a month, for a tenor who can't sing! Who'll perform your opera now? No one! £350 a month! We might as well start an agency for layabouts.

Martha   Albert, Albert, you get worked up too easily. He's probably just tired.

Ernestine   The journey ... the change of air.

Julie   He's hardly had time to catch his breath.

Martha   They probably breathe very slowly in the mountains.

Julie   Besides, if he's famous in Argentina, he must have something ...

Wembley   He'll have something all right when I see him ... that windbag ... that Aztec ...

Enter **Pennyfeather**, *very cheerful, sketching tango steps and humming to himself.*

Wembley   that ... tenor! Leave us alone, would you?

Exeunt all but **Wembley** *and* **Pennyfeather**.

Wembley   Now then, you ...

Pennyfeather   I'm glad that's over. Covent Garden, eh? I didn't enjoy that place at all. Did you?

Wembley (*through his teeth*)   No, I didn't.

Pennyfeather   One good thing is, it's given me an appetite.

He tangoes for a moment, then gets back to his conversational tone. He really is cheerful today.

I could eat a llama.

Wembley   Oh? A llama? Eat a llama? Aren't you ashamed, you ... parasite?

Pennyfeather   They taste very nice.

Wembley   I suppose you think you were brilliant, at Covent Garden just now?

Pennyfeather (*smugly*)   They will remember me, I theenk.

Wembley   Oh, they will? Because you were so marvellous? Well, I could see the faces that commissionaire was making, and they weren't marvellous. It was a scandal, d'you hear me, a scandal!

Pennyfeather   I'm sorry his faces were scandalous.

Wembley   Not his faces! Your singing!

Pennyfeather   Ah, that was your fault. You told me to sing.

Wembley   I never imagined tenors were put into this world to polish boots.

Pennyfeather   D'you know, that is a solemn truth. We must each do the job God ordains for us.

Wembley   You could have said ... We could have waited a day or two.

Pennyfeather   For what, please?

Wembley   Until you were used to the altitude.

Pennyfeather   I don't understand. In Argentina we

have a saying, '*Son locos todos los Britannicos qué pasa qué nada*'.

Wembley   Oh, do you indeed? And what does it mean?

Pennyfeather   Well, it's obvious: 'No practical joker like a Britisher'. I could hardly keep my face straight.

Wembley   You thought I was playing a joke?

Pennyfeather   No reason not to go along with it. I *like* you.

Wembley   Thanks. Perhaps you can tell me what to do with you now? I'm not feeding you and keeping you just for the fun of it. After this morning, you'll never sing at Covent Garden again.

Pennyfeather   Oh. Thank you so much.

Wembley   So what other talents have you got? Is your handwriting neat? How's your arithmetic?

Pennyfeather   My fractions are vulgar.

Wembley   35 and 9 . . . how much is that?

Pennyfeather   35 and 9 . . . ? Let me see . . . (*Counting on his fingers.*) 35 . . . 36 . . . 37 . . .

Wembley   Surely you don't need to use your fingers.

Pennyfeather   D'you want the answer right, or soon?

Wembley   I know! I've got the very job for you. You can be a flunkey. Run errands . . . help with the housework . . . Ask George for a duster.

Pennyfeather   Who, me?

Wembley   Yes, you. Hiring a tenor at £350 a month just to dust furniture isn't cheap, you know.

Pennyfeather   I'll write to Father.

Wembley   And one other thing . . .

Pennyfeather   What now?

Wembley   Don't breathe a word to George about the wages I'm paying you. I can't afford to give *him* a rise.

He glares at **Pennyfeather** *and stalks out.*

Pennyfeather   Well, that's too much. Treating me like that. Yesterday nothing was too good for me ... scarves, hot drinks, all that tripe. Now he treats me like a llama at a wedding.

He sulks. Enter **Julie**. *She finds him at it.*

Julie   Mr Pennyfeather! Is something the matter?

Pennyfeather   Your father's the matter. He wants me to dust the furniture.

Julie   Is that all?

Pennyfeather   It is not all. He called me a flunkey.

Julie   Poor darling. Father never did watch his tongue.

Pennyfeather   I'm wounded. Deep down. If I wasn't held here by the charms of a certain person ...

Julie (*enraptured*)   A ... young person? A young ... lady person?

Pennyfeather   Well, to be sure a lady. I can't tell you her name.

Julie   Of course you can't. It would make me blush.

Pennyfeather   Thees ees as you please.

Julie   I'm overwhelmed by what you've just told me ... overwhelmed and delighted. Your discretion does you credit.

Pennyfeather   Thank you.

Julie   I'm quite overwhelmed.

Pennyfeather   And I'm quite starving.

He stamps out, brushing past **Martha** *and* **Ernestine**, *who are entering.*

Ernestine Gracious! Who was that?

Julie Mr Pennyfeather. He's just had a row with Father. He's wounded, deep down. He's gone to get something to eat.

Ernestine That proves he's a man of feeling.

Martha And appetite. Isn't your father here?

Julie No. Were you looking for him?

Martha Yes. I need him.

She brandishes a piece of chalk.

Ernestine I'm looking for my husband too.

She brandishes her own piece of chalk, then hides it as **Wembley** *and* **Pennyfeather** *come back.*

Wembley You can eat later. Go and spray the greenfly. More useless parasites, but at least you can get rid of them!

Martha Albert! That was unkind.

Julie Poor boy.

Ernestine Making him spray greenfly.

Pennyfeather What degradation! Oh, if only I wasn't held back. (*Aside to* **Martha**.) I have your garters.

Martha Pardon?

Before he can answer, **Ernestine** *draws him aside.*

Ernestine Be careful. My husband's suspicious. Your guilty love. I think he knows.

Pennyfeather Of course he does. I told him myself.

Ernestine You told him? How did he take it?

Pennyfeather How should he have taken it? He mutteréd something about 'the way of the world'.

Ernestine What? The way of the world? He said, the way of the ...? I see I was wrong to have scruples. My dear Mr Pennyfeather, I'm throwing my scruples out of the window.

Pennyfeather Very nice.

Ernestine And I'm waiting for those garters. Thirty-two. Round the leg.

Pennyfeather Oh ... I ... you ...? You're 32? Round the ...? Very nice.

He backs away, and bumps into **Wembley**.

Wembley Stop fiddling and faddling, and spray the greenfly. I've something else for you to do when you've finished.

Pennyfeather Oh, have you?

Wembley You can buy me some garters. One of mine has snapped. It must be the strain.

Pennyfeather (*hysterically to himself*) Haha! It must be something in the blood.

Exit.

Martha You're really making him do it?

Wembley Yes.

Julie Oh Father, that poor young man ...

Wembley Poor? *Poor*? Do you know what he earns from me?

All three women £350 a month.

Wembley Exactly. If you think that's poor ... What about George? He gets five.

Ernestine That's no reason for humiliating the poor,

dear boy.

Julie   You've wounded him. Deep down.

Martha   You think of no one but yourself. I've always said so. You're interested in nothing but business.

Julie   We artists have feelings you'll never understand.

Ernestine   It's very unkind.

Wembley   What d'you mean, unkind?

Women   Unkind, unkind, unkind.

Wembley   All right, all right. Calm down.

Julie   Poor boy. I'm going into the garden after him. A word or two of comfort. Artist to artist . . .

Exit.

Ernestine   And I'm going to find my husband. Where's that chalk? Way of the world, indeed!

Exit.

Wembley   Why are you all so sorry for *him*? It's me you should be sorry for. What am I to do with him? Opera companies aren't all that keen on tenors who can't sing.

Martha   He's been travelling. He's tired. You made him sing too soon.

Enter **George**.

Wembley   Sooner or later, what's the difference? Whoever heard of a voice like that?

George   Excuse me, sir, but whatever the business, there's always a way to spice things up.

Wembley   Eh?

George   My father was a horse-dealer, and whenever he had a broken-down old nag to sell, he put a pinch of pepper under its tail. Always did the trick. I recommend it.

Wembley   Did you really come in here just to tell me that?

George   Oh, no sir. Mr Winstanley's here.

Wembley   Then don't just stand there. Show him in.

George   Yes sir.

He does, and goes.

Winstanley (*bowing left and right*)   Father-in-law-to-be . . . Step-mother-in-law-to-be . . .

Martha   Oh, do call me something else.

Wembley   What d'you want now?

Winstanley   Have you seen my fiancée? I've been waiting in the potting shed. But she never came.

Martha   She's in the garden, watching them kill greenfly.

Winstanley   How nice. Well, excuse me . . .

Wembley   Just a minute. You don't by any chance want a tenor, do you?

Winstanley   A tenor? H'm. Whatever for?

Wembley   Never mind. Do you or don't you?

Winstanley   My mother *is* looking for a cook.

Wembley (*at once*)   She can have my tenor. He's outstanding: cheerful . . . light on his feet . . .

Winstanley   H'm. A tenor, you say?

Wembley   He hardly ever sings.

Winstanley   What does he charge?

Wembley   Nothing really. £350 a month.

Winstanley   For cooking? (*Judiciously.*) It's steep.

Wembley   Plus board and lodging.

Winstanley   *Board* and lodging? (*Idiotically.*) I've always thought that such an odd phrase. Haven't *you*? I mean, at home we have feather mattresses.

Wembley *stares at him.*

Winstanley   I mean, not *hard*, d'you see. If anything, *ticklish*.

Wembley   You don't suppose any of your friends ... ?

Winstanley   No, no. Excuse me. It's time I went.

Exit.

Wembley   If he'd only get his voice back for twenty-four hours ... If only he was a horse, a pinch of pepper ... Twenty-four hours, that's all.

Martha (*snatching her chance*)   You really need him to get his voice back, don't you?

Wembley   Of course I do. For Julie's sake.

Martha   I think I know a way. A gypsy told me once ... selling clothes-pegs at the door ...

Wembley   That's the way to get your voice back?

Martha   No, the gypsy was. This is what you do: when Pennyfeather comes in, wave your handkerchief like this, turn round, and sing 'Goosy Goosy Gander'.

Wembley   Then what?

Martha   That's all.

Wembley   It's absurd.

Martha   What about Beethoven?

Wembley   It worked for him? I'll do it. I'll try anything. £350 a month ... !

Martha (*suddenly*)   Good gracious! Look!

Wembley   What?

Martha   There.

He turns round, and she draws two chalk lines on his back.

One, two. Two o'clock.

Wembley   What's the matter?

Martha   I thought I saw a caterpillar.

Wembley   In the garden. Spraying greenfly.

Martha   It's all right, it was a green thread. There.

He makes to speak, but she goes out, leaving him looking after her with his mouth open and his arm upraised. Behind his back, enter **Ernestine** *and* **Oakleigh**. *He doesn't see them.*

Ernestine   You've got it right, have you? Wave your handkerchief, turn around . . .

Oakleigh *does so. He has three chalk stripes on his back.*

Ernestine   . . . and sing . . .

Oakleigh   Yes, yes, Teenie. If this brings back his voice, I'll give up medicine, that's all.

Ernestine   You'll see.

Exit. **Oakleigh** *and* **Wembley** *find each other dancing in circles, waving handkerchiefs.*

Wembley   Whatever are you doing that for?

Oakleigh   The same as you.

Wembley   Hay fever. It's in case of hay fever.

Oakleigh   Oh. Well, you'll never believe this, but mine's for Pennyfeather.

Wembley   Oh. So's mine, actually.

Oakleigh   Apparently, waving a handkerchief will get his voice back.

Wembley   Exactly.

Oakleigh   You think so too?

Wembley   My dear fellow, if *you* believe it . . . the scientist's trained mind . . .

Oakleigh   All we do is wave?

Wembley   And sing 'Goosy Goosy Gander'.

Oakleigh   Ah. No.

Wembley   What?

Oakleigh   Those aren't the words at all.

Wembley   Of course they are. I always know the words.

Oakleigh   No, no. 'The Grand Old Duke of York'.

Wembley   That must be the army version. There are so many branches of medicine.

*They practise. Then **Oakleigh** freezes.*

Oakleigh   Here he comes! Shh!

*They look nonchalant. Enter **Pennyfeather**, wearing a gardener's spraying equipment.*

Pennyfeather   There. I hope you're satisfied. I've killed your wretched greenfly.

Wembley *and* **Oakleigh** *start dancing round, waving their handkerchiefs.*

Wembley   'Goosy Goosy Gander.'

Oakleigh (*simultaneously*)   'Oh, the Grand Old Duke of York.'

Pennyfeather (*hugging himself excitedly*)   It's the signal. The signal! She agrees!

Wembley (*still twirling, to **Oakleigh***)   Look how excited he is.

Oakleigh Something must be happening to his voice.

Pennyfeather *is dancing with glee. They go cautiously up to him.*

Wembley Well, how are you? D'you feel anything?

Pennyfeather Oh yes. Something seems to be unfolding and growing inside of me.

Wembley There you are!

Oakleigh Incredible. I must try this on my patients.

They start twirling and waving and singing again.

Pennyfeather No, no. It's all right. That's enough. No need to tire yourselves out. That's enough, really.

Wembley It's a pleasure, my dear fellow. Anything to help.

*He moves upstage so that **Pennyfeather** can see his back.*

Pennyfeather Ah! One ... two ... two o'clock.

Oakleigh 'He had ten thousand men.'

He too moves upstage.

Pennyfeather One, two, three. He's got three. Is it two o'clock, or three?

Wembley (*twirling downstage again*) 'Whither do you wander?'

Pennyfeather Three and two ... three and two ... er ...

Wembley (*still pirouetting*) Five! Your maths! Three and two are five!

Pennyfeather So they are. Five o'clock! Marvellous!

He starts to sing, in a magnificent tenor voice, an aria from The Yeomen of the Guard *Act II.*

   'When a wooer goes a-wooing ...'

Wembley   He's singing.

Pennyfeather   'Naught is truer than his joy . . .'

Oakleigh   It's come back. What a voice!

Wembley   Pennyfeather, my dear chap . . .

They surround him and shake his hand.

Pennyfeather   What's the matter?

Enter **Winstanley**.

Wembley   Ah, Winstanley, come in, come in. He's got his voice back.

Winstanley   Who?

Wembley   My tenor.

Winstanley   The cook?

Wembley   Sing it again, from the start, so that we can all hear. Oakleigh, come along: wave. You too, Winstanley. Don't argue, man. Wave it about.

All three start prancing up and down, waving.

Winstanley (*as he prances*)   What's going on?

Wembley   What's going on? A wooer's going a-wooing, that's what's going on. Isn't that so, Pennyfeather?

Pennyfeather   You *want* me to sing now? Anything to oblige. It's better than killing greenfly. (*Singing, as they all wave:*)

'Maiden blushing, hushing all his suing,
Boldly blushing, bravely coy . . .'

Oakleigh *and* **Wembley** *stop, stunned. Then* **Winstanley**.

Wembley   Is that really how it goes on?

Winstanley (*eagerly*)   Yes, yes. (*He too begins to sing.*)

'Oh the happy days of doing . . .'

Oakleigh Good lord, it's worked on him too.

Wembley It's unbelievable! Martha, Julie, Teenie . . .

Enter the three women, and **George**.

Women What is it? What's happened? What's the matter?

Wembley Come in, come in. He's got his voice back. Listen.

He and **Oakleigh** *dance and wave.*

Winstanley (*singing*)
  'Oh the sighing and the suing,
  When a wooer goes a-wooing,
  Oh the sweets that never cloy.'

Wembley Not you, for heaven's sake. It's Pennyfeather we're talking about. (*To* **Martha**, *but so that it could appear to be to any of the women, or indeed to* **George**.) Your cure worked wonders.

Martha I don't believe it.

George You tried pepper then, sir?

Pennyfeather *is still dancing and singing. He contrives to sidle past* **Martha**.

Pennyfeather (*singing, aside to* **Martha**) My dear lady, I'm delighted. I'll be prompt. I've got your garters.

Martha Oh . . . thank you.

Pennyfeather *moves on.* **Ernestine** *draws him aside.*

Ernestine (*aside to* **Pennyfeather**) Young man, whatever can you think of me?

Pennyfeather (*singing*) Nothing at all.

Ernestine Say it once more. Sing it, if you like. (*Singing, operatically.*) 'Good grief, how lumpy Nelson's Column is.'

Pennyfeather (*singing, baffled*) 'Good grief, how lumpy

Nelson's Column is.'

He dances out of range.

Ernestine   It's the same voice. No doubt of it. Enthralling!

Pennyfeather *twirls to a stop, breathless, and mops his brow.*

Pennyfeather (*singing breathlessly*)   You really must excuse me. The dusting's waiting.

Wembley   Dusting? You? Never again. An artist like you? George will see to the dusting. Your path leads to glory, Covent Garden, the world. Ready, everyone?

They all start waving, dancing and singing. Total consternation of **Pennyfeather**. *Curtain.*

Act Three

Next morning, early. **Wembley** *comes from the house, in a very sunny mood, with a cup of coffee. He sips.* **Pennyfeather** *comes in from the garden, very cross.*

Wembley Morning.

Pennyfeather Morning. Hah! Three hours! Women!

He goes into the house, leaving **Wembley** *baffled. Enter* **Oakleigh***. Mutual embarrassment.*

Oakleigh Ah.

Wembley Ah.

Oakleigh Good morning, Albert.

Wembley Good morning, Osbert.

Pause. Then they speak together.

Both Have you seen Pennyfeather?

Oakleigh Pardon?

Wembley I said have you seen Pennyfeather?

Oakleigh So did I.

Wembley Pardon?

Oakleigh So did I.

Wembley No no. Did you?

Oakleigh I just said I did.

Wembley Not said, saw. Did you see?

Oakleigh Seesaw?

Wembley Not see saw. See Pennyfeather. Did you see Pennyfeather?

Oakleigh That's funny. I just asked *you* that.

Wembley   Don't start again. Have you seen him?

Oakleigh   No. Have you?

Wembley   Not since last night.

Oakleigh   Has he still got his voice?

Wembley   That hardly matters, now we have the cure. I hope it works at Covent Garden.

Oakleigh (*darkly*)   It may, or it may not.

Wembley   What does that mean?

Oakleigh   He may be trying to fool you.

Wembley (*jumping as if stung*)   What?

Oakleigh   Having a voice and hiding it.

Wembley (*uncomfortably*)   I don't understand.

Oakleigh   He's *pretending* to lose his voice. It's because of . . . women.

Wembley   Oh my God!

Oakleigh (*relieved to have got to the point at last*)   He's after anything in petticoats.

Wembley (*looking at him pointedly*)   You mean . . . other men's wives?

Oakleigh   Exactly. (*He looks all round, then says conspiratorially:*) And one . . . other man's wife . . . in particular.

Wembley   Ah. Yes. I see exactly what you mean.

Pause. Mutual embarrassment.

Both (*blurting it, together*)   *Your* wife, old man.

Neither has heard. They're so eager to tell each other the bad news, they've not been listening.

Oakleigh   Yes.

Wembley Yes.

Oakleigh Under the circumstances, of course, one can't name names.

Wembley You mean you know?

Oakleigh You mean *you* know?

Both (*together*) Yes.

Oakleigh He didn't tell you, surely?

Wembley Of course he told me. How else would I have found out? He said 'You know, Wembley, I've got a feeling that . . .' Er, well, never mind. I assure you it's nothing, nothing at all.

Oakleigh (*airily*) Oh, I believe you. In any case, it's none of my business really, is it?

Wembley None of your business? I say!

Oakleigh You're taking it very calmly.

Wembley Well, actually, it's none of my business, really, either.

They look at each other, trying to figure it out. Enter **Pennyfeather**.

Pennyfeather Ah, coffee.

He goes for a cup, but **Wembley** *snatches it out of his hand.*

Wembley (*jumping*) You can't do that! Your voice.

Oakleigh Are you taking proper care of it?

Pennyfeather Pardon?

Wembley You must take proper care of it.

Oakleigh It's a gift from God.

Wembley It's a magnificent instrument.

Oakleigh You've no idea what a blessing –

Both Such a magnificent voice can be.

Pennyfeather Oh, but I have. A perfect idea. I have. You don't find them in this country, though. You have to go to Italy. When I was in the Sistine Chapel . . .

Consternation of **Wembley** *and* **Oakleigh**.

Oakleigh What? You . . . ?

Wembley The Sis . . . Sis . . . Sis . . . You the Sis . . .

Pennyfeather I'm sorry, I don't quite catch . . .

Wembley I said in the Sis . . . Sis . . . Sis . . . What did you just say?

Pennyfeather I said I don't quite catch . . .

Wembley Before that.

Pennyfeather I said, when I was in the Sistine Chapel . . .

Oakleigh That's it! You mean you've been in the Sistine Chapel? You . . . to sing . . . ?

Pennyfeather Pardon?

Oakleigh You . . . to . . .

Wembley Sing . . .

Pennyfeather If you insist. (*Singing, falsetto.*) 'O salutaris hostia . . .'

Wembley (*aside to* **Oakleigh**) Did you hear that?

Oakleigh No doubt about it.

Wembley Best pretend we haven't noticed. Poor fellow. I wonder how they do it . . .

Pennyfeather To get back to the Sistine Chapel . . . You know, of course, that all the singers there are . . .

Wembley (*hastily*) Yes, yes, we know . . .

Pennyfeather　You can't imagine the intensity of harmony produced by so many pure voices, freed from the trappings of the flesh . . . singing their parts with a soulfulness . . .

Wembley　I'm not surprised. Soulfulness . . .

Pennyfeather　It stands to reason.

Oakleigh　But you've just come from Argentina. How did you get to Rome?

Wembley　Not to mention the Sistine Chapel?

Pennyfeather　Oh, that's easy. There was a girl on the boat. From Argentina. Dorabella, she said her name was. We found each other, our hearts beat as one, and then, as soon as the boat docked, she ran off with a Neapolitan dentist. Well, what could I do? I ran right after them. All the way to Rome.

Wembley　I thought you said he was Neapolitan.

Pennyfeather　I caught the wrong train. I couldn't think straight.

Wembley　Love's despair. I know what you mean.

Pennyfeather　That's right. Put yourself in my place.

Wembley　No, no. I'm all right here, thanks.

Pennyfeather　You can understand how I felt. I wandered all over Rome, alone, in despair, disgusted by life, women and dentists . . .

Oakleigh　(*really caught up in it*)　Yes. Yes.

Pennyfeather　All at once, what did I see ahead of me? The Vatican. The Sistine Chapel. Well, for a man alone in Rome, fed up with life, women and dentists, it seemed a heaven-sent opportunity. A way of salvation. I shouted 'My God! The Sistine Chapel!'

Oakleigh　Well, you would, old chap, you would.

Pennyfeather   'It's the only answer!' I shouted. 'I'll go in there!'

Wembley   Just like that? Into the Sistine Chapel? Phht?

Pennyfeather   It was a crushing experience.

Wembley (*weakly*)   Crushing . . .

Pennyfeather   As soon as I entered the choir, I felt drawn by the singers into the very voice of heaven. How can I put it? I was sublimated. I was a man no longer. I was . . . I was . . . Oh, I can't tell you what I was.

Oakleigh (*aside to* **Wembley**)   Don't enquire too closely.

Wembley (*aside to* **Oakleigh**)   Phht, just like that.

Pennyfeather   I tell you I cried like a pig at that moment.

Oakleigh (*surprised*)   I didn't know pigs cried, at that moment . . .

Pennyfeather   It was a moment of ecstasy. I reached the point where I didn't even notice what happened to me any more.

Wembley   What a Spartan.

Pennyfeather   I'll never forget it. (*Singing, falsetto.*) 'O salutaris hostia . . .'

Wembley (*hastily*)   That's exactly how it is.

Pennyfeather   No, that's only a rough idea.

Wembley (*taking him aside*)   D'you know, I was certain you were courting Mrs Oakleigh.

Pennyfeather (*taken aback*)   I don't see the connection.

Wembley (*crowing at his own joke*)   There isn't one! There isn't one!

Oakleigh (*drawing* **Pennyfeather** *aside*)   I say. Can you imagine, I was sure you were laying siege to Mrs Wembley.

Pennyfeather   Now you *must* be joking.

Oakleigh *and* **Wembley** (*shaking one hand each*)   My poor fellow . . .

Wembley   I'll write to Covent Garden again. Perhaps they have some soprano parts . . . Are you coming, Oakleigh?

Oakleigh   What? Oh. Yes.

They shake **Pennyfeather**'s *hands again, then catch each other's eyes and exeunt, tangoing ever so slightly.*

Pennyfeather (*grumpily*)   I can't take much more. First last night, and now this about my voice. And I've been up since five o'clock. I leapt out of bed, crept down to the greenhouse . . . My heart was thumping . . . I thought, 'She's due any minute. I'll wait.' Wait, hah! I waited till eight o'clock. Just me and the greenfly. If she never intended to come, what was the point of getting her husband and Wembley to wave those confounded handkerchiefs?

Enter **Martha**. *She too is furious.*

Martha   Ah, there you are. At last!

Pennyfeather   I was going to say the same to you.

Martha   I suppose you think nothing of keeping a lady waiting.

Pennyfeather   I like that! Hah! I like that!

Martha   An hour. A whole hour. I would have been even longer, if it hadn't been for Teenie.

Pennyfeather   Teenie?

Martha   On the stroke of three Teenie appeared in the greenhouse. She said she'd raging toothache and couldn't sleep – so I said I had a migraine, for appearances' sake.

We started pacing up and down, the pair of us, up and down among the tomato plants. In the end, since she clearly had no intention of going, I left her there and went back to bed.

Pennyfeather That's all very well, but I waited for three hours. Three hours, alone with the greenfly.

Martha You waited for me?

Pennyfeather Precisely.

Martha In the greenhouse?

Pennyfeather There is only one, I take it.

Martha You Argentinians are all the same.

Pennyfeather It's no good trying to put the blame on Argentina. Or on me.

Martha It was your idea in the first place.

They glare. Enter **Wembley**.

Wembley Now then, whatever's the matter?

Martha Nothing. We're having an argument.

Pennyfeather This lady she say I . . .

Martha Exactly. *Lady*. Albert, perhaps you can settle it. As a general rule, when a lady agrees to meet a gentleman . . . you understand what I mean . . . and the gentleman doesn't turn up, what then?

Wembley He's not a gentleman, he's a bounder.

Martha (*to* **Pennyfeather**) There you are.

Pennyfeather Ah, but just a minute. Suppose it's the lady who doesn't turn up?

Wembley He's still a bounder.

Pennyfeather Why?

Wembley Because a gentleman always takes the blame.

Martha   You see.

Wembley   Who are you talking about, in any case?

Martha   No one. Just a lady Mr Pennyfeather knows, who agreed, in a moment of weakness, to ...

Wembley   Aha! You mean a married lady?

Martha   Yes.

Wembley (*laughing*)   Hahahaha! What a joke! What was the husband's name?

Martha   I can't tell you.

Wembley   I'll keep it a secret.

Martha   I think you would.

Wembley (*jovially, aside to* **Pennyfeather**)   In any case, there'd be no harm done, eh? You arranged a rendezvous? A ... chap ... in your condition? What on earth *for*?

Pennyfeather   I ...

Martha   You see: it *is* your fault. I'm so glad that's settled. Come along, Albert.

Exeunt **Martha** *and* **Wembley**.

Pennyfeather   It's too much. What is thees now? What have I *done*?

Enter **Ernestine**. *She too is furious.*

Ernestine   Ah, there you are. At last!

Pennyfeather   Ai marmelita. The other one, now.

Ernestine   You're a bounder! It's all your fault.

Pennyfeather   What's the matter?

Ernestine   What's the matter? Answer me one question. One simple question.

Pennyfeather Certainly.

Ernestine What does a clock sound like when it strikes three?

Pennyfeather It goes 'bong, bong, bong', of course. If all you wanted was a lesson in clock-bonging...

Ernestine Of course not! At three o'clock last night, what exactly were you doing?

Pennyfeather I was esleeping.

Ernestine Esleeping? Sleeping? Hah! Three o'clock, and he has the nerve to be esleeping!

Pennyfeather My eyes were shut. My breathing was peaceful. Like thees: ah-hoo, ah-hoo. What else should I be doing at three o'clock? Oh yais: I was dreaming, too.

Ernestine Don't tell me you were dreaming of me.

Pennyfeather *stares at her with disdain.*

Ernestine I see! Well, while you had the nerve to be sleeping, I was awake.

Pennyfeather I know thees. I hear yust now. Toothache.

Ernestine I was awake, wide awake! What d'you say to that?

Pennyfeather I say, 'Ha!' I say, 'Ho!' I say thees ees not my fault.

Ernestine Of course it's your fault. I spent all night walking up and down, up and down, like a goose.

Pennyfeather No, please.

Ernestine Don't contradict. A goose.

Pennyfeather Well, if you insist, a goose.

Ernestine I see! Insult me now! Add insult to injury!

Pennyfeather (*aside*) This is getting out of hand.

Ernestine (*tearfully*) I know what it is: you're tired of me already.

Pennyfeather How can you theenk so?

She wails even louder. He casts his eyes to heaven.

Look, I understand how it is, if you don't get much sleep, what a nuisance it is . . .

Ernestine A nuisance? Aaaaaaaahhhh.

Pennyfeather I know exactly what it's like. It was the same for me.

Ernestine Really? You sweet boy! The same for you?

Pennyfeather (*warming to his theme*) Yes, yes, I know exactly what it's like. You can't settle . . . you toss and turn . . .

Ernestine Oh yes . . . yes . . .

Pennyfeather You're too hot . . . your skin burns . . . you plump up your pillow . . . don't know which side of the bed to lie on . . . in the end you just have to get up.

Ernestine That's it exactly.

Pennyfeather And I can tell you the reason, too.

Ernestine You can?

Pennyfeather My landlady in Buenos Aires . . . it was the same for her. Coffee, last theeng at night.

Ernestine Oh, you bounder! Coffee! I hate you!

She rushes out.

Pennyfeather I theenk thees is a madhouse yust a leetle.

Enter **Martha**.

Martha Bounder! Are you still here?

Pennyfeather You want to talk more?

Martha Of course I don't. Mr Wembley – an impartial judge – told you exactly where you stand.

Pennyfeather But it's not my fault. I got to the greenhouse on the stroke of five, and you'd gone.

Martha Three hours late! What's the point of arriving at five for a rendezvous fixed for two?

Pennyfeather I'm sorry: five.

Martha Two!

Pennyfeather Five. I counted the stripes.

Martha Your maths is entirely hopeless.

Pennyfeather Señor Wembley did the addition for me. In person.

Martha I put two stripes.

Pennyfeather Two on one, yes. And three on the other one. That makes five. Two and three are five.

Martha What other one?

Pennyfeather For heaven's sake! Three on one and two on the other one.

Martha Excuse me. I didn't put three stripes on anyone.

Pennyfeather He can't have put them on himself.

Martha Maybe he leaned against a wall.

Pennyfeather And this wall was estripy, yes?

Martha I put two stripes. It's baffling.

Pennyfeather Really?

Martha Really.

Pennyfeather Well, those other stripes must be how

you call it, an act of God. Dear lady, please accept my apologies.

Martha   With pleasure.

Pennyfeather (*flirting*)   I was a leetle cross with you . . .

Martha   I was *furious* with you.

Pennyfeather (*eagerly*)   My darling. My darling, darling Ernestine . . .

Martha   You're making a serious mistake.

Pennyfeather   Pardon?

Martha   Why d'you call me Ernestine?

Pennyfeather   Because in all the wide world, it's my favourite name. I love my darling Ernestine.

Martha   He admits it! He admits it – to me!

Pennyfeather   Who else would I admit it to?

Martha   You really are a bounder. Leave me alone.

Pennyfeather   Leave you alone? Never!

He falls on his knees in front of her.

I'll spend the rest of my life at your feet.

He embraces her legs. Enter **Wembley**.

Martha   Albert! Get up, quickly.

Pennyfeather   It's all right. He knows everything.

He stays on his knees. Enter **Oakleigh**.

Oakleigh   Good lord! (*Aside to* **Pennyfeather**.) Get up, you fool.

Pennyfeather   Ah! Her husband!

Oakleigh   Exactly, her husband. You're crazy. Can't you see that Wembley's watching every move?

Pennyfeather I'm not worried about Wembley.

Wembley And I'm not worried about *him*. Haha. Little chapel-boy!

Oakleigh You're taking this very calmly.

Martha (*to* **Wembley**) I hope you didn't think . . .

Wembley It's a magnificent joke, that's all.

Pennyfeather *gets up, and takes* **Oakleigh** *aside.*

Pennyfeather Please don't believe what you see. I'm not really . . .

Oakleigh I should hope not.

Pennyfeather Appearances are against me. But I had to do something. It's *his* wife I'm in love with.

Oakleigh No need to tell me that, old chap. It's obvious.

Pennyfeather I know you saw me kneeling at this lady's feet . . . but it was only to keep Wembley from suspecting.

Oakleigh Damn funny way of going about it.

He and **Pennyfeather** *look at each other blankly. Upstage,* **Martha** *is arguing with* **Wembley**.

Martha I see! Well let me tell you something: I don't like the calm way you're taking this.

Wembley I'm taking it calmly because I know I've nothing to fear from him.

Enter **Ernestine**, *still cross.*

Ernestine No no, not coffee. I won't swallow that.

Pennyfeather (*to* **Oakleigh**) Here she is . . . heaven-sent!

He draws **Wembley** *aside.*

Pennyfeather   Look, I'd like to warn you in advance
... your wife ... I don't care a pebb-el for your wife.

Wembley   Pardon?

Pennyfeather   I ask you in advance to forgive what I'm
going to do. It's to stop her husband suspecting.

He leaps on **Ernestine** *and embraces her.*

Pennyfeather   Martha darling, I love you!

Ernestine   Good gracious!

Oakleigh   Good heavens, *my* wife now.

Ernestine (*trying to dislodge* **Pennyfeather**)   You're
crazy. My husband's ...

Pennyfeather   It's all right. I've warned him.

Oakleigh   I say. Just a minute. Are you out of your
mind?

Pennyfeather   It's all right, I keep telling you: I've
warned him. (*To* **Ernestine**.) Martha, you're adorable.

Ernestine (*breaking free at last*)   You keep calling me
Martha. My name's Ernestine.

She goes upstage in a huff.

Pennyfeather   What d'you mean, Ernestine? This is
Ernestine.

Martha (*with dignity*)   This is Martha. Martha Wembley.

Pennyfeather What? Martha? Wembley? You're
Martha-Wem ... ? And that's Ernestine? Ai Pepita.
Marmelito mio. Ai-ai-ai.

Martha *and* **Ernestine**   Bounder.

Exeunt. **Oakleigh** *and* **Wembley** *are highly amused.*

Pennyfeather   Er ... gentlemen ... I assure you, it was
all a ...

Wembley (*as he goes to leave*) No no, my dear fellow.
You carry on. Phht, phht, phht. I don't mind in the least.

Oakleigh (*following him*) Yes, carry on. Phht, phht, phht.
Carry on. We're not jealous.

He and **Wembley** *exeunt, chortling and singing 'O salutaris
hostia'.*

Pennyfeather Whatever next? It is a madhouse. Look,
I come from Buenos Aires to London to learn the
business. On the tram I see her. I give her sixpence. I say
goodbye, I think I never see her again. I go to Wembley,
my father's oldest friend. And there I find her. I write her
a note. She gives me the signal. The greenhouse, the dead
of night. She doesn't turn up. Next morning she's here.
She shouts. Then the other one comes. She's here, she
shouts. Then her husband comes, but he laughs. Then the
other husband comes. And he laughs. Phht, phht, phht.
What is all this 'Phht, phht, phht'? (*Sings.*) 'O salutaris
hostia . . .' I'm humiliated! I'm mortified! I'm . . . crushéd!
Is this what it means to learn the black-pudding business
from the bottom up?

Enter **Winstanley**, *tangoing gently.*

Winstanley (*cheerily*) Good morning, Mr Pennyfeather.

Pennyfeather Ah! Good morning. It's you. Just a
minute! You *are* quite sure it's you?

Winstanley (*sudden panic*) Pardon?

Pennyfeather You're not actually someone else?

Winstanley Just a minute. (*He checks in a mirror.*) No,
I'm me all right.

Pennyfeather Thank goodness, eh?

Winstanley Phew. Yes. Thank goodness. Er . . . you
haven't seen Mr Wembley, have you?

Pennyfeather He's just gone out. If it was him.

(*Singing.*) 'Come into the garden, Ma-ood . . .'

Winstanley (*nervously*) Are you sure you're all right? Would you like a throat lozenge?

Pennyfeather No thank you. Just airing my voice . . .

Enter **Wembley**.

Wembley My dear Winstanley . . . George told me you'd arrived. I rushed downstairs four at a time, to shake your hand and bring you your fiancée. Four at a time. And five at the bottom. I do hope you're well. To say nothing of your sister . . .

Winstanley I haven't got a sister.

Wembley There you are then.

Winstanley *sags, completely defeated. Enter* **Julie**.

Julie Mr Winstanley! Good morning.

Winstanley *goes gratefully to her.*

Winstanley Oh, good morning, Miss Wembley.

Julie (*imitating his earlier stammer*) I h-h-hope you're w-w-well.

Winstanley Hee-hee-hee. Fine, thank you.

They stand there.

Wembley Well, children, I see you have a lot to discuss. I'll leave you alone.

He takes **Pennyfeather** *aside.*

Wembley Look, my dear chap, you don't mind keeping an eye on them, do you? I mean, a man in your condition . . . it would be like the guard in a harem.

Pennyfeather What d'you mean?

Wembley You know.

Pennyfeather A man in what condition?

Wembley Just limp up and down.

Exit. **Pennyfeather** *paces crossly.*

Julie Well, any news?

Winstanley None. The time's not right. Until it comes, we must keep up the pretence.

Julie I daren't tell Father.

Winstanley I daren't tell Mama.

Pennyfeather (*pacing*) I must look like the changing of the guard.

Julie I mean, it's obvious. You lack every single one of the requirements of a future husband.

Winstanley You're a charming gel, but you're not the gel for me.

Julie Your nose is too big, for a start.

Winstanley I always did prefer blondes. Gentlemen do, you know.

Pennyfeather (*as he paces*) Hup-2-3-4, hup-2-3-4 . . .

Julie I never did like artists. They're always covered in paint. Far too colourful.

Winstanley Oh, yes. Ra-THER.

Pause. Then **Julie** *hands him her engagement ring. He pockets it. Pause, then:*

Winstanley Tell me something. Why is that gentleman pacing up and down? It can't be doing him any good.

Julie Shh! He's jealous, that's what it is. He thinks I'm going to marry you. And he loves me himself. Or so he told me.

Winstanley What about you?

Julie Me? I wouldn't mind a bit.

Winstanley   Well, tell him.

Julie   What, now? In front of you?

Winstanley   It's none of my business, is it?

Julie   It would put his mind at rest. Poor man, he does look uncomfortable.

They look at **Pennyfeather**, *who continues to pace, pathetically. Then* **Julie** *diffidently clears her throat.*

Julie   Ahem.

Pennyfeather   Eh? Sorry. Was that for me?

Winstanley   Yes. Yes. Come along. Don't break the rhythm.

He marches up and down in **Pennyfeather**'s *place.*

Pennyfeather (*to* **Julie**)   Did you want me?

Julie   I wanted to set your mind at rest. You didn't look comfortable. I don't love Winstanley.

Pennyfeather   Oh?

Julie   I'll never be his.

Pennyfeather   Good. But why tell me?

Julie   It would be cruel to let you suffer a moment longer.

Pennyfeather   Pardon?

Julie   I should be piling red-hot coals on your passion, not your head.

Pennyfeather (*working his way towards it*)   You mean you ... me ... I ... you ... ai Carmelita mia ...

Julie   That pacing is so bad for the circulation. I thought I'd speak out, to put your mind at rest. I'm sorry if it seemed forward.

Pennyfeather   Ola-qué-bola, qué confusión. My dear

Miss Wembley, dare I trust my ears?

Winstanley (*humming softly as he paces*)   'Boots, boots, boots, boots, marching over Africa . . .'

Pennyfeather (*with formality*)   It's unbelievable, my dear young lady, that anyone should be so blind as to enter this house without falling in love with you right away.

Julie   I know. But you were different.

Pennyfeather   I was?

Julie   You had to restrain your real feelings, because of him.

Pennyfeather   Who?

Winstanley   Me.

He resumes pacing.

Pennyfeather   Oh.

Julie   But now you can say it. He's not listening . . . are you?

Winstanley (*ostentatiously to himself*)   'Boots, boots, boots, boots . . .'

Julie   Go on, then.

Pennyfeather   Ah. I . . . love you.

Julie   Oh, tell me properly, please!

Pennyfeather   Ah, I see.

He kneels.

My dear Miss Wembley . . .

Enter **Wembley**.

Wembley   You should get a job in a shoe shop.

Pennyfeather (*pursuing him on his knees*)   Oh, Mr Wembley, love . . .

Wembley   Not me as well! Get up!

Pennyfeather   No no, I mean love is a funny thing. It only took me a moment for me to fall headlong in love with your daughter.

Wembley   What are you talking about now? And what's *he* doing?

He goes to **Winstanley***, who is still 'Boots'-ing, and adjusts to his pace.*

Wembley   What on earth . . . d'you think . . . you're doing?

Winstanley (*without slackening*)   You can see for yourself. I took the second watch.

Wembley   You're supposed to be courting your fiancée.

Winstanley   Talk to *him* about that. Excuse me.

Pennyfeather   Señor Wembley, you're my father's oldest friend. Don't reject me. I ask for your daughter's hand.

Wembley   You can't have it. What nonsense! You?

Pennyfeather   What's wrong with me?

Julie   Father, please say yes. You said I could choose.

Wembley (*aside to her, embarrassed*)   Julie, you can't choose him. I can't explain. You just can't. (*Aside to* **Pennyfeather**.) Little chapel-boy!

Pennyfeather   What is all this about chapels?

Enter **Oakleigh**.

Oakleigh   I say, Wembley, look at this.

Wembley   The paper? Not now, thank you. Listen, you'll be amazed. Pennyfeather here . . . wants to marry Julie.

Oakleigh   Does he, by jove? Hahaha. That's rich.

That's really rich. (*To* **Winstanley**, *who is still pacing.*) Isn't it?

Winstanley (*without breaking his rhythm*)   It's rich, it's rich, it's really rather rich.

Julie (*to* **Oakleigh**)   Father doesn't like him.

Oakleigh   And he's right, of course. (*To* **Wembley**.) Look, this is important. Read this, won't you?

Wembley   The paper? What is it? 'The engagement is anounced ...' What? My God! (*To* **Pennyfeather**.) Here, you. Read that.

Pennyfeather   'The engagement is announced by Covent Garden of the famous tenor Amoroso, for a season, at a monthly salary of £600.' What about it?

Wembley   What about it? You owe me £4000 for a start.

Pennyfeather   Me? Why?

Wembley   The penalty clause.

Pennyfeather   What penalty clause? I'm not leaving you, am I?

Wembley   You can't work for me and for Covent Garden at the same time.

Pennyfeather   I'm not working for Covent Garden. I'm not Amoroso.

Wembley   What d'you mean, you're not ...? In that case, what are you doing here, eating me out of house and home?

Pennyfeather   Señor Wembley...

Wembley   You told me distinctly that your name was Pennyfeather.

Pennyfeather   Pennyfeather isn't Amoroso.

Wembley   Amoroso is a stage-name, you fool. Didn't you tell me you were Pennyfeather's bastard son?

Pennyfeather   Bastard son? Good lord, who gave you that idea?

Wembley   You, of course. How can you be Pennyfeather's real son? He only has one real son.

Pennyfeather   Of course he has. Me.

Wembley   You? That little boy who thirteen years ago ...? You weren't a tenor then.

Pennyfeather   I'm not a tenor now.

Wembley   Pardon?

Pennyfeather   I can't sing a note.

Wembley   Why d'you pass yourself off as one, then? It's too much! I ask Pennyfeather to engage me a tenor, and he sends me his idiot son instead.

Pennyfeather   My father sent me to England to learn the black-pudding business. He didn't say one word about being a tenor. I've a letter for you, at the bottom of my suitcase. As soon as I arrived you offered me a fortune to stay and sing. I take life as it comes.

Wembley   But what about the telegram?

Pennyfeather   Father didn't get any telegram.

Wembley   George! George!

Enter **George**.

George   Yes, sir?

Wembley   That telegram I gave you the other day, to send to Argentina ...

George   Yes, sir.

Wembley   You do remember it, don't you?

George   Oh, I remember it.

Wembley   What did you do with it?

George   I . . . well, I . . .

Wembley   Well?

George   I . . . ate it.

Exit.

Pennyfeather   So that's why Father never mentioned it. Never mind, back to business. Once again I have the honour to ask for your daughter's hand.

Wembley (*shouting*)   Never!

Pennyfeather (*also shouting*)   What's wrong with me?

Wembley   A man who's sung in the Sistine Chapel?

Pennyfeather   Me?

Wembley   Yes. You.

Oakleigh (*also shouting*)   You told us so yourself.

Pennyfeather   I said I'd *been* there. I didn't say I'd *sung* there.

Enter **Martha** *and* **Ernestine**.

Martha   What's all the shouting for?

Pennyfeather   Dear lady, please try to persuade Señor Wembley to give me Miss Julie's hand in marriage.

Ernestine   What was that?

Martha   I'm sorry: I forbid it.

Pennyfeather (*aside to her*)   Oh, don't be silly. This is no time for petty yealousy.

Martha   Jealousy? Me? She's engaged to be married to Mr Winstanley here. Do stand still, man.

Winstanley (*who has been idly 'Boots'-ing*)   Sorry. Mr

Wembley, I'm deeply honoured. But if Miss Julie loves this gentleman —

Julie   Which I do.

Winstanley (*flustered*)   Which I do ... which she does ... who am I to stand in their way? I ask for your younger daughter's hand instead.

Wembley   I haven't got one.

Winstanley   I'll wait.

Julie   Please, Daddy. I'll take him for what he is.

Wembley   Look, Pennyfeather, I'm not saying no. I just need time to think.

Pennyfeather   Good idea. (*Slyly.*) My father would be very pleased.

Wembley   Aha. Yes. The River Plate and Bolsover ... no, the Bolsover and River Plate Fine Wines, Black Pudding and Glucose Company. I like the sound of — just a minute.

He pulls **Pennyfeather** *aside.*

Wembley   Just a minute, you bounder. Exactly why were you kneeling at my wife's feet just now?

Pennyfeather   Shh! It was ... to pull the wool over Oakleigh's eyes.

Oakleigh (*pulling him aside*)   I say, look, old chap, I gather you've been kissing my wife. What d'you say to that?

Pennyfeather   Shhh! It was ... only to stop Wembley suspecting.

Oakleigh   Ah! I'd a feeling everything would turn out tickety-boo.

Wembley   Ahem. Ladies and gentlemen, it gives me great pleasure ... that is, it gives my dear wife and me great pleasure ... to announce the engagement of our only daughter, Julie, to ... what were those names again?

Pennyfeather   Miguel Rodrigo Jesus-Maria –

Wembley   Yes. To Mr Pennyfeather here. (*To the audience.*) Well, I grant you I didn't have much luck with my tenor. But this whole affair has taught me – has taught us all – a most important lesson. It doesn't matter what business you're in, whether you're taking on tenors or purchasing parsnips. Make sure you inspect the goods before you buy. If you don't, you could be getting a pig in a poke. (*To the others.*) And now, my friends, that dance we've all been practising so hard. George, the furniture. Ladies and gentlemen, take your partners for ... the tango!

George *clears the furniture.* **Winstanley** *goes to play a tango on the piano, and the others pair up and dance. Much business between the couples. With a final flourish, and a tableau, the curtain falls.*

Entracte (*between Acts One and Two*)

In front of the tabs. Music. **Wembley** *and* **Pennyfeather** *appear from the wings.* (*NB Important for continuity: NOT through tabs.*) **Wembley** *is talking to someone, off.*

Wembley On here, you mean? Right. Thank you. Thank you. (*To* **Pennyfeather**.) What a friendly man. And what a uniform. They know how to treat their staff.

He gazes out into the audience.

So this is Covent Garden. All that plush. All those cherubs. That gold paint. D'you see the royal box, up there? No, no, I was forgetting: you're used to this. You've done it all before.

Pennyfeather Done all what before?

Wembley In Argentina. Stood on a stage, bowed, smiled, this way, that way –

Pennyfeather It's new to me.

Wembley No, don't be modest. You've blown kisses, the adulation, the crowds, the beautiful women . . .

Pennyfeather Ah. I *have* done *that* before.

Wembley And now you're here. We're here. You'll be doing it again in a moment. All for me. The contract. My tenor. They won't know *what* to say.

Pennyfeather *That's* for sure.

Wembley Where are they? They said ten o'clock. (*Out into audience.*) Hello? Anybody there? Pardon? Ten minutes? What d'you mean, ten minutes? Oh. (*To* **Pennyfeather**.) They're waiting for the conductor. Ten minutes.

Pennyfeather It's all right. I wait.

Wembley It's too much to ask. You, with your voice. (*Out.*) It's a delicate instrument.

Pennyfeather   Don't make trouble. I wait.

Wembley   I wish I had your patience. In business, we never wait. We act.

Pennyfeather   You see, me, I practise patience in the pampas.

Wembley   Patience? In the pampas?

Pennyfeather   Armadillo hunting. You set out your bait ... ants, perhaps, or termites. You move into ambush, into the tall, tall grass. You draw your armadillo-knife. You hone the blade. You check your bolas. And then ... you wait.

Wembley   Wait.

Pennyfeather   Wait. Like this.

He waits, sleekly.

Wembley   Like that.

He waits, awkwardly.

I can't get the hang of it.

Pennyfeather   No problem. I'll wait for both of us.

Wembley   It's all right. They're coming. (*Out.*) Hello? Good morning. Are you the conductor? Wembley, yes. Albert Sleightholme Wembley. That's right. Not me, him. You'll be amazed. Amazed. Pardon? Oh, right. (*To* **Pennyfeather**.) He says it's up to you now. I'll wait over here. Now take it calmly. I'll just be ... over here ...

He moves aside. **Pennyfeather** *strikes a pose. Blackout.*

* * *

Dumbshow (*before Act Three*)

In front of the tabs. Music. **George**, *in dumb show, with a cheval glass. He is spiffing himself up. He has been watching* **Pennyfeather**, *and is trying to put into practice all the things he's learned, in order to turn himself from a servant into a famous tenor. He strikes poses, he slicks his hair, he shoots his cuffs, he struts, he preens – and every so often he checks anxiously in the mirror, adjusting and perfecting. Finally, satisfied that he looks like Amoroso, he strikes a pose and opens his mouth to sing 'Come into the garden, Ma-ood'. The voice (which of course we can't hear) clearly isn't right. He tries again. No. He walks round, pondering. Tries again. No. Remembers the handkerchief waving, the turning round, the 'Goosy Goosy Gander'. Rehearses it. Runs it. Does it for real. Looks anxiously in the mirror. It's worked! He comes centre stage, bows, flings open his arms and opens his mouth to sing.*

Wembley (*off*)   George!

Blackout.